Windows Mobile Game Development

Building Games for the Windows Phone and Other Mobile Devices

Adam Dawes

Apress®

Windows Mobile Game Development: Building Games for the Windows Phone and Other Mobile Devices

ISBN-13 (pbk): 978-1-4302-2928-5

ISBN-13 (electronic): 978-1-4302-2929-2

Printed and bound in the United States of America 9 8 7 6 5 4 3 2 1

Distributed to the book trade worldwide by Springer-Verlag New York, Inc., 233 Spring Street, 6th Floor, New York, NY 10013. Phone 1-800-SPRINGER, fax 201-348-4505, e-mail orders-ny@springer-sbm.com, or visit www.springeronline.com.

For information on translations, please e-mail rights@apress.com, or visit www.apress.com.

Apress and friends of ED books may be purchased in bulk for academic, corporate, or promotional use. eBook versions and licenses are also available for most titles. For more information, reference our Special Bulk Sales–eBook Licensing web page at www.apress.com/info/bulksales.

The source code for this book is available to readers at www.apress.com.

For Ritu and Kieran

Contents at a Glance

Contents

About the Author

Photograph copyright ©
Dave Parker, 2009

Adam Dawes is a software developer and systems architect working at a cutting-edge online service development company.

He has been a compulsive programmer since the age of four, when he was first introduced to a monochrome Commodore PET. The love affair has continued through three subsequent decades, flourishing through the days of the 8-bit dinosaurs to today's era of multicore processors and pocket supercomputers.

A constant for all of this time has been Adam's fondness for computer games. From the very first time Nightmare Park displayed its devious maze of pathways in green symbols back in 1980, he has been a game player across a variety of genres and styles. These days, he spends his spare time playing the latest 3D titles on his PC or enjoying some of the classics in his stand-up arcade machine or sit-in cockpit driving cabinet. Creating his own games has always been a hobby, and while he has no intention of becoming part of the professional games industry, he has a lot of fun developing his own titles nonetheless.

Adam lives with his wife, Ritu, and son, Kieran, in the southeast of England. His web site is at `www.adamdawes.com` (and all of his finished projects can be downloaded there), and he can be e-mailed at `adam@adamdawes.com`. He would particularly like to see the results of your own game development projects.

About the Technical Reviewer

■ **Don Sorcinelli** has been involved with planning, developing, and deploying enterprise applications for more than 15 years. His involvement in these processes expanded to include the PDA platforms starting in the late 1990s. He is currently a Mobility Consultant for Enterprise Mobile in Watertown, MA, where he works regularly with large enterprises on all aspects of mobility, including the design and development of Windows Mobile line of business applications.

Don frequently presents on Windows Mobile topics for users, developers, and IT professionals. As a result, he was awarded Most Valuable Professional status for Windows Mobile Devices by Microsoft Corporation in January 2004 for his work with the Windows Mobile community.

Don currently is co-manager of the Boston/New England Windows Mobile User and Developer Group, and webmaster of BostonPocketPC.com (http://www.bostonpocketpc.com). He can be contacted at donsorcinelli@bostonpocketpc.com.

Acknowledgments

I must start by thanking my parents for all of the opportunities they gave me when I was growing up and for encouraging my computer habit from a very young age.

Thank you to everyone at Apress for your assistance in getting this book written and delivered, in particular to Mark Beckner for allowing me the opportunity in the first place and to Debra Kelly for her tireless assistance and encouragement.

And finally, of course, huge thanks to my wife, Ritu, and my son, Kieran, for tolerating me shutting myself in my study and writing every evening and weekend—I'll be spending much more time with you both now; I promise!

Introduction

Goal of This Book

Gaming on the move has become very popular over recent years. With the arrival of the Nintendo Gameboy, people realized that they could take their games with them, and as technology has become more sophisticated these games have grown too, encompassing complex game mechanics, advanced 2D and 3D graphics, and engrossing stories and game worlds that the player can literally become lost within.

Alongside these game improvements is the explosion in popularity of mobile communication devices. Nearly everyone carries a phone with every time they leave the house. These devices have become much more than just phones however; they provide contact management, e-mail, Web browsing, satellite navigation, and entertainment.

Writing games for mobile devices allows both of these trends to be brought together into the same place. It is very easy for people to pick up and play games on mobile devices, as they always have the devices in their pockets. Whether they are progressing through a sprawling role-playing game on a train or simply want a few minutes casual diversion waiting for an appointment, mobile gaming can provide.

This book aims to bring you the knowledge and techniques that you will need to create your own games for Windows Mobile and Windows Phone classic devices. Starting with the basics of the platform and its development environment and progressing through to advanced topics such as 3D graphics, this book will guide you step by step toward creating a simple and manageable environment into which you can write your own mobile games and distribute them to the world for fun or profit. Example projects are provided to demonstrate all of the techniques discussed, and are ideal as a basis for experimentation.

It can be difficult to cater for the diversity of hardware available running Windows Mobile. This book will show you how to create games that work on the largest possible array of devices, catering for different screen resolutions, devices with and without touch screens, and accommodating all sorts of other hardware capabilities that your games may need to work with.

Who This Book Is For

This book is written for those who are already familiar with programming one of the two main managed Visual Studio languages, C# or Visual Basic.NET. It is assumed that you already have a grasp of the fundamentals of programming and are familiar with using the environment for PC-based application development. This book is not an introduction to programming or to Visual Studio itself.

You will, however, be given a complete guide to setting up the development environment for Windows Mobile programming, getting your first programs to compile, and interactively debugging your games as they run either on the Windows Mobile emulators included with Visual Studio or on a real device.

To develop software for your device, you will need access to either Visual Studio 2005 Standard or Visual Studio 2008 Professional. While many of the projects in this book can be developed using the Windows Mobile emulators, I strongly recommended that you do have access to a real device to test your games.

For developing games using OpenGL, as discussed toward the end of the book, you will need a device that has OpenGL hardware acceleration available, as no emulators currently offer this. Most recent devices do have OpenGL support—check the Internet if you are unsure.

The examples in this book are all written using C#, but the vast majority are capable of being converted to VB.NET without any problems. Tips and advice for VB.NET programmers are offered within the text, and workarounds are provided for the few cases where a direct VB.NET conversion is not available.

Chapter Overview

The following is a brief description of each chapter. The chapters tend to build on one another, so I recommend that you read them in sequence to avoid knowledge gaps in later chapters.

Chapter 1 introduces Windows Mobile and using the Visual Studio development environment to create Windows Mobile games applications. It covers some of the different hardware configurations that you may need to work with and explains how to set up simple .NET Compact Framework projects running against the emulators and hardware devices.

Chapter 2 explores the user interface, explaining how to use forms and controls, menus, and timers as well as more specialized subjects such as capturing pictures using the camera.

Chapter 3 introduces the first game development concepts, exploring the Graphics Device Interface (GDI) graphics system. While the GDI is fairly primitive in its abilities, it is still capable of producing interesting and playable games and works across all Windows Mobile devices, and the mechanisms for creating these are investigated.

Chapter 4 starts to build a reusable game engine that will provide simplification for lots of the features that we need to use to make complex and flexible games. It provides a simple mechanism for creating lots of independent and interdependent objects within a game environment and optimizes the GDI rendering process to get games running as fast as possible.

Chapter 5 shows how the timing of games can be made consistent across all devices, regardless of their speed, graphical capabilities, or processor load from other parts of the system. The speed of animation is made entirely predictable without any loss of flexibility or fluidity.

Chapter 6 covers the subject of user input. All sorts of input devices are available on Windows Mobile devices, from touch screens and keyboards through to accelerometers, and all of these are explored in detail to show how they can be used to allow your games to be controlled.

Chapter 7 turns up the volume and reveals the options for game audio, covering simple sound effects to MP3 and music playback. Everything you need to know about sound for your games can be found here.

Chapter 8 combines everything that has been covered so far into a full working game called GemDrops. Featuring colorful graphics, a variety of control mechanisms for different device capabilities, screen resolution independence, sound effects and music, the whole game is built step by step to show how an actual game can be developed.

Chapter 9 provides a series of reusable components that may be used in any game. A simple mechanism for loading and saving user settings, a message presentation window, a flexible high score table, and an application information page are all provided to allow you to focus on writing your game rather than having to reinvent these features yourself.

Chapter 10 opens the door to the world of OpenGL for Embedded Systems (OpenGL ES) graphics programming. Beginning by exploring the concepts and mechanisms behind OpenGL ES and comparing and contrasting these to GDI, everything you need to initialize an OpenGL ES environment and present colorful texture-mapped graphics can be found here.

Chapter 11 integrates the OpenGL ES features from Chapter 10 into the game engine, providing a series of reusable functions to simplify OpenGL ES game development. The focus of this chapter is using the game engine for 2D graphics, exploring the features that are opened up in this area by OpenGL ES beyond those provided by GDI.

Chapter 12 lifts up the OpenGL ES feature set into the third dimension, explaining how to create 3D game worlds. Subjects covered include perspective, the depth buffer, and lighting so that your scenes really come to life.

Chapter 13 continues the exploration of OpenGL ES in the third dimension and introduces a number of useful new features to the game engine. These include importing 3D objects and third-party modeling packages, moving and manipulating the cameras within a game world, and applying fog to a 3D scene.

Chapter 14 wraps up everything with tips and techniques for distributing your game to the world, covering subjects such as version control, creating installation packages, registration code systems, reverse engineering, and promotion of your game.

PART 1

Windows Mobile Development

CHAPTER 1

■ ■ ■

Windows Mobile and .NET

It is a genuine pleasure to develop software for Windows Mobile devices using Visual Studio .NET.

For a substantial part of its lifetime, programming for Microsoft's mobile operating system involved using the suite of eMbedded Visual Tools. These came supporting two different languages: eMbedded Visual Basic and eMbedded Visual C++.

eMbedded Visual Basic was based on the same technologies as Visual Basic for Applications (VBA). This was similar in a number of ways to Visual Basic 6 (VB6), the desktop version of VB that was current at the time, but with many shortcomings, such as the lack of strongly typed variables and poor object orientation features. Programs were written using a stand-alone IDE, which had its own peculiarities and different ways of working to VB6 itself.

eMbedded Visual C++ presented more of a challenge because of differences not only in the IDE but in the code too. While established C++ programmers would no doubt have managed to pick up this language without too many problems, those less-well-versed in the intricacies of C++ would have found that the amount of new information they needed to learn proved a significant barrier to entry.

All of this changed with the release of Visual Studio .NET and the .NET Compact Framework (.NET CF).

.NET CF provides a set of class libraries that are parallel to the desktop .NET Framework. The libraries are not identical, as large parts of the full .NET Framework functionality are missing from .NET CF. However, a substantial set of identical functionality does exist, and any programmer who is comfortable developing C# or Visual Basic .NET applications for Windows will be instantly at home developing for Windows Mobile too.

The .NET Framework has met resistance from some quarters in the Windows desktop world. While various versions of the framework come preinstalled with recent versions of Windows, getting users to accept .NET as a requirement of an application can still be difficult. Fortunately, there seems to be no such reluctance to install .NET CF on Windows Mobile devices, perhaps in part due to the huge amount of software that requires it in order to run.

A major advantage of developing for Windows Mobile using Visual Studio .NET is that the exact same IDE is used as for Windows desktop development. There no need to learn the details or keyboard shortcuts of a new IDE: instead, you will be working within the environment you are already used to, which includes all of your user interface tweaks and preferences changes. Developing an application for Windows Mobile is simply a question of creating a different project type.

Programming within Visual Studio .NET also means that the Windows Mobile developer is able to take advantage of the maturity of the Visual Studio.NET development environment. Microsoft has spent many years improving the user interfaces and functionality of Visual Studio, and countless versions and releases have cumulated in an extremely powerful and user-friendly studio for application design, development, and debugging. All of this is at your disposal when developing Windows Mobile applications.

The framework itself also retains much of the power of its desktop cousin, including extensive object orientation features, strong variable typing, generics, flexible collections, and powerful XML processing functions.

In this chapter, we will take a closer look at the .NET Framework, at the past and present of the Windows Mobile platform, and at some of the challenges that must be overcome to create games for the wide variety of hardware capable of running Microsoft's mobile operating system. You will create your first simple Windows Mobile application and examine some of the options that are available for game development.

Looking Closely at .NET for Windows Mobile

Let's start by taking a look at the various different versions of Visual Studio that we can use for developing software for Windows Mobile.

These are two versions of Visual Studio that we are able to use for mobile development:

- Visual Studio 2005 Standard

- Visual Studio 2008 Professional

Visual Studio 2005 targets version 2.0 of the .NET CF. Visual Studio 2008 is able to target either version 2.0 or 3.5. Version 3.5 introduces a number of new areas of functionality and language enhancements.

Unfortunately, Microsoft decided to remove smart device support for the Standard edition of Visual Studio 2008, requiring instead that the more expensive Professional edition be purchased. If you are working within a budget and would prefer to avoid the expense of buying Visual Studio 2008 Professional, the vast majority of the content of this book is compatible with .NET CF version 2.0 and Visual Studio 2005 Standard. Any exceptions to this will be highlighted as each new feature is introduced.

The real shame is that the free Express versions of Visual Studio do not support smart device development. If such functionality were available, the possibilities of Windows Mobile development would be opened up to a vast number of additional developers who either cannot or will not purchase a full version of Visual Studio.

It remains to be seen whether this will continue to be the case with the forthcoming release of Visual Studio 2010. Windows Mobile application development has not seen anything like the explosion in popularity that other mobile platforms have undergone in recent years, and hopefully Microsoft will realize that giving their development tools away for free will stimulate development for the platform.

Language Choices

Just as with desktop .NET development, a number of different languages are supported:

- C#

- Visual Basic

- C++

When a new project is being created, the language to use for the project must be selected. When compiling managed .NET projects, the resulting executable code is functionally identical regardless of which language has been selected.

The .NET Runtime Libraries

In order for your programs to run on a Windows Mobile device, the appropriate .NET CF runtime libraries will need to be installed. The libraries can be downloaded from Microsoft's web site and are not excessively large (24.5MB for the .NET CF 2.0 runtime, 33.3MB for .NET 3.5). Once these are installed on the device, your .NET CF applications will be able to run.

■ **NOTE** The .NET Framework installers contain support for all older versions of the framework. Installing the .NET CF 3.5 runtime will allow programs written for earlier versions of .NET to run too; the older versions of .NET do not need to be individually installed.

IDE Features

As would be expected from Visual Studio, a number of very useful features are available to help with developing and debugging Windows Mobile applications.

Emulators

Visual Studio offers a number of Windows Mobile emulators to help test your programs. As you will soon see, quite a diverse range of different hardware form factors are able to run Windows Mobile, and chances are that you will only have access to one or two of these, depending on your individual circumstances. Making sure that your game runs on other devices, therefore, has the potential to be a problem. Emulators, such as the one shown in Figure 1–1, neatly solve this by allowing you to run your code against all sorts of different types of virtual hardware and different versions of Windows Mobile.

Figure 1–1. One of the Visual Studio emulators showing the Today screen

These emulators actually offer a full implementation of the emulated device and are capable of running genuine Windows Mobile applications. They offer full access to a substantial subset of features of the device, including the ability to simulate things such as networking, battery levels, and screen rotation.

Running your application in an emulator is as simple as could be—just select the emulator that you wish to use and start your application. The emulator will appear, and your program will run. We will look at how to use these emulators in much more detail in the "Working with the Emulators" section later on in this chapter.

Form Designer

A fully featured form designer is available to lay out windows and controls for use within your program. The form designer goes as far as to display an image of the device around the edge of your form to help visualize its appearance (though you can switch this off if you prefer).

Breakpoints

Another extremely useful tool is Visual Studio's breakpoint feature. No doubt familiar to any desktop developer, breakpoints are fully supported for Windows Mobile development too and can be used both when running against an emulator and against a physical device. It can be extremely useful to break into your code, examine your variables and step through the instructions while watching the results on a real device on the desk next to you.

Debug Output

Access to the Visual Studio Output window is available from Windows Mobile applications running inside the IDE. Text can be written to the Output window at any time, allowing you to easily keep track of what you program is doing. Pairing this with the ability to effectively have two independent screens (your PC screen and your mobile device screen) makes this particularly powerful.

Preparing for Windows Mobile Development Challenges

Perhaps the biggest challenge facing the Windows Mobile developer is the huge diversity of hardware to be found in the available devices. Let's take a look at what we are up against. Don't be too put off by any of this, as we will tackle these problems head on later in this book and provide some solutions to reduce or eliminate their impact.

Numerous Windows Mobile Versions and Editions

A somewhat bewildering selection of names has been applied to Microsoft's operating system over the years, which can make it difficult to know exactly what you are developing for. In particular, searching for information on the Web can be tricky due to this naming inconsistency. The following sections explain the various terms and versions relating to the operating system.

Windows CE

The underlying operating system in all versions of Windows Mobile is Windows CE. "CE" does not in fact officially stand for anything, but instead, according to Microsoft, "…implies a number of the precepts around which Windows CE is designed, including Compact, Connectable, Compatible, Companion, and Efficient."

Windows CE is able to power all sorts of embedded and low-resource devices and is capable of running inside set top boxes, point-of-sale systems, information terminals, and other similar pieces of hardware.

Despite its similar name, it is not part of the desktop Windows family of operating systems. It does, however, have many design similarities, which even extend as far as a common application programming interface (API) for many classes between Windows and Windows CE.

Windows CE forms the underlying platform for Windows Mobile devices. These use many of the features and services provided by the core operating system, but add a significant amount of additional functionality that is appropriate for modern device use, such as the Today screen, e-mail and phone systems, Office Mobile applications, and so on.

Pocket PC

Pocket PC is that name that was used by Microsoft to describe their mobile devices prior to Windows Mobile 6. Pocket PC devices offered the same kind of functionality and user experience that we have become familiar with on Windows Mobile devices but had no requirement for any integrated phone hardware. Such devices were, therefore, more usually classed as PDAs, rather than smart phones or personal Internet devices, as we would expect in more recent hardware.

Windows Mobile

The Windows Mobile name was first introduced as a new version of the Pocket PC platform as Windows Mobile 2003. Various versions have appeared since then up to the current version, Windows Mobile 6.5

Versions 2003, 2003SE and 5.0 came in three separate editions:

- *Windows Mobile for Pocket PC*: This version was for devices with no telephone capability.

- *Windows Mobile for Pocket PC Phone*: This version targeted devices that did include telephone capability.

- *Windows Mobile for Smartphone*: This version was for telephone devices that did not offer a touch screen.

With the arrival of Windows Mobile 6, the terminology changed:

- *Windows Mobile Classic*: This is for devices with no phone capability.

- *Windows Mobile Professional*: This is the version for devices with phones and touch screens.

- *Windows Mobile Standard*: This is for devices with phones but no touch screens.

Windows Phones

Starting with Windows Mobile 6.5, Microsoft has begun to brand their devices as Windows Phones. The underlying technology is still Windows Mobile however.

Hardware Considerations

Many of the smart phones running competing operating systems have consistent hardware form factors across their ranges of available devices. This dramatically simplifies the task of writing applications for those platforms, as the number of variables and unknowns that the software has to deal with is close to zero.

This unfortunately is not the case with Windows Mobile devices, whose capabilities and hardware can vary massively. Even the latest devices have huge differences in their abilities, and if you want to allow users of older hardware to play your games too, you have even more complexity to deal with.

Once again, we will tackle these problems later on, but here are some of the things that need to be considered when designing your game and planning the user's interaction with it.

Touch Screens

The majority of new hardware devices have touch screens as standard, but large numbers of devices still do not have any touch screen support. These, instead, provide an interface much closer to standard mobile phones, with a numeric keypad and a small number of other hardware buttons used to control the device.

The presence of a touch screen has an important impact on the way users will interact with your game: the different between controlling a game by touching the screen or by pressing one of a fixed number of buttons is significant.

Some types of games will be impractical to play without a touch screen; others will benefit from having some hardware buttons that the user can use to control things. You will need to decide what is practical for your game, but do be aware that by requiring a touch screen you will prevent some of your potential audience from being able to play your game.

Hardware Buttons

The availability of hardware buttons on a device can be highly variable. It is common to expect devices to have a four-directional navigation pad, but this is not always the case: many recent devices make the screen as large as possible, leaving no space left for input mechanisms such as this. Many recent devices from manufacturer HTC for example have buttons to pick up or drop a call, a back button, and a Windows button, and virtually nothing else.

At the other extreme are devices with built-in keyboards, which either slide out or are positioned below the screen. These have more buttons than you will generally know what to do with but are much less common.

When planning your game, you will need to cater for all of these different possibilities to support as many devices as possible.

Processors

A problem much more familiar to desktop game developers is that if processor capability. Just as desktop CPUs have seen enormous increases in power over time, embedded CPUs have also become substantially more powerful (though they are still a long way behind their desktop counterparts).

Without taking these factors into consideration, a program that runs well on a new device may well suffer on an older device simply because the processor is unable to handle data as quickly as the developer expected. Similarly, games written for older hardware may run too quickly on new devices.

Screen Size

For a long time, it was standard for Windows Mobile devices to use Quarter VGA (QVGA) resolution, that is, 240×320 pixels. Advances in technology have put this firmly into the past now, with a number of new resolutions in wide use.

Full VGA resolution (480×640 pixels) is now available on many devices as is Wide VGA (WVGA) at 480×800 pixels. Back in the lower resolution arena, we now have Wide Quarter VGA (WQVGA) at 240×400 pixels and Square QVGA at 240×240 pixels or 480×480 pixels. That's a lot of different resolutions to keep track of and a lot of headache for a game designer to deal with.

It is essential to ensure that your game looks good and functions well on as wide a range of different screen resolutions as possible. It is very common (and disappointing) to see older games that run in the top/left quarter of the screen on newer devices.

We also have to consider the uncertainty of future devices too: what resolution will we be using one or two years from now? Obviously, we can go only so far to accommodate devices with higher resolutions than are currently available on the market, but we should at least provide some sensible provision to stop our games from looking bad on such hardware.

An important consideration when designing a game for a mobile platform is that the screen orientation is generally rotated when compared to that of a desktop PC: the screen is tall rather than wide. This benefits some types of games (Tetris-style games, for example) but can be problematic for others. Don't overlook this basic but important detail when planning your game structure.

Graphics Hardware

Hardware-accelerated graphics are a relatively modern development in the world of Windows Mobile. Many new devices do offer some level of accelerated graphics, meaning that 3-D rendering starts to become a viable option. It is safe to assume that older devices will not have such hardware and will be more limited in their capabilities.

If you wish to target newer graphics hardware, be prepared for the fact you will be limiting your target audience. Hopefully, the proportion of devices that support hardware acceleration will continue to increase over time.

We will examine the various graphics technologies and APIs that are available for Windows Mobile development in the "Graphics APIs" section later in this chapter.

Cooperation with Devices

Let's not forget an extremely important fact: your game is running on someone's phone and personal organizer. They are going to place more importance on tasks such as answering a phone call or responding to a calendar reminder alert than they are in continuing to play your game. It is essential that you play nicely with the rest of the device to avoid irritating your user.

There are a number of things we can do to reduce the impact of this type of interruption: automatically pause the game if another application comes to the foreground, or save your game state to the device if your game closes and automatically restore it the next time your game starts. People will appreciate details like this.

This kind of feature often becomes invisible when it works well but is much more likely to be very visible when it *doesn't* work—make sure you take these unexpected interactions into consideration.

Using Visual Studio for Windows Mobile Development

Let's take a look now at the steps required to begin development of Windows Mobile games and applications.

Installing Visual Studio

Configuring Visual Studio to support mobile devices is very easy. If you have not yet installed Visual Studio, you simply need to ensure that the Smart Device Programmability option is selected for the language(s) in which you wish to be able to develop (see Figure 1–2). You can find these options by selecting to perform a Custom Installation of Visual Studio.

Figure 1–2. Selecting the Smart Device Programmability options in Visual Studio's installation window

If Visual Studio is already installed on your system, you can check to see whether support for mobile development is available by selecting to create a new project (see Figure 1–3). If this project type is available then everything is installed and ready for you to use.

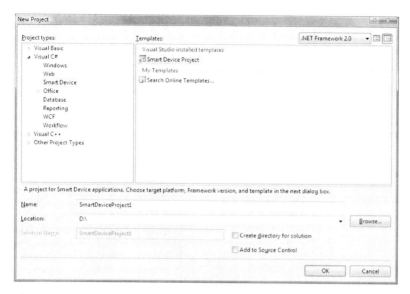

Figure 1–3. *Creating a new Smart Device project*

If the Smart Device project type is not available, you can easily add the missing feature by opening the Add/Remove Programs feature in Control Panel (Programs and Features in Windows Vista and Windows 7) and selecting the Uninstall/Change option. Follow the instructions in the installer application to add the Smart Device Programmability feature as shown in Figure 1–2.

Once everything is installed as required, we are ready to begin.

Creating a Windows Mobile Project

With our tools all in place, it is time to finally create a Windows Mobile application and take a look at how we interact with both the emulators and real devices.

To begin, select File ➤ New ➤ Project, and choose to locate the C# Smart Device project type. Exactly how we proceed towards creation of our empty project now depends on which version of Visual Studio is in use.

Visual Studio 2005

In Visual Studio 2005, the Smart Device item contains several different suboptions. For now, choose Windows Mobile 6 Professional and then the Device Application template, as shown in Figure 1–4.

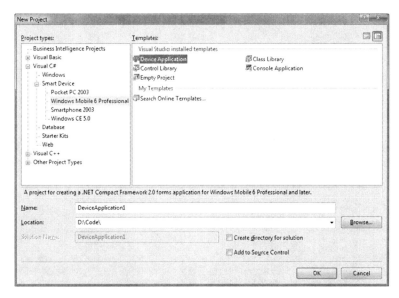

Figure 1–4. *Creating a Smart Device project in Visual Studio 2005*

With these options selected, set the Name of your project to whatever you wish (**FirstProject**, for example) and set the Location to wherever you want your project files to be created.

Click the OK button, and after a few seconds, your project will be created, and an empty form designer window will appear.

Visual Studio 2008

In Visual Studio 2008, we have no project template options available for our smart device project; these are instead chosen in the next step. One option that is present in this window is the .NET Framework version that we wish to target. We can actually ignore this however, as this setting is not used for smart device projects. The .NET CF version we want to compile against will be chosen in a moment.

Enter a Name and Location for your project, and then click OK to continue to the next dialog.

The Add New Smart Device Project window now appears (see Figure 1–5), in which we select the platform and .NET Compact Framework version that we wish to target and the type of project that we wish to create.

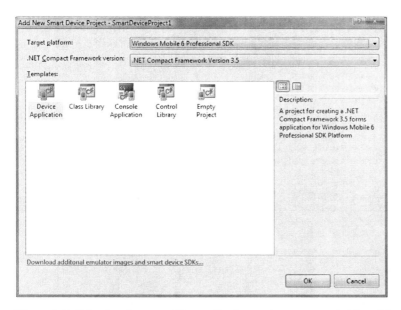

Figure 1–5. Selecting the type of Smart Device project to create in Visual Studio 2008

The target platform will allow you to choose which set of emulators are available for working on your project. Note that the emulator selection doesn't have any effect on the ability of your application to run on older or newer versions of Windows Mobile: projects that target the Pocket PC 2003 platform will still work perfectly well on Windows Mobile 6 devices and vice versa (providing you do not use any features of a newer version of the operating system that are not available on older versions). For our test project, select to target Windows Mobile 6 Professional.

This is also the stage at which we actually select the version of the .NET Compact Framework that we wish to target. To ensure you have the largest set of features available, select version 3.5.

■ **NOTE** You may choose to target .NET CF version 2.0 if you wish to allow your application to run on devices that only have this older framework version installed, but .NET CF version 3.5 is compatible with devices running right back to Windows Mobile 2003 SE, so in hardware terms, you are unlikely to exclude a significant number of users by developing against .NET 3.5. The target framework can be changed after your project has been created if required.

Finally, we select the template that we wish to use. Select to create a Device Application. Click the OK button, and the empty form designer window will appear.

Project Templates

As you have seen when creating a project, a number of different templates are provided by Visual Studio for your new project. Each of these will result in a different initial project for you to start working on, as follows:

- *Device Application*: This will create a project that will compile into an executable application (.exe file). Whenever you are developing, you will need to have such an application in your solution set as your startup project in order to be able to begin execution of your code. This is one of the most frequently used templates.

- *Class Library*: This is another commonly used template and will allow your project to compile into a reusable code library (.dll file). Class libraries generally contain code that you wish to share between multiple applications.

- *Console Application*: The description of this template is somewhat misleading, as Windows Mobile doesn't have a console in the way that Windows does. Console application projects will compile to executable applications but will not have any user input or output, including no forms displayed on the screen. Such applications are useful for noninteractive background processes.

- *Control Library*: Just like the desktop .NET Framework, .NET CF has support for creating user controls, user-defined form control elements that can be placed on to a form. These are compiled into .dll files.

- *Empty Project*: Use this template to create a completely empty project with no initial files present at all.

If you need to change the project type after it has been created, this can be accomplished from the Project Properties window. This window is opened by right-clicking the project node within the Solution Explorer and selecting Properties. From within the Application tab, the project type can be altered by changing the setting of the "Output type" field.

Designing a Form

Now, we are ready to create our test application's form. As you can see, the form designer includes an image around the outside of the form which shows you how the form will appear when running inside the target device. Personally, I find this quite pleasant, but if you would prefer to design your forms without this, you can switch it off by opening the Tools/Options window, selecting the Device Tools item in the options tree, and then unchecking the "Show skin in Windows Forms Designer" option. Note that you will need to close and reopen your form designer windows for this change to have any effect.

For the purposes of our simple application, we will simply place a Button control on to the form and get it to display a message when clicked. The Button is added from the toolbox exactly as it would be for a desktop application (see Figure 1–6).

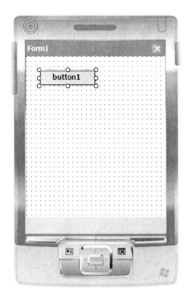

Figure 1–6. The Smart Device form designer

Once you have added your Button, take a look at its properties in the Properties window (see Figure 1–7). Everything should look familiar, and you will find that a subset of the standard desktop Button control properties is available.

Figure 1–7. The Button's properties

■ **TIP** If the Properties window is not open, it can be opened by selecting the View/Properties Window item from Visual Studio's main menus. Under the default key mappings, it can also be opened by pressing F4 on the keyboard.

Double-click the button to open the code designer and create the button's Click event handler. Once again, the code should all be exactly as you would expect when developing a desktop application. Hopefully, at this stage, it is clear how much the IDE and the way it is used for smart device projects is the same as for desktop application development.

Complete the implementation of the button1_Click procedure so that it simply displays a MessageBox (see Listing 1–1).

Listing 1–1. The button1_Click procedure

```csharp
private void button1_Click(object sender, EventArgs e)
{
    MessageBox.Show("Hello mobile world!");
}
```

Running the Application

We are now ready to compile and run the project. Press F5 to begin the process. After compilation (assuming there are no errors!), Visual Studio opens the deployment device selection window. We use this to decide whether we want to run in an emulator (and if so, which one) or on a real device (see Figure 1–8).

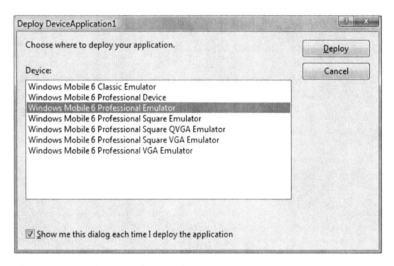

Figure 1–8. Deployment device selection

For the moment, select to run on one of the emulators. The list of available emulators will vary depending on the platform that you chose to target when you created your project.

After you click Deploy, the selected emulator will be opened. Visual Studio will deploy everything that your project needs to run, including the .NET CF itself. Once this is all complete (which may take a few seconds), your program will launch. Clicking the button will display the MessageBox as you would expect (see Figure 1–9).

Figure 1–9. Our test application showing off its full range of abilities

To stop the program running, click the Stop Debugging button in Visual Studio. The IDE will return to edit mode, and your program will close on the emulator. The emulator itself will keep running, ready for any further programs that you start.

Let's take a look at some of the more subtle behavior of the application. Start your program running again, switch back to the emulator, and wait until your program's window appears. This time, instead of stopping the program within the IDE, click the form close button in the top-right corner of the application within the emulator window. Your program disappears and the Today page is displayed once again.

Note, however, that the Visual Studio IDE is still in run mode, because the close button on a Windows Mobile program generally just minimizes the application, leaving it running in the background. This behavior can be very confusing if you are not expecting it (both as a developer and as a user) because it is not at all what would be expected based on experience with Windows running on the desktop. As a developer, it can be useful under some circumstances to put your application into this state to test that it works properly.

To redisplay the application, you need to navigate around the emulator a little. First, click the Start button, and then choose the Settings option. Inside the Settings window, open the System tab, and then click the Memory icon. Finally, select the Running Programs tab. The Running Programs List will display Form1 (the caption of our test form). Click this and then click the Activate button to redisplay your program window.

If all you want to do is close your application after it has been minimized, you can, of course, still just click the Stop Debugging button in the Visual Studio IDE.

Working with the Emulators

The device emulators offer an extremely useful service, allowing you to test your application inside all sorts of different hardware and operating system configurations without need access to any physical hardware. Let's take a closer look at some of the emulator features.

Device Selection

Each time you run your application, Visual Studio will prompt you to select which device you wish to use to host the application. After a while, this can become quite annoying, particularly if you wish to use the same device over and over again.

Instead of repeatedly answering this question, you can uncheck the "Show me this dialog each time I deploy the application" check box at the bottom of the form. Visual Studio will then remember your selected device and automatically use it when you launch your application in the future.

To actually change the selected device after doing this, the Device toolbar needs to be added to the Visual Studio IDE (although I would advise adding this toolbar even if you prefer to use the emulator selection window). To add the toolbar, right-click anywhere within one of your existing toolbars, and check the Device item in the menu that appears.

The Device toolbar displays the currently active device and allows different devices to be selected.

▒ **TIP** The device selection in the toolbar relates to the individual project that you have selected within the Solution Explorer and not to the solution or the IDE as a whole. If you have multiple projects open in your solution, it is important to select the Startup Project when choosing the active device, as this is the project whose device will be observed when the application launches.

If you subsequently wish to use the device selection window once again, click the Device Options button in the Device toolbar (or select Tools/Options from the menu and then Device Tools) and check the "Show device choices before deploying a device project" check box. This will reactivate the selection window.

Note that the emulators are happy to run side by side. If you need to repeatedly switch between devices, you can leave multiple emulators open and just switch the focus to the one that you need each time your application runs.

Sharing Files with an Emulated Device

If you need to copy files to or from one of your emulated devices, this can be achieved by configuring a shared folder within the emulator. Select the File/Configure menu item inside the emulator window and then inside the "Shared folder" box, browse to a directory on your hard drive.

Using a shared folder gives the emulator access to the selected directory as if it were a storage card within the device. Using File Explorer, open the Storage Card item and you will find that you have live access to the files in your specified directory.

As the emulator now has full access to this part of your hard drive, I recommend creating a new folder specifically for the purpose of exchanging files. This removes any danger of the emulator damaging or modifying any files on your computer unexpectedly.

Re-enabling Alt-Tab

If you find that the Alt-Tab keyboard combination stops working when an emulator has the focus, you can fix this by editing the emulator configuration and changing the Host key to Left Alt. You will then be able to task switch as normal.

Emulator State

When you close one of your emulators, a dialog window will appear asking if you wish to save the emulator state before existing. Just as a real device remembers what it is doing when you switch it off by pressing the power button, so the emulators are able to store the exact state that they are in and recall this the next time the device is started.

Normally, it is sensible to get the emulator to save its state only when it is in an idle state and does not have an instance of your application running. It is a good idea to save the state after having first used an emulator to run one of your programs, as this will result in the state being saved with the .NET CF installed, speeding up deployment the next time you use the emulator.

After this initial state has been saved, you can then continue to close the emulator without saving the state unless you have modified the device in some way that you want to retain for future use.

Note that the configuration options (within the File/Configure menu) are treated as part of the device state. If you modify these and want to keep the changes, you will need to save the device's state.

Obtaining More Emulators

A number of emulators and platforms are included with Visual Studio itself, but additional emulators are released by Microsoft whenever new versions of Windows Mobile are released. For example, emulators for Windows Mobile 6.5 are now available, but these had not been completed when Visual Studio was released and so that are not included by default.

These additional emulators can be downloaded from Microsoft's web site. Once installed, they will appear either as new platforms (alongside the choice of Windows Mobile 5.0 Pocket PC SDK, Windows Mobile 6 Professional SDK, and so on) or as new devices within an existing platform.

The easiest way to locate the updated SDKs is to search for them within Google. For example, to find the download for the Windows Mobile 6.5 SDK, use the search term, "windows mobile 6.5 sdk."

Generally speaking, later versions of a Windows Mobile operating system will require the original version of that operating system to be installed before they will appear. In order to use the Windows Mobile 6.5 SDK, the Windows Mobile 6.0 Professional or Standard SDK must already be installed.

Targeting Different Platforms

The Windows Mobile platform that your application will run against is selected at the time your project is created, but it can be useful to choose a different platform for an existing project. This can be achieved using the Project ➤ Change Target Platform menu option.

Visual Studio will display its Change Target Platform window, and any of the available platforms can be selected. Your project will then close and reopen, and all of the devices for the new platform will appear in the device selection list. Note that this only affects the project that is currently selected in the Solution Explorer, so make sure you select your startup project before using this option.

Be aware that not all platforms support all of the features that you may wish to use. For example, changing to one of the smart phone platforms will already cause a problem, as smart phone devices do not allow Button controls to be used. We will explore how to deal with this situation and how to prevent Visual Studio making unexpected changes to your project as a result of this when we examine the user interface controls in more detail in the next chapter.

Running on a Real Device

You will no doubt be please to hear that running your application on a real device is no more difficult than running it within an emulator. Let's try it out now.

First plug your device into the PC and ensure it is connected and recognized within Windows (this assumes that you have previously established a relationship between the device and Windows itself). If data synchronization begins, it may be wise to allow this to finish first, as it can cause the performance of your application to deteriorate until it completes.

Once everything is ready, select to deploy your application to a device rather than an emulator. For example, with the Windows Mobile 6 platform, you would select to deploy to Windows Mobile Professional 6 Device. Visual Studio will connect to the device and automatically install everything your project needs—the .NET CF, any DLLs that you are referencing, and the application executable.

Depending on the version of Windows Mobile on your device, you may now receive a security dialog warning you that a component from an unknown publisher is being started (see Figure 1–10). There might, in fact, be a series of these relating to different components that Visual Studio has installed. You will need to respond Yes to each of these in order for your application deployment to succeed.

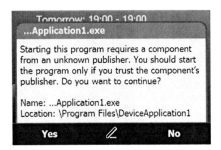

Figure 1–10. Deployment security warnings

Once these dialogs have been acknowledged, they will not appear again unless the component they refer to has been modified. In practice, this means that you will be asked to confirm only your application (as this will be changing very frequently) and not any of the other .NET CF components. These warnings can be disabled, and we will discuss how to do this shortly.

With these dialogs out of the way, the program finally launches. Unsurprisingly, it looks and behaves just as it did in the emulator. Congratulations, you have written and deployed your first Windows Mobile application!

The executable itself gets deployed to the Program Files directory in the main memory of your device. If you explore there with File Explorer, you will find that a directory has been created matching the name of your application. Inside here is the program that has been compiled. You can run it directly from within File Explorer if you wish.

Deployment Problems

If you receive an error message when you try to launch your application, one possible problem is that the program is actually already running on the device. When this occurs, Visual Studio displays a rather unhelpful message stating that it is unable to start the program because "The data necessary to complete this operation is not yet available."

If you receive this error message, use the Running Programs window to check that your application is not already running, as described in the "Running the Application" section.

Another possible cause of errors is the connection type that is configured for your device within the Windows-based ActiveSync (Windows XP) or Windows Mobile Device Centre (Windows Vista and Windows 7) applications. If deployment fails, open whichever of these applications you are using, edit the connection settings, and select the option to "Allow connections to use one of the following: DMA". Apply the settings, disconnect and reconnect your device, and then try deploying your application again.

Any connection failures that occur while your application is running (if the USB cable is disconnected, for example) will leave the application running on the device, as will manually launching it. Either of these scenarios can result in this unhelpful error message appearing.

Removing the Security Warnings

The security warnings that may be displayed each time you launch your application can become quite frustrating after a while, but it is possible to disable them. Exactly how you do this will depend on the version of Visual Studio that you are using.

Using Visual Studio 2008, select the Tools ➤ Device Security Manager menu item. In the window that opens, select the Security Configuration tab, and right-click the Connected Devices item below (see Figure 1–11). Then, choose Connect to Device (making sure first of all that your device is connected to your PC). Choose your device from the list (rather than any of the emulators) and select Connect. After a few seconds the connection should be established and you can click the Close button.

The current security configuration for your device will now be selected within the window. To remove the warnings, click the Security Off configuration. Finally, right-click your device within the Connected Devices list, and select Deploy to Device. The updated configuration will be written to the device and no further warnings should appear.

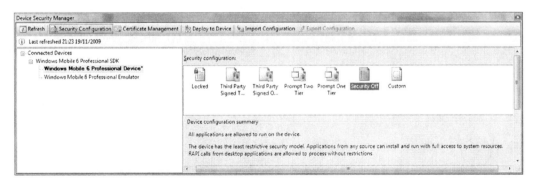

Figure 1–11. Visual Studio 2008's Device Security Manager

Visual Studio 2005 is unfortunately missing this configuration window, but the same result can be achieved by making a change to the system registry.

■ **CAUTION** Exercise extreme caution when editing the registry on your device. Incorrect changes to the registry can cause your device to malfunction or stop working. If you are not confident with editing the registry or at any stage become unsure as to whether the change you are making is correct, please do not continue with this procedure.

If you wish to make this change, you will need to obtain a third-party registry editor. One such editor which is available free of change is CeRegEditor. This runs on your PC (not on the device itself) and provides access to the whole of the device registry. To disable the warnings, navigate to the following key within your registry editor:

HKEY_LOCAL_MACHINE/Security/Policies/Policies

Here, you should find a value 0000101a containing the value data 0. Change the data to 1. If the value does not exist, create it as a DWORD type value and set its data as to 1. Once this change has been made, no further warnings will be displayed.

This change will, of course, affect all applications, removing the warnings for any third-party software that you install as well as your own applications, so be sure that you wish to make this change before doing so.

■ **TIP** If when attempting to edit the registry you receive an "access denied" error, this is because the registry is locked. To unlock it, you can use the Unlock registry tool inside CeRegEditor.

Changing the Deployment Directory

If you need to change the directory to which your program is deployed when you run it (for example, if you rename your project), you can do so within the properties for your project. Select the project in the Solution Explorer and then look in the Properties window. The deployment path is specified in the Output File Folder property. The property value will be set as follows:

    %CSIDL_PROGRAM_FILES%\ProjectName

To modify the deployment folder, simply modify the project name (after the backslash) as required.

Debugging

Now that you have a simple application written and working, let's take a closer look at some of the debugging features that are available.

The powerful debugging tools that can be used within the Visual Studio IDE make development systems from the past look extremely primitive in comparison. We are able to use all of these tools for Windows Mobile development, making tracking down problems simple.

Breakpoints

First of all, try setting a breakpoint on the line of code containing the MessageBox function call. Launch the program (on a real device or one of the emulators), and click the button within the form. As you would expect, the breakpoint triggers just as it would on a desktop application.

From here, you can explore all of the usual attributes of your application: the call stack, object property windows, visualizers, immediate window commands: everything is present and working.

The one useful feature that is not available however is "edit and continue." Unfortunately, as the application is actually running outside of Visual Studio's controlled environment, such changes cannot be applied at runtime and will need to be held back until the IDE returns to edit mode.

Debug Output

At any stage within your application you can display text in Visual Studio's Output window. This is done in just the same way as for a desktop application, using the System.Diagnostics.Debug object. To test this out, modify the button click handler as shown in Listing 1–2.

Listing 1–2. Writing Text to the Debug Output wiçndow

```
private void button1_Click(object sender, EventArgs e)
{
    System.Diagnostics.Debug.WriteLine("Debug text");
    MessageBox.Show("Hello mobile world!");
}
```

Each time you click the button, you will now see your debug text appear within the IDE (see Figure 1–12).

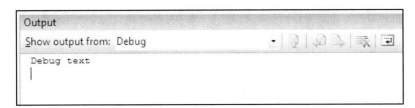

Figure 1–12. Debug text appearing in the Debug Output window

▓ **TIP** If the Output window is not displayed, it can be opened by selecting View ➤ Output from Visual Studio's menu. If the Output window is open but no text is appearing, ensure the "Show output from" value is set to Debug.

Getting Help

It is inevitable that sooner or later you will run into a development problem that you cannot solve on your own. A number of great resources at your disposal can provide insight and inspiration to keep you moving. Here are some of them.

MSDN

As you would expect from one of Microsoft's products, comprehensive and detailed documentation is available for all aspects of Windows Mobile development and the .NET Compact Framework. Providing you have it installed, MSDN is an excellent source of help and is never further away than a quick press of the F1 key.

Search Engines

The Web is, as ever, an indispensible fountain of information. When searching, try accompanying your search phrase with "windows mobile" (including the quotation marks) or "netcf" (without quotes)—this works particularly well in Google, which broadens it to cover a range of appropriate terms—to help find relevant information. If that bears no fruit, try "pocket pc" (though this will often bring back very old information).

Microsoft's Windows Mobile Developer Center

The Developer Center can be found at the following URL:

`http://msdn.microsoft.com/en-us/windowsmobile/`

The site hosts a large variety of articles, development tips, frequently asked questions and code samples. Also of particular interest here is the Forums link, which leads to a number of active message forums. There's a good chance that someone here will be able to offer you some assistance.

Newsgroups

Microsoft provides various newsgroups relating to .NET CF development. The group that is best for Windows Mobile programming discussions is

`microsoft.public.pocketpc.development`

You can subscribe to this using any NNTP client (such as Windows Live Mail or Mozilla Thunderbird) on the `msnews.microsoft.com` server or on the web via Google Groups. Microsoft does not reply to questions directly, but a number of other developers regularly respond to messages and may be able to help solve any problems that are posted.

Windows Mobile Game Development

We've spent a lot of time discussing development in general, but we have not yet looked at game development. We will start preparing to actually write a game in Chapter 3, but let's conclude this overview of Windows Mobile software development by thinking about what types of games we can create and the technologies available to create them.

Suitable Games

Unfortunately, the hardware capabilities of even the latest devices are not approaching the capabilities required to mirror the 3-D action games seen on desktop PCs or dedicated handheld game consoles such as Sony's PlayStation Portable or Nintendo's DS. However, lots of game styles work wonderfully on a Windows Mobile device.

We can do great things with the more laid -back game genres such as strategy, role playing, and puzzle games. Well-crafted games such as these can become extremely popular, as the immediate "switch on and play" nature of the device is ideal for people who have only a few spare minutes to dedicate to gaming before real life gets in the way. This type of game is well suited to most hardware, even older devices, and has a potentially large audience.

Board and card games are examples of other styles that are easily accessible to a wide audience, and they convert well to handheld devices. In particular, the ability to drag cards around the game on touch screen devices leads to a satisfying feeling of involvement.

Action and platform games require a bit more processing and graphical power and may not be suitable for older hardware. Nevertheless, newer systems can really do justice to this kind of game and lots of opportunities await in these areas.

Novelty games have recently become popular on other platforms such as the iPhone, allowing users to create and distort photographs of their friends, to create sound effects in response to interactions with the device, and a variety of other unusual things. Relatively few examples of this kind of application exist on Windows Mobile at the moment, but for those of you with creative flair and imagination to spare, this could be an interesting area to explore!

It is important to bear in mind how users are going to interact with your game. How do you control a platform game if you only have a touch screen and no directional movement pad? How do you play a card game on a smart phone with no touch screen? We'll consider some ways of interacting with different devices in Chapter 6.

Graphics APIs

One of the first decisions that you need to make when you begin programming a game is which graphics API to use.

The history of graphics APIs on Windows Mobile is just about as twisted and complex as that of the operating system itself, so this question can be difficult to answer. A number of APIs could potentially be used, and the details of each follow.

GDI

The Graphics Device Interface (GDI) is the API on which Windows Mobile itself bases its graphical output. It is simple to use and very flexible but not particularly fast.

Due to the lower resolution of Windows Mobile devices, it is actually possible to get acceptable results from GDI for certain types of games. In particular, GDI handles puzzle, strategy, board, and card games very well. When smooth animation or full-screen updates are required however, GDI is not really good enough and will result in slow and jerky animation.

GAPI

Microsoft's Game API (GAPI) was, as you might expect, ideally suited for game development. The API was introduced for Windows Mobile 2003 and was required to be supported for all hardware devices. With the arrival of Windows Mobile 5.0, however, Microsoft deprecated GAPI and removed it from the hardware requirements. GAPI-driven games may still work on newer hardware, but there is no certainty that they will now or in the future.

There is no managed interface to GAPI for Visual Studio .NET.

DirectDraw

The placement for GAPI is DirectDraw, a scaled-down version of the desktop DirectX component, introduced with Windows Mobile 5.0. DirectDraw would potentially be ideal for game development, but unfortunately, there are a number of issues with it at the current time. Many of the devices that are able to support DirectDraw have insufficient memory available to be able to reliably initialize a DirectDraw application (particularly once large WVGA screens are introduced into the mix), so this technology is not currently suitable for us to use.

There is no managed interface to DirectDraw for Visual Studio .NET.

Direct3D

Direct3D was introduced alongside DirectDraw. Just as with DirectDraw, this is a cut-down version of the desktop DirectX component. It would be an ideal candidate for game development for both 2-D and 3-D games and has a managed interface too. But here comes the problem: Microsoft has never required any of the hardware vendors producing Windows Mobile devices to include any hardware support for Direct3D acceleration. A number of devices do include such support, but many others (notably those from HTC, who currently are arguably the brand leaders in Windows Mobile devices) ship only the reference driver for Direct3D. This software implementation takes no advantage of graphics hardware at all.

As a result, many devices render Direct3D graphics at a terribly slow rate, taking several seconds to produce a single frame of animation in some cases.

In the future, Direct3D may become a viable graphics API for game development, but for the time being, only a small subsection of your potential audience will be able to use it.

OpenGL ES

OpenGL for Embedded Systems (OpenGL ES) is a cut-down version of the industry standard OpenGL graphics API. It supports 3-D graphics and can be easily used for 2-D graphics too.

This is not a Microsoft technology but is starting to become established as the graphics API of choice on Windows Mobile devices. The majority of recent devices have hardware support for OpenGL ES, allowing comparatively demanding graphics to be rendered. OpenGL ES is also capable of producing smooth animation, resulting in very pleasing movement on the screen.

No managed interface is provided for OpenGL ES, but a managed wrapper has been created that allows access to all of the underlying functionality from within Visual Studio .NET.

Technologies Used in This book

We will be focusing on using two of these graphics technologies: GDI and OpenGL.

Initially, we will use GDI, as it is simple to use and will allow us to focus on creating a reusable game framework inside which our projects can be created. We will examine how to make GDI work efficiently for game development and how to create a consistent game experience across all sorts of different devices.

Afterward, we will take a closer look at OpenGL ES and extend our game engine to support it, using all of the tricks and techniques you have learned along the way.

Welcome to the World of Windows Mobile Development

This concludes our overview of .NET Compact Framework development and hopefully has provided you with enthusiasm and excitement about the opportunities of developing for the Windows Mobile platform.

Please spend some time experimenting with the capabilities of the environment and the .NET CF libraries. We will look at exactly what we can do with .NET CF in much more detail in the following chapters, but for now, do get comfortable with building and launching applications.
Have fun!

■ ■ ■

CHAPTER 2

Mastering the User Interface

Although I know you are primarily interested in writing games (and we will get to that soon I promise!), our masterpieces of entertainment will all still run within the humble Windows Mobile form. In this chapter, we will examine the form and some of the controls that are available to use within it in detail. We'll also consider when and how these are relevant in our game design.

In many ways, working with the form designer is very similar to its desktop counterpart. However, some subtle and important differences need to be taken into consideration. Many of the controls that Visual Studio offers are unlikely to be of use to us in the context of game design, and we'll skip over these. Others may be used in almost every game you write.

Developing for Touch Screen and Smart Phone Devices

There are a number of behavioral variations between the controls and properties available on touch screen and smart phone devices, and in some cases, these are significant. If you wish to include smart phone users in your target audience (which I would encourage you to do wherever possible), it is necessary to understand the implications of these variations.

It is entirely possible to develop a single application that works on both classes of hardware, and as part of the examination of UI design in this chapter, we will look at how this can be achieved. Each of the sections in this chapter will highlight things that you need to be aware of when designing your forms.

The general problem is that lots of functionality is available only in touch screen versions of the operating system. A couple of simple examples here are the form's ControlBox (the "X" button in the top-right corner of the screen) and Button controls. Neither of these exists in the smart phone world, as there is no way for the user to click them (although you could argue that the button could easily have been supported, as the user is able to move the focus between controls, but that is a discussion for another time).

For this reason, unless you want to develop *only* for smart phone devices, you should always design and code your software using a touch screen platform (such as Windows Mobile 6 Professional) rather than a smart phone platform. Those properties that smart phones do not support will simply be ignored when your code executes in that environment. However, if you develop against a smart phone platform, the options will not be presented to you in the first place.

In some instances, we will have to provide separate code for each of the types of device. We can determine whether we are running on a smart phone or a touch screen device by using one of Windows Mobile's API calls (surprisingly, there is no built-in .NET function to retrieve this information for us).

Listing 2–1 will query the device type and return a bool value telling us whether we are running on a smart phone.

Listing 2–1. Determining Whether Code Is Running on a Smart Phone Device

```
Using System.Runtime.InteropServices;

// Declaration of the SystemParametersInfo API function
[DllImport("Coredll.dll")]
static extern private int SystemParametersInfo(uint uiAction, uint uiParam,
    System.Text.StringBuilder pvParam, uint fWinIni);

// Constants required for SystemParametersInfo
private const uint SPI_GETPLATFORMTYPE = 257;

/// <summary>
/// Determine whether this device is a smart phone
/// </summary>
/// <returns>Returns true for smart phone devices, false for devices with
/// touch screens</returns>
public bool IsSmartphone()
{
    // Declare a StringBuilder to receive the platform type string
    StringBuilder platformType = new StringBuilder(255);

    // Call SystemParametersInfo and check the return value
    if (SystemParametersInfo(SPI_GETPLATFORMTYPE, (uint)platformType.Capacity,
                                                  platformType, 0) == 0)
    {
        // No data returned so we are unable to determine the platform type.
        // Guess that we are not a smartphone as this is the most common
        // device type.
        return false;
    }

    // Return a bool depending upon the string that we have received
    return (platformType.ToString() == "SmartPhone");
}
```

For a working example of this code, see the project 2_1_IsSmartPhone in the accompanying code download. This simple application determines the platform type and displays an appropriate message on the screen.

In practice, it would be more efficient to cache the result of the call to SystemParametersInfo so as to avoid the need to repeatedly call it. We will wrap up a nice efficient version of this function once we start developing a framework into which our game development code can grow.

Once we have this information at our disposal, we can quickly check whether we are running on a touch screen or smart phone device and then switch our code execution path depending on the result.

The User Interface Controls

Now, let's take a look at the forms themselves and the controls we can place within them.

Forms

Just like when developing for the desktop, we will use a form to provide the container for all of our applications. Some of the relevant properties of Windows Mobile forms differ in functionality from their desktop counterparts however, as detailed in the following sections.

AutoScaleMode Property

To assist with form layouts on devices with different resolutions, .NET CF will, if you wish, automatically scale all of the controls on your form so that they retain the same proportions relative to the runtime form size that they had at design time.

For example, if you place a PictureBox control so that it fills the top-left quarter of the form designer, this scaling will ensure that, regardless of the resolution of your target device, the control still occupies the same quarter of the screen at runtime. To activate this scaling, provide a value of DPI for the AutoScaleMode property (this is its default setting).

Alternatively, setting this property to None will cause the pixel sizes that you define at design time to be retained exactly at runtime. This may mean that controls appear much larger or smaller than you expected.

Note that font sizes will always be scaled to match the DPI setting of the device regardless of how this property is configured, which may result in text that no longer fits within the bounds of its control if AutoScaleMode is set to None.

NOTE The scaling of controls takes place when the form is first being displayed. Once the form initialization is complete, all control dimensions will be measured in device pixels. This means that if you programmatically change the size of controls, you will need to take different screen resolutions into account when working out how much the control sizes need to be altered.

ControlBox Property

The ControlBox property allows you to set whether the form minimize or close button (that is, the "X" or OK button) appears in the top-right corner of the form. Unless you have a very good reason to remove these buttons, you should always leave the value of this property set to True. It can be unsettling for users to find that they cannot leave the form by using the control box.

In smart phone projects, this property is not available, as the user is unable to use the button without touch screen capability. Minimizing or closing the form is always handled in a different manner (by either using a menu option to close the application or switching to another application by pressing the Home or Back hardware buttons).

FormFactor Property

By default, the form designer shows a device with a 240 × 320–pixel resolution. If you intend to target a different size screen than this, it can be useful to change the form designer to match the target resolution.

The FormFactor property allows any of the emulated devices available for the selected platform to be chosen for form design purposes. The form designer will immediately change its size to match that of the device you have selected.

Note that if the AutoScaleMode property is set to DPI when you change this then the controls placed within your form will scale to match the new form resolution; otherwise, they will be left at their current pixel sizes.

If you frequently wish to use a FormFactor other than this, the default can be changed. Select the Tools ➤ Options item from Visual Studio's menu bar, and then navigate to Device Tools ➤ Form Factors. The Default Form Factor can be changed to whichever form factor you most commonly use (see Figure 2–1). All new forms that are created will default to whichever target you have selected.

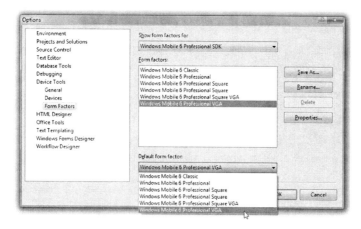

Figure 2–1. *Setting the default form factor*

MinimizeBox Property

The ControlBox property controls whether the Close or Minimize button in displayed in the top-right corner of the form. If so, The MinimizeBox property controls which of the two buttons will be displayed. When MinimizeBox is set to True, the button will display as an "X", which minimizes the form (this differs from the behavior in Windows, in which the same button closes the form). When MinimizeBox is False, the button will display OK instead and will close the form when clicked.

In general, the minimize box should always be displayed for main application windows, and the close box retained for dialog windows.

This property is not available for smart phone projects and has no effect on such devices.

Text Property

A form's Text property controls the caption displayed at the top of the form. It also controls the way the form is referred to in other parts of the operating system. When the Running Programs tab in the

Windows Mobile's Settings pages is open, the form caption will be displayed to identify your program to the user.

It is important, therefore, to make sure you set this value sensibly for every form you create, even if the caption is not actually displayed within the window. Users won't be impressed by an application referred to as Form1.

WindowState Property

Two options are available for the WindowState property: Normal and Maximized. When set to Maximized, the form will expand in size so that it covers the status bar across the top of the screen.

In many situations, covering the status bar might be frowned upon, but for the purposes of games, doing so can be extremely useful. Using the full screen like this can give the user a greater feeling of immersion within the game, hiding away the intrusion of the operating system. Be aware, though, that going full screen can also be disorienting for users, as normally the status bar is available at all times. You should ensure the user always has a clear route out of your application if you maximize your window. Additionally, it is usually a good idea to offer to maximize your form as a user preference rather than forcing the window into this state.

Resize Event

A standard feature of Windows Mobile is the ability to rotate the screen to different orientations than the default. This can happen at any time: many devices will automatically rotate the screen when certain events occur (for example, if a hardware keyboard is slid out), or if the device is fitted with an accelerometer, rotation may be a result of simply physically turning the device.

As a result, such rotation may occur while your game is running. When this happens, you will need to respond to it in some way. Otherwise, your game will suddenly find that it no longer fits within the bounds of the screen.

We'll deal with how to respond to rotation later on, but for now, it is worth knowing how to detect that the device has rotated. This information can easily be picked up by responding to the form's Resize event. When the rotation takes place, the window's width and height will effectively swap, resulting in this event being fired.

The one exception to this is with devices that have square screens. How do we deal with rotation on such devices? The simple answer is that we don't need to worry about it. The window size will be exactly the same after rotation as it was before, and so we can just carry on with our game without having to change anything at all.

Creating Non-Full-Screen Forms

Although it is not immediately obvious how, non-full-screen windows can be created within your application if you wish. These can be useful for in-game dialogs, showing high scores and so on, without pulling the user completely away from your game.

To configure a form to display in this way, set its properties as follows:

```
FormBorderStyle = None
MinimizeBox = False
Size = (100, 100)
WindowState = Normal
```

The Size property can of course be set to whatever size you want your window to be.

With these settings in place, your window will appear floating in front of whatever is behind it. The "X" button required to close the window will still appear in the top-right corner of the screen, not within the window itself.

The Location property can then be used to position the window. Note that there is no equivalent to the desktop StartupPosition property, so if you want to center your window, you will have to calculate its position manually. This can be easily achieved by setting up a Form Load event containing the code in Listing 2–2.

Listing 2–2. Automatically Center a Non-Full-Screen Form

```
private void Form1_Load(object sender, EventArgs e)
{
    // Calculate the position required to center the from
    int left = (Screen.PrimaryScreen.WorkingArea.Width - this.Width) / 2;
    int top = (Screen.PrimaryScreen.WorkingArea.Height - this.Height) / 2;
    // Set the form's location
    this.Location = new Point(left, top);
}
```

■ **NOTE** The FormBorderStyle, MinimizeBox, and Location properties are not supported on smart phone platforms and do not appear within the form designer's Properties window. They can be set through code but will have no effect on the form and will generate warnings when compiling with a smart phone device set as the target platform. If you are supporting smart phone devices, make sure you account for the lack of support for this feature.

To return your form to being full screen, set its FormBorderStyle property back to FixedSingle. The form will immediately revert to its original size.

This functionality cannot be replicated on smart phones, which force the window to fill the screen regardless of how these properties are set.

Losing and Gaining Focus

Each time your form becomes the foremost form and gains focus, its Activated event will fire. When the user switches away from your application or something else jumps in front, the form's Deactivate event fires. This behavior makes it simple for individual forms to track whether they are active or not. After all, if your form is not in the foreground, there's no point in spending lots of CPU time processing game logic the user is not even seeing—in fact, it would probably be better to suspend the game entirely until the user returns.

Telling whether your application has the focus gets slightly more complex when you add multiple forms into your code. If you need to know whether *any* of your forms are active, there is no built-in way to determine this. Fortunately, this limitation can be easily solved because of the way in which .NET CF fires these two events. When focus changes from one of your forms to another, the first form's Deactivate event will consistently fire before the new form's Activate event. We can keep track of whether one of our forms has the focus by creating a variable and setting it to true each time a form is activated and false each time it is deactivated. If we create this variable as a static variable, we can see it at all times from any part of our project.

For a working example of this code, see the project 2_2_AppFocus in the accompanying code download. This piece of code writes a message to the Visual Studio Output window once per second, identifying whether or not the application has focus. Try opening the second window or minimizing the application and then switching back to it. The application focus value always identifies whether the application is in the foreground.

A useful alternative to using multiple forms is to use a single form with Panel controls placed on it. Each panel can then be treated as if it were a virtual form in its own right. To display one of these "forms," simply set the panel so that it has its Visible property set to true and its Dock property set to Fill. To hide it again, simply set its Visible property back to false. Other controls can be placed within these panels exactly as they would be into real forms, simulating form switching without any of the complexities of having to actually manage multiple forms.

Labels

The humble Label performs the same basic tasks on Windows Mobile applications as it does on the desktop: displaying text. While the label may be low-tech, don't underestimate its use in displaying textual information in your games: it can often be much easier and more efficient to put a label on to your form to show the player's score instead of using graphical routines to draw the text on.

One very useful feature that is sadly missing from the CF Label is the AutoSize property. On the desktop .NET Framework, this automatically sizes the control to match the text that is contained within; in .NET CF, the label's size is always set manually.

It is possible to work around this by measuring the size of the text within the label and adjusting the label size to match. A little extra work also allows the TextAlign setting to be taken into account, so that if the text is centered, the center point of the label is maintained, and if the text is right-aligned, the right edge of the label stays put. The 2_3_AutoSizeLabel sample project in the accompanying code download provides a demonstration of this and a working autosize function, which you can use in your projects.

Buttons

For the most part, buttons also function in much the way you would expect in .NET CF. Many of their properties are missing compared to the desktop Button control (for example, buttons in .NET CF do not offer support for using images instead of text, nor for aligning the button text). Other properties remain (such as the very useful DialogResult property).

The main point to note about buttons, as has already been briefly touched on, is that they are not supported at all on smart phone devices. Any attempt to open a form containing a button on such a device will result in a NotSupportedException being thrown by the framework.

Throwing this exception strikes me as unnecessary, since the smart phone UI already supports the concept of moving the focus through the fields within a form using the up and down navigation buttons, so buttons could easily be implemented by allowing them to gain the focus in this way and then clicked by pressing the selection button.

Opening a form containing an unsupported control within the Visual Studio Form designer when a smart phone platform is selected will replace the control within the designer with a warning icon, such as the one shown in Figure 2–2. All of the control's properties will be disabled. Visual Studio doesn't actually change or damage the control properties however, and switching back to a non-smart-phone platform will restore all of the control functionality.

Figure 2–2. Controls in the form designer that are not supported on smart phone platforms

The alternative to buttons recommended by Microsoft is to use a MainMenu control (which we will be looking at next). Usually, it will provide a sufficient substitute, but if you plan to include buttons within your game forms, please bear this limitation in mind.

Menu Bars

Menus are one of the most widely used controls in the Windows Mobile environment and are a key user interface feature of virtually all mobile applications. They provide a straightforward mechanism for allowing the user to navigate around the system, execute commands that an application offers, and switch configuration settings on and off.

It is, therefore, very useful to be able to implement menus into your own software, and the MainMenu control allows you to do this.

Depending on the style and presentation of your game, you may well decide to implement your own menu system. This is fine if you prefer, but do bear in mind that your users will already be familiar with the standard menu system and will understand exactly how to use it; your own menus may look nice but may not be as simple to use. On the other hand, the standard menu may take up space that you wish to use for your game and can provide a distraction from whatever is happening on the screen.

Menu Design Considerations

The way menus are used has changed over the course of the various releases of Windows Mobile. In earlier versions, it was common to provide a whole series of top-level menu items in a menu bar area, providing access to all of the different functions within an application. With the arrival of Windows Mobile 5.0, this approach changed so that just two top-level items are present in the new soft key bar. This system fits in much better with the smart phone model, which offers two hardware buttons solely for the purpose of opening such top-level menus; on touch screen devices, the on-screen buttons themselves are pressed to activate the corresponding item.

Figure 2–3 shows a side-by-side comparison of two different MainMenu implementations for the same application on different versions of the operating system.

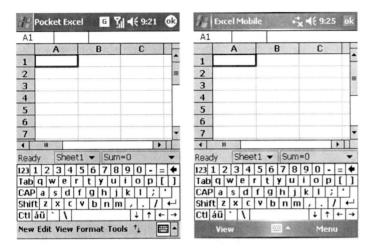

Figure 2–3. The MainMenu implementation in Pocket Excel (running in Windows Mobile 2003) and Excel Mobile (running in Windows Mobile 5.0).

Microsoft's design guidelines for menus state that the item on the left should be used to provide the most likely user action command, and the item on the right to open a menu containing further commands. It is not necessary to strictly adhere to this policy, but in general, it should be considered when designing your menus. If you find that you have a series of unrelated actions, such as user preferences and file selection, put them in a menu on the right; if you have one or more actions that specifically apply to the user's current scenario within your game, put these on the left.

If you particularly want to, you can include more than two top-level items within the Visual Studio MainMenu control. These will look and work just like the old-style menus when running on a touch screen device. When on a smart phone however, any form using such a menu will fail on loading with a NotSupportedException.

The menu also supports having just a single item (which will appear on the left) or no items at all.

There is one other important feature of the menu bar and the soft key bar: on touch screen devices, they include the button that opens the Soft Input Panel (SIP). This panel is shown in both of the screen shots in Figure 2–3, and it allows the user to enter text using the on-screen keyboard or one of the other input mechanisms. If the bar is hidden, the user has no way to request the SIP to appear, which one reason that Microsoft recommends leaving the bar active even if there are no items within it.

Submenus

The MainMenu control supports unlimited levels of submenus. These allow a potentially sprawling and complex menu structure to be derived. Such structures should be avoided if possible, as navigating them becomes time-consuming and frustrating. Due to the limited size of the screen, submenus very quickly begin to overlap with their parent elements, which can be confusing to visually interpret.

Try not to use more than a single level of submenu if you can. If possible, avoid using submenus in the soft button on the left of the menu, as this should be reserved for straightforward commands instead of more complex menu hierarchies.

Smart Phone Menus

When menus are used on a smart phone device, each menu item is automatically given a numeric shortcut alongside its item text. Pressing the appropriate key on the numeric keypad will immediately activate the corresponding menu item. This provides the user with a quick way of selecting each item without having to scroll up and down through the list. No additional code is required to activate these shortcuts; the platform will add them itself.

The items within each menu will be given shortcut numbers starting from 1 (the top-most item) through to 0 (the item at the bottom). If your menu has more than ten items, they will appear unnumbered and will need to be accessed using the up and down buttons. In practical terms, menus with this many items are probably too large anyway.

Working with MainMenu Controls

All new forms initially contain a MainMenu form when they are created. It may be removed if you wish, and once this has been done, the control may be re-added from the Toolbox.

It is also possible to add multiple MainMenu controls to the same form. Each of these will appear in the icon-tray below the form designer and may be edited by first selecting its icon and then changing its items as required. Only one MainMenu may be active at any time however. The active menu is set using the form's Menu property, which can be set both at design time and at runtime. If you need to display different sets of menu options at different times in your game, creating multiple MainMenu controls is the simplest way to achieve this.

MainMenu items at any level may be disabled to prevent them from being selected. If a disabled MainMenu control has any child items, the child menu will become inaccessible. Items may be enabled or disabled both at design time and at runtime.

There is no support for making menu items invisible. If you wish to hide a menu item, you will need to entirely remove it from the menu and re-add it (and rewire its event handlers) if you wish to make it visible again.

Items may be checked or unchecked by setting their Checked property. Top-level menu items and items that contain subitems are not eligible for becoming checked and will result in an exception being thrown if an attempt is made to check one.

Separators may be added by creating a menu item whose caption is a dash (–). These will be displayed as an unselectable horizontal line. On smart phone platforms, no shortcut number will be assigned to separator items.

MainMenu Events

Items within the menu support two events: Click and Popup.

Click is fired each time the user activates a menu item. If the menu is a parent item containing submenus however, this event does not fire.

Instead, to catch the opening of a submenu, listen for the Popup event on the menu item that contains the submenu. This is actually a good way of initializing your menu for use: if you have various options that may be enabled, disabled, checked, or otherwise configured within the menu, you can simply hook into the Popup event of your top-level menu items and use this to configure all of the items within the whole menu structure. This lets you keep all of the menu manipulation logic together in a single place, reducing the complexity of the code.

Menu Item Naming

As you will potentially end up with a lot of menu items (especially if you use multiple MainMenu controls), using a consistent naming scheme for your menu items is worthwhile.

My preferred approach is to provide a name for the menu control itself, such as mnuMain. Within here, I name the two top-level items with the same name, followed by an underscore and then an item-specific name. For example, I may call my items mnuMain_Restart and mnuMain_Menu. Each subitem then takes its parent item name followed by another underscore and an item-specific name. So the items that appear within the top-level mnuMain_Menu item will be given names such as mnuMain_Menu_ShowScores, mnuMain_Menu_Settings, and mnuMain_Menu_About. This system provides a consistent way of identifying and referring to your menu items and makes for much more readable code.

Visual Studio's Document Outline window, shown in Figure 2–4, provides a useful tool for viewing and changing the names of your menu items. It can be opened by selecting View ➤ Other Windows ➤ Document Outline from Visual Studio's main menu. Within the Document Outline window, menu items can be selected (and highlighted within the form designer) by clicking the item within the list and renamed by single-clicking the item again once it has been selected. This can be used for any other controls placed on your form, too.

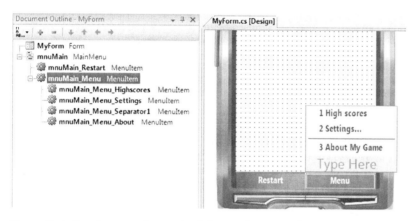

Figure 2–4. *Consistent and meaningful menu item naming*

Context Menus

The ContextMenu is very similar in function to the MainMenu control, but instead of appearing constantly at the bottom of the form, it appears when the user touches an area of the form for a couple of seconds. Windows Mobile draws a ring of dots around the point that has been touched, and after a brief pause, the context menu appears.

Due to the way users control games, context menus are unlikely to feature prominently in all of your programs. However, they can be useful in certain circumstances where the user needs to interact in some way with one of the items in your game. Using a context menu is much more probable in slower games (a character based role-playing game, for example) than in action games. On those occasions where it fits in with the user interface, it can provide a handy input mechanism.

ContextMenu controls are added to your form in the same way as MainMenu controls and appear in the icon tray below the form design. When the control is selected, a menu editor will appear within the form designer itself, and the items you wish to include can be entered in this editor.

The easiest way to display a context menu is to set the ContextMenu property of the form (or one of the controls to which you wish to attach the menu) so that it refers to your ContextMenu control. Pressing and holding on the control will trigger the display of the menu.

An alternative method is to call the ContextMenu control's Show() method. This provides a simple mechanism for displaying the menu on demand (for example, within a Click event handler) without having to wait for Windows Mobile to display its ring of dots. You can also use this method if you wish to dynamically select one of a number of context menus depending on the state of your game.

The Show() method expects two parameters: the control over which the context menu is to display and the coordinate of the top-left corner of the menu relative to the top-left corner of the specified control. To display the context menu so that it appears with its corner exactly where the user has tapped, the position can be calculated as shown in Listing 2–3.

Listing 2–3. Calculating the Position for a ContextMenu Control

```
// Get the position of the 'mouse' within the window
Point mousePos = this.PointToClient(MousePosition);
// Display the menu at the appropriate position
contextMenu1.Show(this, mousePos);
```

ContextMenu controls support the same events as MainMenu controls (Click and Popup), and they fire under the same circumstances. The Popup event for the top-level ContextMenu can be found by selecting the control within the icon tray below the form designer.

As you have probably guessed, ContextMenu controls are not supported on smart phone platforms. Forms containing such controls will display without error, but any attempt to display the menu will result in yet another NotSupportedException.

Timers

Timers perform the same task as on the desktop .NET Framework, allowing a piece of code to run at a specific time interval. The Interval property defines the frequency at which the timer ticks, measured in thousandths of a second. Setting this to 1000, therefore, causes the timer to tick once every second. Each time the interval time elapses, the Tick event is fired.

Timer Initialization

Usually, it is a good idea to leave your timer's Enabled property set to false at design time and set it to true once your game has initialized. Without following this approach, the timer could potentially begin ticking before you have finished setting up your game environment. Enabling the timer only once you are ready for it will prevent any problems occurring for this reason.

Concurrent Tick Events

Here's a question worth knowing the answer to: what happens if it takes longer to process a timer tick than the timer interval itself?

The answer is generally very simple—any ticks that occur while a previous tick is still being executed are discarded. However, the next tick's execution is based on intervals elapsed from when the first tick *began* executing code rather than when it finished. Therefore, the interval between the first tick finishing and the next tick beginning will likely be much smaller than the defined interval.

There is an exception to this tick behavior: if any code within the tick executes a call to `System.Windows.Forms.Application.DoEvents()`, any pending window messages will be processed. If the timer was due to fire by this point, it will begin executing its own timer code immediately. If this in turn makes another call to `DoEvents()`, it is possible to get into a state where none of the timer ticks ever complete their processing.

To avoid both of these situations, disable the timer at the beginning of its `Tick` event code. This stops the timer for the next tick (removing the part-interval tick problem) and prevents any further ticks from firing (removing the `DoEvents()` problem). Once all the processing required by the event is complete, the timer can be enabled once again. It is sensible to use a `try/finally` block to ensure that the timer is reenabled regardless of what happens within the procedure (see Listing 2–4).

Listing 2–4. Disabling and Reenabling a Timer During Its Tick Event

```
private void timerMain_Tick(object sender, EventArgs e)
{
    try
    {
        // Disable the timer while we work
        timerMain.Enabled = false;
        // Do whatever work is required
        DoGameProcessing();
    }
    finally
    {
        // Re-enable the timer for the next tick
        timerMain.Enabled = true;
    }
}
```

Timers on Inactive Forms

When a form that contains a timer becomes in active, the timer will continue to tick regardless. If you are performing any intensive work or updating your game, you will want to stop your timers from working when the window loses focus. Continuing to update your game will result in wasted CPU time and could result in your game ending without the player even seeing it. For example, if a phone call interrupts the user, who then switches back into the device to do something else and forgets that the game is running, your game may not gets any further attention for hours or days, yet it will be left running in the background the whole time the phone is switched on.

You should, therefore, disable your timers when your form is deactivated and reenable them when it is activated. The "Losing and Gaining Focus" section provides information about the events that will be triggered when each of these actions occurs.

Other Timers

In addition to the `Timer` control, .NET CF also offers a class that allows code to be executed at regular intervals. The `System.Threading.Timer` class can be instantiated, providing a time interval and a function to call each time the interval has elapsed.

When the callback is triggered by the timer, it will run in a different thread to the one that created the timer. This means that the timer is potentially useful for background operations but cannot directly interact with any user interface components without delegating back to the main user interface thread.

For general purpose updates, the `Timer` control is often a more practical solution.

File Dialog Controls

The Windows Mobile file dialogs are very simplistic but are still workable mechanisms for allowing the user to select a file in the device's memory to be used for reading or writing data. While these dialogs may not be something that you will frequently use in your games, one common purpose is for allowing the user to load and save a game's state.

In .NET CF, the dialogs are accessed using the OpenFileDialog and SaveFileDialog controls. The dialog controls are programmatically invoked in similar ways to their desktop equivalents and allow filenames, filters, and directories to be set and retrieved.

Sadly, for reasons known best to Microsoft, there is no support at all for either of these controls on smart phone devices. In fact, if you place either of these controls on your form, you will once again see the same old NotSupportedException that you've encountered several times already during this chapter.

To allow such dialogs to function when you are running on a touch screen device, you can simply declare and instantiate the dialog in code rather than placing a control on a form. The amount of additional code required for this is very small. If you detect that the user is running on a smart phone device, you will need to tell them that the function is unavailable or find an alternative mechanism for identifying the filename to read from or write to, like the one shown in Listing 2–5.

Listing 2–5. Using OpenFileDialog Without Failing on Smart Phone Devices

```
private bool LoadGameData()
{
    String filename;
    // Are we running on a smart phone?
    if (IsSmartphone())
    {
        // No OpenFileDialog available -- use a default filename in the My Documents folder
        filename = Environment.GetFolderPath(Environment.SpecialFolder.Personal).ToString();
        filename = System.IO.Path.Combine(filename, "MyGameData.save");
        // Does the file exist?
        if (System.IO.File.Exists(filename))
        {
            // Read the game data
            ReadGameDataFromFile(filename);
            return true;
        }
    }
    else
    {
        // We can use the OpenFileDialog to select the file
        using (OpenFileDialog openFileDlg = new OpenFileDialog())
        {
            // Configure the dialog
            openFileDlg.FileName = filename;
            openFileDlg.Filter = "Game saves|*.save|All files|*.*";
            // Show the dialog
            if (openFileDlg.ShowDialog() == DialogResult.OK)
            {
                // A file was selected so read the game data
                ReadGameDataFromFile(openFileDlg.FileName);
```

```
                    return true;
                }
            }
        }
    }
}
```

Some implementations of `OpenFileDialog`-like dialogs written in C# available on the Internet are designed to work on smart phones. In fact, the built-in dialogs on touch screen devices are so basic that, in some ways, these custom dialog windows are actually preferable to the real thing, but genuine Windows Mobile dialogs are at least standard and probably best used when the hardware supports it.

For examples of such custom dialogs, see the following web sites:

```
http://www.eggheadcafe.com/articles/20050624.asp
http://www.devx.com/wireless/Article/17104/1763/page/1
```

Input Panels

When entering text on Windows Mobile devices, users without hardware keyboards will use one of the on-screen text entry panels. These include the on-screen keyboard, letter recognizer, and phone keypad input panels—each of these is known as a Soft Input Panel (SIP).

Being able to interact with an SIP is sometimes useful. For example, when prompting the user to enter some text, you can automatically open the SIP to save the user from needing to manually. Another useful thing is to be able to tell when the SIP is opened or closed by the user and to tell how much space it occupies. This gives you the option of moving things that would otherwise be obscured behind it out of the way.

The `InputPanel` control provides a simple way of performing these interactions. It can be added to your form and appears in the icon tray below the form designer. A couple of properties are available at design time, but the most useful features of the `InputPanel` are available when your program is running.

Your code can, at any time, detect whether the SIP is open by checking its `Enabled` property, which will return `true` when the SIP is open and `false` when it is closed. The value of this property can be set too, so you can use this to programmatically show or hide the SIP as required.

To make responding to this easier, the control provides an event called `EnabledChanged`. This event fires each time the `Enabled` property value is changed (either by the user or your program code).

If you need to respond to the SIP appearing or disappearing, the `InputPanel` provides two useful properties that allow you to determine exactly where it is located on the screen. The `VisibleDesktop` property returns a `Rectangle` whose position and size match that of the screen area that is not occupied by the SIP or by the status bar at the top of the screen. It will take into account whether the SIP is currently visible and adjust its coordinates accordingly.

The second similar property is the `Bounds` property. It also returns a `Rectangle`, but this time, the position and size of the SIP itself is specified. In particular, this property is very useful for simply finding the height of the SIP so that you can move things out of the way. The value returned by the `Bounds` property is not dependent on whether the SIP is currently open: it will still return the location information that would be occupied by the SIP even if it is currently closed.

Figure 2–5 shows `VisibleDesktop` and `Bounds` in action.

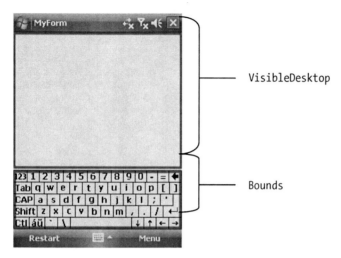

Figure 2–5. TheVisibleDesktop and Bounds areas

And yes, you've guessed it; there's obviously no support for the SIP on smart phones. The input panels are all about getting text from the user via the touch screen, so smart phones would have no use for them at all. Unfortunately, this is yet another instance where simply placing an InputPanel control on your form will result in a NotSupportedException being thrown.

As always, there is a simple work-around for this problem (see Listing 2–6). Instead of placing the InputPanel control on your form, you can define it as a variable within your code. At form initialization, you can then instantiate the object only if you are running on a touch screen device. When interacting with the object later, ensure that it is not null before calling any of its properties or methods.

Listing 2–6. InputPanel Compatibility with Smart Phone Devices

```
public partial class MyForm : Form
{
    // Declare our InputPanel variable
    private Microsoft.WindowsCE.Forms.InputPanel _inputPanel;

    public MyForm()
    {
        InitializeComponent();
        // If we are running on a touch-screen device, instantiate the inputpanel
        if (!IsSmartphone())
        {
            _inputPanel = new Microsoft.WindowsCE.Forms.InputPanel();
            // Add event handler (if required)
            _inputPanel.EnabledChanged += new System.EventHandler(EnabledChanged);
        }
    }

    /// <summary>
    /// Determine whether the SIP is currently open
```

```
        /// </summary>
        private bool IsSIPOpen
        {
            get
            {
                // If we have an inputpanel, return its Enabled property
                if (_inputPanel != null) return _inputPanel.Enabled;
                // No input panel present so always return false
                return false;
            }
        }
}
```

■ **NOTE** If you can't find the InputPanel class, make sure you have a reference to Microsoft.WindowsCE.Forms, as this is where InputPanel's classes are defined.

Capturing Camera Images

A popular feature for novelty games is to allow the users to take a photograph of themselves (or of a handy victim) and then distort or otherwise modify this photograph for comic effect. Other uses can be made of photos too, allowing users to save a picture of themselves into a high score table, for example. As cameras are fitted into a huge number of mobile devices these days, let's take a quick look at how you can take advantage of them within your games.

Prior to Windows Mobile 5.0, there was no standard mechanism for accessing the camera. Each vendor and device would implement their own API for this, and so writing code that worked on multiple devices was problematic and time-consuming. With the arrival of Windows Mobile 5.0, Microsoft introduced a standard API to allow applications to access the camera.

The implementation of this API is still entirely down to each device vendor to implement, so the user interface presented and the specific functionality available may vary considerably from one device to the next. Furthermore, even with the standardized API, not all devices support access to the camera using this mechanism and will throw unhelpful InvalidOperationException messages when the camera functionality is invoked. For this reason, you should either ensure that the use of the camera in your game is optional or accept that some of your potential audience will be unable to use your game. Allowing an option to import a photo from a file will provide a useful alternative when the camera can't be accessed.

Taking all of this into account, interacting with the camera within your code is very straightforward. The CameraCaptureDialog control provides a simple mechanism for retrieving pictures that is broadly similar to the other dialog controls within .NET (see Figure 2–6). CameraCaptureDialog is defined in Microsoft.WindowsMobile.Forms, so add a reference if you need to.

Figure 2–6. The CameraDialog in action on an HTC Touch Pro2 device

If the picture is successfully taken, a result of OK is returned from the ShowDialog() method. Unfortunately, the dialog doesn't return the image that has been taken. Instead, the image is saved to the device's memory and its filename returned. Once you have read in this image file, it is a good idea to delete it to prevent the memory from jamming up with old photos.

Ensure that the camera code is wrapped in a try/catch block that appropriately handles the exceptions that are thrown when the dialog cannot be used. This will trap problems both from older devices (earlier than Windows Mobile 5.0) and devices on which the camera interaction fails.

See the project 2_4_CameraCaptureDialog in the accompanying code download for a simple working example of capturing a picture using the CameraCaptureDialog and transferring the resulting image to a PictureBox control.

The "Busy" Cursor

Windows Mobile's standard "busy" indicator is to display the spinning color wheel in the centre of the screen. If your game needs to perform any takes that may be time-consuming, you can easily display the same indicator from within your code.

The "busy" indicator is implemented using the same concept as the hourglass cursor on desktop Windows and is therefore set using an object called Cursor. To display the indicator, execute the following code:

```
Cursor.Current = Cursors.WaitCursor;
```

To remove the indicator, use this:

```
Cursor.Current = Cursors.Default;
```

On with the Game

In this chapter, we have looked at a variety of different aspects and features of user interface design and this should give you a good idea of how to construct forms for use within your games. There are lots of things to take into account when designing your user interface, from device capabilities to general layout and design.

Microsoft has published a series of "Design Guidelines" for Windows Mobile applications, addressing all sorts of techniques and practices that can be employed when creating your games. The guidelines are well worth reading through and can be found at the following URL:

`http://msdn.microsoft.com/en-us/library/bb158602.aspx`

Now that you are fully up to speed with how to develop for Windows Mobile, let's take the next step forward and begin our journey into writing some games.

PART 2

Creating Games

CHAPTER 3

■■■

GDI Graphics

Now, it is time to start putting the knowledge you have acquired so far into writing a game. The approach that we will take over the next few chapters is to build a straightforward and easy-to-use game framework that we can use to develop our creations. This framework will take care of all the problems and device diversity that you have discovered in your journey so far, keeping as many of these details as possible tidied away so that we don't need to worry about them.

In this chapter, we will look at the Graphics Device Interface (GDI), one of Windows Mobile's fundamental graphics technologies.

All About GDI

Let's not kid ourselves: GDI is not a high performance graphics interface. We're not going to create fast-moving 3D games using it (we'll get to those later on when we look at OpenGL ES). However, it isn't a waste of time either. For a huge number of games and game styles, GDI is perfectly adequate and well suited. It is simple to use and supported on all versions of Windows Mobile, and with a little bit of care, it can be tuned to give perfectly reasonable performance on virtually all devices.

Historically, mobile devices have significantly lacked in power and ability compared to desktop PCs. While the desktop has undergone a major 3D revolution with huge power available from even very cheap graphics cards, mobile devices have remained limited both by power consumption and physical size. While APIs such as DirectX and OpenGL offer a substantial set of powerful and flexible features, many devices are simply not able to handle the kind of complex operations that such technologies require. The features offered by GDI may be simple in comparison, but they will work well on hardware old and new, and with a little effort can produce very enjoyable and attractive games.

GDI is a set of classes and functions that allow simple graphical operations to be performed. The Windows Mobile operating system itself uses GDI for many of its display functions.

In the following sections, we will discuss how to use GDI and examine the functionality that it offers us as game developers.

Let's Paint

The starting point for all our graphical updates is the Form's Paint event, which is called every time the form (or any part of the form) needs to be redrawn. Inside this event, we can draw everything we need to our window and be certain that it will be constantly displayed whenever our window is visible.

The Paint event is invoked with two parameters, as follows:

```
private void Form1_Paint(object sender, PaintEventArgs e)
{
}
```

As with all standard .NET events, our sender object provides a reference to whatever invoked the event (which in this case will be the form being painted). The second parameter, of type PaintEventArgs, is our route into getting our graphics on to the screen. It contains a property called Graphics (whose class name is also Graphics), and via this object, all of the drawing functions and properties that GDI has to offer are made available.

We'll start with a very simple example that draws some lines inside our form (see Listing 3–1).

Listing 3–1. Painting Lines to a Form

```
private void Form1_Paint(object sender, PaintEventArgs e)
{
    // Create a black pen
    using (Pen myPen = new Pen(Color.Black))
    {
        // Draw a line from the top left (0, 0) to the bottom right
        // (Width, Height) of the form
        e.Graphics.DrawLine(myPen, 0, 0, this.Width, this.Height);
        // Draw a line from the top right (Width, 0) to the bottom left
        // (0, Height) of the form
        e.Graphics.DrawLine(myPen, this.Width,0, 0, this.Height);
    }
}
```

If you try adding this code to a form and then running your code, you will find the form displays as shown in Figure 3–1.

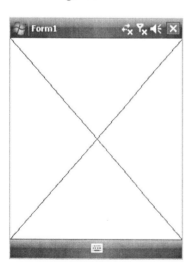

Figure 3–1. A painted form

Using this outline framework, we will now examine the functionality and methods available for drawing on our forms and look at some of the related classes and data structures that come into play.

Invalidating a Form

Listing 3–1 relies on the form automatically painting itself. This takes place when the form is first opened, so if we hook into the Paint event and render to the form at that point, our graphics are displayed.

In less trivial examples, however, we will need to repaint the form over and over again. This will allow us to move and animate the graphics that are displayed on the screen. To force the form to repaint, call its Invalidate method. This tells GDI that all of the current form content is out of date, so the Paint event will fire once again in order for it to be updated. As a simple example, this method could be called from within a Timer control to update the graphics displayed on the screen.

The Invalidate method provides a second overload into which a Rectangle can be passed to indicate that just a section of the form should be repainted. This offers us potential to improve performance of our game by repainting only parts of the form that have actually changed. We will take advantage of this to optimize our display updates in the next chapter.

The Drawing Coordinate System

Locations within a Form are specified using standard x axis (horizontal) and y axis (vertical) coordinate system. Parameter names for functions throughout GDI will use the names x and y to request the position within the form at which their drawing operations are to update.

When coordinates are written down, they are enclosed within parentheses inside which two values are placed, separated by a comma. The first value is the x coordinate, and the second is the y coordinate. For example, (20, 50) represents a point with an x coordinate of 20 and a y coordinate of 50.

The coordinate system used by GDI starts from (0, 0) at the top-left corner of the form. This then extends across the form's width and height such that the point at the bottom right corner of the form is (Form.Width - 1, Form.Height - 1).

All coordinates are measured in pixels, regardless of the form's AutoScaleMode property. If your game is running on a display with a different resolution to the one it was designed on, your graphics will need to be scaled to fit the new display. We won't worry about that just yet, though we will look at ways to deal with this in Chapter 8 when we come to implement a full game.

Colors

Everything we draw will require us to provide a color for drawing. There are two ways that we can specify a color to use:

- Using one of the named color values from System.Drawing.Color
- Specifying the individual levels of red, green, and blue that will make up the color

A large range of named colors is provided, from standard colors such as Black and Blue to those with more extravagant names including the sublime PapayaWhip and the unmistakable BlanchedAlmond. This list of named colors is actually the full list of X11 colors, which also form the predefined named colors used for HTML and Cascading Style Sheets (CSS). For further information about these colors, see the Wikipedia page at http://en.wikipedia.org/wiki/Web_colors where a full list and an example of each can be seen.

Colors may alternatively be specified by providing the levels of red, green, and blue intensity (the additive primary colors) that are required to form the required color. Each of these is specified independently and ranges from 0 (no intensity) to 255 (full intensity). For example, creating a color with its red component set to 255 and its green and blue components set to 0 will result in a pure red. By varying the intensity of each color, all of the available shades that the device is able to display can be created.

▓ **NOTE** There are various different models in which colors can be specified. In printing, the most common model is the CMYK model. "CMYK" is an abbreviation for "Cyan, Magenta, Yellow, and Key-black." Cyan, magenta, and yellow are the primary *subtractive colors*—so named because when additional color is applied, they reduce the amount of light that is reflected and result in a darker color. The model that is most commonly used in computer devices is RGB, an abbreviation for "Red, Green, and Blue." Red, green, and blue are the primary *additive colors*, which result in an increased amount of light when the colors are mixed together (so that, in fact, mixing all three results in white light). The .NET framework supports color specifications using the RGB model.

As we can specify 256 levels of each of the three color components, we are able to create colors from a total palette of 16,777,216 different colors ($256 \times 256 \times 256 = 16,777,216$). This is the same color depth as used on virtually all modern desktop PC displays. As each of the three color components requires 8 bits of data (to store a value from 0 to 255), this is known as 24-bit color.

However, Windows Mobile devices generally do not display their colors using all of this information. Color detail is sacrificed to avoid the extra processing overhead and memory requirements needed to display the entire palette. The majority of devices display either 65,536 colors or 262,244 colors. To obtain 65,536 colors, you have 16 bits in total, divided into 5 bits for red, 6 for green, and 5 for blue (the reason they are weighted toward green is because the eye is more susceptible to subtle differences in shades of green than in either blue or red). For 262,244 colors, there are 18 bits in total, formed from 6 bits each for red, green, and blue.

Despite this lower color detail, and for both consistency and future-proofing, the .NET color functions accept 8-bit values for their red, green, and blue color intensities. The loss of color precision is handled by the device itself and not imposed by the operating system. As faster and more powerful devices are produced in the future, we may see the color palette increase, and colors created in this way will automatically take advantage of the extra shades of color that are available.

In practical terms, the difference between 16- or 18-bit color and the full 24-bit color palette is hard to distinguish in most cases.

To create a color using RGB values, call the `static System.Drawing.Color.FromArgb` function. There are various overloads of this, but the one we are interested in at the moment takes three parameters named `red`, `green`, and `blue`. Pass in the color intensity levels that you require, and a `Color` object will be returned. You must ensure that all of your values fall within the range of 0 to 255 or an `ArgumentOutOfRange` exception will be thrown.

The project `3_1_ColorFromArgb` in this chapter's downloads demonstrates creating colors from their RGB values and using them to create a gradient that fades across the form. The menu options can be used to select which color components should be included within the fade. The screen produced by the program looks like the one shown in Figure 3–2.

Figure 3–2. *Gradient graphics produced by the ColorFromArgb program*

Smooth gradient fills are one of the cases in which the restricted color palette is more clearly visible. You will most likely notice that the gradient is not entirely smooth and instead consists of bands of color a few pixels thick.

Incidentally, the mysterious A component in FromArgb is for the alpha level, which controls the level of transparency of the color: a fully opaque color will entirely replace whatever is behind it, while semitransparent colors will allow the background to be seen through. Unfortunately, GDI on Windows Mobile does not support alpha transparency, so we will not be exploring it any further at the moment. We'll look at alpha values more closely later on when we begin working with OpenGL ES in Chapter 10.

Pens and Brushes

All graphics operations require either a Pen object (for functions which fundamentally draw lines) or a Brush object (for functions which fill a region of the form in a solid color). These objects must be created within our code when required and disposed of when we have finished using them.

Pens

To create a pen, we simply instantiate a new System.Drawing.Pen object, providing the color that we want the pen to draw in (as we discussed in the "Colors" section).

In addition to specifying just the pen color, we can also specify its width in pixels. If this is not specified, it will default to a width of 1 pixel.

Once a pen has been created, its color and width can be modified by setting the Pen's Color or Width properties. There is no need to create a new Pen object to change one of these properties.

Pens also offer support for creating dashed lines. These can be controlled using the DashStyle property.

Once you have finished using a Pen, don't forget to call its Dispose method to release any resources that it has allocated.

Brushes

Unlike the similar Pen class, System.Drawing.Brush is actually an abstract base class. This allows the .NET framework to provide several different types of brushes, and it is one of these derived types that we must actually instantiate.

Two such brush classes are available in .NET CF: SolidBrush and TextureBrush. The SolidBrush is the one that we will use the most: instantiated by passing a Color to its constructor, it creates a single solid color that is used to fill the interior area of whatever we draw. TextureBrush is created with a Bitmap object passed to its constructor instead of a Color, and it uses tiled copies of the bitmap image to create a pattern within the drawn interior (we'll be looking at Bitmap objects shortly).

Both brush classes offer properties to allow their appearance to be changed (using the Color property for SolidBrush and the Image property for TextureBrush). Once again, don't forget to call Dispose to release resources of your brushes when you have finished with them.

Unfortunately, the set of derived brush classes in .NET CF is smaller than the one offered for the desktop .NET Framework. If you are familiar with using GDI on the desktop, you will note that, in particular, the LinearGradientBrush is missing, which is a pity as it can be used to create some useful and attractive filled regions. We will have to simulate the effects of this in our own code.

Drawing Lines

Lines form one of the simplest graphical structures that we are able to render within our forms. A line consists of several properties:

- The Pen with which the line is to be drawn
- The start coordinate of the line
- The end coordinate of the line

These are passed to the Graphics object's DrawLine method as the code in Listing 3–2 from within a form's Paint event shows.

Listing 3–2. Using the DrawLine Method

```
private void MyForm_Paint(object sender, PaintEventArgs e)
{
    // Draw a line from point (10, 10) to point (40, 40)
    using (Pen linePen = new Pen(Color.Black))
    {
        e.Graphics.DrawLine(linePen, 10, 10, 40, 40);
    }
}
```

The code shown here draws a blank line from the coordinate (10, 10) to the coordinate (40, 40), as shown in Figure 3–3. Note that both of these coordinates are inclusive: the actual width and height of the line is 41 pixels. This may seem like a trivial detail, but it can be important if you are drawing lots of lines that need to adjoin to one another.

Figure 3–3. *The output from the DrawLine example in Listing 3–2*

A further method, DrawLines, is able to draw a series of connected lines in a single operation. An array of Point variables is provided, and DrawLines will draw a line from the first point to the second, the second point to the third, and so on until all of the points have been processed. This method does not draw a line from the final point back to the first, so if you wish to draw a closed series of lines you will need to either specify the first coordinate again at the end of your array, or use the DrawPolygon method described in the next section. The example in Listing 3–3 draws the zigzag line shown in Figure 3–4.

Listing 3–3. *Using the DrawLines Method*

```
private void MyForm_Paint(object sender, PaintEventArgs e)
{
    // Declare an array of points
    Point[] points = { new Point(20, 20), new Point(50, 50),
                        new Point(80, 20), new Point(110, 50),
                        new Point(140, 20) , new Point(170, 50) };

    using (Pen linePen = new Pen(Color.Black))
    {
        // Draw a series of lines between each defined point
        e.Graphics.DrawLines(linePen, points);
    }
}
```

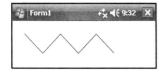

Figure 3–4. *The output from the DrawLines example in Listing 3–3*

Drawing Polygons

A *polygon* is any shape that can be formed by drawing straight lines, such that the series of lines loops back to the beginning. The lines that form a polygon may cross over one another. Polygons, therefore, include shapes such as triangles, squares, and rectangles.

In many ways, drawing a polygon in GDI is very similar to drawing lines using the DrawLines method, but there are two key differences:

- Polygons are always closed, meaning the final point is joined back to the first point.

- Polygons can be drawn so that their interior is filled with color; this cannot be achieved with DrawLines.

Polygons are defined as an array of Point structures (in just the same way you saw for the DrawLines method) and are rendered to the form using the DrawPolygon method. If the first and last points within the array are not at the same location, they will be automatically joined with an additional line.

To fill the interior of a polygon, we first create a brush as described previously in the Brushes section, and then call the FillPolygon method. If you wish to also display an outline around the edge of the polygon, use both FillPolygon and DrawPolygon one after the other (make sure you draw the outline after drawing the interior however, as otherwise the filled polygon will completely overwrite the outline).

Listing 3–4 shows an example of using drawing and filling a polygon to create the graphic shown in Figure 3–5.

Listing 3–4. Filled and Outline Polygons

```
private void Form1_Paint(object sender, PaintEventArgs e)
{
    // Define the points for our polygon
    Point[] points = { new Point(40, 20), new Point(90, 80),
                       new Point(110, 50), new Point(20, 50) };

    // First draw the filled polygon...
    using (SolidBrush polyBrush = new SolidBrush(Color.LightBlue))
    {
        e.Graphics.FillPolygon(polyBrush, points);
    }
    // ...and then draw the outline in black on top of it
    using (Pen polyPen = new Pen(Color.Black))
    {
        e.Graphics.DrawPolygon(polyPen, points);
    }
}
```

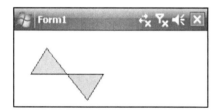

Figure 3–5. The polygon generated by Listing 3–4

This simple example uses four points to create its polygon, but there is no limit to the number of points that you use (though obviously the larger the point count, the slower it will be to render the polygon).

Drawing Rectangles

Rectangles are another of GDI's simple graphical structures. Mirroring the function structure that we have already seen with polygons, we are able to draw outline rectangles with the DrawRectangle function or filled rectangles with FillRectangle.

The location and size of the rectangle can be specified in two different ways: by passing in a Rectangle structure populated with the required information or by specifying the x, y, width, and height values.

NOTE Observe that, while the first corner of the rectangle is specified as part of the data provided to these methods, we don't specify the opposite corner by its coordinate. Instead, we imply it by specifying the rectangle's width and height. If you have a coordinate that you wish to use for the rectangle's opposite corner, the width and height can be calculated by using these formulas: width = (x2 − x1) and height = (y2 − y1).

Be aware that the width and height of the rectangle is inclusive of both bounds of the rectangle when using the DrawRectangle method: if you specify a rectangle to have a y value of 10 and a height of 20, the resulting rectangle will be 21 pixels high (including all the positions from 10 to 30 inclusive). When using FillRectangle, the rectangle will exclude the right and bottom edges, resulting in the same rectangle being 20 pixels high (including the pixels from 10 to 29 inclusive).

Width and height values may be negative if you wish and may also be 0 (in which case a horizontal or vertical line will be displayed). Note that if both dimensions are 0, nothing will be drawn at all; see the "Working with Pixels" section for more information.

GDI doesn't make any specific allowance for drawing squares; squares are simply rectangles whose width and height are equal to one another. There is also no way of drawing rotated rectangles (whose lines are at angles that are not perpendicular to the edges of the screen) using these methods; this can be achieved instead using the previously discussed polygon methods.

Drawing Ellipses

Ellipses and circles are created in a very similar way to rectangles. They are created using the function DrawEllipse and FillEllipse, and the parameters passed to these methods are identical to those passed to the corresponding rectangle functions. The resulting ellipse is created such that it exactly fills the bounds of the rectangle, as shown in Figure 3–6.

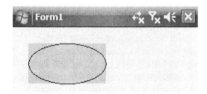

Figure 3–6. *An ellipse drawn on top of an identically-sized rectangle*

59

Like squares, circles are created simply by specifying width and height values that are equal. There is no support for drawing rotated ellipses; such ellipses could be generated by using polygons with a series of small lines to approximate the shape of the ellipse or by writing a custom drawing algorithm to produce the required shape pixel by pixel, but GDI won't do it for us on its own.

Working with Pixels

Addressing individual pixels within the form is surprisingly tricky, as the Graphics object provides no mechanism for reading or setting pixels. You might believe you can work around this by trying to draw a line whose start and end coordinate are both in the same location; unfortunately, due to an oddity in the way GDI handles single-pixel drawing requests, it decides under this circumstance not to draw anything at all. The same occurs for rectangles and ellipses whose width and height are both 0 and for polygons where all the points are at the same coordinate.

One way that it is possible to draw a single pixel is by using the FillRectangle method with width and height both set to 1. This will result in a one-pixel rectangle appearing at the specified location. This is a particularly inefficient way of writing pixels, however, and should be avoided if possible.

We will be looking at the Bitmap class later on in this chapter, and it does offer much more useful GetPixel and SetPixel methods, which are a more straightforward way of performing this task.

Displaying Text

We are also able to paint text to the form using the DrawString method. A number of overloads of this method are provided to allow finer control over the way the text is rendered.

All of these overloads have their first three parameters in common: they all require a text string to display, a font to use, and a brush to draw the text with.

The simplest version of DrawString requires us to specify the position of the text to be displayed as an (x, y) coordinate. Listing 3–5 displays some red text at coordinate (10, 10) in the form's default font.

Listing 3–5. *Printing Text to the Screen*

```
private void MyForm_Paint(object sender, PaintEventArgs e)
{
    using (SolidBrush textBrush = new SolidBrush(Color.Red))
    {
        e.Graphics.DrawString("Hello world!", this.Font, textBrush, 10, 10);
    }
}
```

The coordinate we provide will be the top-left corner of the area in which the text is printed. If the text is too wide to fit on the screen, it will simply run off the right edge of the display. We can insert line breaks into the text at any point by using C#'s \n character sequence—changing the printed text in the Listing 3–5 to read "Hello\nworld!" will cause the two words to appear one above the other. Line breaks will cause the text to resume printing a line lower but still starting at the x coordinate that was provided to DrawString.

If we need to have finer control over the layout of the text, we can take advantage of some of the other overloads of this function that are provided. These allow a Rectangle to be provided, into which the text will be drawn. This listing creates a rectangle at coordinate (10, 10) with width and height values of 100. The end result is that the text is wrapped so that it fits inside the defined area. GDI automatically breaks the text after the nearest whole word, so you don't have to worry about text wrapping midword (see Listing 3–6). If the text is long enough that it reaches the bottom of the rectangle, any further text will be clipped.

Listing 3–6. Wrapped Test Inside a Rectangular Area

```
private void MyForm_Paint(object sender, PaintEventArgs e)
{
    using (SolidBrush textBrush = new SolidBrush(Color.Red))
    {
        // Print the text into a square
        e.Graphics.DrawString("The quick brown fox jumps over the lazy dog",
                this.Font, textBrush, new Rectangle(10, 10, 100, 100));
        // Print the text into a rectangle with insufficient height
        e.Graphics.DrawString("The quick brown fox jumps over the lazy dog",
                this.Font, textBrush, new Rectangle(130, 10, 100, 35));
    }
}
```

The result from this listing is shown in Figure 3–7; note that the text on the right has overrun its rectangle, so the bottom section of text is missing.

Figure 3–7. Text drawn into rectangles using DrawString

We are also able to provide one further parameter to control how text is rendered within the rectangle, using a `StringFormat` object. Two flags are available for use by this object:

- `NoClip`: If this is specified, text will be allowed to run outside of the defined rectangle. It will still wrap within the rectangle's width but will continue past the defined height of required.

- `NoWrap`: This flag prevents the text from wrapping in the rectangle. Any text that falls outside of the rectangle will be clipped.

These flags can both be specified by combining them with C#'s binary OR operator (using the vertical bar character: |). However, this results in exactly the same effect as simply providing a point to `DrawString` rather than a rectangle.

Using Different Fonts

All of the text examples we have looked at so far have used the form's default font. It is, however, possible to change the type, size, and style of font that your text is printed with.

Our examples have all used `this.Font` as their font specification. We can of course provide a different font if we want. However, the properties of the `Font` object are all read-only, so we must provide all the required information as part of the font's instantiation. We need to provide details about which font to use, the size of the font, and the font style (bold, italicized, and so on).

If you know the name of the font you wish to use, you can specify it directly. However, the set of available fonts can vary fairly significantly between devices, even those running the same version of Windows Mobile. You may, therefore, find that your named font doesn't exist when you distribute your

61

game to other users. This won't result in an error but will instead drop back to the system default font. Named fonts are created as follows:

```
Font textFont = new Font("Tahoma", 12, FontStyle.Regular);
```

A slightly more predictable way to specify a font is using the FontFamily parameter, which allows one of three different types of font to be specified: serif, sans-serif, or monospace. Using one of these, GDI will attempt to find a suitable font of the requested type. There is still no guarantee that such a font will exist, but if one does, it will be selected without you needing to know its name. Fonts are created from a font family as follows:

```
Font textFont = new Font(FontFamily.GenericSansSerif, 12, FontStyle.Regular);
```

Both of the examples in this section also show how the font size is specified; in this case, it is being set to be 12 points. Points are a resolution-independent measurement, so your fonts should appear at approximately the same physical size regardless of the screen resolution of your target device.

The final parameter allows the font style to be chosen. This can be either Regular (no style applied) or any combination of Bold, Italic, Underline, or Strikeout. These flags may be combined to create fonts with multiple styles; for example, the following code creates a font that uses bold and italic text:

```
Font textFont = new Font(FontFamily.GenericSansSerif, 12,
                        FontStyle.Bold | FontStyle.Italic);
```

Centering Text

When working with text in GDI on the full desktop .NET Framework, the StringFormat object has all sorts of additional properties, including the very useful ability to center or right-align text on a specified point on the screen. This functionality is sadly missing from .NET CF, so we have to implement it ourselves. Fortunately, this is not very difficult. We can use the MeasureString function within the Graphics object to tell us the width and height that a piece of text will occupy when it is displayed on the screen. Once we know the width of the text, it is easy to align it however we need.

For example, if we want to print some text so that it is centered on screen, we can first find the screen's center point by dividing its width by two. If we then subtract from that half the width of the text, the result will be that half of the text is printed to the left half of the screen and half to the right—in other words, the text is centered (see Figure 3–8).

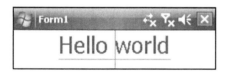

Figure 3–8. *Text centered within a form with the center point and the text width drawn alongside*

The code required to center text at a point is show in Listing 3–7.

Listing 3–7. *Centering Text*

```
private void MyForm_Paint(object sender, PaintEventArgs e)
{
    int x;
    SizeF textSize;
```

```
        int xAlignPoint;

        // Create a brush for our text
        using (SolidBrush textBrush = new SolidBrush(Color.Red))
        {
            // Create a font for our text
            using (Font textFont = new Font(FontFamily.GenericSansSerif, 20, FontStyle.Regular))
            {
                // Measure the size of the text
                textSize = e.Graphics.MeasureString("Hello world", textFont);
                // Calculate the position on which we want the text to be centered.
                // We will use the point halfway across the screen.
                xAlignPoint = this.Width / 2;
                // Determine the x position for the text
                x = xAlignPoint - ((int)textSize.Width / 2);
                // Draw the text at the resulting position
                e.Graphics.DrawString("Hello world", textFont, textBrush, x, 0);
            }
        }
}
```

To right-align text, simple change the line of code that works out the value for x so that it no longer divides the measured text width by two:

```
        [...]
        // Determine the x position for the text
        x = xAlignPoint - (int)textSize.Width;
        [...]
```

MeasureString also returns the height of the text, so it is easy to see how much vertical space your text requires too. It is also able to deal with line breaks, but be aware that with line break present, the returned size is for the entire string, not for any of the individual lines; if you want to centre a string with line breaks, you will need to split the string into each separate line and measure each one independently in order for all of the lines to be centered.

Having said all of this, there is one gotcha to be aware of: the size returned by MeasureString is unfortunately not always accurate, and sometimes returns values that are a little smaller than the text actually requires. For the purposes of aligning text, this is unlikely to cause a problem, but if you need to ensure that the size is large enough to hold the text (for example, if you are using it to build a Rectangle structure to pass into DrawString), it is advisable to add a small percentage to the returned width and height to ensure that the text actually fits.

Clearing the Background

One last very simple method is Clear. This erases the entire content of the area you are drawing on and fills it with a single color, passed as a parameter. This is effectively the same as using FillRectangle to fill the entire area but is simpler to call and doesn't require the creation of a Pen or Brush.

Painting in Action

The sample project 3_2_GDIShapes in the accompanying source code provides a demonstration of each of the different drawing functions that we have looked at so far in this chapter (see Figure 3–9). When launched, a random shape will be generated. You can then choose which method of drawing to use in order to display the shape on the screen and whether the shape should be filled or outlined (where appropriate). To create a new shape, use the New menu option.

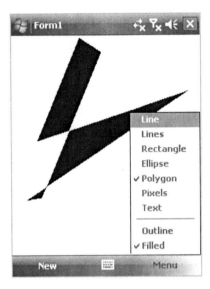

Figure 3–9. The GDIShapes sample project

Bitmaps

Armed with all of this knowledge about drawing primitives such as rectangles and ellipses, we now reach one of the most useful drawing facilities that GDI has to offer: the bitmap.

GDI's Bitmap object allows us to create an off-screen image (using the draw and fill methods we have been using throughout the Let's Paint section, loading predrawn graphics, or using a combination of these methods) and then paint copies of this image on to the screen. Bitmaps provide us with a mechanism for loading external graphics into our game or constructing complex graphics using graphics primitives. We can then efficiently rendering them on to the screen in a single function call. These are the closest to *sprites* (moving graphical objects) that we have available to us using GDI. By changing the image that we draw each time we update the screen, we are able to create effective animated graphics too.

Creating Bitmaps Using Graphics Primitives

It is easy to create an image using the drawing functions that we have already been using within this chapter. Once this image is ready, drawing it to the screen is a quick and efficient task, much more so than repeatedly invoking the drawing functions.

To create a bitmap in this way, we first instantiate a Bitmap object, stating the width and height that we desire (in pixels) as part of the object constructor. This will create an empty bitmap, which initially is filled in black.

In order for us to be able to draw on the bitmap, we need to obtain a Graphics object. We can get hold of this object by calling the static Graphics.FromImage function. Once this is done, all of the drawing methods can be used to draw whatever shapes (or text) are required. Remember that this is all taking place into the bitmap and not on to the screen; the bitmap won't be visible at all until we draw it at a later time (which we will do shortly).

Listing 3–8 creates a Bitmap, sets its background to be white, and draws a circle within it.

Listing 3–8. Creating and Drawing on a Bitmap

```
// Declare the Bitmap object that we are going to create
Bitmap myBitmap;

private void InitializeBitmap()
{
    // Create the bitmap and set its width and height
    myBitmap = new Bitmap(50, 50);
    // Create a Graphics object for our bitmap
    using (Graphics gfx = Graphics.FromImage(myBitmap))
    {
        // Fill the entire bitmap in white
        gfx.Clear(Color.White);
        // Create a pen for drawing
        using (Pen b = new Pen(Color.Black))
        {
            // Draw a circle within our bitmap
            gfx.DrawEllipse(b, 0, 0, myBitmap.Width, myBitmap.Height);
        }
    }
}
```

You can also see from this code listing that we are able to interrogate the Bitmap using its Width and Height properties in order to retrieve its size; there is no need to store this information separately.

Creating Bitmaps from Predrawn Graphics

The second way that graphics can be created is by loading their image using a graphics file. This method allows you to draw your graphics using an art package of some description and then import them into your game, which allows you far greater flexibility with the graphics that you display in your game than you would achieve just using lines, circles, and rectangles.

■ **TIP** There are lots of graphics packages that you can use to create your graphics, from the lowly Microsoft Paint all the way up to professional packages such as Adobe Photoshop. If you are looking for a flexible and powerful image editor on a budget, try the freeware application Paint.NET. Visit the http://www.getpaint.net/ web site to download.

.NET CF offers two different mechanisms for loading graphics into a Bitmap: you can either specify the filename of the image that you wish to load or provide a Stream object containing the image data. If the latter approach is used, the stream should contain the data of an actual image file in one of the supported formats. Both of these methods support images in BMP, GIF, PNG, or JPG format.

Generally, embedding your graphics as resources in your project is much quicker and easier. This makes it easier to deploy your game as it still consists of a single executable, simplifies locating the graphics files within the device's memory, and takes away any problems such as the graphics files being deleted.

Embedding Graphic Resources

To use this approach, first open a Windows Explorer window from within Visual Studio and locate the directory in which all your source code is saved (the easiest way to do this is to right-click the tab for one of your source-code windows and select the Open Containing Folder menu item). See Figure 3–10.

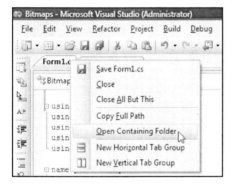

Figure 3–10. *Opening an Explorer window to your source code directory*

Within the Explorer window, create a directory called Resources and save your image into it. Now return to Visual Studio and click the Show All Files button at the top of the Solution Explorer panel (see Figure 3–11). This will then allow you to see the Resources directory that you have created. Click the plus (+) button to expand this, and right-click your graphics file contained inside. Select "Include in Project" to add the file to your solution.

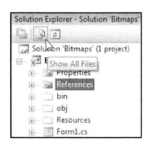 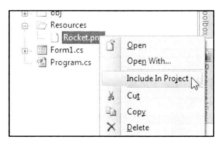

Figure 3–11. Using the Show All Files button to display the whole contents of your source code directory (left) and then adding a graphic file into your solution (right)

Once your graphics file has been added, you can click the Show All Files button once again to hide the nonproject files. The Resources directory and your graphic file will remain within the Solution Explorer tree.

The graphic has been added to your solution, but it is not yet an embedded resource. To change this, select the graphic file in Solution Explorer and then take a look at its properties. Ensure that the Build Action property is set to Embedded Resource, and Copy to Output Directory is set to "Do not copy" as shown in Figure 3–12. When you compile, the graphic file will now be included within the executable that is created.

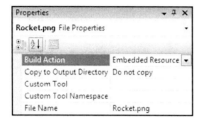

Figure 3–12. Setting the image resource properties

If you wish to modify the graphic file, simply open it from the Resources directory on disk using your image editor, make whatever changes are required, and then save it again. Visual Studio will automatically pick up the latest version of the file each time you compile.

With the graphic embedded, we now need to figure out how to read access it within your code. This is achieved using the Assembly.GetManifestResourceStream function. We need to pass into this a string containing the path within our assembly of the graphic file. The path consists of several elements, each separated by a period:

- The assembly name

- The name of the directory within Solution Explorer containing the resource file, if required (subdirectories are separated using a period, not a backslash as would be the case in a DOS-style path.)

- The filename of the resource file

All of these elements are case-sensitive.

We can programmatically retrieve the assembly name using the following code:

```
String AssemblyName = Assembly.GetExecutingAssembly().GetName().Name;
```

Finding the assembly name through code means that if you ever decide to change the name of your assembly, your code will continue to work. I, therefore, recommend this approach. Once we have this, we can concatenate the directory and filename in order to generate the full resource name. The resource name can then be provided to GetManifestResourceStream to retrieve the graphic resource as a Stream, which is one of the constructors understood by the Bitmap object. Putting all these pieces of the jigsaw puzzle together, we arrive at the code in Listing 3–9.

Listing 3–9. Loading a Bitmap Image from an Embedded Resource

```
// Declare the Bitmap object that we are going to create
Bitmap myBitmap;

private void InitializeBitmap()
{
    // Get the assembly name
    String AssemblyName = Assembly.GetExecutingAssembly().GetName().Name;
```

```
    // Add the resource path and name
    String ResourceName = AssemblyName + ".Resources.Rocket.png";
    // Generate the resource bitmap -- this will contain our spaceship image
    using (System.IO.Stream str =
            Assembly.GetExecutingAssembly().GetManifestResourceStream(ResourceName))
    {
        myBitmap = new Bitmap(str);
    }
}
```

If the resource name that you specify is incorrect, the GetManifestResourceStream function doesn't throw an exception and instead returns null. If you experience a NullReferenceException when instantiating the Bitmap object, this is the most likely cause. To provide a useful response in this situation, it is a good idea to wrap this operation in a try/catch block; if you catch a NullReferenceException then you can provide a more useful error message. Putting this in place can save a lot of headaches later on when you can't understand why your project won't start!

Reading Graphics from Files

On some occasions, you may still wish to store your graphics in separate files. For example, maybe you wish to allow users to choose between different sets of graphics or to provide their own graphics. To load an image into a Bitmap from a file, simply provide the filename when instantiating the object:

```
    myBitmap = new Bitmap("Graphics.png");
```

If the specified image file doesn't exist, a FileNotFoundException will be thrown.

A Note About Graphic File Formats

We have a choice of graphic file format to use when saving images for use within our games. Some are distinctly better than others. Here is a summary of each:

- *BMP* (bitmap) files have a simple structure internally and are, therefore, easy for graphics libraries to interact with. One of the reasons for this simplicity is that they do not employ any form of compression at all. For this result, BMP files can be huge in terms of file size compared to the other graphics formats that are available. There are no compelling reasons to use BMP files, so please avoid using them.

- *GIF* (Graphics Interchange Format) files have become a very widely used graphics format, not least of which due to their adoption within the Web. They store graphics up to a maximum of 256 colors and compress the content to reduce file size. This compression is *lossless*, so no degradation of the image occurs as a result. Simple animations can be stored within GIF files, but these will be ignored by .NET CF, so this offers us no benefits in this environment. These are a reasonable format for storage of graphics, but the compression offered by PNG files is superior.

- *PNG* (Portable Network Graphics) files are the most recently developed file format supported by .NET CF. They are able to store graphics using the full 24-bit color palette and are additionally able to support alpha (transparency) information. Like GIF files, they store their data using lossless compression but will result in smaller files then equivalent GIF images. For nonphotographic images, this is the file format that I recommend.

- **JPG** (an abbreviation for JPEG, the Joint Photographic Experts Group that developed the format) files revolutionized the Web and have been an enabling technology in a range of other areas too, such as digital cameras. The format's strength is the ability to hugely compress images to file sizes that are substantially smaller than their uncompressed originals, far more so than GIF or PNG are able to offer. The problem with this however is that JPG uses a *lossy* compression technique: after decompressing the image, you don't get back exactly what you started with. Compressed JPGs quickly start to exhibit graphics distortions, and this is most strongly apparent with graphics that contain highly contrasting areas of color, such as those within a computer game often do. JPG files can be useful for reducing the size of photographic images but are not well suited to hand-drawn game graphics. Even with photographs, be careful not to compress the image to a point where distortion begins to appear.

Painting Bitmaps to the Screen

Once we have our `Bitmap` ready, we are now ready to paint it to the screen. This is a simple matter of using the `Graphics.DrawImage` function, as shown in Listing 3–10.

Listing 3–10. Drawing a Bitmap to the Screen

```
private void MyForm_Paint(object sender, PaintEventArgs e)
{
    e.Graphics.DrawImage(myBitmap, 50, 50);
}
```

This code draws a copy of the bitmap image to the form at coordinate (50, 50). This coordinate forms the top-left corner of the image.

There are a number of additional features that we can use when we call `DrawImage`, so let's take a look at each of these now.

Partial Bitmap Copying

The example in Listing 3–10 simply instructs GDI to copy the whole bitmap image to a point on the form. We are also able to copy just a subsection of the bitmap to the screen. This is very useful as it allows us to create a multiframe animation within a single image and then copy each individual frame to the screen one after another (see Figure 3–13).

Figure 3–13. Multiple animation frames stored within a single image file

We can copy a subsection of the source image by providing two rectangles when we call DrawImage: the first defines the position and size of the output image that is created, and the second defines the position and size of the image to copy from the source bitmap.

In the example animation frames shown in Figure 3–13, each image is 75 pixels wide and 75 pixels high. We can, therefore, copy a single frame of the animation using the code shown in Listing 3–11.

Listing 3–11. Drawing a Single Frame of Animation from a Bitmap Containing Multiple Frames

```
// A variable to store the current animation frame.
int animFrame = 0;

Private void Form1_Paint(object sender, PaintEventArgs e)
{
    const int frameWidth = 75;      // The width of each animation frame
    const int frameHeight = 75;     // The height of each animation frame
    // Create the source rectangle.
    // This will have a width and height of 75 (the size of our animation frame).
    // The x-coordinate will specify the position within the source image from which we
    // want to copy. Multiplying the animation frame number by the frame width results
    // in a coordinate at the left of the frame that we are going to copy.
    Rectangle srcRect = new Rectangle(animFrame * frameWidth, 0, frameWidth, frameHeight);
    // Draw the bitmap at coordinate (100, 100)
    e.Graphics.DrawImage(myBitmap, 100, 100, srcRect, GraphicsUnit.Pixel);
    // Move to the next animation frame for the next Paint
    animFrame += 1;
}
```

The parameters being passed to DrawImage follow:

- The Bitmap whose image we are going to draw to the screen (myBitmap) is required first.

- Next, we specify the x and y positions at which we are to draw the image, (100, 100).

- The position and size of the region within the source image that is to be drawn (srcRect) are specified next.

- In common with the desktop versions of this function, .NET CF asks us to provide the GraphicsUnit with which we are measuring our Rectangles. Pixel is the only value currently supported within .NET CF, so we have no choice but to pass GraphicsUnit.Pixel for this parameter.

Scaling

As well as providing a rectangle to read a section of the source image, we can also provide a rectangle for the target drawing area, instead of the simple coordinate that we used previously. If the target rectangle is a different size to the source rectangle, the bitmap will be stretched or shrunk (*scaled*) to fit the requested rectangle size.

This is potentially useful, but unfortunately, the scaling of the source bitmap is a comparatively slow operation, which may impact the performance of your game. Used sparingly and appropriately, scaling can be a useful effect, but don't rely on it for large numbers of images, as the frame rate of your game will fall dramatically.

To use this feature, specify the destination `Rectangle` as well as the source `Rectangle`, as shown in Listing 3–12. If the two rectangles do not exactly match in size then the image will be scaled as required.

Listing 3–12. Drawing a Bitmap Stretched to Double Its Original Width and Height

```
private void Form1_Paint(object sender, PaintEventArgs e)
{
    // Create the source rectangle to match the size of the bitmap.
    Rectangle srcRect = new Rectangle(0, 0, myBitmap.Width, myBitmap.Height);
    // Create the destination rectangle at double the size of the source rectangle.
    Rectangle destRect = new Rectangle(100, 100, srcRect.Width * 2, srcRect.Height * 3);
    // Draw the bitmap
    e.Graphics.DrawImage(myBitmap, destRect, srcRect, GraphicsUnit.Pixel);
}
```

Color Keys

The final remaining `DrawImage` feature is perhaps the most important: the ability to draw images with transparent regions. The code samples we have used so far will all copy to rectangular areas on the form, and any graphics that were already contained within that area will be overwritten. It is almost certain that we will want to allow images to overlap with existing content without cutting out these rectangular holes.

Figure 3–14 shows the standard behavior of `DrawImage`. You can see that the second circle image on the left has cut a section out of the first image. In the right-hand image, the two circles overlap without obstructing one another.

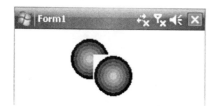 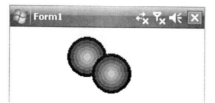

Figure 3–14. Drawing images without a color key (left) and with a color key (right)

We achieve the effect shown in Figure 3–14 using a *color key*. We designate a single color within our source image that we want to become transparent and provide this color to `DrawImage`. Any pixels that match that color will be transparent when drawn to the screen. These transparent pixels do not have to just form the outside of the image as shown in this example; they may appear anywhere at all that transparency is required. You, therefore, need to choose a color that is not already in use within your image.

The color key only allows our bitmap pixels to be fully transparent (for pixels matching the color key) or fully opaque (for all other pixels). No support for translucency or semitransparent drawing is provided by GDI (once again, you will see how to draw with translucency when we look at OpenGL ES in Chapter 10.

To specify the color that is to form the color key, we create an `ImageAttributes` object. This is yet another cut-down version of a desktop .NET class, and in fact, the only useful functions that remain are `SetColorKey` and `ClearColorKey`.

We call `SetColorKey` to identify our transparency color. You will find that this function actually takes two `Color` parameters, named `colorLow` and `colorHigh`. The reason for providing two colors is due yet again to mirroring the desktop .NET function, which allows a color range to be specified. However, .NET CF only supports a single color, so the same color should be specified for both of these parameters.

The code in Listing 3–13 draws an image to the screen with all white pixels left transparent.

Listing 3–13. Drawing a Bitmap with a Color Key

```
private void Form1_Paint(object sender, PaintEventArgs e)
{
    // Create the destination rectangle at double the size of the source rectangle.
    Rectangle destRect = new Rectangle(100, 100, myBitmap.Width, myBitmap.Height);
    // Create an ImageAttributes object
    using (ImageAttributes imgAttributes = new ImageAttributes())
    {
        // Set the color key to White.
        imgAttributes.SetColorKey(Color.White, Color.White);
        // Draw the bitmap
        e.Graphics.DrawImage(myBitmap, destRect, 0, 0, myBitmap.Width, myBitmap.Height,
                                         GraphicsUnit.Pixel, imgAttributes);
    }
}
```

Irritatingly, the parameters used for this version of `DrawImage` are inconsistent with those we have already looked at, requiring us to provide individual coordinates and size values for the source image rather than a source `Rectangle`. Despite this minor annoyance, all the functionality offered by the other versions of this function is still present, including the ability to copy subsections of the bitmap or perform scaling if required.

Bitmaps in Action

To see many of the `Bitmap` features we have discussed here in action, take a look at the `3_3_Bitmaps` sample project provided with the accompanying code download. This creates two different bitmaps, one using graphics primitives and the other from an embedded resource. These are then displayed on the screen using a color key.

Smooth Animation

All of the examples we have looked at so far in this chapter have resulted in static images. Now, it's time to get animated and start moving some graphics around the screen. There are a couple of challenges that we will face when we start using moving graphics, so let's explore the problems and find solutions to each.

We will create a simple example that moves a filled box around the screen, bouncing off each of the edges when it reaches them. We can implement this by storing the coordinate at which our box currently resides and the direction in which it is moving (its velocity).

In order to know an object's velocity, we need to know both the direction in which it is moving and the speed with which it is traveling. There are two straightforward methods in which we can describe an object's velocity: either by storing its direction (as an angle from 0 to 360 degrees) and its speed of movement in that direction, or by storing its speed as a value along each of the axes, x and y.

The first of these methods provides for a simulation of movement that is closer to how things move in reality, and in many scenarios, this will be an appropriate system to use. For the sake of simplicity in our example, however, we will use the second method. This simply tracks the x and y distances that we wish to move the object each time it updates. To bounce an object off the side of the screen, we can simply negate the speed in that particular axis: if we are adding a value of 1 to the x position and we hit the right side of the screen, we then start subtracting 1 to move to the left again. Subtracting 1 is the same as adding –1, so changing the x speed from 1 to –1 will reverse the direction on that axis. Exactly the same function applies to the y axis. The calculation is illustrated in Figure 3–15.

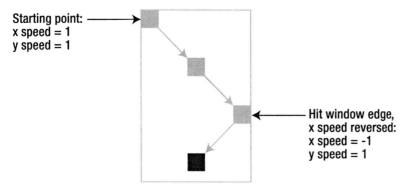

Figure 3–15. *The motion of our box, as controlled using x and y axis speeds*

We can animate our simple bouncing box by using the code in Listing 3–14.

Listing 3–14. *Updating the Position of Our Box*

```
// The position of our box
private int xpos, ypos;
// The direction in which our box is moving
private int xadd = 1, yadd = 1;
// The size of our box
private const int boxSize = 50;

/// <summary>
/// Update the position of the box that we are rendering
/// </summary>
private void UpdateScene()
{
    // Add the velocity to the box's position
    xpos += xadd;
    ypos += yadd;
```

```
    // If the box has reached the left or right edge of the screen,
    // reverse its horizontal velocity so that it bounces back into the screen.
    if (xpos <= 0) xadd = -xadd;
    if (xpos + boxSize >= this.Width) xadd = -xadd;
    // If the box has reached the top or bottom edge of the screen,
    // reverse its vertical velocity so that it bounces back into the screen.
    if (ypos <= 0) yadd = -yadd;
    if (ypos + boxSize >= this.Height) yadd = -yadd;
}
```

That takes care of the movement of our box, so now we need to actually draw it. Based on the Graphics object methods that we have been working with, you might expect that the required code for this to look like Listing 3–15.

Listing 3–15. Drawing the Bouncing Box to the Screen

```
private void Method1_SimpleDraw_Paint(object sender, PaintEventArgs e)
{
    // Draw our box at its current location
    using (Brush b = new SolidBrush(Color.Blue))
    {
        gfx.FillRectangle(b, xpos, ypos, boxSize, boxSize);
    }
}
```

Fundamentally this does work. However, the animation is extremely flickery. You can see this for yourself by running the 3_4_RenderingMethods sample from the accompanying code and selecting to use the SimpleDraw rendering method. The box moves in the way that we expect but flashes horribly while moving. This certainly isn't the type of graphical presentation we want to use in any of our games!

■ **NOTE** Due to the way the emulators buffer updates to the screen, the flicker is not particularly noticeable when running this example in one of them. To see how the animation in this section really looks, make sure you run the code on an actual device.

How do we stop this flicker from occurring? Let's take a look at what is actually happening when we render.

You will notice that our Paint event isn't actually clearing the form, yet we don't have a trail of old boxes left behind. This is because GDI is automatically clearing the screen each time we paint, and we are then drawing our new box into the cleared space. Because all of this is happening directly on the form, right where we can see it, the clearing and painting of the form are fighting one another: between the point at which the clear finishes and our box is drawn, the form is blank.

To avoid this conflict, we change the way that we draw our graphics. Instead of drawing straight to the screen, we instead create an off-screen buffer to draw in, and we perform all of our painting operations there. While this is happening, whatever was previously displayed on the screen can remain in place.

Once we have fully completed all of our painting, we copy the entire buffer image on to the screen in a single operation. This allows each rendered scene to switch directly to the next without any partly finished graphics operations ever becoming visible. The technique is known as *double buffering*, because we have two graphics buffers: the visible buffer (displayed on the screen) and the invisible back buffer (into which we render our graphics).

There is another difference in the way we draw using double buffering. As we have created the back buffer ourselves, we are completely in control of it. Unlike when we painted directly on to the form, GDI will leave any existing content of our buffer alone, meaning that whatever we drew in the previous scene is still present the next time we draw on it. This is extremely useful, because it means that any graphics that are not actively moving can be left in place without any need to redraw them. We will look at how we can efficiently optimize our game based around this approach in the next chapter.

The immediate implication of this is that we need to clear the buffer before we render our box. Otherwise, we will be left with a trail of old box images as we perform our animation. The code in Listing 3–16 initializes the back buffer, draws on it, and then copies it to the form so that it can be seen.

Listing 3–16. Drawing the Bouncing Box to the Screen Using Double-Buffering

```
/// <summary>
/// Draw all of the graphics for our scene
/// </summary>
private void DrawScene(Graphics gfx)
{
    // Have we initialised our back buffer yet?
    if (backBuffer == null)
    {
        // We haven't, so initialise it now.
        backBuffer = new Bitmap(this.Width, this.Height);
    }

    // Create a graphics object for the backbuffer
    using (Graphics buffergfx = Graphics.FromImage(backBuffer))
    {
        // Clear the back buffer
        buffergfx.Clear(Color.White);
        // Draw our box into the back buffer at its current location
        using (Brush b = new SolidBrush(Color.Blue))
        {
            buffergfx.FillRectangle(b, xpos, ypos, boxSize, boxSize);
        }
    }

    // Finally, copy the content of the entire backbuffer to the window
    gfx.DrawImage(backBuffer, 0, 0);
}

private void Method2_DoubleBuffering_Paint(object sender, PaintEventArgs e)
{
    // Call DrawScene to do the drawing for us
    DrawScene(e.Graphics);
}
```

Try running the sample application once again, and this time choose the DoubleBuffer rendering method. There are two things to note from this:

- The box moves more slowly than in the previous example.

- The animation is still horribly flickery—in fact, it's even worse than before.

The box moves slower than in the first method, because we have more work to do: instead of simply drawing a box, we now additionally have to both clear and copy the whole of the back buffer to the screen, and this takes some time to do. Minimizing this overhead is another part of the optimization that we will look at in the next chapter. In Chapter 5, we will also look at ways of making the speed consistent regardless of the environment in which we are working.

The reason for the flicker is that, even though we are creating all of our graphics in our back buffer, GDI is still automatically clearing the form each time we repaint. We need to properly address this flicker to be able to display any form of smooth animation.

Fortunately, it is very easy to switch off the automatic form clearing. We can override the Form's OnPaintBackground method, and instead of calling into the base class (where the clear actually takes place), we simply do nothing. Whatever was displayed on the screen prior to the Paint event now remains in place while the event is being processed.

With the background painting switched off, we are now able to copy our back buffer to the form itself without any flickering occurring at all. The back buffer directly replaces the previously displayed image with no intermediate painting getting in the way. Try the SmoothDraw rendering method in the sample application to see this working. At last we have smooth, flicker-free movement of our box.

This is the approach we will take when we create a game using GDI. The back buffer contains a complete image of the entire scene, and we copy it to the form each time anything within our game moves.

Getting the Most From GDI

This chapter has covered all of the mechanics of displaying graphics on the screen, from simple graphics primitives through to bitmap graphics and smooth animation. You are now ready to start using it to create more complex animations. Then, the animation can be made interactive, and you will have the beginnings of your first games.

However, there are some other important performance implications that we need to address before we get too much further. In its raw form, GDI might be too slow for us to use for game development, but with some planning, we can not only gain noticeable speed improvements but also make tracking and working with moving objects in our games much easier to handle.

In the next chapter, we will begin the construction of a reusable game engine that will look after all of this for us.

CHAPTER 4

■■■

Taming the Device with the Game Engine

We have covered a lot of the technology foundations so far, and you have a good understanding of the functions required for displaying content to the screen. Now, it is time to start organizing and structuring what you have learned.

It would be very easy to launch straight into our first game at this point, but instead of diving straight in, we will take a rather more planned approach.

In this chapter, we will begin the creation of a *game engine*, a framework that will host our games for us. The engine will be able to simplify the code that we write for each game, speeding up development time and allowing us to focus on the game itself rather than getting caught up in fiddly technical details. We can address all of these details in the engine just once, and then we don't have to worry about them when we are developing.

The game engine can also take care of lots of other complexities for us: device capabilities, graphics optimization, object management, and interaction with the operating system to name but a few.

We will continue to both develop and use the game engine throughout the rest of this book. Once we are finished, we will have created a DLL class library that you can use for your own games, plunder for ideas, or customize in whatever way you wish.

■ **NOTE** We will continue to evolve this game engine right up to the end of this book. If you wish to create your own projects before we reach that point, you should use the final version of the game engine code, although this will contain a number of features we haven't yet covered. This can be found in the accompanying source code in the GameEngine directory. To save confusion, each of the versions we build along the way will include the chapter name as part of the project and DLL names.

Designing the Game Engine

We will take advantage of .NET's object orientation features in the design of the engine. The engine itself will provide an abstract class that supports a core set of functions that will be generally useful in any game. We will then derive another game engine class from this engine and set up this derived class to provide support for creating games using GDI. Later on in this book in Chapter 10, we will derive another class for OpenGL ES games, allowing us to keep a significant part of the functionality and methodology that we have discussed and developed along the way.

Next to the engine class, we will define another abstract class that provides support for *game objects*. These objects will be used for all elements of the game that we need to draw (they will be the falling tiles in a game of Tetris; the ghosts, dots, and player in Pac Man, and all the spaceships and bullets in Space Invaders). Objects will know various things about themselves (such as where they are on the screen) and will allow us to manage a consistent and simple mechanism for moving and rendering efficiently. Just as with the engine, a derived version of the class will provide additional support for GDI object handling.

Figure 4–1 shows each of the classes and their relationships to one another.

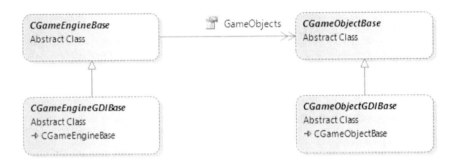

Figure 4–1. Engine class diagram

The main functions of each of the classes we will create for the initial GDI implementation of the engine will be as shown in Table 4–1.

Table 4–1. The Game Engine Classes

Class	Purpose
CGameEngineBase	The class at the heart of the whole game engine is CGameEngineBase. It has responsibility for managing all of the objects within the game, providing timing functionality so that things move at a consistent speed, and providing standard mechanisms for initializing and updating the contents of the game.
CGameEngineGDIBase	The CGameEngineGDIBase class derives from CGameEngineBase and supplements it with functionality specific for GDI. This class contains our back buffer for off-screen rendering and keeps track of which areas of the screen need to be redrawn in order for us to achieve efficient screen updates.
CGameObjectBase	This class contains the fundamental information we need to represent a graphical object within our game, tracking its position and allowing for it to be rendered and updated.
CGameObjectGDIBase	CGameObjectGDIBase is a class derived from CGameObjectBase specifically to support GDI game objects. This adds information about the width and height of each object and allows us to determine whether an object has moved and exactly where its graphics are to be drawn on the screen.

When we actually implement a game using the engine, we will add several more components specific to the game itself, as shown in Table 4–2.

Table 4–2. Components Created For a Game Project

Game Component	Purpose
Engine	Our game will create an engine class of its own derived from CGameEngineGDIBase into which all of the game logic will be placed. This is where we will create our game objects and define how the player interacts with them, how they move, the player's score, game over conditions, and everything else that the game will need.
Objects	We will create a class derived from CGameObjectGDIBase for each of the game objects we need to use. Thinking once again about the classic Space Invaders, we would create one class for the invaders, another for the invader bullets, one for the player, and another for the player's bullets. Each game will provide a completely different set of game object classes.
Form	We also need to create the form inside which our game will be played. It is passed to the game engine class so that it knows where to draw the game.

The basic program flow within the engine will be as shown in Figure 4–2.

Implementing the Engine

Let's start putting all of this together by beginning to code up the CGameEngineBase class. Don't worry if any of this doesn't make sense at this stage, as we'll be building some examples based on this engine later on in this chapter. The engine is necessarily complex in places, so that the code we write within our game can remain as simple as possible.

CGameEngineBase

An overview of the CGameEngineBase class is as follows:

- *Purpose*: The heart of the game engine; provides functions for managing the game and objects contained within it

- *Type*: Abstract base class

- *Derived from*: Not derived

- *Inherited by*: Graphics API-specific game implementations, such as for the GDI engine

- *Main functionality*:

    - Prepare: Initializes data for the engine

    - Reset: Initializes data for a new game

    - Advance: Steps forward all elements of the game simulation

- Update: Updates the state of the game
- Render: Draws the game

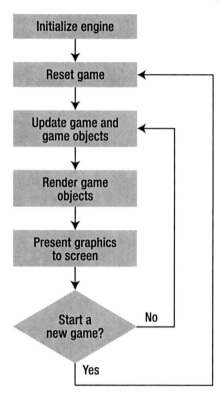

Figure 4–2. Engine control flow chart

This class will be created as an abstract class; we will never create an actual instance of this class, as it doesn't have enough functionality contained within it to support our game development. Instead, it will become a building block for the game classes created for GDI and OpenGL (and indeed any other rendering technology that we may wish to apply to it in the future).

We will, therefore, provide a core set of functions that all of our derived game engines will need to support and provide a set of virtual functions that can be overridden in the derived classes to perform tasks specific to the rendering method in question.

Something that will be common to all of our derived engine classes is the requirement to access the Form inside which our game is running. We may need to check the size of the form in order to know when things are about to run off its edge or to access controls that have been placed within the form.

To guarantee that we always have a form available, we will parameterize the class constructor and require the form to be passed in. The class therefore begins off quite simply, as shown in Listing 4–1.

Listing 4–1. The Very Beginning of Our CGameEngineBase Class

```
namespace GameEngineCh4
{
    public abstract class CGameEngineBase
    {
        /// <summary>
        /// Store a reference to the form against which this GameEngine instance is running
        /// </summary>
        private Form _gameForm;

        /// <summary>
        /// Class constructor -- require an instance of the form that we will be running
        /// within to be provided.
        /// </summary>
        /// <param name="gameForm"></param>
        public CGameEngineBase(Form gameForm)
        {
            // Store a reference to the form
            _gameForm = gameForm;
        }
    }
}
```

The constructor stores a reference to the provided gameForm object in the class-level private variable _gameForm. To keep tight control over our objects, we will store all class-level variables with the private scope and then expose properties to allow code outside of the class to access the values contained within. We, therefore, need to add a property so that code outside of the base class is able to retrieve this form reference.

We will use a public read-only property for this. The property is made public so that all other classes within both the engine assembly and any external game assemblies that derive from here are able to access it; see Listing 4–2.

Listing 4–2. The Very Beginning of our CGameEngineBase Class

```
        /// <summary>
        /// Return our game form object
        /// </summary>
        public Form GameForm
        {
            get
            {
                // Return our game form instance
                return _gameForm;
            }
        }
    }
```

Now that we have dealt with the way the engine will be created, we can start looking at the functionality that we need to provide from the class. To start with, we will build two main areas of functionality into the class: object management and game mechanics. Let's start by looking at the object management.

Managing Game Objects

Each object within our game represents a single on-screen graphical entity. Each object has a position on the screen and knows how to draw itself and potentially move itself too.

We will store a collection within the game engine containing all the objects that are active within the game at any time. The engine is then able to interact with each of these objects when one is required to do something.

Our games can add new objects to the game environment simply by creating such an object and adding it to the object collection. This provides an extremely simple and flexible mechanism for handling potentially large numbers of objects: each time we want to add something to the game we can add it to the object collection and then essentially forget about it. No extra code is required outside of the game engine to manage all of these objects.

All game objects are implemented in classes derived from the CGameObjectBase class, which we will look at in closer detail shortly. To store the collection of these objects, we add a class variable and a corresponding access property to the CGameEngineBase class, as shown in Listing 4–3.

Listing 4–3. The Engine's Object Collection and Accessor Property

```
/// <summary>
/// Store a collection of game objects that are currently active
/// </summary>
private System.Collections.Generic.List<CGameObjectBase> _gameObjects;

/// <summary>
/// Retrieves the list of active game objects
/// </summary>
public System.Collections.Generic.List<CGameObjectBase> GameObjects
{
    get
    {
        return _gameObjects;
    }
}
```

We then modify the class constructor to create a new instance of the _gameObjects collection when the class is instantiated.

A little extra code is needed to manage the objects that are placed within this object list; we will see this in the Advance function, described in the next section.

Game Mechanics

In order for our game to run, we need to be able to ask it to do the following things:

- Perform start-up initialization.
- Reset for a new game to begin.
- Update the game state as it is being played.
- Draw everything to the screen.

Let's look at how each of these is implemented and used.

Initializing Start-Up

When a game first launches, it may need to do a number of things: load graphics, prepare a high-score table, or set variables that will control how the game is going to play.

We split those into two different categories: those that need to happen just once when the game first loads and those that potentially need to be repeated after the game has started.

Functions such as preparing the high-score table can be carried out in the class constructor function and don't need to override any engine functions.

Functions that may potentially need to be reevaluated can be placed into the overridden Prepare function (see Listing 4–4). This function will be called again at certain stages during the engine's processing; for example, when the form resizes, the Prepare method will be called again. This is, therefore, the place to handle loading different graphics depending on the form dimensions and setting up a game coordinate system based on the form size. We'll look at this more closely when we build a game using the engine in a Chapter 9.

If you wish to support multiple different sets of graphics, you may also want to call into Prepare from your own game code to reinitialize the graphics each time the selected graphics set changes.

The base class itself doesn't have any preparation to perform, so we simply provide an empty virtual function that derived classes can override.

Listing 4–4. The Prepare Function

```
/// <summary>
/// Virtual function to allow the game to prepare itself for rendering.
/// This includes loading graphics, setting coordinate systems, etc.
/// </summary>
public virtual void Prepare()
{
    // Nothing to do for the base class.
}
```

Resetting the Game

This is the function that we will use to prepare the engine state so that a new game is ready to begin. Tasks that will be attended to in this function include resetting the player's score to zero and clearing or randomizing the level that is to be encountered. Any information that is left over from a previously running game will need to be cleared so that it doesn't affect the new game that is starting up.

Our class constructor is modified to call into Reset when the class is instantiated.

As with the Prepare function, we will simply provide an empty virtual function called Reset within the base class, which the derived engine can override to perform these tasks.

Rendering

Once the game has updated itself, we need to draw everything that our game requires to the screen. We will use a function called Render function to perform this. As you will see, the rendering-type-specific derived classes will override this function and perform everything that is required within the derived engine itself, keeping things as simple as possible for the games that are using the engine.

As with the game reset, we don't actually have anything to do in the base class, so we simply provide an empty virtual function.

Updating the Game State

All the game functionality that relates to the game as a whole (such as checking whether the game has finished) will be performed in the Update function. Our game will override this to perform any necessary tasks, but once again, we have nothing to do here in the base class, so this function is left empty.

Advancing the Game

Once a game has started, it will enter a loop whereby the game state is continuously updated: all of the spaceships will move; the player's character will change position; new objects will be created and existing ones destroyed. To make all of this happen, we will call into the Advance function (see Listing 4–5).

This function is not responsible for directly performing these updates, but instead triggers each one to take place. We will need to update both the game as a whole (so that we can check things such as the game over state being triggered) and all of the individual objects in the game (allowing each one to move and interact with other objects in whatever way is required).

Listing 4–5. The Advance Function

```
/// <summary>
/// Virtual function to allow the game itself and all objects within
/// the game to be updated.
/// </summary>
public virtual void Advance()
{
    // Update the game itself
    Update();
    // Update all objects that are within our object collection
    foreach (CGameObjectGDIBase gameObj in _gameObjects)
    {
        // Ignore objects that have been flagged as terminated
        if (!gameObj.Terminate)
        {
            // Update the object's last position
            gameObj.UpdatePreviousPosition();
            // Perform any update processing required upon the object
            gameObj.Update();
        }
    }

    // Now that everything is updated, render the scene
    Render();

    // Remove any objects that have been flagged for termination
    RemoveTerminatedObjects();

    // Update the Frames Per Second information
    UpdateFPS();
}
```

The code here calls into the game's Update function for the game itself (as we discussed previously) and enters a loop for each of the objects within our game object list. For each one of these, it first checks whether the object has been terminated; this happens when an object is waiting to be destroyed and removed from the game, so we don't need to perform any further processing on these objects. For all objects that are still active, we do two things:

- Copy the object's position into its previous position variables. We'll examine the reasons for this when we look at the CGameObjectBase class later in this chapter.

- Call each object's Update method so that the object can perform whatever processing it needs.

Adding Other Functions

We will include a small set of further features in the base class that can be of use to the engine or to the games themselves.

First of all, we will include a random number generator. This will simply be an instance of .NET's System.Random class, but exposing it from the engine provides us with two advantages: First, we can call it without having to create a local instance each time we need a random number, slightly simplifying the code requirement. Second (and most usefully), this gives us the opportunity to seed the random number generator with a fixed seed. Seeded in this way, the exact same sequence of random numbers will be generated by the application, so (player interaction aside) it is possible to repeat the same game scenarios for testing purposes.

We also add some code to allow the frames-per-second rate that our game is running at to be returned (using the FramesPerSecond property). This keeps track of the number of times we update the graphical imagery on screen within each second. We will want to try to obtain the highest possible frames-per-second reading, as this will result in smoother animation. When the frames-per-second value drops too low, the animation of the game will start to look jerky and slow, so it is useful to able to monitor this value.

Finally, we have another object management function, RemoveTerminatedObjects. When an object is no longer required within the game, we set a flag within it to indicate to the engine that it is to be terminated. RemoveTerminatedObjects will remove any such objects from our object collection. Objects must be removed in this way (rather then immediately removing them from the collection), because we need to clean them up before they are destroyed; this task is executed at the end of the Advance function. You'll see why removing objects in this way is necessary when we optimize the graphics rendering later in this chapter.

CGameObjectBase

An overview of the CGameObjectBase class is as follows:

- *Purpose*: Represents a graphical object within a game

- *Type*: Abstract base class

- *Derived from*: Not derived

- *Inherited by*: Graphics API-specific game implementations, such as for the GDI engine

- *Main functionality*:

    - XPos, YPos, ZPos, LastXPos, LastYPos, LastZPos: Properties to define the position of objects

- IsNew, Terminate: Properties to define the state of an object

- Render: Allows the object to be drawn into the game

- Update: Allows the object to move and animate itself

There have been a number of references to game objects, so let's now look at the base class for these objects.

CGameObjectBase is another abstract class from which all our actual game object classes will derive. It is constructed by passing in a reference to the CGameEngineBase game engine (or a class derived from there), which it stores in a private class variable, _gameEngine, and exposes through the protected GameEngine property. This allows all objects to access the engine instance inside which they are running.

Positioning Objects

The CGameObjectBase class contains a series of property values to track the position of the object. For each object, we store the current x, y, and z coordinates. We discussed x and y coordinates in the previous chapter; z coordinates are used to provide a position in the third dimension, in and out of the screen. The z coordinate won't play a significant role until we start working the 3D graphics in OpenGL ES later in this book.

For each coordinate, we store both the object's current and previous positions. There are two significant reasons for this. First, having both positions allows us to tell whether an object has moved. We will use this information later on in this chapter to make our rendering engine more efficient. Second, storing both coordinates allows us to smoothly move an object between its previous position and its current position. This is something that will come into play in the next chapter when we look at different timing mechanisms that the game can use.

The position values are exposed using six properties: XPos, YPos, ZPos, LastXPos, LastYPos, and LastZPos. The first three of these set or return the current object position; they are defined as virtual properties and so may be overridden in derived object classes if desired. The remaining functions set or return the object's previous position.

Related to the position properties is a function named UpdatePreviousPosition. This copies all of the current position values into the previous position properties. This function will be called by the game engine each time we update the object positions, prior to their new positions being calculated, which ensures that the previous object position properties are always accurate and up to date.

All of these coordinate properties use the float type to store their values. This may seem unnecessary—after all, we can't draw half a pixel, so why allow objects to be positioned at fractional pixel locations?

One reason is that, although objects cannot be drawn at fractional pixel positions, it is still very useful to be able to update their positions using noninteger numbers. For example, say you wanted to move an image of the sun across the screen very slowly. You find that if you move it one pixel per frame, it is going much too quickly. Instead of implementing any complex logic that moves it once only a number of frames has passed, you can now just increment its position by 0.1 or 0.01. This results in it moving at one-tenth or one-hundredth the speed, without requiring any extra code.

Another reason will become clear when we begin using OpenGL ES later on. OpenGL ES uses a coordinate system that doesn't necessarily correspond to the pixels on the screen. Changing an object's position by a fractional value, therefore, can actually have an impact on its display position.

Storing Object States

In addition to the object's position, we store two other properties that relate to its state within the game engine. These are called IsNew and Terminate.

IsNew indicates that the object has been added to the game engine since it was last updated. This allows us to ensure that it is initially displayed correctly on the screen. The property is automatically set to true for new objects and will be set to false once the game engine has processed an update for the object.

Terminate, as already mentioned, allows us to request that an object be removed from the simulation. Termination can be requested simply by setting the property value to true. After the next game update takes place, the object will be removed from the game.

Object Mechanics

Finally, we have two virtual functions that the engine can call to instruct the object to perform its operational tasks.

The first of these is Render, which is used by the object to draw itself to the back buffer. As with the Render method in CGameEngineBase, the method takes a Graphics object as a parameter and doesn't actually do anything at this stage; rather, it will be used by derived object classes.

The other function is Update. You will see soon that we can make many of our objects autonomous (or partly so), allowing them to control their own movement with a degree of independence from the controlling engine. This function, therefore, will be called by the engine in order for the object to perform any processing that it needs. Once again, this function contains no code in the base class and instead will be overridden by derived classes.

CGameObjectGDIBase

An overview of the CGameObjectGDIBase class is as follows:

- *Purpose*: An implementation of CGameObjectBase with functionality required for GDI graphics

- *Type*: Abstract base class

- *Derived from*: CGameObjectBase

- *Inherited by*: Game objects within individual games, created in separate assemblies

- *Main functionality*:

  - Width and Height: Size properties

  - HasMoved and GetRenderRectangle: Determines movement state and the area into which the object is drawn

While our discussion of the game object class is still fresh, let's look at the GDI derivation. CGameObjectGDIBase is another abstract class and is fairly light in its content, adding some further properties and methods that we can use to make the GDI rendering engine function efficiently.

Setting the Object State for GDI

The first things we add are properties to track the Width and Height of the object. It is important for us to know this information to be able to track the space that each object occupies on the screen. We will use this as part of our rendering engine optimization later in the chapter.

We also add a function called GetRenderRectangle, which has the responsibility of determining and returning the rectangle inside which the object will draw itself, based on its current position and size. We use this for both drawing within the object's own Render method and helping to optimize the game engine, as you will see later on in this chapter. Internally, the object also keeps track of its previous position, which will be updated each time the object moves. This will also help with optimization later on.

Object movement

We then declare a property called HasMoved. We will use this to identify whether the object has moved in any way. Movement not only includes changes to its position but also whether it has been added to the game engine or has been terminated. Any of these conditions will require the object to be repainted to the form.

This property is updated using a function called CheckIfMoved. It examines each of the relevant object state properties, and if any of them are set such that the object is considered to have moved, the HasMoved property is set to true. The code for this function is shown in Listing 4–6.

Listing 4–6. The CheckIfMoved Function

```
/// <summary>
/// Determine whether any of our object state has changed in a way that would
/// require the object to be redrawn. If so, set the HasMoved flag to true.
/// </summary>
internal virtual void CheckIfMoved()
{
    if (XPos != LastXPos) HasMoved = true;
    if (YPos != LastYPos) HasMoved = true;
    if (ZPos != LastZPos) HasMoved = true;
    if (IsNew) HasMoved = true;
    if (Terminate) HasMoved = true;
}
```

Additionally, modifying any of the position properties (XPos, YPos, or ZPos) will cause the HasMoved property to be set to true.

CGameEngineGDIBase

An overview of the CGameEngineGDIBase class is as follows:

- *Purpose*: An implementation of CGameEngineBase with functionality required for GDI graphics

- *Type*: Abstract base class

- *Derived from*: CGameEngineBase

- *Inherited by*: Individual games, created in separate assemblies

- *Main functionality:*
  - Prepare: Initializes for GDI rendering
  - Render: Provides efficient graphics rendering techniques
  - Present: Copies rendered graphics to the screen

With our abstract engine and game objects all in place, it's time to start adding the functionality for the GDI rendering engine. The CGameEngineGDIBase class is still declared as abstract, but we will derive our actual game class from it.

The most significant area of additional functionality in this class is within Render method. Let's take a look at this and the other changes that are implemented here.

Rendering

The Render function is where everything needed to update our back buffer takes place. We have a number of required operations here:

- Initialize the back buffer if that has not already been done.
- Clear the background.
- Draw all objects to the back buffer.
- Invalidate the game form to trigger a Paint event, which allows us to copy our modified back buffer to the form.

First, let's discuss the back buffer. As mentioned in the previous chapter, this off-screen Bitmap is where we will render all of our graphics. This will always maintain an image of the current displayed game content. At the start of the Render function, we call into InitBackBuffer to prepare the buffer if it is not already available. In this case, the buffer will be created to match the size of the game form, as shown in Listing 4–7.

Listing 4–7. Initialization of the Back Buffer

```
/// <summary>
/// If not already ready, creates and initialises the back buffer that we use
/// for off-screen rendering.
/// </summary>
private void InitBackBuffer()
{
    // Make a new back buffer if needed.
    if (_backBuffer == null)
    {
        _backBuffer = new Bitmap(GameForm.ClientSize.Width, GameForm.ClientSize.Height);
        // Ensure we repaint the whole form
        ForceRepaint();
    }
}
```

Next, we clear the background. We have two possible mechanisms here: clear it to a solid background color, or display a background image behind our moving graphics.

If no image has been provided to us, we will call into the virtual CreateBackgroundImage function. The derived game class may override this and return a Bitmap containing the background image if one is required. This will then be used to clear the back buffer prior to drawing our graphics.

Alternatively, if the game finds that it still has no background image after calling into this function, it will simply clear the back buffer using a solid color. The color can be specified by setting the class's BackgroundColor property.

The third step is to draw all the objects to the back buffer. We'll actually skip over the detail of the implementation for the moment, as it will be examine more closely in the "Optimizing Rendering" section later in this chapter. Suffice it to say for the moment that all the objects that need to be redrawn are rendered to the back buffer.

Finally, we call the game form's Invalidate method to trigger it to repaint. This is the mechanism by which the back buffer changes that we have just made actually reach the screen so that they can be seen. When this event fires, the form will call into the CGameEngineGDIBase.Present method, passing in the form's Graphics instance. We will look at how the form is wired into the engine shortly.

Advancing the Game

We also override the Advance method. In this method, we check every object in the game to see whether its position has moved, or anything else has occurred that requires it to be rendered again. The reason for this will be shown in the "Optimizing Rendering" section.

CGameFunctions

An overview of the CGameFunctions class is as follows:

- *Purpose*: Provides utility functions to the game engine project

- *Type*: Internal class containing static members

- *Derived from*: Not derived

- *Inherited by*: Not inherited

- *Main functionality*:

    - IsSmartphone: Determines whether the device is a touch screen or smart phone device

    - CombineRectangles: Helps us to manipulate rectangular areas

The final class present within the game engine is CGameFunction, which provides various general-purpose utility functions to the engine. This in an internal class and so is invisible outside of the engine assembly. It has a private constructor, so instances of this class cannot be created: all the functions contained within the class are static and so can be called without a class instance.

We will build additional functionality into this class as we enhance the engine in the coming chapters, but for the time being, we have two functions available:

- IsSmartphone: Just as you saw in Chapter 2, this function identifies whether the device is a touch screen or smart phone device.

- CombineRectangles: This function takes two Rectangle parameters and returns another Rectangle that exactly encompasses those provided. This is essentially a wrapper around the Rectangle.Union method, but it treats empty rectangles (those with Top, Left, Width, and Height all set to 0) as special cases and excludes these from the union.

This concludes our initial examination of the game engine—hopefully, that wasn't too taxing! Now, we will briefly examine how we actually attach to the engine within a game.

Using the Game Engine

Games are implemented in separate projects from the game engine itself, accessing the game engine classes via a reference to the game engine project or DLL.

Our game project will then consist of a *game class*, which derives from CGameEngineGDIBase. This is the class into which we will put the code that controls the overall flow of the game itself.

To this we add one or more additional *object class*es to cover the objects within our game (one each for the asteroids, the missiles, the Earth-pounding aliens, and so on). Instances of these classes can be added to the game by the game class.

We then finally need to wire the game up to a .NET CF form. We need a small amount of code in the form, most of which should be familiar and straightforward:

- Within the form's constructor, we instantiate the game class that we have defined in our game project and pass a reference to the form itself as a parameter.

- We override the OnPaintBackground method, as discussed in the previous chapter.

- A handler needs to be added for the Paint event, and here, we call into the game's Present method in order for its back buffer to be displayed on the screen.

- We create a game loop that repeatedly updates the game. In this loop, we call the game's Advance function. We will look at this loop in detail in a moment.

And that's it. Outside of the engine itself this hopefully all looks very simple so far!

Creating the Bounce Example Game

Let's build an example project that uses the game engine. We'll create a ball and bounce it around the game window. This is similar to the moving box that we created in the last chapter, but we'll apply a rudimentary simulation of gravity so that the balls accelerate toward the bottom of the window.

The Bounce project is a separate assembly from the game engine, with a reference to GameEngineCh4 (the version of the engine we have built for this chapter). The reference is already present within the provided project, but can be added to your own projects by right-clicking the References node for your game project in the Solution Explorer and picking Add Reference (in VB.NET, double-click the My Project node, select the References tab, and click the Add button). If the game engine project is part of your solution then you can select it from the Projects tab; otherwise, locate its compiled DLL within the Browse tab. The game engine can then be used by your game project.

The Bounce project consists of a form to display the output of the game, and two classes to run the game (one derived from GameEngineCh4.CGameEngineGDIBase and the other from CGameObjectGDIBase). The project can be found in the 4_1_Bounce directory within the accompanying code download.

CBounceGame

First of all, we will create our game engine. This is implemented in the class CBounceGame, which derives from the game engine's CGameEngineGDIBase. In addition to the class constructor, we have only two functions within the class, overrides for Prepare and Reset. Listing 4–8 shows the code for the Prepare function.

Listing 4–8. The Bounce Game's Prepare Function

```
/// <summary>
/// Prepare the game
/// </summary>
public override void Prepare()
{
    Assembly asm;

    // Allow the base class to do its work
    base.Prepare();

    // Initialise graphics library
    if (GameGraphics.Count == 0)
    {
        asm = Assembly.GetExecutingAssembly();
        GameGraphics.Add("Ball",
            new Bitmap(asm.GetManifestResourceStream("Bounce.Graphics.Ball.png")));
    }
}
```

The code is very simple: it checks to see whether we have already loaded the game graphics by querying the GameGraphics.Count property, and if not, adds the graphic from the Ball.png resource. Listing 4–9 shows the Reset function.

Listing 4–9. The Bounce Game's Reset Function

```
/// <summary>
/// Reset the game
/// </summary>
public override void Reset()
{
    CObjBall ball;

    // Allow the base class to do its work
    base.Reset();

    // Clear any existing game objects.
    GameObjects.Clear();

    // Create a new ball. This will automatically generate a random position for itself.
    ball = new CObjBall(this);
    // Add the ball to the game engine
    GameObjects.Add(ball);
}
```

The code here first removes any existing game objects by calling GameObjects.Clear. It then creates an instance of our project's CObjBall class (which we'll look at in a moment) and adds it to the GameObjects collection.

CObjBall

The CObjBall class derives from the game engine's CGameObjectGDIBase and provides the functionality we need to move and display the ball within the game. We start off by declaring some class-level variables as shown in Listing 4–10.

Listing 4–10. Class-Level Variable Declarations for CObjBall

```
// The velocity of the ball in the x and y axes
private float _xadd = 0;
private float _yadd = 0;

// Our reference to the game engine.
// Note that this is typed as CBounceGame, not as CGameEngineGDIBase
private CBounceGame _myGameEngine;
```

The class constructor for the ball is defined to accept a gameEngine parameter of type CBounceGame, not of type CGameEngineGDIBase as you might expect. As CBounceGame derives from the base engine class, we have no problems using it for the call to the base class, and declaring the engine reference in this way allows us to call into any additional functions that have been created in our derived class.

After storing a reference to the engine in the _myGameEngine variable, the constructor then initializes the ball. This consists of determining its Width and Height (both retrieved from the loaded Bitmap) and then setting a random position and velocity. The code is shown in Listing 4–11.

Listing 4–11. The Ball Object's Class Constructor

```
/// <summary>
/// Constructor. Require an instance of our own CBounceGame class as a parameter.
/// </summary>
public CObjBall(CBounceGame gameEngine) : base(gameEngine)
{
    // Store a reference to the game engine as its derived type
    _myGameEngine = gameEngine;

    // Set the width and height of the ball. Retrieve these from the loaded bitmap.
    Width = _myGameEngine.GameGraphics["Ball"].Width;
    Height = _myGameEngine.GameGraphics["Ball"].Height;

    // Set a random position for the ball's starting location.
    XPos = _myGameEngine.Random.Next(0, (int)(_myGameEngine.GameForm.Width - Width));
    YPos = _myGameEngine.Random.Next(0, (int)(_myGameEngine.GameForm.Height / 2));

    // Set a random x velocity. Keep looping until we get a non-zero value.
    while (_xadd == 0)
    {
        _xadd = _myGameEngine.Random.Next(-4, 4);
    }
```

```
        // Set a random y velocity. Zero values don't matter here as this value will
        // be affected by our simulation of gravity.
        _yadd = (_myGameEngine.Random.Next(5, 15)) / 10;
    }
```

As the code shows, the Width and Height properties are set by interrogating the Ball bitmap that has been loaded into the GameGraphics collection. This is a better mechanism than hard-coding these dimensions, as it allows us to change the image's size without needing any code to be changed.

Now, we provide an override for the Render function. This uses the techniques we examined in the last chapter to draw the loaded graphic to the provided Graphics object using a color key for transparency; see Listing 4–12.

Listing 4–12. The Ball Object's Render Function

```
/// <summary>
/// Render the ball to the provided Graphics object
/// </summary>
public override void Render(Graphics gfx)
{
    base.Render(gfx);

    // Create an ImageAttributes object so that we can set a transparency color key
    ImageAttributes imgAttributes = new ImageAttributes();
    // The color key is Fuchsia (Red=255, Green=0, Blue=255). This is the color that is
    // used within the ball graphic to represent the transparent background.
    imgAttributes.SetColorKey(Color.Fuchsia, Color.Fuchsia);
    // Draw the ball to the current render rectangle
    gfx.DrawImage(_myGameEngine.GameGraphics["Ball"], GetRenderRectangle(),
                        0, 0, Width, Height, GraphicsUnit.Pixel, imgAttributes);
}
```

Once again, we take advantage of information that is available to us to avoid having to hard-code anything into this function. We work out where to draw the ball by calling the base class's GetRenderRectangle function (which is quite able to work out where we are drawing without us needing to figure it out again). We also provide the source image Width and Height values for the call to DrawImage by reading back our own object properties, as we set in the constructor.

All that is left now is to actually move the ball. We allow the ball to control its own movement; the game engine itself can simply add a ball object to the game and then let the ball do whatever it wants. This movement is handled within the object Update function shown in Listing 4–13.

Listing 4–13. The Ball Object's Update Function

```
/// <summary>
/// Update the state of the ball
/// </summary>
public override void Update()
{
    // Allow the base class to perform any processing it needs
    base.Update();

    // Add the ball's velocity in each axis to its position
    XPos += _xadd;
    YPos += _yadd;
```

```
// If we have passed the left edge of the window, reset back to the edge
// and reverse the x velocity.
if (XPos < 0)
{
    _xadd = -_xadd;
    XPos = 0;
}
// If we have passed the right edge of the window, reset back to the edge
// and reverse the x velocity.
if (XPos > _myGameEngine.GameForm.ClientSize.Width - Width)
{
    _xadd = -_xadd;
    XPos = _myGameEngine.GameForm.ClientSize.Width - Width;
}
// If we have passed the bottom of the form, reset back to the bottom
// and reverse the y velocity. This time we also reduce the velocity
// slightly to simulate drag. The ball will eventually run out of
// vertical velocity and stop bouncing.
if (YPos + Height > _myGameEngine.GameForm.ClientSize.Height)
{
    _yadd = _yadd * -0.9f;
    YPos = _myGameEngine.GameForm.ClientSize.Height - Height;
}

// This is our very simple gravity simulation.
// We just modify the vertical velocity to move it slightly into
// the downward direction.
_yadd += 0.25f;
}
```

The code comments should sufficiently describe what is going on in this class. There is nothing that is really any more complex than the bouncing box example from the previous chapter.

Getting the Game Running

That is all the code we require within the game itself to run our demonstration. The only component that is missing is the game form. This is set up with its constructor, OnPaintBackground method and Paint event as described at the beginning of this section. We also add a label to the form into which the current Frames Per Second measurement will be displayed. This is handled using a Timer, set to update once per second.

Now, we need to set up a loop to actually drive the game. One simple way that we could do this would be to put another Timer on to the form with its interval set to 1 so that it ticks as fast as possible. This will work, but doesn't deliver the best performance possible, because there are always small delays between one tick finishing and the next beginning.

Instead, we create a loop that runs constantly, advancing the game each time it loops around. The loop will continue until the game form closes, at which point it will exit to allow the application to close. This loop is created within a function called RenderLoop, shown in Listing 4–14.

Listing 4–14. Driving The Game with the RenderLoop Function

```
/// <summary>
/// Drive the game
/// </summary>
private void RenderLoop()
{
    do
    {
        // If we lose focus, stop rendering
        if (!this.Focused)
        {
            System.Threading.Thread.Sleep(100);
        }
        else
        {
            // Advance the game
            _game.Advance();
        }

        // Process pending events
        Application.DoEvents();

        // If our window has been closed then return without doing anything more
        if (_formClosed) return;

        // Loop forever (or at least, until our game form is closed).
    } while (true);
}
```

RenderLoop first checks that the form actually has focus. If it is minimized, we don't want to spend a lot of CPU time updating the game while the user is not playing it. If we detect that we do not have focus, the thread is put to sleep for one-tenth of a second, and no further processing takes place. Because we don't call the game's Advance function, we also effectively pause the game while it is out of focus.

Assuming that we do have focus, the game engine's Advance function is called so that the game can be updated. This update will also trigger the form's Paint event because of calls to the form's Invalidate method contained within the game engine.

Next, we make a call to Application.DoEvents. This call is very important, as without it, all events for the game form will queue up waiting for the RenderLoop function to finish. This would mean we would be unable to process any input events or other form events that might take place, such as the form resizing, minimizing, or closing.

Finally, we check to see if the form has been closed. In .NET CF 3.5, we can easily tell this by looking at the form's IsDisposed property, but sadly, this property is unavailable in .NET CF 2.0. To keep the code working across both versions of the framework, we handle this in a slightly different way. The _formClosed variable is a class-level variable and is set to true in the form's Closed event. This triggers the loop to exit.

To initiate the render loop, we call it from the form's Load event. Prior to this we make sure that the form is visible and fully repainted by calling its Show and Invalidate methods. The code for this, along with the Frames Per Second timer initialization, is shown in Listing 4–15.

Listing 4–15. Starting the Render Loop from the Form Load Event

```
private void Form1_Load(object sender, EventArgs e)
{
    // Enable both of the timers used within the form
    fpsTimer.Enabled = true;

    // Show the game form and ensure that it repaints itself
    this.Show();
    this.Invalidate();

    // Begin the game's render loop
    RenderLoop();
}
```

The project can now be launched, and our bouncing ball appears. That might sound like a lot of work to achieve what is essentially the same as in the last chapter. But one of the advantages of the engine can be shown by making a small change to CBounceGame's Reset method. It instead of adding the single ball, we add 20 balls in a loop, we suddenly find a lot more activity is taking place within the form (see Listing 4–16).

Listing 4–16. Adding Lots of Balls to the Game Within CBounceGame.Reset

```
[...]
// Add some balls
for (int i = 0; i < 20; i++)
{
    // Create a new ball. This will auto-generate a random position for itself.
    ball = new CObjBall(this);
    // Add the ball to the game engine
    GameObjects.Add(ball);
}
[...]
```

A screenshot of the running project is shown in Figure 4–3.

Figure 4–3. The Bounce project running with 20 balls

Optimizing Rendering

The code that we have discussed so far renders graphics for each update as follows:

- Clear the back buffer.
- Draw all the game objects to the back buffer.
- Present the back buffer to the screen.

This is very simple but not very efficient. Imagine a game like Tetris: we have the player's block falling toward the bottom of the screen and a series of other blocks already present within the game area that are completely static. Using our current rendering steps, we would need to completely redraw all of those static blocks for each update, even though they are identical to the previous update. We could achieve a significant degree of extra efficiency by just redrawing the parts of the back buffer that have actually changed.

So how do we do this? The steps required are as follows:

- Determine the area in which game objects have moved since the previous frame.
- Clear the back buffer but only in the movement area.
- Draw all objects that overlap with the movement area.
- Present the movement area to the screen, preserving any graphics that fall outside of the movement area.

Implementing this change can result in a substantial improvement in performance within the engine, particularly in games where there are static elements that we can regularly avoid redrawing altogether.

All of the changes required to implement this optimization are made within the `CGameEngineGDIBase` class, primarily within the `Render` function. The first thing that we need to do is to determine the area in which movement has taken place since the last render.

This area actually consists of both the space objects have moved into (the area into which they will be rendered) and the area that they have moved away from (which will also need to be rendered so that the background or any other objects displayed in that position can be redisplayed). Rendering the area that the object has moved from is important, or we will leave a trail of old objects behind.

■ **NOTE** In our implementation, we will calculate just a single movement area for the game. An alternative approach would be to calculate lots of smaller movement areas, perhaps even one per object. In most cases, optimizing the rendering with one single area actually turns out to be a more efficient approach, as GDI doesn't have to keep track of lots of individual clip areas. The code using this technique is also much simpler, which keeps the complexity of the `Render` function to a minimum.

The diagram in Figure 4–4 highlights the movement area for a ball, with its position in the previous call to `Render` shown in gray and in the current call shown in black. It is clear that we need to redraw both the box that was previously being obscured by the ball and the background in this area. The movement area is highlighted by the dashed rectangle.

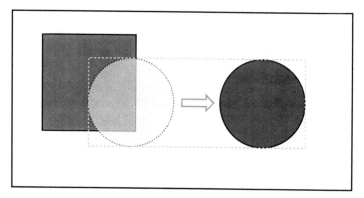

Figure 4–4. The movement area for a ball

The information we need to calculate this area is all already available to us. We can determine which objects have moved by querying their HasMoved property. The area into which these objects have moved can be found by examining each of their current render rectangles; the objects will return this to us from their GetRenderRectangle function. If we use our CombineRectangles function, we can build all of these into a single large render rectangle. This then forms the area into which objects have moved.

Determining the area that objects have moved *from* is easy too. We just combine each object's PreviousRenderRect as scan through them. After retrieving this information, the object's current render rectangle is copied to its previous render rectangle, ready for us to look at in the next render call.

All of this is taken care in the FindCurrentRenderRectangle function, shown in Listing 4–17.

Listing 4–17. Finding the Rectangle Inside Which We Need to Render

```
/// <summary>
/// Calculate the bounds of the rectangle inside which all of the moving objects reside.
/// </summary>
/// <returns></returns>
private Rectangle FindCurrentRenderRectangle()
{
    Rectangle renderRect = new Rectangle();
    Rectangle objectRenderRect;

    // Loop through all items, combining the positions of those that have moved or
    // created into the render rectangle
    foreach (CGameObjectGDIBase gameObj in GameObjects)
    {
        // Has this object been moved (or created) since the last update?
        gameObj.CheckIfMoved();
        if (gameObj.HasMoved)
        {
            // The object has moved so we need to add the its rectangle to the render
            // rectangle. Retrieve its current rectangle
            objectRenderRect = gameObj.GetRenderRectangle();
            // Add to the overall rectangle
            renderRect = CGameFunctions.CombineRectangles(renderRect, objectRenderRect);
            // Include the object's previous rectangle too.
            // (We can't rely on its LastX/Y position as it may have been updated
```

```
                    // multiple times since the last render)
                    renderRect = CGameFunctions.CombineRectangles(renderRect,
                                                    gameObj.PreviousRenderRect);
                    // Store the current render rectangle into the object as its previous
                    // rectangle for the next call.
                    gameObj.PreviousRenderRect = objectRenderRect;

                    // Clear the HasMoved flag now that we have observed this object's movement
                    gameObj.HasMoved = false;
                }

                // This object has now been processed so it is no longer new
                gameObj.IsNew = false;
            }

        return renderRect;
    }
```

Now that you know all of the areas into and from which our objects have moved, we can check to see whether it is empty; if so, we have no further drawing to do at all.

Assuming there is something to draw, we set the Graphics.ClipRegion property with our drawing area. Any attempts to draw outside of this region will have no effect: drawing operations will be clipped within the specified area. This feature is important, as we may need to redraw objects inside the update area that are themselves overlapped by objects outside of the update area. The ClipRegion allows us to do this without needing to redraw all of the overlapped objects until the frontmost one is reached, as shown in Figure 4–5. In this diagram, we have a stack of boxes and a ball that overlaps them. The ball moves away when the scene is updated, and the ClipRegion saves us from having to render the entire stack of boxes again.

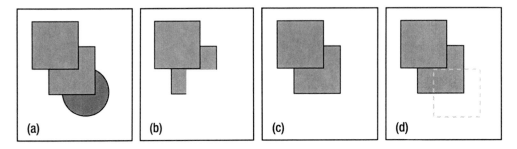

Figure 4–5. Redrawing the scene with and without the ClipRegion.

Figure 4–5(a) shows the original scene. Two boxes are present with a ball behind them. Part (b) shows the scene with the ball having moved away. The movement area is cut out, as it has not yet been rendered. This leaves a section of the lower box missing. Part (c) shows the result of rendering the lower box *without* a ClipRegion active. The box is redrawn, but it now appears in front of the upper box, which is not where we want it to be. To correct this, we would have to redraw the upper box too, and any objects that happen to fall in front of it, and so on. This could potentially result in a long chain of extra object rendering. Finally, part (d) shows what happens if we repeat the render from (c) but this time with a ClipRegion active (shown as a dotted rectangle). The lower box is redrawn but only the section that falls within the ClipRegion is updated. This prevents it from jumping in front of the upper box, so no further rendering is required.

With the movement area determined and the ClipRegion set, the second step in our optimized rendering process (clearing the update area) is very simple. If we are using a background image, we just copy it for the movement area; if not, we can just call the Graphics.Clear method (which will only affect the required area due to our ClipRegion).

Now, we need to draw the game objects. We can reduce the amount of work here to identifying those objects that overlap the movement area and just redrawing these. Objects that fall completely outside of this area will not have been altered from when they were drawn in the previous Render, so they can be left alone. This saves a lot of GDI processing.

The back buffer at this stage is completely updated and is finally ready to be shown to the user. We can optimize this process too however. As you know, the movement area that was rendered to, we can pass just this area into the form's Invalidate call at the end of the Render method. This triggers a call to Present, inside which we copy just this area from the back buffer to the game form. Once again, these changes can result in a noticeable saving of effort for GDI and a faster frame rate as a result.

We also accumulate the rectangular areas into a class variable called _presentRect. This will be used by Present to identify which areas of the form require copying from the back buffer.

To help visualize exactly which areas are being redrawn, some debug code is present inside CGameEngineGDIBase.Render that draws a rectangle around the outside of the movement area each frame. This is commented out by default but can be enabled if you wish to see exactly which part of the screen is being updated. To enable this, remove the comments from the call to DrawRectangle near the end of the Render code shown in Listing 4–18.

Listing 4–18. The ClipRegion Visualization Debug Code

```
// Debug: draw a rectangle around the clip area so we can see what we have redrawn
using (Pen p = new Pen(Color.Blue))
{
    backGfx.DrawRectangle(p, renderRect.X, renderRect.Y,
                          renderRect.Width - 1, renderRect.Height - 1);
}
```

Running the Bounce project with this enabled results in a display like the one shown in Figure 4–6.

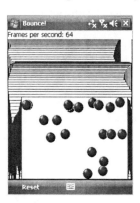

Figure 4–6. The Bounce project with ClipRegion visualization debug code active

The trail of boxes left behind with this rectangle being drawn shows the ClipRegion that was in place during each frame. As we are only updating the movement area, we end up with this trail of old render area rectangles left behind on the screen. This makes it very easy to see exactly where the rendering effort is being focused as the game runs.

Adding, Updating, and Deleting Objects

There are three further operations that can affect the movement rectangle but don't directly relate to objects moving: adding new objects, deleting existing objects, and updating the imagery of stationary objects.

When a new object is added, even if it is completely motionless, we need to render it, or it will be remain invisible until it happens to fall within the movement rectangle. We therefore set a flag called IsNew inside each object when it is created. Any object found with this flag set will be included within the movement rectangle calculation regardless of changes to its coordinates.

At the other end of the objects' lifetimes is their termination. When an object is no longer required, we need to redraw its screen area so that it disappears from the scene. This is the reason for the Terminate flag, which I have mentioned several times already in this chapter. Objects that are flagged for termination are not redrawn but are considered as part of the movement rectangle. After this processing has taken place, the RemoveTerminatedObjects function is used to remove them from the game object list. Any objects that are directly removed from this list without using the Terminate flag will be left behind on the screen until the movement rectangle eventually wipes them out, so it is important to remember to use this mechanism for terminating objects.

CGameObjectGDIBase contains the CheckIfMoved function, which is called by the engine each time it is advanced. This function looks for the conditions that require the object to be redrawn (movement, new object, or terminated object), and if any are found to match, the object's HasMoved property is set to true. This is then checked in the next call to Render.

Finally, we have the situation where an object has changed its imagery but not changed its position. In this scenario, we need to redraw it so that its new graphic can be seen, but with the conditions we have described so far, this would not take place as it is not new or terminated and has not moved.

For this circumstance, we can force the redraw of an object by setting its HasMoved property to true. The next time Render is called, it will see that this flag is set and redraw the object regardless of any of its other properties.

Forcing a Repaint

There are times when we will need to force the entire back buffer to be presented to the game form, instead of just the movement rectangle. Such instances include the following:

- *When the game first launches*: Without repainting the entire form at launch, we can end up with objects that are initially stationary failing to be drawn, and we will find ourselves drawing on the Windows Mobile Today screen rather than in a blank window.

- *When the game resets*: We can make significant changes to the game objects during this phase. Performing a full repaint ensures that everything is displayed properly.

- *When the game form resizes*: If the form size changes (for example, due to the device orientation switching between portrait and landscape), we will need to re-render and redisplay the entire game to ensure that it can accommodate the new dimensions of the form.

We achieve this by calling the CGameEngineGDIBase.ForceRepaint method. This method does three things:

- It sets a class variable called _forceRerender to true. This will be picked up by the next call to Render and will ensure that the entire back buffer is recreated.

- It sets a class variable called _forceRepaint to true. This will be picked up by the next call to Present and will ensure that the entire back buffer is presented.

- It invalidates the game form in its entirety.

Performance Impact

The game engine project included with the Bounce project already contains all the code required to optimize the rendering as described within this section, and the frame rate displayed when the project is running therefore includes the effects of the resulting performance gain. To see the contrast between this and unoptimized rendering, we can simply insert a call to ForceRepaint at the start of the code in CGameEngineGDIBase.Advance.

Try running the code on your device both with and without the optimizations. On a couple of test devices, my results for this comparison are as follows:

- *HTC Touch Pro2 (WVGA)*: 31 frames per second without optimization and 45 with it (a 45 percent improvement)

- *i-mate PDA2 (QVGA)*: 32 frames per second without optimization and 40 with it (a 25 percent improvement)

This implies (perhaps not unexpectedly) that the performance gain is greater in devices with larger screens. Games that have smaller areas of movement will have even more significant improvements than this example.

Other Engine Features

Our game engine provides us with a simple and optimized graphical framework, but we can also get it to perform some other tasks for us. Let's take a look at some other functionality that we can add.

Interacting with the Device

As we discussed in Chapter 1, we cannot forget that we are running in a multitasking device that performs all sorts of other functions, some of which will be classed as more important than our game. Therefore, we need to be able to handle various device interaction events that may occur. The following sections will provide the missing pieces required to ensure our game interacts well with the device.

Minimizing and Restoring

The user may decide, at any time, to minimize the game by clicking the "X" button or otherwise navigating away from our game. Similarly, another application may take the focus away and force us to minimize (for example, in incoming phone call). When this happens, there are two things that we need to do:

- Stop running the game. Pause any action, and reduce CPU usage as far as possible.

- Wait until the game is reactivated, and then resume and force a repaint of the screen so that everything is displayed.

The responsibility for suspending the game lies within the game itself, as the engine has no control over whether or not it gets called. We already saw how this is handled in the form's RenderLoop function.

What the engine can do, however, is confirm that the game form does has focus in its Advance method. If not, it can prevent any further engine advancement and yield to the operating system. This happens within the CGameEngineGDIBase.Advance method, by the addition of the code in Listing 4–19.

Listing 4–19. Focus Checking in the Advance Method

```
/// <summary>
/// Advance the simulation by one frame
/// </summary>
public override void Advance()
{
    // If the game form doesn't have focus, sleep for a moment and
    // return without any further processing
    if (!GameForm.Focused)
    {
        System.Threading.Thread.Sleep(100);
        return;
    }

    [... - the rest of the Advance procedure continues here ...]
}
```

The call to Sleep suspends the application for one-tenth of a second, allowing the operating system to perform any other tasks it has waiting. As the game will essentially just enter a loop that sleeps repeatedly, the actual CPU usage will be very low. I would still recommend that your main game form checks this itself rather than rely on this approach, however.

At the point at which our game form is reactivated, we need to force a repaint so that the background is fully rendered. This is achieved by adding an event handler for the game form's Activated event in the CGameEngineGDIBase constructor. Note that as it is the engine base class that is adding this handler rather than the form itself, we cannot use the normal Events section of the form's Properties window to add this, but must add it programmatically instead:

```
// Add an Activated handler for the game form
gameForm.Activated += new System.EventHandler(GameFormActivated);
```

When the form is reactivated, the GameFormActivated method is called, in which we simply force a repaint (see Listing 4–20).

Listing 4–20. Responding to the Game Form Becoming Reactivated

```
/// <summary>
/// Respond to the game form Activate event
/// <summary>
private void GameFormActivated(object sender, EventArgs e)
{
    // Force the whole form to repaint
    ForceRepaint();
}
```

Resizing the Form

As discussed in Chapter 2, our form will resize if the device orientation changes. This may occur if the user minimizes the application and reconfigures the device or by simply physically rotating the device in newer devices fitted with accelerometers.

When a form resize occurs, we need to reorganize the game for the new dimensions. This may require us to reposition our graphics (or even load entirely new graphics) or display a message stating that the game doesn't work in the new orientation.

However we need to respond, we can get the game engine to intercept this event and prompt us to do whatever we need. Just us with the Activated event, we add a handler for the form's Resize event in the CGameEngineGDIBase constructor. This time we call the GameFormResize function as shown in Listing 4–21.

Listing 4–21. Responding to the Game Form Resizing

```
/// <summary>
/// Respond to the game form resize event
/// </summary>
private void GameFormResize(object sender, EventArgs e)
{
    // If we have no back buffer or its size differs from
    // that of the game form, we need to re-prepare the game.
    if (_backBuffer == null ||
            GameForm.ClientSize.Width != _backBuffer.Width ||
            GameForm.ClientSize.Height != _backBuffer.Height)
    {
        // Re-prepare the game.
        Prepare();
        // Force the whole form to repaint
        ForceRepaint();
    }
}
```

The main purpose of this function is to call into the Prepare method once again (this is where our game engine can do whatever it needs in response to the resize) and force a repaint so that everything is rendered into the newly sized form.

The resize event will however sometimes fire at unexpected times (such as when the form is first opened). To ignore spurious calls, we compare the form dimensions to those of the back buffer. If they match, we ignore the resize calls. Only once we have detected that there definitely has been a change do we call the Prepare and ForceRepaint methods.

Handling the SIP

On touch screen devices, the SIP may open and close at any time. When it closes, the area behind the SIP will remain unpainted if it is not included within the movement area, which looks horrible and is quite disconcerting for the user. We, therefore, need to trap the closure of the SIP and force a repaint whenever this occurs.

We respond to the event in just the same way as with the form events previously, with the slight additional complication of the InputPanel throwing an exception if any attempt is made to interact with it on a smart phone device. We, therefore, check to see whether we are on a smart phone platform before adding the event handler (if we are, then there is no SIP and so no need to handle its events).

To implement this, an InputPanel variable named _inputPanel is added to the class, and it is initialized in the class CGameEngineGDIBase class constructor using the code segment in Listing 4–22.

Listing 4–22. Initializing the SIP Event Handler

```
// If we are running on a touch-screen device, instantiate the inputpanel
if (!IsSmartphone)
{
    _inputPanel = new Microsoft.WindowsCE.Forms.InputPanel();
    // Add the event handler
    _inputPanel.EnabledChanged += new System.EventHandler(SIPEnabledChanged);
}
```

This code calls into the SIPEnabledChanged function each time the SIP is opened or closed. The function contains the code shown in Listing 4–23.

Listing 4–23. Responding to the SIP EnabledChanged Event

```
/// <summary>
/// Respond to the SIP opening or closing
/// </summary>
private void SIPEnabledChanged(object sender, EventArgs e)
{
    // Has the input panel enabled state changed to false?
    if (_inputPanel != null && _inputPanel.Enabled == false)
    {
        // The SIP has closed so force a repaint of the whole window.
        // Otherwise the SIP imagery is left behind on the screen.
        ForceRepaint();
    }
}
```

Checking Device Capabilities

Although it makes sense to target as wide a range of devices as possible, there will be times when you need to enforce minimum hardware requirements for your game. To simplify the task of checking the abilities of the device that is running your came, we will add some capability check functions to the game engine in the CGameEngineBase class.

Your game can use these functions to specify any particular requirements that it has. The engine will then verify that each required capability is actually available and return a value that identifies those capabilities that are *not* present within the device. These can then be used to generate an informational message to the user explaining why the game is unable to run.

We will check for a number of capabilities, falling into the following categories:

- Screen resolution

- Input capabilities

- Windows Mobile version

The capabilities check will be written in such a way that it can be expanded in the future (indeed, we'll add some additional options to it as we continue to develop the engine in the following chapters).

We identify each capability by using an enumeration. Each capability is given a value that is a power of 2. This allows us to perform a bitwise OR operation on the capability values to combine them into a single value from which each individual identity can be retrieved. We apply the Flags attribute to the enumeration to indicate to .NET that we are using the enumeration in this way.

The enumeration for our capabilities is shown in Listing 4–24.

Listing 4–24. *The Capabilities Enumeration*

```
/// <summary>
/// Capabilities flags for the CheckCapabilities and ReportMissingCapabilities functions
/// </summary>
[Flags()]
public enum Capabilities
{
    SquareQVGA = 1,
    QVGA = 2,
    WQVGA = 4,
    SquareVGA = 8,
    VGA = 16,
    WVGA = 32,
    TouchScreen = 64,
    WindowsMobile2003 = 128,
    WindowsMobile5 = 256,
    WindowsMobile6 = 512
}
```

The function that checks the required capabilities against those actually present within the device is CheckCapabilities. This expects a parameter to be passed with all of the required capabilities encoded within it. The code then checks each specified capability against the actual device hardware. This function can be found near the end of the source code inside CGameEngineBase if you wish to examine it.

It works by checking each requested capability in turn. First, for the screen resolution checks, it retrieves the screen's width and height in pixels and ensures that we have the screen in portrait mode (taller rather than wider). The code then compares the required screen size against the actual screen size for each one of the resolution capability flags that is set, setting the capability flag in the missingCaps variable for each resolution that is found to be unavailable.

The TouchScreen flag simply checks the IsSmartphone function—if this returns true, we have no touch screen, so this flag is added to missingCaps.

To determine the version of Windows Mobile, we check the Environment.OSVersion.Version object. This returns major and minor version numbers for each operating system as shown in Table 4–3.

Table 4–3. *Windows Mobile Operating System Version Identification Values*

Operating system	Environment.OSVersion.Version major.minor Value
Windows Mobile 2003 SE	4.x
Windows Mobile 5	5.1
Windows Mobile 6	5.2

We can use the Version object's CompareTo function to easily verify which version of the operating system is running. Once again, all operating system version capability flags that are not met are added to the missingCaps variable, which is then returned back to the calling procedure.

Checking the device in this way allows our code to see exactly which capabilities are missing, but we need a way to report this information back to the user. A second function, ReportMissingCapabilities, is available within the engine to translate these missing capabilities into a readable report that can be presented on the screen.

ReportMissingCapabilities expects another Capabilities parameter; this time, it expects those capabilities that were returned from CheckCapabilities as being unavailable. It first looks for the lowest missing resolution, and if one is found, this is added to a string to be returned. Subsequent resolutions do not need to be displayed, as it is the lowest one that the game actually needs.

The same approach is taken for the Windows Mobile version check: only the lowest required version will be specified.

Once the touch screen check has been catered for too, the requirement string is returned.

We can use the capability check in our game by calling these two functions in our form's Load event. If we find that the required capabilities are not met, we tell the user what is missing, close the form, and exit. The example in Listing 4–25 is for a game which requires VGA resolution or greater, a touch screen, and Windows Mobile 6.

Listing 4–25. Device Capabilities Check

```
private void GameForm_Load(object sender, EventArgs e)
{
    GameEngine.CGameEngineBase.Capabilities missingCaps;
    // Check game capabilities -- OR each required capability together
    missingCaps = game.CheckCapabilities(GameEngine.CGameEngineBase.Capabilities.VGA
            | GameEngine.CGameEngineBase.Capabilities. TouchScreen
            | GameEngine.CGameEngineBase.Capabilities. WindowsMobile6);
    // Are any required capabilities missing?
    if (missingCaps > 0)
    {
        // Yes, so report the problem to the user
        MessageBox.Show("Unable to launch the game as your device does not meet "
            + "all of the hardware requirements:\n\n"
            + game.ReportMissingCapabilities(missingCaps), "Unable to launch");
        // Close the form and exit
        this.Close();
        return;
    }

    [...]
    // Other Form Load code goes here.
    [...]
}
```

This results in the message shown in Figure 4–7 appearing when run on a Windows Mobile 6 QVGA smart phone.

Figure 4–7. *Missing device capabilities*

It is nearly always worth the extra effort required to make your device requirements as low as possible, but when there are some requirements that you simply cannot work without, use this check to ensure that everything you need is available.

Future Enhancements

The engine is designed to be as open-ended as possible. Anything that we add to the engine is immediately available to all of the games that are derived from it. In the coming chapters, we will add code to allow us to read user input, play music and sound effects and later on use OpenGL ES for displaying graphics as an alternative to GDI. The fundamental elements of the engine remain the same throughout all of this.

Next Steps

We are now well on the way to being able to write efficient games with a minimum of effort. The game engine allows us to concentrate just on our game code, without having to worry about how our game interacts with the device.

The Bounce example hopefully goes some way to demonstrate how little code we actually need in our game assembly to get graphical elements animating on the screen. Please spend a little time experimenting with this code, adding your own objects, and changing the way the objects are animated within the game, so that you begin to feel comfortable with the engine that we have built so far.

Of course, we need to allow the user to interact with the engine so that we can produce an actual game rather than simple animations, and we will get to that very shortly. But first, we need to solve a problem that all games encounter: how do we make sure our game runs at the correct speed on every device? This is the area we will focus on in the next chapter.

CHAPTER 5

■ ■ ■

Timing to Perfection

You may have noticed when running the Bounce project from the previous chapter that the speed at which the balls move can be very inconsistent. If you run the project on one of the emulators, the balls move at one speed, and when running on a real device, they move at another. If you try the game on multiple devices, you will find that they all perform completely differently.

If we cannot make our game run at exactly the speed we want, how do we fine-tune the way it plays? The difficulty level of the game can be substantially affected by the speed at which things move, and it's no good spending a lot of time tweaking the speed on your device only to find that everyone else sees the game running at an entirely different speed.

In this chapter, we will examine different mechanisms for keeping your games running at a precise and consistent speed and identify the mechanism that offers the highest performance with the greatest code simplicity. Then, we'll integrate this into the game engine and run some example code to demonstrate the timing between devices.

Affirming the Need for Consistent Timing

In the early days of game development, the systems that games were being written for were entirely standard and identical in terms of ability and performance. Developers could guarantee that the speed the game played when they wrote it would be identical to the speed that everyone else playing it would experience.

These days are long gone now, so we have to take a lot of unpredictability into account when we write our games to keep things running at the speed we want. Lots of things can interfere with the speed that our game runs, as shown in the following sections.

Processor Speed

The most obvious cause of speed difference between devices is the processor speed. CPU specifications have become a common feature of desktop computer games, and all PC gamers are used to checking the requirements of each game against the abilities of their computer.

Mobile devices operate across a smaller range of CPU speeds than their desktop equivalents, but speeds can still vary widely from one device to another. The slower the speed, the longer it takes for your game's code to execute, resulting in slower performance.

Graphics Performance

Not all devices are equal in terms of their ability to update graphics on the screen either. Each device will have its own way of interacting with the display, and as a result, graphical operations will vary in speed from one device to the next.

Another important consideration in this area is the screen resolution of the device. A QVGA screen consists of 76,800 individual pixels, whereas a WVGA screen has 384,000—that's five times as many pixels to update. Full screen operations on WVGA devices, therefore, will be slower than on those with lower resolutions.

Multitasking

Windows Mobile devices are constantly working away in the background doing lots of things you are not aware of. These include trivial tasks such as keeping track of when your next calendar reminder is due to be displayed, through to more complex tasks such as downloading your e-mail messages or synchronizing files with a desktop PC.

All of these divert resources away from other tasks that are running, such as your game. Particularly complex background tasks can cause a running game to lose processor resource for more extended periods of time, which can be disruptive to the player and makes the game feel sluggish and laggy.

Processing and Graphical Complexity

Even assuming that you have the full attention of the device, things within your game will still run at different speeds. Large volumes of alien ships on the screen will require more time to update in terms both of game logic and graphical presentation. Having the game get slower and slower when more intensive processing is required can be frustrating for the player.

Development Mode vs. Released Code

Executing your game in debug mode actually has quite an effect on the speed at which your code executes. For pure data processing (ignoring graphical updates), a debug mode application running with the Visual Studio debugger attached can be many times slower than the same code running as a release build with no debugger. This makes performance unpredictable even under otherwise controlled environments.

Overcoming Performance Inconsistencies

The way to fix all of these problems is to use an external timer to drive our game forward. One second lasts exactly the same amount of time regardless of how fast the CPU is or how many graphics are being displayed. As long as we can make our game run with the same number of updates per second, we can ensure that the game will run at the speed we want every time.

We have a number of mechanisms at our disposal with which we can attempt to do this. Let's take a look at some of them and work out which one to add to the game engine.

Fixed Interval Updates

In the Bounce project in the previous chapter, we used a loop that updated the game engine as quickly as possible in order to drive updates to the game. If we could slow these updates down to regular constant intervals so that they fired at much lower frequencies (say, once or twice per second), we would almost certainly gain consistent performance within the game.

The obvious downside to this approach, of course, is that the game's frame rate will plummet. Updating twice per second will result in horrible animation that no one will want to watch.

In a small number of scenarios, this approach may be viable, but for the majority of games, despite its simplicity, this solution will not be workable at all.

Dynamic Update Intervals

If we rule out slow fixed interval updates, we can return to a model where we update the engine as fast as we can, as in the Bounce example. However, we could monitor how much time has actually passed between each update and provide this interval as a parameter to the game engine. The game engine could then move things larger or smaller distances depending on how much time has elapsed.

Let's assume we are displaying a soap bubble graphic within our game, and we want it to rise up the screen at a constant rate. In our previous approaches, we would simply have subtracted a value from the bubble's y coordinate each time the bubble's Update method was called. As a result, fluctuations in the rate at which the bubble was updated resulted in fluctuations in its speed.

But this time, we'll tell the bubble how much time has elapsed each time we update it. Figure 5–1 shows the results.

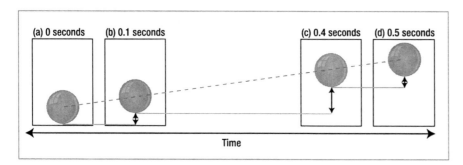

Figure 5–1. *The motion of a bubble using dynamic update intervals*

Figure 5–1 shows four frames of movement for the bubble, each one at a slightly later time in the simulation than the last.

The first frame (a) shows the bubble at its starting point at the bottom of the screen. The second frame (b) is displayed 0.1 seconds later, and the bubble has moved a small distance up the screen. The distance it has moved is shown by the arrows beneath the bubble. The *distance* is calculated by multiplying the amount of *time* that has elapsed (0.1) by the *speed* of the bubble. If we want the bubble to move at a speed of 100 pixels per second, this results in 10 pixels of movement (0.1 × 100 = 10). This is therefore subtracted from the y coordinate when the bubble is updated and rendered.

At this stage, something outside of our application causes us to lose the attention of the processor for a moment, and nothing gets updated for a brief period of time. The next frame that we are able to render, (c), is therefore 0.3 seconds behind frame (b) rather than the 0.1 seconds we would have preferred.

Instead of simply subtracting a constant value from the y coordinate (as we would using fixed interval updates), we continue to apply the formula that we used for frame (b): time × speed = distance. In this case, 0.3 seconds has elapsed, so continuing to use our speed of 100 pixels per second we get a distance of 30 pixels ($0.3 \times 100 = 30$). This increased distance is represented by the larger arrows shown below the bubble in this frame.

Finally, we reach frame (d), which occurs at the expected interval of 0.1 seconds behind frame (c). Our calculation therefore results in a movement of 10 pixels just as in frame (b).

Laying the frames out in a timeline as shown in Figure 5–1, we can draw a line through the center of each bubble and see that its movement speed is indeed constant throughout the simulation.

For the purposes of explaining this approach, I have talked about updating the animation in 0.1-second intervals. In a real simulation we would continue to update the game as quickly as we possibly could. This can therefore result in lots of *additional* frames of animation rather than missed frames as shown in the figure. If we managed to render updates at a rate of 50 frames per second, we would be providing *time* updates of just 0.02 seconds. At this speed, we would gain four additional frames of movement between (a) and (b) shown in Figure 5–1—at 0.02, 0.04, 0.06, and 0.08 seconds. This allows us to keep our rate of movement constant regardless of how fast the game is able to run.

The same applies if the device is unable to handle such high rendering rates. At 20 frames per second, the bubble would move at exactly the same speed but with a time interval of 0.05 for each update. However fast or slow the device is able to go, that's the speed that our game will update, but the actual speed at which things move will be completely constant.

As you can see, the movement speed is now completely independent of the speed of the device—which is exactly what we set out to achieve.

The Problem with Dynamic Intervals

Sounds perfect? Well, it almost is, but unfortunately, it has one major flaw: it works very nicely for linear movement as described here, but for more complex movement patterns, the work that is required inside each update becomes extremely mathematically complicated.

Let's look at this example again, but instead of moving the bubble up at a constant rate, let's make it accelerate as it moves. We'll get it to accelerate so that it increases its speed by 50 percent every 0.1 seconds.

If we were to call our Update method exactly every 0.1 seconds, this would be easy to achieve. We would create a variable to hold the speed, subtract this from the y coordinate and then increase it by 50 percent, as shown in Listing 5–1.

Listing 5–1. Accelerating the Speed of the Bubble

```
class CObjBubble : GameEngine.CGameObjectGDIBase
{
    private float _speed = 1;
[...]
    public override void Update()
    {
        // Allow the base class to perform any processing it needs
        base.Update();
        // Update the y position
        YPos -= _speed;
        // Increase the movement speed by 50%
        _speed *= 1.5f;
    }
}
```

This works well at constant update intervals, but what happens when we introduce dynamic intervals? We can still update the bubble's position easily; we continue to multiply the value of _speed by the time interval just as we did in Listing 5–1. But then what to we do to modify the value of _speed itself? If it increases by 50 percent after 0.1 seconds, how much does it increase by after 0.2 seconds? Or 0.05 seconds? Or 20 seconds?

The answer to these questions can be obtained using differentiation equations. Speaking as a nonmathematician, I don't particularly want to have to get involved with differentiation when writing games (and this is just a simple example of this type of problem). Complex mathematical calculations won't help our performance either; we need to save every CPU cycle for making our game work, not spend it on what should be a just simple acceleration calculation.

This unfortunately makes dynamic intervals unsuitable for our game timing. We need something that has the ability to render the game at whatever speed we require (as the dynamic intervals approach does) but also updates our game logic at a constant rate (as the fixed intervals approach does).

How can we do both of these things at once? Let's take a look at our third and final solution.

Interpolated Updates

Fortunately, there is an answer—and it's really quite simple too. We solve the problem by breaking apart the game logic and the rendering into separate processes. We tell the engine to update itself at regular constant intervals—say, once every tenth of a second, though in practice it would probably be more frequent than this—and continue to render as fast as we can.

But what happens when we try to render multiple times within the same tenth of a second interval? We can certainly expect to need to do this; after all we've already seen our Bounce code running at higher frame rates than this. Multiple updates in the same interval would mean that all of these renders would draw the objects in exactly the same place. The rendering would effectively only update once every tenth of a second. Surely, this is no better than the fixed interval update approach?

We address this using a simple mathematical technique called *interpolation*. Interpolation is the process where a value can be derived on a scale between a starting point and an ending point. There are various types of interpolation and some are quite complex, but we will use the simplest one, called *linear interpolation*.

Although you may not realize it, linear interpolation is probably something that you intuitively use all the time. Take a look at the graph in Figure 5–2.

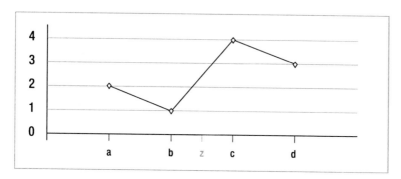

Figure 5–2. Interpolating points upon a graph

The graph has values of 2, 1, 4 and 3 for points a, b, c , and d respectively. However, there is an extra point z marked on the graph too, halfway between points b and c. No value is shown for point z. What is its value? Clearly, it is 2.5. We can see this because point z falls halfway between points b and c, so we can take the value halfway between the values for those two points. 2.5 falls halfway between 1 and 4.

We can describe this is a mathematical calculation by adding the two values together and dividing by two:

```
z = (b + c) / 2
```

This is, of course, simply the calculation to determine the average between the two points.

How does all of this help with our rendering? Well, assume that the points a, b, c and d are the update points of our game. They are all exactly the same distance apart from each other, which meets our requirement to have constant intervals between updates. If we find that we need to render exactly halfway between the update represented by point b and the update represented by point c, we can calculate the midpoint between these two updates and put the object at that location. We have effectively created a new position for our game object, but without having to perform a new update.

Interpolation takes this calculation up a step and allows us to figure out the position anywhere on the line between two points, not just at the midpoint. To interpolate between two values (say, two x coordinates) we take an *interpolation factor* between 0 and 1. A factor of 0 will mean that we are exactly on the first value (which we'll call x_1). A factor of 1 will mean that we are exactly on the second value (which we'll call x_2). If we can now create a calculation that allows any factor within this range to be provided and the appropriate value returned, we can smoothly slide our x coordinate from one value to the next. We'll call the interpolation factor f and the resulting value x_{new}.

The calculation is not too difficult. Its formula is as follows:

```
Xnew = (x2 * f) + (x1 * (1 - f))
```

Let's try evaluating this for same sample values. We'll use the same values as we did in our example above, and so give x_1 a value of 1 and x_2 a value of 4 (see Table 5–1).

Table 5–1. Testing Our Interpolation Function Between Two Values

f	Calculation	x_{new}
0	(4 * 0) + (1 * (1 - 0)) == (0) + (1)	1 (this is exactly on the point x_1)
1	(4 * 1) + (1 * (1 - 1)) == (4) + (0)	4 (this is exactly on the point x_2)
0.5	(4 * 0.5) + (1 * (1 - 0.5)) == (2) + (0.5)	2.5 (this is exactly halfway between x_1 and x_2)
0.25	(4 * 0.25) + (1 * (1 - 0.25)) == (1) + (0.75)	1.75 (this is a quarter of the way between x_1 and x_2)

The calculation achieved everything that we wanted it to: with interpolation factor values of 0 and 1, we find ourselves exactly at the start and end points respectively. Any value between this provides a smooth transition between the first point and the second point. Using this formula, we can smoothly slide between any two values.

Applying the same calculation to both the x and y coordinate values for a game object will result in a calculated position at any point we wish between the two screen coordinates.

Applying Interpolated Updates to a Game

Let's use this technique within the scenario presented by our game engine. When we are rendering, we know what each object's current position is, but we don't know what its next position will be as we haven't calculated it yet. So how do we interpolate our object positions? We do it by interpolating the current position against the *previous* position instead. We smoothly slide our objects from where they were on the previous update toward where they are on the current update. And as you may recall, our objects already store their previous position. How convenient!

What value should we use for our interpolation factor? We will calculate this by seeing how much time has elapsed since we last performed an Update. If we then take this as the proportion of the update interval, we get our value between 0 and 1, which is what we need.

There is still the problem of how we should respond if the regular updates are delayed. Everything in this section so far has assumed that the updates will fire exactly on the schedule that we define for them. In practice of course this is not how things work, and we will find that the program gets interrupted at times such that our update gets delayed a little—or even a lot.

In fact, the interruptions don't actually matter. As long as we process the correct *number* of updates between each render and know what our interpolation factor is from when the most recent update was *scheduled* to take place, everything will flow smoothly as each render will know from the external timer exactly where everything should be displayed on the screen.

Putting this all together, we end up with a flow of events as shown in Figure 5–3.

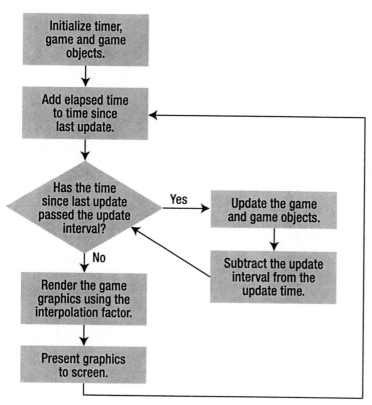

Figure 5–3. Program flow with interpolated updates

The end result of this approach is that we can update our game and all our objects as if they were running at fixed interval updates but keep the rendering moving smoothly and at the fastest rate possible.

Figure 5–4 shows how this may actually be presented to the screen. Once again, this example uses the motion of a ball affected by gravity, starting off moving upward.

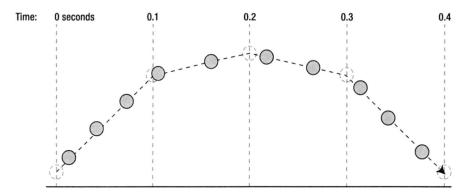

***Figure 5–4.** Interpolated positions between calculated updates*

Figure 5–4 shows the calculated positions for the ball at five different time points (at 0.1 second intervals from 0 seconds to 0.4 seconds). The gray outline ball at each time point shows the calculated vertical position of the ball at that interval, and the dashed line that connects these shows the interpolation path along which the ball will travel.

Drawn on this is a series of filled balls, which represent the locations at which the ball is actually rendered. All of these fall directly on the interpolation line. Note, however, that none of them fall directly on the calculated position for the ball. As every single render is performed using an interpolation factor, it is entirely possible that none of the moving graphics will ever be displayed exactly where they are calculated (though in practice their interpolated positions will often miss their targets by only fractions of a pixel and will therefore appear exactly correct on the screen regardless of this).

Update Frequency

Our discussions thus far have used an update frequency of a tenth of a second. Is this interval fast enough? It generally depends on the nature of your game. In many cases, it may be, but if you have fast moving objects (particularly user-controlled objects), this interval may feel a bit sluggish.

We can increase the frame update frequency to smooth out the curve shown in Figure 5–4 and make out game objects feel more responsive. Repeating the example above with update intervals at 0.025 seconds (a fortieth of a second) results in a much smoother movement curve, as shown in Figure 5–5.

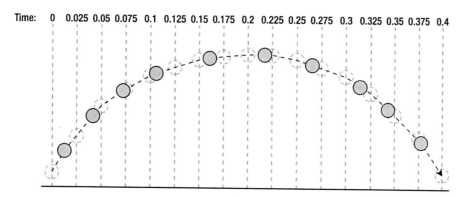

Figure 5–5. Interpolated positions between calculated updates

Figure 5–5 shows the balls rendered at exactly the same points in time as before, but running against a higher frequency update. The *interpolation curve* (the dashed black line) clearly approximates a smooth curve much more closely than in the previous diagram. Having a sufficiently high update frequency is, therefore, important for smooth movement.

The other thing that the frequency affects is the speed at which objects within your game move. If you move a ball 1 pixel across the screen 50 times a second, it will clearly move further than if you move it 1 pixel only 10 seconds a second.

Therefore, it is important to decide on your update frequency before you start putting any substantial amounts of code into your game; if you decide later that you need a higher frequency, you will need to change the amounts you add to all of your objects when you move them in order to retain your initial speeds.

On the other hand, changing the update frequency can be useful in some cases. A lower frequency will make your game run slower, and a higher frequency will make it run faster. This is a simple way in which you can affect the difficulty level of your game should you wish to.

When your game is actually running, the majority of the game's processor time will usually be spent in graphic rendering tasks as this is a much more expensive process than updating your game objects. We will set the engine is to run by default at a frequency of 60 updates per second. This should be fast enough that interpolation inaccuracies never present themselves and that the game always feels responsive, but without performing too much unnecessary work in updates that are never displayed to the screen.

Distinguishing Between Updates and Frames

It's important to keep the distinction between updates and frames.

Updates are performed at a constant rate within the game in order to update the game state and all the objects to new positions. We want our updates to run as close as possible to a fixed time schedule, which we can set at a number of updates per second.

Frames are performed as fast as the device is able and are part of the process of rendering the game to the screen. We can measure the frames per second to see how smoothly our game is running.

We want to aim to have a fixed number of updates per second and the highest frames per second that we can manage.

Making a clear distinction between these two terms will help to clarify the work that we are going to get the game engine to do for us.

Using an External Timer

We discussed some of the features of the Timer form control back in Chapter 2. This control, however, is not very suitable for our requirements here. It is useful for triggering some of your code to run at regular intervals, but it is not hugely accurate and is unable to give us a time reading on demand (if we are partway between two of its intervals, we can't find how far through we are).

Instead, we need to use something that can give us a precise time reading whenever we want it. We have various options available, so let's take a look at each.

DateTime.Now

The simplest such timer is provided by the static DateTime.Now property. This supports a Milliseconds property, so in theory, it could be used by our code to track how much timer has elapsed each time the game is advanced.

In practice, this property turns out to be no use whatsoever, as .NET CF (unlike the desktop version) returns only whole seconds. Although this timer would have been easy to use, even on the desktop this is not a particularly high-resolution timer, so it isn't a great loss to us in this case.

Environment.TickCount

A much more accurate timer is provided by the Environment.TickCount property. This returns back to use the number of milliseconds that have passed since the device was last soft reset. The value is returned as a signed integer, which gives us a maximum possible value of int.MaxValue milliseconds (2,147,483,647). This means that the value is able to count up to a total of 24.85 days before reaching its upper limit, at which point it resets to 0 once again.

This is a respectable choice of timer and will generally provide sufficiently accurate results for our game. However, there is one other timer available that is even more accurate than this.

The High-Performance Timer

Windows Mobile, just like the full desktop Windows, also has a high-performance timer that runs at a substantially higher resolution than even the millisecond timing provided by Environment.TickCount. The timer is not exposed via .NET CF itself but can be accessed using some simple P/Invoke calls.

Not all devices support the high-performance timer, though devices without are likely to be few and far between. Any device running Windows Mobile 5.0 or later should have access to such a timer, but for any device lacking this capability, we will need to fall back to using Environment.TickCount instead.

To use this timer, we need to call two functions: QueryPerformanceFrequency tells us the actual frequency at which the timer runs. It returns a value of either 1 or 0; 0 indicates that the timer is not available and 1 that it is. It also returns out by reference a long value, which is the number of updates per second at which the timer is running. This value will usually be in the millions and will depend on the processor speed and device capabilities. My test devices return values between 3,250,000 and 19,200,000. That's very fast—substantially faster than we will ever need!

The second function is QueryPerformanceCounter. This returns to us by reference another long, which is the current timer value. We can easily convert this into a value in seconds by dividing the QueryPerformanceCounter value by the QueryPerformanceFrequency value.

In theory, it would be possible for this timer to exceed the upper limit of long.MaxValue and loop back to 0. You would however need to wait a particularly long time for this to happen. Even at a frequency of 19,200,000 updates per second, it would take over 15,000 years for the timer to loop around. It's unlikely that your game will be running when that occurs.

Using the high-performance timer when it is available gives us the highest level of accuracy that we could wish for. This should guarantee that we never get misleading timer readings, which could cause our game to stutter or judder when things are moving on the screen.

Timing in the Game Engine

Let's put everything we have discussed in this chapter into the game engine so that we can gain full control over the speed at which everything moves.

The functions we will use that involve the timer fall into three sections:

- Timer initialization and interrogation

- Interpolation-based functions (rendering and calculating object positions)

- Noninterpolation functions (updating the game state and presenting graphics to the screen)

Let's start off with the timer functions.

Initializing and Interrogating the Timer

All of the code relating to timers is added to the CGameEngineBase class.

Before we can use the high performance timer, we need to declare the P/Invoke functions described above. These are declared as shown in Listing 5–2.

Listing 5–2. P/Invoke Declarations for the High-Performance Timer Functions

```
[DllImport("coredll.dll", EntryPoint = "QueryPerformanceFrequency")]
private static extern bool QueryPerformanceFrequency(out long countsPerSecond);

[DllImport("coredll.dll", EntryPoint = "QueryPerformanceCounter")]
private static extern bool QueryPerformanceCounter(out long count);
```

Following this is a series of private class-level variables that will store all the information we need to operate our timers, as shown in Listing 5–3.

Listing 5–3. Timer Variables

```
/// <summary>
/// The high performance counter's frequency, if available, or zero if not.
/// Dividing the timer values by this will give us a value in seconds.
/// </summary>
private float _timerFrequency;
/// <summary>
/// The time value that was returned in the previous timer call
/// </summary>
private long _timerLastTime;
/// <summary>
/// The amount of time (in seconds) that has elapsed since the last render
/// </summary>
private float _renderElapsedTime;
/// <summary>
```

```
/// The amount of time (in seconds) that has elapsed since the last game update
/// </summary>
private float _updateElapsedTime;
/// <summary>
/// The number of game updates to perform per second
/// </summary>
private int _updatesPerSecond;
/// <summary>
/// The duration (in seconds) for each game update.
/// This is calculated as 1 / _updatesPerSecond
/// </summary>
private float _updateTime;
```

Each of these variables will be examined in more detail as we continue to explore out implementation of the timer functions.

The timer will be initialized in a new InitTimer function contained within CGameEngineBase. This is called from the class's constructor to ensure that everything is ready for action and contains the code in Listing 5–4.

Listing 5–4. Timer Initialization

```
/// <summary>
/// Initialize the system timer that we will use for our game
/// </summary>
private void InitTimer()
{
    long Frequency;

    // Do we have access to a high-performance timer?
    if (QueryPerformanceFrequency(out Frequency))
    {
        // High-performance timer available -- calculate the time scale value
        _timerFrequency = Frequency;
        7/ Obtain the current time
        QueryPerformanceCounter(out _timerLastTime);
    }
    else
    {
        // No high-performance timer is available so we'll use tick counts instead
        _timerFrequency = 0;
        7/ Obtain the current time
        _timerLastTime = Environment.TickCount;
    }

    // We are exactly at the beginning of the next game update
    _updateElapsedTime = 0;
}
```

The code first determines whether the high performance counter is available by calling the QueryPerformanceFrequency function. If it is, we store in the _timerFrequency variable. At any stage later on, we can convert a performance counter reading into seconds by dividing by this value. We then store the current time in the _timerLastTime variable by calling QueryPerformaneCounter function.

Alternatively, we may find that the high performance timer is not available on our device. In this case, we store 0 in the _timerFrequency variable to indicate this and read the current TickCount value into _timerLastTime instead.

Whichever way through we go, we end up with information stored that tells us whether we are using the high-performance timer (and if so, its frequency) and the current time reading from whichever timer is being utilized.

To actually read out the time, we use another function, GetElapsedTime. This will return to us the number of seconds that have elapsed since the function was last called (or since the timer was initialized if it has not previously been called). The code for this function is in Listing 5–5.

Listing 5–5. Timer Interrogation

```
/// <summary>
/// Determine how much time (in seconds) has elapsed since we last called GetElapsed().
/// </summary>
protected float GetElapsedTime()
{
    long newTime;
    float fElapsed;

    // Do we have a high performance timer?
    if (_timerFrequency > 0)
    {
        // Yes, so get the new performance counter
        QueryPerformanceCounter(out newTime);
        // Scale accordingly to give us a value in seconds
        fElapsed = (float)(newTime - _timerLastTime) / _timerFrequency;
    }
    else
    {
        // No, so get the tick count
        newTime = Environment.TickCount;
        // Scale from 1000ths of a second to seconds
        fElapsed = (float)(newTime - _timerLastTime) / 1000;
    }

    // Save the new time
    _timerLastTime = newTime;

    // Don't allow negative times
    if (fElapsed < 0) fElapsed = 0;
    // Don't allow excessively large times (cap at 0.25 seconds)
    if (fElapsed > 0.25f) fElapsed = 0.25f;

    return fElapsed;
}
```

The code path is very similar for both timers. First of all, we retrieve a new current time reading into the newTime variable. We then subtract from this the _timerLastTime value to find out how much additional time has elapsed since the timer was initialized or since we last called GetElapsedTime. This value is then divided by the timer frequency to return a value in seconds (though it will most likely be a very small fraction of a second).

With this calculation made, we store the new time reading into the _timerLastTime variable, which effectively resets the reading. The next time we call into this function (where we will compare this stored value against the new current timer), we will receive just the time that has elapsed since this variable was updated.

Before returning the time interval that we have calculated, we perform a couple of sanity checks on it. First, we ensure that it is not negative. The most likely scenario for this is the TickCount value passing its upper limit. This may happen very infrequently but it is still possible, and we don't want our game to go berserk when it happens by trying to move everything backward by a month.

We also check that the time interval doesn't get too large. This is most likely to occur when the device is busy performing CPU-intensive background tasks (such as running an ActiveSync operation with the desktop). Allowing large elapsed values could cause the game to jump forward in huge steps, which would disrupt the game for the player. Capping the value at 0.25 seconds means that if the time intervals become any larger than this, we will slow the game down to compensate by pretending that only this fraction of a second has passed regardless of how much time has actually elapsed.

The code in the game engine also performs a simple frames-per-second calculation within this function; for more details of what this does, have a look at the GameEngineCh5 source code in this chapter's accompanying download. The current reading can be retrieved at any time by calling on the engine's FramesPerSecond property.

We also add a property named UpdatesPerSecond to the class. As we discussed in the "Update Frequency" section, we need to make sure that enough updates are processed per second to keep our animation smooth but not perform so many that the update processing overwhelms the game engine. The required number of updates can be set in this property. The engine defaults to 30 per second.

Changes to the Interpolation-Based Functions

The timer is now ready and waiting for us to use. In order to take advantage of it, several other changes are required to the functions within the engine.

CGameEngineBase

The CGameEngineBase.Advance function undergoes a number of changes. Remember that this function will be called from the game form as many times as can possibly be managed. Whereas in the previous chapter, this function always performed a game update and moved all our objects, now we only want to move the object once sufficient time has elapsed for a whole update to take place; in between these updates, we will use interpolation to move objects between their previous and current positions. The rendering takes place as fast as possible, but the updates only at their preset intervals.

The code for the modified Advance function is shown in Listing 5–6.

Listing 5–6. The CGameEngineBase.Advance Function

```
/// <summary>
/// Virtual function to allow the game and all objects within the game to be updated.
/// <summary>
public virtual void Advance()
{
    // Work out how much time has elaspsed since the last call to Advance
    _renderElapsedTime = GetElapsedTime();
    // Add this to any partial elapsed time already present from the last update.
    _updateElapsedTime += _renderElapsedTime;

    // Has sufficient time has passed for us to render a new frame?
```

```
        while (_updateElapsedTime >= _updateTime)
        {
            // Increment the update counter
            _updateCount += 1;
            // Update the game
            Update();

            // Update all objects that remain within our collection.
            foreach (CGameObjectBase gameObj in _gameObjects)
            {
                // Ignore objects that have been flagged as terminated
                // (We need to retain these however until the next render to ensures
                // that the space they leave behind is re-rendered properly)
                if (!gameObj.Terminate)
                {
                    // Update the object's last position (copy its current position)
                    gameObj.UpdatePreviousPosition();
                    // Perform any update processing required upon the object
                    gameObj.Update();
                }
            }

            // Subtract the frame time from the elapsed time
            _updateElapsedTime -= _updateTime;

            // If we still have elapsed time in excess of the update interval,
            // loop around and process another update.
        }

        // Now that everything is updated, render the scene.
        // Pass the interpolation factor as the proportion of the update time that has
        // elapsed.
        Render(_updateElapsedTime / _updateTime);

        // Remove any objects which have been requested for termination
        RemoveTerminatedObjects();
    }
```

You can see that the function first determines how much time has passed since the last call to Advance and then adds this to the class-level _updateElapsedTime variable. If the time elapsed since the last update exceeds the update time, a game update takes place—calling the Update method on the engine itself and all of the game objects.

The update time is then subtracted from the update elapsed time, and this value is once again compared to the update time. If it still exceeds the update time, another update is performed. This process is repeated as many times as is necessary for the elapsed time to fall below the update time. This ensures that even if we experience a significant processing delay, the number of updates is always in line with the amount of time that has passed.

With any and all required updates processed, we are ready to render the scene. To keep objects moving smoothly between updates, we calculate the interpolation factor to use for rendering. This is calculated by dividing the time that has elapsed since the last update by the update time interval.

Once any terminated objects have been removed, Advance's work is finished.

The other change made to this class is to add the interpolation factor as a parameter to the Render function, so that it may be called as described above. As the base class implementation of Render contains no actual code, no further changes are needed here.

CGameEngineGDIBase

We need to make some minor changes in CGameEngineGDIBase to respond to the interpolation factor that is now being passed into the Render function.

This factor is used in two places, both related to calculating the positions of objects. First, when we calculate the render rectangle for drawing to the back buffer, we now need to tell each object the interpolation factor when it calculates its individual render rectangle. This ensures that the rectangle (and therefore the back buffer clip region) is placed exactly around the objects' actual positions, maximizing the rendering efficiency technique as far as is possible.

The second place this is used is when we actually render each object. When determining whether each object falls within our render rectangle and when calling into each one's Render method, the interpolation factor is used to calculate the actual position on the screen at which rendering is required.

Both of these changes simply require us to pass the interpolation factor into the calls to the CGameObjectGDIBase.GetRenderRectangle function; the changes to that function are described in the "CGameObjectGDIBase" section in a moment.

CGameObjectBase

The changes to the CGameObjectBase class are minimal.

The interpolation factor parameter is added to the Render method. As this doesn't actually do anything within this class, no further changes are required here.

Three new methods are made available, named GetDisplayXPos, GetDisplayYPos, and GetDisplayZPos. Each of these requires the interpolation factor to be provided as a parameter and uses it to calculate the actual screen position at which the object is to be rendered, using its previous and current position and the interpolation factor to calculate this as discussed in the preceding sections (see Listing 5–7).

Listing 5–7. The New Interpolated Position Calculation Functions in CGameObjectBase

```
/// <summary>
/// Retrieve the actual x position of the object based on the interpolation factor
/// for the current update
/// </summary>
/// <param name="interpFactor">The interpolation factor for the current update</param>
public float GetDisplayXPos(float interpFactor)
{
    // If we have no previous x position then return the current x position
    if (LastXPos == float.MinValue) return XPos;
    // Otherwise interpolate between the previous position and the current position
    return CGameFunctions.Interpolate(interpFactor, XPos, LastXPos);
}

/// <summary>
/// Retrieve the actual y position of the object based on the interpolation factor
/// for the current update
/// </summary>
/// <param name="interpFactor">The interpolation factor for the current update</param>
```

```
public float GetDisplayYPos(float interpFactor)
{
    // If we have no previous y position then return the current y position
    if (LastYPos == float.MinValue) return YPos;
    // Otherwise interpolate between the previous position and the current position
    return CGameFunctions.Interpolate(interpFactor, YPos, LastYPos);
}

/// <summary>
/// Retrieve the actual z position of the object based on the interpolation factor
/// for the current update
/// </summary>
/// <param name="interpFactor">The interpolation factor for the current update</param>
public float GetDisplayZPos(float interpFactor)
{
    // If we have no previous z position then return the current z position
    if (LastZPos == float.MinValue) return ZPos;
    // Otherwise interpolate between the previous position and the current position
    return CGameFunctions.Interpolate(interpFactor, ZPos, LastZPos);
}
```

All three of the "last position" variables (LastXPos, LastYPos, and LastZPos) initially hold the value float.MinValue, so we can tell when these have not yet been updated. If this initial value is found to be present, the stored coordinate is returned without any interpolation being performed (as we have no previous point to interpolate from). Otherwise, interpolation between the previous and current point is performed as described earlier in the chapter.

No further changes are required in this class.

CGameObjectGDIBase

A single change is required here, to the GetRenderRectangle function. This now requires the interpolation factor to be provided as a parameter so that the actual on-screen coordinates can be determined. This uses the GetDisplayXPos, GetDisplayYPos, and GetDisplayZPos functions from the base class to perform the calculation (see Listing 5–8).

Listing 5–8. *GetRenderRectangle Taking Advantage of the Interpolated Object Positions*

```
/// <summary>
/// Determine the rectangle inside which the render of the object will take place at its
/// current position for specified interpolation factor.
/// </summary>
/// <param name="interpFactor">The interpolation factor for the current update</param>
public virtual Rectangle GetRenderRectangle(float interpFactor)
{
    // Return the object's render rectangle
    return new Rectangle((int)GetDisplayXPos(interpFactor),
                         (int)GetDisplayYPos(interpFactor), Width, Height);
}
```

Changes to the Noninterpolation Functions

The remaining functions (the game engine's Update and Present functions and the object's Update function) remain entirely unchanged. These are not affected by interpolation and work just as they did when we examined them in the previous chapter.

Using the Game Engine

Developing a game against the modified engine is almost identical with the timing implementation in place to how it was without it. Classes derived from CGameEngineGDIBase will most likely need no modification at all. Unless they happen to override the Render method, everything that the class will be required to do is unchanged.

Game objects derived from CGameObjectGDIBase will need to accept the new interpolation factor parameter in their Render functions and pass this in to any calls to GetRenderRectangle. The only other change that will need to be made to the class is to tweak the movement of the objects to ensure that they are now moving at the desired speeds on the screen. Once the speed has been set, it will remain consistent across all devices, regardless of their processing power and graphical abilities.

There is one other change that needs to be considered within game objects however. If you wish to make an object instantaneously move from one position to another, we need to do something extra when we change the object's position. Its default behavior will be to interpolate from the old position to the new one, causing it to slide across the screen rather than to jump.

Any time you wish to instantly relocate an object, make sure to call into its UpdatePreviousPosition function once you have set the new coordinates. This will update the previous coordinates to match the new current coordinates, removing the transition from the old location to the new one.

Let's Bounce Again

The accompanying code download for this chapter includes a new version of the game engine containing all the timing functionality we have discussed in this chapter and a new version of the Bounce project that takes advantage of it.

You will see that the Bounce project itself is very similar to the version from Chapter 4. Although internally, the timing adds some complexity to the game engine, from the perspective of the games themselves, there is very little extra to do. The game engine provides this functionality for us virtually free of charge.

■ ■ ■

CHAPTER 6

Exploring User Input

We've given Windows Mobile plenty of opportunity to tell us what it is thinking. Now, let's even things up and let it know what's going on inside our human brains. Input is, of course, an essential part of any game and will add interactivity and excitement to our projects.

The ways in which we can get information from the user are no less diverse than the ways we display things on the screen. We have all sorts of hardware form factors to deal with, from devices with keyboards through to those with directional pads to others with barely any hardware buttons at all, from touch screen devices to others with numeric keypads.

More recent devices offer some other interesting options such as accelerometers, which allow us to tell which way up the device is and detect whether it is being moved.

As with everything we've done so far, this chapter will focus on the options available and how to make your game work on the largest selection of hardware we can manage.

Touch Screen Input

On devices that support it, the most obvious way of allowing the user to interact with your game is via the touch screen. The screen is large and is where all the action is taking place, so using this as an input area provides a great opportunity for your game to take on a physical, tangible quality.

There are lots of interesting game mechanics that can be brought to life by allowing the player to actually touch the game as it unfolds. Let's see how we allow the user to control our games using this input method.

Touch Screen Events

From a technical perspective, interaction via the touch screen is handled in exactly the same way as interaction with a mouse on the desktop version of .NET. In fact, even the event names are the same, so if you're used to desktop mouse events, you should feel at home straight away.

Just as with desktop programming, many of the Windows Mobile Forms controls have mouse events that they can respond to, and the control that receives the event will be the one that the user has touched on the screen. Generally, in our games, we will have the form itself covering the majority of the screen, so it is this that receives most of the mouse events.

The relevant events within .NET CF are explained in the following sections.

Click

When the user taps the screen, a Click event will fire against whatever control was tapped. As most of our games will consist of a mostly empty form (with our game graphics rendered inside it), this will usually be the form itself.

Most of the time, it won't be much use knowing that a click occurred without also knowing where on the screen the click actually took place. Unfortunately, this information is not passed to us as part of the event parameters; we receive just an EventArgs object, which doesn't contain any information at all.

We can use another mechanism to retrieve the position that was clicked however. The Form class has a static property called MousePosition that returns the most recent point at which the screen was tapped. This returns the appropriate coordinate back to us, but if you try using it, you will find that it is actually the *screen* coordinate, not the coordinate within our window. We know that the top-left corner inside our window is at coordinate (0,0), but tapping the corner and querying the MousePosition returns a coordinate of (0, 27) (or thereabouts). This query has not taken into account the height of the status bar displayed above the window, so the locations will be out of alignment with what we are drawing within the form.

To retrieve the coordinate within the form's client area, we can use the form's PointToClient function. This is actually defined as a member of the System.Windows.Forms.Control class from which all form controls (including the form itself) are derived.

The function expects a screen coordinate to be passed in as a parameter (such as the one we retrieve from Form.MousePosition) and returns the corresponding coordinate relative to the client area of the control on which the function is called. Calling this function on the form itself, therefore, returns the coordinate within the client area of the form.

Listing 6–1 shows how to use this function to determine the actual coordinate within the form.

Listing 6–1. Retrieving the Click Coordinate Within the Form Client Area

```
private void MyForm_Click(object sender, EventArgs e)
{
    Point formPoint;

    // Translate the mouse position into client coordinates within the form
    formPoint = this.PointToClient(Form.MousePosition);

    // Display the coordinate to the user
    MessageBox.Show("Click: " + formPoint.X.ToString() + "," + formPoint.Y.ToString());
}
```

Note that clicks are not timed: a Click event will always fire when the screen is touched and released regardless of how much time elapses between the two events.

DoubleClick

The DoubleClick event unsurprisingly occurs when the user double-taps the screen. Just as with the Click event, no location information is passed in the event parameters, so the same Form.MousePosition approach is required to work out where on the form the double-click actually took place.

When the user double-clicks the screen, both the Click and DoubleClick events will actually fire. The Click event will fire for the first tap on the screen and the DoubleClick straight afterward for the second tap (the Click event fires only once).

MouseDown

To get the user's screen interaction at a lower level, we can use the MouseDown and MouseUp events. These correspond exactly with the taps and releases on the screen, unlike Click and DoubleClick, which both require multiple steps to fire (pressing and releasing for Click, or pressing and releasing twice for DoubleClick).

The MouseDown event provides a MouseEventArgs object as its second parameter, which provides us with some actual information. The first thing it tells us is which mouse button was pressed. This is clearly present to maintain interface compatibility with the desktop version of .NET (and perhaps for future-proofing too—there's no reason why Windows Mobile devices may not commonly support mice one day in the future) but is of very limited use to us at present.

More usefully, we can query the X and Y properties of the object to find the coordinate in which the screen was touched. This provides the coordinate relative to its sender's client area, so there is no need to translate the coordinate using the PointToClient method as we had to with the Click event.

MouseUp

What goes down must come up (I think that's how the saying goes), and the same applies to taps on the screen too. The MouseUp event also receives a MouseEventArgs object containing details of the last touch position when contact was released.

If you touch the screen and then slide your stylus or finger off the edge of the screen without ever actually releasing contact, the MouseUp event will fire as soon as the point of contact leaves the touch screen area. This isn't perfectly simulated in the device emulators, which will fire the event only once the left mouse button is actually released, even if the mouse cursor is moved outside of the bounds of the window. This does mean, of course, that all MouseDown events will be paired with a corresponding MouseUp event.

Unfortunately, the MouseUp event doesn't provide us with any more information than this. It would have been very useful to be told the coordinate at which the mouse went down and how long ago this event took place. We need to track this data ourselves, but this is all very easy to do, and we'll look at an example of this shortly.

When all four of these events are used together, the sequence in which they fire when the use double-clicks the screen is as follows:

- MouseDown
- Click
- MouseUp
- MouseDown
- DoubleClick
- MouseUp

MoveMove

The MouseMove event fires continuously each time the point of contact with the screen moves. Just as with the MouseDown and MouseUp events, it is passed a MouseEventArgs object from which the current contact coordinate can be retrieved.

Unlike .NET on the desktop, this event is only triggered when there is actually contact with the screen. Windows has an on-screen mouse cursor, so its forms are able to detect movement when the mouse button is not pressed, but Windows Mobile by default has no such concept (it cannot detect your finger hovering in front of the screen!) and so MouseMove events will not fire except between MouseDown and MouseUp events.

However, as I have already mentioned, we shouldn't preclude the possibility of Windows Mobile supporting mouse cursors in the future, so you should still ensure that the mouse is actually down prior to processing MouseMove events. This is simple to do and will help to future-proof your application.

Selecting, Dragging, and Swiping

These events provide a mechanism for simple control over objects within our game. Frequent requirements for our games will include:

- Allowing the user to touch a game object in order to select it

- Allowing the user to hold down on an object and drag it to move its position

- Allowing the user to "swipe" an object by releasing contact with the screen while moving an object (this is commonly known as *kinetic movement*)

Let's take a look at how we can implement each of these into a game.

Selecting an Object

To allow the user to select an object within the game, we need to be able to identify which object (if any) occupies the point on the screen that has been touched. As objects may be different sizes and shapes, we will allow each object to perform its own test to determine if the touch point actually falls within its area. For those objects that don't want or need to provide special processing for this, we'll simply see if the point is within the object's render rectangle.

This object detection is implemented by adding a new virtual function named IsPointInObject to the CGameObjectGDIBase class. The implementation within the base class itself simply checks whether the point falls within the rectangle returned by the GetRenderRectangle function.

Of course, as the position of the object on the screen is affected by the interpolation described in the last chapter, we need to know the interpolation factor for the most recent render. The game engine itself will provide this value when it calls into the function.

The base class code is shown in Listing 6–2.

Listing 6–2. The Base Class Implementation of the IsPointInObject Function

```
/// <summary>
/// Determine whether the specified point falls within the boundaries of the object.
/// </summary>
/// <param name="interpFactor">The current interpolation factor</param>
/// <param name="testPoint">The point to test</param>
/// <remarks>The implementation in this function simply looks to see if the point is
/// within theobject's render rectangle. To perform more sophisticated checking, the
/// functioncan be overridden in the derived object class.</remarks>
protected internal virtual bool IsPointInObject(float interpFactor, Point testPoint)
{
    // By default we'll see if the point falls within the current render rectangle
    return (GetRenderRectangle(interpFactor).Contains(testPoint));
}
```

This works fine when our objects fill their render rectangle, but frequently, they will have more complex shapes. In many cases, this doesn't actually matter: the selection area of an object doesn't have to exactly correspond to the graphics displayed on the screen, so often it is not worth the development or processing time required to perform exact testing for the objects.

One test that can be useful, however, is a circular hit test. We can determine whether a touch point falls within a circular region by using the Pythagorean theorem. If a circle is drawn with a known radius, we can use this mathematical approach to find the distance between the circle's center and the touch point. If the distance is less than or equal to the radius, the point is within the bounds of the circle; otherwise, it is not.

The Pythagorean theorem allows the length of the hypotenuse (the long edge) of a right-angled triangle to be calculated if the length of the other two sides are known. It states that the square of the hypotenuse is equal to the squares of the other two sides added together. The length of the hypotenuse can, therefore, be found by adding together the square of the other two sides and then finding the square root of the result.

We can use this to determine the distance between the circle center and a touch point as shown in Figure 6–1.

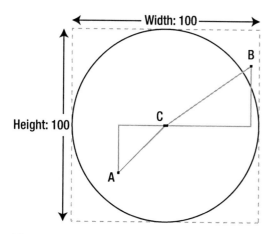

Figure 6–1. Testing whether points fall inside a circle

In Figure 6-1, the center of the circle is marked as point C. Our circle has a width and height of 100 pixels, and a top-left coordinate of (100, 100). This means that the centre is at (150, 150) (the top-left coordinate offset by half the width and half the height of the circle).

We can now test the two other points shown, A and B. Note that both of these fall within the render rectangle (shown as the dashed square), but only point A is actually within the circle. Points that fall outside of the render rectangle can be immediately eliminated without any further processing, as these cannot be within the circle. Eliminating these points saves us the need to perform this relatively expensive calculation for all of the circular objects active within the game.

To calculate the distance between each of these points and the center point C, we first find the distance along the x and y axes by subtracting the center point coordinates from the test point coordinates. These are shown in Table 6–1.

Table 6–1. Calculating the Horizontal and Vertical Distances Between the Center and Vertex Points in Figure 6–1.

Point	X distance	Y distance
A	$150 - 125 = 25$	$150 - 175 = -25$
B	$150 - 195 = -45$	$150 - 120 = 30$

We then calculate the distance as the square root of X distance^2 + Y distance^2, as shown in Table 6–2.

Table 6–2. Calculating the Distance from the Center to the Vertex Points

Point	X distance^2 + Y distance^2	$\sqrt{\text{X distance}^2 + \text{Y distance}^2}$
A	$(25 \times 25) + (-25 \times -25) = 1250$	$\sqrt{1250} = 35.35$
B	$(-45 \times -45) + (30 \times 30) = 2925$	$\sqrt{2925} = 54.08$

The results here show that point A is 35.35 pixels away from the center point. This is less than the circle radius of 50 pixels, so point A is calculated as being within the circle. Point B has a distance of 54.08 pixels, greater than the radius, so it is calculated as being outside the circle.

This calculation can be implemented into a derived game object as shown in Listing 6–3.

Listing 6–3. Determining Whether a Point Falls Within a Circular Region

```
/// <summary>
/// Determine whether the testPoint falls inside a circular area within the object
/// </summary>
protected override bool IsPointInObject(float interpFactor, Point testPoint)
{
    Rectangle rect;
    Point center;
    float radius;
    int xdist, ydist;
    float pointDistance;

    // See if we are in the render rectangle. If not, we can exit without
    // processing any further. The base class can check this for us.
    if (!base.IsPointInObject(interpFactor, testPoint))
    {
        return false;
    }

    // Find the current render rectangle
    rect = GetRenderRectangle(interpFactor);
    // Calculate the center point of the rectangle (and therefore of the circle)
    center = new Point(rect.X + rect.Width / 2 - 1, rect.Y + rect.Height / 2 - 1);
    // The radius is half the width of the circle
```

```
    radius = rect.Width / 2;

    // Find the distance along the x and y axis between the test point and the center
    xdist = testPoint.X - center.X;
    ydist = testPoint.Y - center.Y;

    // Find the distance between the touch point and the center of the circle
    pointDistance = (float)Math.Sqrt(xdist * xdist + ydist * ydist);

    // Return true if this is less than or equal to the radius, false if it is greater
    return (pointDistance <= radius);
}
```

More sophisticated point tests can be created if required by comparing the testPoint against multiple circles or rectangles within the render rectangle of the shape.

Now that we have a way to find whether a point falls within an individual object, we can now add a function to CGameEngineGDIBase that determines which object is underneath the point that has been touched. The code for this is shown in Listing 6–4.

Listing 6–4. *GetObjectAtPoint Determines Which Object, If Any, Is At a Specified Location*

```
/// <summary>
/// Find which object is at the specified location.
/// </summary>
/// <param name="testPoint">The point to check</param>
/// <returns>If an object exists at the testPoint location then it will
/// be returned; otherwise returns null.</returns>
public CGameObjectGDIBase GetObjectAtPoint(Point testPoint)
{
    float interpFactor;
    CGameObjectGDIBase gameObj;

    // Get the most recent render interpolation factor
    interpFactor = GetInterpFactor();

    // Scan all objects within the object collection.
    // Loop backwards so that the frontmost objects are processed first.
    for (int i = GameObjects.Count - 1; i >= 0; i--)
    {
        // Get a reference to the object at this position.
        gameObj = (CGameObjectGDIBase)GameObjects[i];

        // Ignore objects that have been flagged as terminated
        if (!gameObj.Terminate)
        {
            // Ask the object whether it contains the specified point
            if (gameObj.IsPointInObject(interpFactor, testPoint))
            {
                // The point is contained within this object
                return gameObj;
            }
        }
    }
}
```

```
        // The point was not contained within any of the game objects.
        return null;
    }
```

The code is straightforward, simply looping through the objects and asking each one if it contains the specified touch point. Note that the loop is performed backward: this is to handle scenarios where multiple objects overlap and occupy the same space. When we render the objects, the ones at the end of the object list are drawn last, and therefore draw over any objects earlier in the list and appear in front. In order to ensure we locate the object in the front, we need to consider those at the end of the list before the earlier objects.

Sometimes, it is useful to be able to find *all* of the objects that occupy a point on the screen, irrespective of whether or not they are the front-most objects. To deal with this, a second function named GetAllObjectsAtPoint can be used. The code for this is virtually identical to that of GetObjectAtPoint, except that it returns a List<CGameObjectGDIBase> rather than a game object instance. The loop still executes backward so that the objects within the returned list will be sorted front-to-back.

The ObjectSelection project in the accompanying code demonstrates using these object selection functions. It defines a new abstract object class, CObjSelectableBase, which derives from CGameObjectGDIBase and adds a Selected property. Two object classes are then derived from here, CObjBall and CObjBox, representing a circular and square object respectively. CObjBall provides as override for IsPointInObject, which uses the circular point test described previously, whereas CObjBox has no override and just uses the simple rectangular region test. Both of the object types are filled in white if they are selected or in violet if they are not.

The form has code within a function called SelectObject, called from the MouseDown event, which finds the object at the touched coordinate, checks that it is derived from CObjSelectableBase, and then ensures that it is selected and that all other objects are not. If no (selectable) object is under the coordinate, all the objects are unselected. The code for this function is shown in Listing 6–5.

Listing 6–5. Selecting the Object at the Touched Screen Position

```
/// <summary>
/// Select the object at the specified position
/// </summary>
private CObjSelectableBase SelectObject(Point testPoint)
{
    GameEngine.CGameObjectGDIBase touchedObject;

    // Find the object at the position (or null if nothing is there)
    touchedObject = _game.GetObjectAtPoint(testPoint);

    // Select or deselect each objects as needed
    foreach (GameEngine.CGameObjectGDIBase obj in _game.GameObjects)
    {
        // Is this a selectable object?
        if (obj is CObjSelectableBase)
        {
            if (((CObjSelectableBase)obj).Selected && obj != touchedObject)
            {
                // This object was selected but is no longer, so redraw it
                ((CObjSelectableBase)obj).Selected = false;
                obj.HasMoved = true;
            }
            if (!((CObjSelectableBase)obj).Selected && obj == touchedObject)
```

```
            {
                // This object was not selected but now is, so redraw it
                ((CObjSelectableBase)obj).Selected = true;
                obj.HasMoved = true;
            }
        }
    }

    // Return whatever object we found, or null if no object was selected
    if (touchedObject is CObjSelectableBase)
    {
        // A selectable object was touched, so return a reference to it
        return (CObjSelectableBase)touchedObject;
    }
    else
    {
        // Either no object selected or not a selectable object, so return null
        return null;
    }
}
```

Try running the code and then touching the objects on the screen: each one highlights when it is touched (see Figure 6–2). Observe that the balls really do become selected only when a point inside them is picked, and that overlapping objects are selected as you would expect them to be.

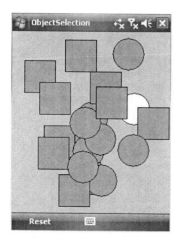

Figure 6–2. The ObjectSelection sample project

When selecting objects, it is often useful to be able to move then in front of the other objects that are being displayed. Figure 6–2 has one of the circular objects selected, and it is clearly still behind some of the other game objects.

To permit objects moving to the front or back of the object group, we add two new functions to CGameObjectGDIBase, called MoveToFront and MoveToBack. The code for these is shown in Listing 6–6.

Listing 6–6. Moving an Object to the Front or Back of the Displayed Objects

```
/// <summary>
/// Move this object to the front of all the objects being rendered
/// </summary>
public void MoveToFront()
{
    // Remove the object from the list...
    GameEngine.GameObjects.Remove(this);
    // ...and then re-add it at the end of the list so that it is rendered last
    GameEngine.GameObjects.Add(this);
    // Mark it as moved so that it is redrawn
    this.HasMoved = true;
}

/// <summary>
/// Move this object to the back of all the objects being rendered
/// </summary>
public void MoveToBack()
{
    // Remove the object from the list...
    GameEngine.GameObjects.Remove(this);
    // ...and then re-add it at the start of the list so that it is rendered first
    GameEngine.GameObjects.Insert(0, this);
    // Mark it as moved so that it is redrawn
    this.HasMoved = true;
}
```

Both of these functions work by simply changing the position of the object within the GameObjects list. Objects are drawn in sequence from the object at index 0 to the object at GameObjects.Count - 1, and any object drawn will render in front of those drawn before it. This sequencing means that the object at index 0 appears at the back, and the one at GameObjects.Count - 1 at the front. Putting an object to the front of the list therefore pushes it to the back of the objects, and putting an object to the end of the list brings it to the front.

■ **NOTE** As these methods modify the order of the GameObjects list, they cannot be used from within a foreach loop. If you need to reorder the objects within such a loop, you will need to store references to the objects to be relocated in local variables and call the MoveToFront or MoveToBack methods once the loop has completed.

Dragging Objects

A common requirement in many types of game is the ability to drag an object around the screen. Let's look at how we can build on the object selection example to implement this.

To simplify handling draggable objects, we first create a new abstract class, CObjDraggable. This is virtually identical to the CObjSelectableBase class that we have just been looking at but will be used to identify whether an object actually is draggable (it can be dragged only if it derives from the CObjDraggable class) and also to provide kinetic movement in the "Swiping Objects" section coming up next.

Dragging is achieved by keeping a reference to the object that is selected in the MouseDown event. All subsequent MouseMove events are then used to update the position of the object. When the MouseUp event fires, we release the reference to the selected object, leaving it in its final position.

However, we cannot simply move the object to the coordinate provided to the MouseMove event; the object coordinate is for the top-left corner of the object, and so moving the object to this position would result in the object jumping so that this corner was aligned with the mouse position. Instead, we keep track of the current and previous positions, and monitor the differences between them. If we find that the touch point has moved 10 pixels to the right, we move the object 10 pixels to the right too. This ensures that it moves in exactly the same direction as the touch point.

This information is stored in two class-level variables declared within GameForm; see Listing 6–7.

Listing 6–7. Variables Required for Object Dragging

```
// The object currently being dragged (or null if no dragging is active)
CObjDraggableBase _dragObject;
// The most recent touch coordinate for dragging
Point _dragPoint;
```

We start off the dragging with a function within GameForm called DragBegin. Called from MouseDown with the touch point as a parameter, this function will store a reference to the object being dragged and track the touch location within the object. It uses a version of the SelectObject function described above to determine which object has been touched, as shown in Listing 6–8.

Listing 6–8. Initiating Dragging of an Object

```
/// <summary>
/// Begin dragging an object
/// <summary>
/// <param name="touchPoint">The point containing an object to drag. If an object is
/// found here then dragging will begin, otherwise the call will be ignored.</param>
private void DragBegin(Point touchPoint)
{
    // Select the object at the specified point and store a reference
    // to it in _dragObject (or null if nothing is at this location)
    _dragObject = SelectObject(touchPoint);
    // Store the point that was touched
    _dragPoint = touchPoint;

    // If an object is selected, move it to the front
    if (_dragObject != null) _dragObject.MoveToFront();
}
```

The function first attempts to select the object at the provided coordinate. It stores this object reference (which may be null if no object was selected) in the _dragObject variable and stores the touched coordinate in _dragPoint. If an object was selected, it is moved to the front of the other objects.

Once dragging has started, the DragMove function is responsible for actually moving the target object. This is called from the form's MouseMove event and is shown in Listing 6–9.

Listing 6–9. Implementing the Movement of a Dragged Object

```
/// <summary>
/// Move an object being dragged
/// </summary>
```

```
private void DragMove(Point touchPoint)
{
    // Are we currently dragging an object? If not, there is nothing more to do
    if (_dragObject == null) return;

    // Update the object position based on how far the touch point has moved
    _dragObject.XPos += (touchPoint.X - _dragPoint.X);
    _dragObject.YPos += (touchPoint.Y - _dragPoint.Y);

    // Update the stored drag point for the next movement
    _dragPoint = touchPoint;
}
```

First, the code checks that an object is actually being dragged; if not, it exits immediately.

If we get past that check, we now look at the difference between the current touch coordinate and the previous touch coordinate. By subtracting one from the other, we can see how far the touch point has moved since dragging was initiated or last processed by this function. The distance is added to the object's XPos and YPos variables, which will cause it to follow the motion of the touch point on the screen.

Finally, we store the touch point back into the _dragPoint variable so that we can refer to this coordinate during the next call to DragMove, allowing us to see any further movement that has taken place.

When the user releases contact with the screen, we call from the form's MouseUp event into the DragEnd function. For the moment, all this does is release the reference we have stored to the dragged object, as shown in Listing 6–10.

Listing 6–10. Releasing a Dragged Object

```
/// <summary>
/// Finish dragging an object
/// </summary>
private void DragEnd(Point releasePoint)
{
    // Release the dragged object reference
    _dragObject = null;
}
```

All the code required to implement dragging objects can be found in the DragsAndSwipes example project in the accompanying code download. Give it a try, and make sure you are comfortable with all of the code that has been put into place in this section.

Swiping Objects

Object dragging is useful and appropriate in many situations, but in others, it can be useful to allow objects to be swiped—dragged and released with momentum so that they continue moving in the direction that they were dragged. Swiping has become a common user interface feature on handheld devices recently, allowing users to push their way through pages of information by quickly swiping across the screen.

Replication of the same kind of movement in a game can be achieved fairly easily. Let's take a look at how we can do this.

To create a swipe, all the time our object is being moved, we keep track of its movement points. We need to keep track of a number of the most recent points; not too many are required. For our sample, we'll keep the five most recent positions of each object. If you have a higher number of updates per second, you may need to increase this value, but it will suffice in most cases.

Retaining the recent positions allows us to track where the touch point was a moment ago and compare this to where it is now. When the touch is released, we calculate the direction that the object was moving and set up velocity variables to keep it moving in the same direction. The object is pushed across the screen as a result.

However, unless we do something to stop it, this calculation will result in the object moving forever. To make it slide to a halt, we apply a simulation of friction to the object. Reducing the velocity each time we apply the velocity variable will cause the object to slide to a stop. We can vary the friction level to allow it to slide further or stop more quickly.

This can be seen in action in the DragsAndSwipes example project. All of the movement information is tracked inside the CObjDraggableBase class. The motion information is stored using the class-level variables shown in Listing 6–11.

Listing 6–11. Variables Required to Implement Kinetic Movement of a Dragged Object

```
// The friction to apply to kinetic object movement
// (1 == virtually none, 99 == extremely high).
private float _kineticFriction = 10;
// The kinetic velocity of the object,
private float _xVelocity = 0;
private float _yVelocity = 0;
// The most recent positions of the object -- used to calculate the direction
// for kinetic movement of the object.
private Queue<Point> _dragPositions = new Queue<Point>();
// The number of points we want to track in the dragPositions queue.
private const int _DraggableQueueSize = 5;
```

The _kineticFriction variable is exposed outside of the class using a public property; all of the other variables are used only within the class itself. The other variables store the current kinetic velocity of the object (zero unless the object has actually been swiped), most recent object positions (stored in a Queue), and a constant defining the size of the queue.

We then add a function called InitializeKineticDragging. This must be called as soon as object dragging begins in order to prepare it to track the object movement. The function is shown in Listing 6–12.

Listing 6–12. Preparing an Object for Kinetic Dragging

```
/// <summary>
/// Prepare the object for kinetic motion. Call this when the object enters drag mode.
/// </summary>
internal void InitializeKineticDragging()
{
    // Clear the queue of recent object positions
    _dragPositions = new Queue<Point>();

    // Cancel any existing kinetic movement
    _xVelocity = 0;
    _yVelocity = 0;
}
```

The function creates the queue of points and ensures that any existing velocity is set to 0. This allows the user to catch any object that is in motion and immediately puts that object back under the user's control without the kinetic motion attempting to pull it away.

Next, we need to add points to the queue in the Update method. The lines of code required are as shown in Listing 6–13.

Listing 6–13. Adding the Object Position to the _dragPositions Queue

```
public override void Update()
{
    [...]

    // Write the current object position into the drag positions queue.
    // This will allow us to apply kinetic movement to the object
    // when it is released from dragging.
    _dragPositions.Enqueue(new Point((int)XPos, (int)YPos));
    if (_dragPositions.Count > _DraggableQueueSize) _dragPositions.Dequeue();

    [...]
}
```

The code first adds the current object position to the queue. It then checks the queue size. If the queue size exceeds the defined maximum, the first point in the queue is removed. This gives us a rolling window into the last five (in this case) points, with the first item in the queue always containing the oldest of the points and the last item containing the most recent.

While the object is being dragged, the queue will ensure that we know where it has been and how fast it is moving. Now, we need to wait until the dragging is completed and work out the kinetic velocity for the object; see Listing 6–14.

Listing 6–14. Calculating and Applying the kinetic Velocity When Dragging Is Finished

```
/// <summary>
/// Apply kinetic motion to the object. Call this when the object leaves drag mode.
/// </summary>
internal void ApplyKineticDragging()
{
    Point first, last;

    // Make sure there is something in the point queue...
    // We need at least 2 points in order to determine the movement direction
    if (_dragPositions.Count < 2)
    {
        // There is not, so no kinetic force is available
        return;
    }

    // Retrieve the oldest position from the drag position queue
    first = _dragPositions.Dequeue();
    // Remove all the other positions until we obtain the most recent
    do
    {
        last = _dragPositions.Dequeue();
    } while (_dragPositions.Count > 0);

    // Set the x and y velocity based upon the difference between these
    // two points. As these represent the last five object positions, divide the
```

```
    // distance by one less than this (four) to maintain the same actual speed.
    _xVelocity = (last.X - first.X) / (_DraggableQueueSize - 1);
    _yVelocity = (last.Y - first.Y) / (_DraggableQueueSize - 1);
}
```

The oldest of the stored object locations is placed into the first variable, and the queue is then emptied so that the most recent location is retrieved into the last variable. By comparing these, we can then find the direction and speed of movement during the most recent five updates. By setting the object to continue to move in the same direction and at the same speed, we achieve the kinetic motion that we are looking to apply.

As these points cover a range of five updates, and we are going to apply the motion during every subsequent update, we need to divide the speed by the number of movements that we are able to see within the queue to find the average distance the object actually moved in each of the previous updates. Each movement is defined by two coordinates—the initial position and the updated position—so there will be one less movement than there are coordinates. By dividing the velocities by one less than the queue size (_DraggableQueueSize - 1), we ensure that the initial kinetic speed will match the drag speed.

For example, assume that the object moved at a constant speed of 10 pixels per update in the x axis and 5 pixels per update in the y axis. The first and last coordinates returned from the queue might therefore be (100, 100) and (140, 120). To scale this overall movement distance down to match the constant speed, we subtract the first x position from the last and divide by the number of movements that we have in the queue. This gives us the constant speed that was being applied, which is 10 in this case: (140 – 100) / 4. The same calculation for the y axis again yields the speed that was applied: (120 – 100) / 4 = 5,

Now that the velocity is calculated and stored within the object, we need to allow it to move when it updates. The remainder of the Update function applies the velocity to the object and gradually reduces the velocity to simulate friction; see Listing 6–15.

Listing 6–15. The complete Update Function, With the Code Required to Move the Object According to Its Stored Kinetic Velocity

```
/// <summary>
/// Provide all of the functionality necessary to implement kinetic
/// motion within the object.
/// </summary>
public override void Update()
{
    base.Update();

    // Write the current object position into the drag positions queue.
    // This will allow us to apply kinetic movement to the object
    // when it is released from dragging.
    _dragPositions.Enqueue(new Point((int)XPos, (int)YPos));
    if (_dragPositions.Count > _DraggableQueueSize) _dragPositions.Dequeue();

    // Apply any existing kinetic velocity set for this object
    if (_xVelocity != 0 || _yVelocity != 0)
    {
        XPos += _xVelocity;
        YPos += _yVelocity;
        // Apply friction to the velocity
        _xVelocity *= (1 - (KineticFriction / 100));
        _yVelocity *= (1 - (KineticFriction / 100));
        // Once the velocity falls to a small enough value, cancel it completely
```

```
            if (Math.Abs(_xVelocity) < 0.25f) _xVelocity = 0;
            if (Math.Abs(_yVelocity) < 0.25f) _yVelocity = 0;
        }
    }
```

The velocity is added to the XPos and YPos values and is then reduced in size based on the friction that has been applied. Once the friction level falls to a suitable low level (0.25), it is cancelled completely to prevent the object from updating with miniscule values.

Once this code has been added to the class, we then need to call it from our game. This simply requires a call to InitializeKineticDragging from the GameForm's DragBegin function and a call to ApplyKineticDragging in the DragEnd function.

To activate kinetic dragging in the **DragsAndSwipes** project, open the Menu and select the Kinetic Movement option. Once this has been selected, the three different friction level menu items become enabled. These use values of 2, 20, and 50 for low, normal, and high friction respectively. Note that because the objects are taking care of the kinetic movement on their own, we can have multiple objects moving under kinetic motion simultaneously without having to put any extra code in place. Objects can be caught while in motion, cancelling their existing momentum.

Adding Context Menus

Menus were discussed in detail back in Chapter 2, but an additional menu construct that can be useful is the ContextMenu. This provides a standard Windows Mobile user interface mechanism whereby the screen is touched and held for a second or so. After a brief pause, a series of dots will be displayed in a ring around the touch point. If the touch is maintained long enough for the full ring to be completed, a pop-up context menu appears so that a menu item can be selected that relates to the touch point as shown in Figure 6–3.

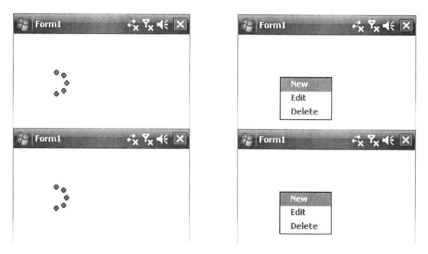

Figure 6–3. A ContextMenu in the progress of being activated (left) and opened (right)

You can use context menus in your games, though there are some things you need to be aware of. Let's look at how to set up and work with these controls.

A context menu can be added to a form by double-clicking its item in the form designer Toolbox. It will appear in the control tray below the form designer and can be selected in order to add the context menu items just as you would with a MainMenu control.

The context menu won't become active until the form's ContextMenu property is set to reference the context menu control. This allows multiple control menus to be created for the same form and then activated based on the current form scenario. The context menu can be deactivated by setting the ContextMenu property to null.

▓ **TIP** While context menus added to a form will be tolerated by smart phone platforms (resulting in a compiler warning but nothing more), actually setting the form's ContextMenu property will result in an exception on such devices. If you wish to maintain compatibility with smart phones, you should therefore set the ContextMenu property at runtime rather than at design time and only once you have determined that the device has a touch screen available.

Once a ContextMenu has been attached to the form, the user can open it using the normal press-and-hold approach described previously. The ring of dots will appear, and if the point is held for sufficient time, the context menu will appear. It will fire its PopUp event immediately upon its appearance on the screen.

▓ **TIP** If you want to allow the user to activate the ContextMenu using this standard mechanism but want to do something else instead of showing a menu, create a ContextMenu with no items within it. The PopUp event will still be triggered, but no menu will appear on the screen; the event can therefore be used to display whatever other information you wish to present in its place.

What does the presence of a ContextMenu do to the sequence of mouse events that fire when the user interacts with the form? This varies depending on how far the user gets through the context menu press-and-hold period.

When the screen is tapped briefly enough that the ring of dots has not yet begun to be displayed, the events are fired exactly as normal: MouseDown, Click, MouseUp. In this instance, the ContextMenu has no effect on the user interaction with the form. The same applies if the user maintains contact with the screen but moves the touch point (for example, to drag an object).

When the screen is pressed for long enough to initiate the ring of dots but released before the whole ring can be completed, the MouseDown, Click, and MouseUp events will again fire in their usual sequence. However, note that none of these events fire until the point where Windows Mobile cancels the ring of dots. This is unlike the normal behavior if no ContextMenu were present, in which case the MouseDown event would fire at the moment contact was made with the screen.

When the screen is pressed for long enough for the context menu to be actually displayed, the context menu's PopUp event is fired. The MouseDown, Click, and MouseUp events do not fire at all under this circumstance.

This is all great, but unfortunately, our approach to rendering games has created a couple of problems. Specifically, as we have overridden the OnPaintBackground method of the form, we end up with the imagery of both the ring of dots and the actual menu itself left behind on the screen after the menu has been used. There is nothing present to automatically tidy these up for us.

The cleanup of the menu can be implemented by calling the game engine's ForceRefresh method from the ContextMenu's PopUp event. That gets rid of the completed ring of dots and the displayed menu very easily.

But we have a bigger problem if the user initiated the ring of dots but didn't maintain contact long enough for the menu to open. In this case, as noted previously, the series of events that fires is exactly the same as it would be if the ring of dots had not been initiated. We are unable to tell that the dots were displayed and so are unable to perform the cleanup required to remove them from the screen.

Unfortunately, there is no efficient way of handling this. Instead, you will need to make sure that the game's ForceRefresh method is called in every single MouseUp event while a context menu is active within the form. This solution is fairly inefficient, but as MouseUp events fire relatively infrequently when compared to the number of Render calls that are made, it shouldn't have a noticeable effect on your game.

Context menus are a potentially useful input mechanism, but they can be unintuitive for the user (who may not even realize that they exist) and can be awkward in practice to use. In many cases, it will be preferable to combine object selection with a normal MainMenu control instead of putting context menus into your game.

If you do decide to use a context menu, it is a good idea to get it into your game as soon as you can to give yourself as much time as possible to deal with the changes in the way your form's events are fired.

Using Finger-Friendly Input

Windows Mobile devices have traditionally required a stylus for interaction via the touch screen. Recent developments in user interface design and functionality available in other competing mobile operating systems has seen a shift away from the use of styluses, towards being able to use the screen entirely with a finger instead.

A finger is unfortunately quite a lot fatter than a stylus, so the accuracy of the screen touch point suffers substantially. When large objects are being displayed with a reasonable distance between them, this isn't too much of a problem, but when objects are smaller or closer together, it can become increasingly difficult for the user to select the desired object without a stylus.

Due consideration should be given to making your game finger friendly if it is likely to be affected by this limitation. The general approach is to allow object selection by dragging over the objects, providing feedback about which is actually selected; the selection is completed when contact with the screen is released, at which point the selected object is positioned far enough from its neighbors that it can be comfortably reselected for operations such as dragging.

For example, consider a card game that displays a stack of cards face up on the screen and allows the user to drag a card into the main game area. A game that is not finger friendly would allow the user to press the stylus down to choose a card, drag the stylus to move it, and then release to drop the card in its new location.

If the cards are positioned such that they overlap and only a small section of each is visible, this interface can be very difficult to interact with when using a finger, as the user will repeatedly select the wrong card due to the inaccuracy of finger selection.

To allow the game to be finger friendly, the select-and-drag operation can be split into two parts. First, the user selects the card by making contact with the screen and moving the touch point until the appropriate card is selected. While this is taking place, the actual selected card is clearly highlighted. The user can gently slide a finger across the cards until the desired card highlights, at which point contact is released. The highlighted card moves slightly to allow easier access.

The drag operation can then be performed by dragging the selected card. As this card has distanced itself from the others, it is much easier to select for movement.

Not all games have any need to consider finger friendliness, but those that have lots of small or overlapping objects that need selection can benefit greatly from taking this into consideration.

Using Multitouch Input?

Sadly, you can't use multitouch yet.

Multitouch is an input mechanism that allows multiple points of contact with the screen to be made simultaneously. The device then tracks each of these touch points independently to allow the user to perform operations such as grabbing two edges of a photo with two fingers and moving the fingers further apart or closer together to enlarge or shrink the image.

Multitouch has not made any significant inroads into Windows Mobile (at the time of this writing, the HTC Touch HD2 is the only device released that supports it) and as such, there is not yet a mechanism for reading multitouch inputs even on those devices that are capable of such interaction.

Multitouch is much more likely to be widely used in Windows Mobile 7, so support for interacting with such devices will hopefully be added to .NET CF in the future. Until then, it is unfortunately not an option for Windows Mobile development.

Using Button and Keyboard Input

Input via buttons and keyboards can also be handled using form events. The main problem with using this input mechanism is that the available keys and buttons can vary widely from one device to another.

It is common (though not guaranteed) for devices to have a directional pad (d-pad). This consists of a four-way input button that acts in a similar way to the cursor keys on a normal keyboard. Additionally, the center of the pad can usually be pressed in to perform a selection function.

Other devices may have other hardware buttons, and smart phones in particular will have numeric keypads that allow numbers to be easily entered.

It is become more frequent to find full keyboards present on devices these days too, which allows data entry to be performed much like it would be on a PC keyboard.

A series of special buttons are almost certain to be present on all devices, offering features such as picking up and hanging up the phone, changing the volume level, and opening the Windows menu. These keys are not easily handled within an application but are better left alone anyway—the user will expect these to perform their normal functions and probably won't appreciate having them hijacked for the purposes of a game.

Let's look at the mechanisms for reading input from hardware buttons.

Button and Keyboard Events

As with the mouse events, the keyboard and button events are identical in name and function to those on the desktop version of .NET. The functions that can be used are described in the following sections.

KeyPress

The KeyPress event will be fired each time a character key or button is pressed on the device. Character keys are those that have an ASCII character representation and contain the visible symbols (numeric digits, the letters of the alphabet, and punctuation) as well as the Enter, Tab, and Backspace keys. This event will not however be triggered for the cursor keys, the Delete key, or individual shift keys (such as Ctrl or Shift).

Passed into the KeyPress event handler is a KeyPressEventArgs object that contains information about which key was pressed. The KeyChar property of this object tells you the character that was generated by the pressed key. Note that this character will the shift keys into account, so on a device with a keyboard, pressing the A key along with the Shift key will result in the capitalized A character being returned from this property.

If a key is held down, the device's key-repeat feature will activate after a short delay. As a result, KeyPress will be called repeatedly until the user releases the key. This might sound ideal for allowing the user to control a player object within a game, but in truth, it is not. The initial delay before the key repeat activates can be frustrating and makes the game control feel sluggish, and even once the repeat begins, the frequency at which the KeyPress event fires will be out of your control and will vary between devices.

An alternative mechanism for reading the keyboard that doesn't suffer from these delays is discussed in a moment.

KeyDown

The KeyDown event fires each time a key or button is pressed down on the device. The KeyDown provides a KeyEventArgs object as one of its parameters, from which information about the pressed key can be retrieved.

Unlike KeyPress, which gives access to an actual character, KeyDown allows the pressed key to be retrieved via the KeyCode property, as a value from the System.Windows.Forms.Keys enumeration. This means that a much wider range of keys can be detected (including cursor keys, the Shift and Ctrl keys, etc.) but means that the keycode is raw —pressing A along with the Shift key with this event will indicate that the A and Shift keys are pressed but won't actually translate the keypress into a capitalized character.

The Keys enumeration includes a huge range of keys that might potentially be pressed, even though some of them won't exist on any given target device. The alphabetical characters have values in the enumeration with names A through to Z. The numeric digits are represented by the names D0 to D9 (enumerations do not allow names starting with digits, so a prefix had to be applied to these items to make their names valid). The cursor keys are represented by the values named Up, Down, Left, and Right.

To determine which modifier keys were pressed, the Alt, Control, and Shift properties of the KeyEventArgs object can be interrogated.

■ **TIP** If you are unsure as to which enumeration item corresponds to a key on the keyboard, place a breakpoint into the KeyDown event, press the key in question, and see what the value of the KeyEventArgs.KeyCode property is when the breakpoint triggers.

The same key-repeat behavior that we described for the KeyPress event applies to KeyDown too. If a key is held down, multiple KeyDown events will fire.

KeyDown may sound like it is a more useful event than KeyPress in many circumstances, as it can see the noncharacter keys that KeyPress is blind to. But unfortunately, the event has a problem. On devices with actual keyboards, all of the character keys that KeyPress is able to see are returned as the Keys.ProcessKey enumeration value when KeyDown is called. Therefore, while it is able to see the noncharacter keys just fine, it cannot distinguish between the majority of other keys on the keyboard.

Used together, KeyPress and KeyDown are able to handle the whole set of possible inputs between them, but having to split keyboard processing between two different events is a nuisance.

We're nearly at the promised alternative mechanism, but let's just take a quick glance at the final keyboard event first.

KeyUp

This event is very similar in function to KeyDown, except as you can probably guess, it fires when the key is released rather than when it is pressed. If a key is held down, it will generate multiple KeyPress and KeyDown events for the duration of the keypress but will trigger only a single KeyUp when the key is finally released.

All of the features and shortcomings of KeyDown apply to KeyUp too.

Reading the Keyboard State

So the keyboard events are workable but have limitations. Each event can see only certain types of keys, and using key-repeat for player movement is not always ideal. What alternative is there?

Windows Mobile offers a very useful function called GetAsyncKeyState. This allows us to query the state of any key or button and returns a value indicating whether that key is currently pressed. It is able to see all of the keys and buttons that a device is able to support, and as we are asking it for information rather than relying on something to tell us about a keypress (as is the case with the form events), we don't need to rely on key-repeat at all.

The function is unfortunately not made available through .NET CF but can be accessed very easily using a P/Invoke call, as shown in Listing 6–16.

Listing 6–16. The Declaration of the GetAsyncKeyState Function

```
using System.Runtime.InteropServices;

[DllImport("coredll.dll")]
public static extern int GetAsyncKeyState(Keys vkey);
```

Using this function, we can now at any time ask whether a key is being pressed. We provide the identity of the key to check as a parameter to the function call (using the same Keys enumeration that we looked at for the KeyDown event), and we receive a value back that tells us whether or not the key is pressed. If the return value is 0, the key is not pressed; any nonzero value indicates that it is.

■ **TIP** To check whether the keyboard Shift, Ctrl, or Alt keys are pressed, use the Keys.ShiftKey, Keys.ControlKey, and Keys.AltKey enumeration values rather than Keys.Shift, Keys.Control, and Keys.Alt. The former values refer to specific keys on the keyboard, whereas the latter are modifier values that can be combined with other keys using a logical OR operation to represent shifted characters within a single value.

Being able to query the key state on demand means that we no longer have to keep our key processing code within the form. Using this mechanism, we can put it directly into our derived game's Update method, which is where you are most likely to also need to respond to the keypresses. This allows you to keep the reading of the buttons and reacting to the buttons all together in the same piece of code, which improves the readability and maintainability of your program.

There is one other consideration to take into account using the GetAsyncKeyState function however: if the user presses the key very quickly, such that it is pressed and released before your code has any chance to interrogate the key state, it is possible that the keypress may be entirely missed. If your game's update frequency is running at a reasonable rate, it will be unlikely for this to be a problem (it is difficult to press and release a key in under one-thirtieth of a second) but if every keypress is important (such as when the user is entering text on a keyboard), the KeyPress and KeyDown events may be a more accurate way of retrieving key press information.

To see the difference between the KeyDown and GetAsyncKeyState input mechanisms in action, run the ButtonPresses sample from the accompanying code download. The program displays a ball on the screen and lets you move it around by pressing the cursor keys (the d-pad on most devices). The menu allows you to switch between using the two different mechanisms. Object movement is performed within the form's KeyDown event when using the KeyDown input mechanism and in the CButtonPressesGame.Update function when using the GetAsyncKeyState mechanism.

The contrast should be immediately obvious, but some of the differences are more subtle. The differences between the two mechanisms are as follows:

- GetAsyncKeyState provides immediate, smooth, and rapid movement, whereas KeyDown has a sluggish feel and jerky movement.

- GetAsyncKeyState has a consistent movement speed, as we are moving the object exactly once per update. Because our updates occur at a fixed interval, the object moves at the same speed on all devices and under all circumstances. KeyDown moves at a speed dictated by the key-repeat rate and is inconsistent across devices.

- GetAsyncKeyState allows for diagonal movement, because it is able to determine that multiple directions are pressed simultaneously. KeyDown does not support this; it only reports on the key that was most recently pressed.

Input from the SIP

How does the SIP interact with everything we have discussed in this section?

When the user enters characters into the Keyboard or Letter Recognizer panels, the KeyPress, KeyDown and KeyUp events will all fire as normal for each entered character. The Transcriber panel works a little differently, as it allows a series of characters to be entered at once. None of the events fire while text is being entered, but once Windows Mobile decides that the text entry is finished and sends it to the application, a KeyPress event will be triggered for each entered character but not any KeyDown or KeyUp events. In general, this shouldn't be a problem, because we already know to use KeyPress events for character keys, and these are what will be entered into the Transcriber panel, but you should be aware of this caveat.

The GetAsyncKeyState mechanism however is generally not compatible with the SIP. The SIP sends its keypresses so quickly that GetAsyncKeyState has no opportunity to detect them. You will need to rely on the event mechanism in order to process input from the SIP.

Choosing the Keyboard Input Method

The following guidelines should help you to choose which of the input mechanisms is better for your game:

- If you need continuous and immediate smooth control over a game, use GetAsyncKeyState. This will give you a high degree of responsiveness and will a consistent speed across all devices.

    An example of a game type that would use this mechanism is controlling a spaceship in a shooting game.

- If you need finer control over movement and smooth object motion is less important, or if you need to be able to read from the SIP, use the key events. These will move less smoothly but will make it easier to make small and precise movements.

  An example of a game type that would use this mechanism is a Tetris game where the player needs to be able to move a shape exactly one position at a time; the repeat delay is a benefit here rather than a drawback. With `GetAsyncKeyState`, it would be easy to move the shape further than you expected.

Reading From an Accelerometer

Accelerometers are becoming more commonplace in devices these days, which is a good thing as they are very useful—not least of which for gaming.

An *accelerometer* is a device contained within a phone that can report the device's current orientation or position. In other words, it can tell if the device is laying flat on a desk, being held upright or rotated onto its side, or is in any other position in between.

This information presents all sorts of opportunities for games. If we can tell the angle of the device, we can use this as a control mechanism. Instead of touching the screen or pressing a button to move objects on the screen, the player can simply tilt the device in whatever direction is needed to affect the gameplay.

Sadly, there is no standard mechanism within Windows Mobile for reading an accelerometer. Some device vendors (such as Samsung) provide public information as to how the accelerometer in their devices can be read, whereas others (such as HTC) provide nothing at all, requiring clever hackers to reverse engineer the device to see how to retrieve its data.

Fortunately, one such clever developer on the Internet by the name of Scott Seligman (www.scottandmichelle.net) managed to reverse engineer the HTC accelerometer. This was then later wrapped up into a .NET CF managed wrapper by Koushik Dutta (www.koushikdutta.com), providing a single programming library that allows both the HTC and Samsung accelerometers to be accessed without the code needing to know which type of device it is running on.

Koushik later released this library as the Windows Mobile Unified Sensor API. It actually includes code for working with some other sensors too (such as light and proximity sensors), but the accelerometer is the one that is useful for game development. The Sensor API code can be downloaded from the CodePlex site: at sensorapi.codeplex.com.

Let's see how we can use this in a game. Note that the sample project won't work on the emulator as no accelerometer simulation is available, you'll need to try this on a real supported device.

Initializing the Accelerometer

The accelerometer is accessed using an interface within a class library called `Sensors`. The interface's name is `IGSensor` (short for Interface for the Gravity Sensor). This interface is implemented by different classes within `Sensors` depending on the brand of device, which means that from within our game, we don't need to worry about how the sensor actually works behind the scenes; we can just access its properties through the interface.

As there are multiple possible classes that may be used to implement the interface (one for each different device vendor), we don't create the object instance directly. Instead, we call the `static` `Sensors.GSensorFactory.CreateGSensor` function, and it will determine the type of object to be created. If no supported accelerometer is found, it instead returns `null` to indicate this.

Creating the object is therefore simply achieved using the code in Listing 6–17.

Listing 6–17. Initializing the _gSensor Object to Read Data from the Accelerometer

```
// A variable to hold our accelerometer sensor object
private Sensors.IGSensor _gSensor;

/// <summary>
/// Class constructor
/// </summary>
public CAccelerometerGame(Form gameForm)
    : base(gameForm)
{
    // Create the GSensor object that will be used by this class
    _gSensor = Sensors.GSensorFactory.CreateGSensor();
}
```

We first declare a class level variable _gSensor in which our sensor instance will be stored. We then create this using the `CreateGSensor` function in the class constructor. When the `CAccelerometerGame` class is instantiated, the accelerometer sensor class will be immediately ready to use.

Reading Data from the Accelerometer

Whenever we want to find the orientation of the device, we call the `IGSensor.GetGVector` function. This returns a GVector object containing a reading of the acceleration of the device relative to freefall. What exactly does that mean?

First, let's look at the vector itself. It contains three properties that can be used to interrogate the device orientation: X, Y, and Z. Each of these is a double value that represents the movement of the device in the real world in the appropriate axis. If the device is lying flat and face up on a table, the values returned for the vector will be approximately as follows:

```
X = 0, Y = 0, Z = -9.8
```

The value 9.8 appears because this is the acceleration provided by the force of gravity on Earth (gravity accelerates objects at 9.8 meters per second, per second). If you were running this on another planet, the value would be different (though you'll probably have to take my word for that unless you have friends at NASA).

The value here is actually –9.8, implying a negative movement of 9.8 along the z axis (the z axis corresponds to up and down, negative values being in the upward direction). But the device isn't moving upward, so why do we get this reading?

The answer is back in the description "relative to freefall." If the device were in freefall, then the z value would be 0. When it is stationary, we get a negative value, as this is the difference in acceleration between a stationary object and a falling object.

This z value is very useful as it means we always get a movement reading relative to the force of gravity, even when the device is not in motion. By working out which of the x, y, and z axes the reading applies to, we can therefore work out which way up the device is.

As you've seen, with the device face up, we get a negative reading on the z axis. With the device upright, the accelerometer returns a value of 9.8 on the y axis (and upright but upside down, it returns the opposite value, –9.8). Turn the device on its side and you'll get a value of –9.8 or 9.8 on the x axis, depending on which way the device has rotated. All orientations between these extremes return values spread across the three axes.

As our screen is only two-dimensional, we can for the most part ignore the value on the z axis. We can instead read out the x and y values and apply these as acceleration to objects in the game. When the device is flat on the desk, x and y are 0, so our objects don't move at all. Tip the device up and the x and y values change based on the tilt angle, providing acceleration for our objects—the steeper the tilt, the faster the acceleration.

To simplify the values returned by the accelerometer, we can *normalize* the vector. Normalizing reduces its length so that it is always 1, instead of the 9.8 we are currently seeing. After normalization, the values on each axis will range from –1 to 1. We can then simply multiply the axis values by a speed factor in order to make the game objects move faster or slower.

The Accelerometer project in the accompanying downloads includes all of the code required to move a ball around on the screen under control of the accelerometer. It also displays the normalized vector values on the screen, so you can easily see the data coming back from the accelerometer as you change the orientation of your device.

The project contains a single game object, CObjBall. There's nothing new in here; we've looked at all the techniques the ball uses in earlier projects. The ball offers XVelocity and YVelocity properties, and in its Update method, it adds these to the ball position, bouncing if the edges of the form are hit. The velocities are gradually reduced during each update to simulate friction on the object.

The code that interacts with the accelerometer is in the CAccelerometerGame.Update function; see Listing 6–18. This reads the GSensor vector, normalizes it, and adds its X and Y values to the velocity of the ball. It scales up these values (by a factor of three in this case) to make the ball move faster. Increasing or decreasing this value will make the ball movement more or less sensitive.

Listing 6–18. Using the _gSensor Object to Read Data from the Accelerometer

```
/// <summary>
/// Update the game
/// </summary>
public override void Update()
{
    // Get the base class to perform its work
    base.Update();

    // Retrieve the GSensor vector
    Sensors.GVector gVector = _gSensor.GetGVector();
    // Normalize the vector so that it has a length of 1
    gVector = gVector.Normalize();

    // Display the vector on the game form
    ((GameForm)GameForm).lblAccelerometerVector.Text = gVector.ToString();

    // Add the x and y values to the ball's velocity
    ((CObjBall)GameObjects[0]).XVelocity += (float)gVector.X * 3;
    ((CObjBall)GameObjects[0]).YVelocity += (float)gVector.Y * 3;
}
```

> ▧ **NOTE** In HTC devices, the accelerometer dislikes being read too frequently. Anything more than about one-twenty-fifth of a second causes it to stop updating, returning old values back each time it is queried. Because our game engine typically runs faster than this, a change has been made to the `Sensors.HTCGSensor.GetGVector` function in the accompanying code to ensure that the accelometer is not read more frequently than this rate. If calls are made too quickly, a cached value will be returned. Using a cached value doesn't have any noticeable effect on our game but ensures that the returned values do not freeze up. This code is not present in the official download of the code from the CodePlex web site, so be aware of this if you use the source code from there.

You now have all the code that is required to simulate a ball rolling around a virtual desktop. If you have a supported device, try running the project and see how the ball reacts to the device being tilted. Observe the way the ball moves faster when the devices is tilted at a steeper angle.

Detecting the Presence of a Supported Accelerometer

If a game is to rely on an accelerometer, checking that one is actually present is important. There is nothing more frustrating than seeing a game running but being unable to interact with it and not understanding why. We'll add a new item to our capabilities check (as discussed back in Chapter 4) to allow us to check for an accelerometer that we are able to work with.

First of all, we'll add a new item to the `CGameEngineBase.Capabilities` enumeration as shown in Listing 6–19.

Listing 6–19. The New Accelerometer Item Within the Capabilities Enumeration

```
/// <summary>
/// Capabilities flags for the CheckCapabilities and ReportMissingCapabilities functions
/// </summary>
[Flags()]
public enum Capabilities
{
    [...]
    Accelerometer = 1024
}
```

Now, we need to update the `CGameEngineBase.CheckCapabilities` function to look for the presence of an accelerometer. However, this presents a small problem. In order for us to determine whether an accelerometer is available, we need to use `Sensors.dll` to check for us. But if we add a reference to `Sensors.dll` then this will become a required dependency of the game engine. All of the games that we create that have no interest in the accelerometer at all will still need to have the DLL available just to compile. This would be a nuisance.

Instead of interacting with `Sensors.dll` like this, we will instead use *reflection* to access the DLL. This allows us to call into its functions without having to add a reference at all. The steps required follow:

- Load the Sensors assembly from the `Sensors.dll` file.

- Locate the `GSensorFactory` class within the Sensors assembly.

- Locate the CreateGSensor method within the GSensorFactory class.

- Call the CreateGSensor method and see whether it returns an object or null.

All of this is wrapped in an exception handler so that, if any problems occur, we can throw a further exception explaining that there is a problem with Sensors.dll. We throw an exception rather than just returning false, as this problem is an indication that the application is misconfigured (for example, if Sensors.dll cannot be found, there is an installation problem). Throwing an exception makes problems much easier to identify if something goes wrong.

CreateGSensor returns a GSensor object if a supported accelerometer was found, or null if not. We can, therefore, simply check the return value from this function and see whether it is null. This tells us all we need to know for the capabilities check. This is all wrapped up inside the CheckCapabilities_CheckForAccelerometer function, as shown in Listing 6–20.

Listing 6–20. Checking for an Accelerometer Without Adding a Reference to Sensors.dll

```
/// <summary>
/// Detect whether a supported accelerometer is available in this device
/// </summary>
/// <returns>Returns true if a supported accelerometer is found, false if not.</returns>
/// <remarks>This function uses reflection to check the accelerometer so that no
/// reference to Sensors.dll needs to be added to the Game Engine. This saves
/// us from having to distribute Sensors.dll with projects that don't use it.</remarks>
private bool CheckCapabilities_CheckForAccelerometer()
{
    Assembly sensorAsm;
    Type sensorType;
    MethodInfo sensorMethod;
    object accelSensor;

    try
    {
        // Attempt to load the Sensors dll
        sensorAsm = Assembly.LoadFrom("Sensors.dll");

        // Find the GSensorFactory type
        sensorType = sensorAsm.GetType("Sensors.GSensorFactory");
        // If the type was not found, throw an exception.
        // This will be picked up by our catch block and reported back to the user.
        if (sensorType == null) throw new Exception();

        // Find the CreateGSensor method within the Sensors.GSensorFactory object
        sensorMethod = sensorType.GetMethod("CreateGSensor");

        // Invoke the method so that it attempts to create out sensor object.
        // If no supported accelerometer is available, this will return null,
        // otherwise we will receive a sensor object.
        accelSensor = sensorMethod.Invoke(null, null);

        // Did we get an object?
        if (accelSensor == null)
        {
            // No, so no supported accelerometer is available
            return false;
```

155

```
            }

            // A supported accelerometer is available
            return true;

        }
        catch
        {
            // The Sensors.dll failed to load or did not contain the expected
            // classes/methods. Throw an exception as we have an application
            // configuration problem rather than just a missing capability.
            throw new Exception("Unable to load Sensors.dll, which is required by
                this application. Please ensure the application is installed correctly.");
        }
    }
```

The CheckCapabilities function is modified to use this new code if the Accelerometer flag is specified. If the flag is not specified (and therefore the accelerometer is not a required capability), then the function is not called at all, so the absence of Sensors.dll doesn't cause any problems.

The final change in this area is to the ReportMissingCapabilities function, which has another check added to report back about a missing accelerometer capability if it is detected.

Supporting Devices With No Accelerometer

Requiring the presence of an accelerometer obviously limits your target audience. Users will not only need to have an accelerometer available, but it must also be one recognized by the Sensors library.

For all those users who do not have the required hardware, it is worth considering an alternative control mechanism. For example, the d-pad could be used to simulate tilting of a device, as could the touch screen (allowing touches further from the center of the device to equate to tilting the device to steeper angles). This allows your game to be enjoyed by everyone instead of just those with devices that happen to support this feature.

Considering Input Design

There are lots of things to take into account when planning how the user will control and interact with your game. Are there certain control mechanisms that are essential, or can alternatives be provided? How do we deal with devices that don't have input mechanisms that we might want to use, such as touch screens, hardware buttons, or accelerometers?

Planning your game control options so that you are as accommodating of different types of device as possible will allow your game to work on a wide range of devices and increase the size of your audience. We will consider a specific example of how alternative input mechanisms can be implemented when we look at a sample game in Chapter 8.

CHAPTER 7

■ ■ ■

Sounding Out with Game Audio

Our worlds have been very quiet so far; apart from the occasional sound of the screen being tapped, everything has moved in complete silence. That's no way for a game to be, so in this chapter, we'll make some noise by adding sound effects and music to our games.

Understanding Sound File Types

Just as there are lots of different graphics image formats, there are also lots of different audio and music formats that we could use within our games. Here is a brief description of the formats that you may wish to use:

- *WAV* files are one of the oldest sound formats used by Microsoft. They usually store sound in an uncompressed format, making them easy to read and write but resulting in large file sizes.

  On desktop PCs, WAV files have largely been replaced by formats offering higher levels of compression such as MP3, but on Windows Mobile, they are still worthy of consideration, as older devices have no built-in support for MP3 decoding.

- *MP3* files have taken over the world during the last decade and must surely form one of the most widely known file formats in existence. Sound files encoded using MP3 are compressed using a *lossy* compression algorithm. This means that there is some degradation of the audio when it is played back (just as there a loss of image quality with JPG images), but in most cases, the quality loss is virtually or completely unnoticeable.

  MP3 can compress audio data to different degrees, and the higher the compression the greater the quality loss on playback. The compression level is set when the MP3 is created by specifying a *bit rate*, which controls how many kilobits of data may be used to store each second of compressed audio. Compressing files at a bit rate of 128 kilobits per second will typically reduce CD quality audio to about 9 percent of its original file size—a massive saving.

- *OGG* (Ogg Vorbis) files are similar to MP3 files in that they are compressed using a lossy algorithm to obtain similarly high levels of compression. The big difference between OGG and MP3 files is that the Ogg Vorbis algorithm is open source and completely free of licensing and patent restrictions, whereas the MP3 standard is closed source and covered by software patents.

  While not nearly as popular as MP3, Ogg Vorbis files are being used in a growing number of high profile PC games.

- Tracker files (most commonly in *MOD, XM, IT* and *S3M* files) use a very different way of storing music. Instead of a single stream of audio (as is used by the other formats we have discussed here), tracker files store multiple individual sound samples, which are then used like instruments within a musical score. These samples might include a single keypress on a piano, a variety of individual drum sounds, and a violin sound. With this library of instruments, a sequence of different sounds and pitches can be constructed to form a piece of music. The file size stays small, as just the individual instruments are stored rather than the sound of the complete music.

  These used to be a very common method for storing music for computer games, but as computer hard drive capacities and network bandwidth have increased, MP3 files have become more common and tracker files have begun to disappear. For Windows Mobile, where file size is more of an issue, tracker files can be a useful format, though a third-party library (such as BASS, described later in this chapter) is required to play them. Lots of tracker files can be found at www.modarchive.org, but don't forget to contact each song's author to check for permission prior to using any of the files in your games.

- *MID* (MIDI) files are similar in some ways to tracker files in that they don't store a single audio stream, but instead a sequence of notes that are then interpreted by the device when playing the file. However unlike tracker files, the instrument samples are not contained within the file; you're relying instead on the device to have its own library of standard instruments to use for playback.

  MIDI files were popular on mobile devices for a brief period when they were used for ringtones, but MP3s have become the common way of storing ringtones now, so support for MIDI files is not considered as important as it used to be. Different devices have different degrees of support for MIDI files, and so while they are a good way of storing music in a small file, they may not deliver a high-quality music experience on all devices.

Exploring the Available Sound APIs

The good news is that we have a number of different APIs that we can use to get sound playing within our devices. The bad news is that all of them have a drawback of some kind. The built-in API that has the best support across devices can only play WAV sounds. The API that has the best of set features is a third-party product that needs to be purchased if you plan to sell your game (though it is free for freeware products). Exactly which API is appropriate for your game will depend on your needs and how you plan to sell or distribute your game.

Before we go into detail, let's take a quick look at the available APIs and see the advantages and disadvantages of each.

PlaySound: The PlaySound function is accessed using P/Invoke, as no direct access to it is provided by the .NET Compact Framework. It is nevertheless easy to use, able to play files from on disk or from memory, and supported across all devices back to Windows Mobile 2003 SE. The significant disadvantages to this function are that it supports only WAV files and is capable of playing only a single sound at a time. If a second sound is started while an existing sound is still playing, the first sound will be stopped.

System.Media.SoundPlayer: Introduced with .NET CF 3.5 was a new class in the System.Media namespace called SoundPlayer. This provides proper managed access to playing sounds and additionally allows multiple sound files to be played at the same time. This class sadly still only supports WAV files, so there is no MP3 playback to be found here despite its recent addition to the .NET Framework. The lack of support in .NET 2.0 means that it is not available in Visual Studio 2005.

AygShell sound functions: With the release of Windows Mobile 6.0, some additional sound functions were added to aygshell.dll, one of the Windows Mobile system DLLs. These functions finally add support for playing back MP3 and MIDI files in addition to WAV files. There are drawbacks however. With support only for Windows Mobile 6, a large slice of your potential audience is excluded if you rely on these functions. Additionally, the functions are only able to play sounds loaded from separate files within the device (it cannot read from embedded resources), and it cannot play more than one sound at a time.

BASS.dll: We don't have to stick just with the functions provided by Microsoft, however. A powerful third-party cross-platform audio library called BASS has a version for Windows CE, and along with a .NET wrapper DLL it works very nicely. It supports a wide range of audio files including MP3, WAV, OGG, and the tracker formats, works on all versions of Windows Mobile, and can load both from external files and embedded resources. This is also the only API that allows control over the volume level of each played sound. The only disadvantage is that if you plan to sell your game, you need to purchase a license in order to use both BASS and its .NET wrapper DLL. The shareware license is however fairly inexpensive and covers you for an unlimited number of products. If you plan to give your game away for free, BASS and the .NET wrapper can both be used free of charge. We'll look at licensing in more detail when we cover how to use this DLL shortly.

Now that we're looked at each of the APIs that are available to use, Table 7–1 summarize everything so that we can easily compare the features of each.

Table 7–1. Feature Comparison of Each of the Sound APIs

Feature	PlaySound	SoundPlayer	AygShell	BASS
Supported file formats	WAV	WAV	WAV, MP3, and MID	WAV, MP3, OGG, and trackers
Windows Mobile versions	Windows Mobile 2003 SE and above	Windows Mobile 2003 SE and above	Windows Mobile 6.0 and above	Windows Mobile 2003 SE and above
.NET/Visual Studio versions	.NET 2.0/VS2005 or later	.NET 3.5/Visual Studio 2008	.NET 2.0/Visual Studio 2005 or later	.NET 2.0/Visual Studio 2005 or later
Multiple simultaneous sound playback	No	Yes	No	Yes
Supported data sources	Files or memory	Files or memory	Files	Files or memory
Volume control	No	No	No	Yes
License required	No	No	No	Yes (except for free games and applications)

Using the Sound APIs

Having briefly looked at each API, let's now examine them in more detail and see how to use them in our code.

PlaySound

The PlaySound function must be used via P/Invoke, so we must first declare the function that we want to use. The same function can be used for playing sounds from in memory (e.g., embedded resources) and from files on disk, but we provide a byte array for the former and a filename string for the latter. The functions are made available with the statements shown in Listing 7–1.

Listing 7–1. P/Invoke Statements Required for Using the PlaySound Function

```
/// <summary>
/// The PlaySound function declaration for embedded resources
/// </summary>
[DllImport("coredll.dll")]
static extern bool PlaySound(byte[] data, IntPtr hMod, SoundFlags sf);
```

```
/// <summary>
/// The PlaySound function declaration for files
/// </summary>
[DllImport("coredll.dll")]
static extern bool PlaySound(string pszSound, IntPtr hMod, SoundFlags sf);
```

As you can see, the PlaySound function requires three parameter values. The first will be either the byte array or filename of the sound to play. The second is a handle for a module containing a resource to be played—we won't be using this (even when playing embedded resources), and so we'll always pass IntPtr.Zero for this parameter. Finally, we have a series of flags that can be passed to tell the function how to operate. These are defined in an enumeration named SoundFlags, which follows in Listing 7–2.

Listing 7–2. The Flags That May Be Passed to PlaySound

```
/// <summary>
/// Flags used by PlaySound
/// </summary>
[Flags]
public enum SoundFlags
{
    SND_SYNC = 0x0000,            // play synchronously (default)
    SND_ASYNC = 0x0001,          // play asynchronously
    SND_NODEFAULT = 0x0002,      // silence (!default) if sound not found
    SND_MEMORY = 0x0004,         // pszSound points to a memory file
    SND_LOOP = 0x0008,           // loop the sound until next sndPlaySound
    SND_NOSTOP = 0x0010,         // don't stop any currently playing sound
    SND_NOWAIT = 0x00002000,     // don't wait if the driver is busy
    SND_ALIAS = 0x00010000,      // name is a registry alias
    SND_ALIAS_ID = 0x00110000,   // alias is a predefined ID
    SND_FILENAME = 0x00020000,   // name is file name
    SND_RESOURCE = 0x00040004    // name is resource name or atom
}
```

We won't use many of these flags, but the useful ones follow:

- SND_SYNC tells PlaySound to play synchronously. The function will not return until the entire sound has been played.

- SND_ASYNC tells PlaySound to play asynchronously. The function will return immediately, leaving the sound playing in the background.

- SND_MEMORY indicates that we are providing a pointer to a block of memory that contains the sound to play.

- SND_FILENAME indicates that we are providing the name of a file that contains the sound to play.

These flags look useful but are sadly unlikely to actually be practical to use:

- SND_LOOP tells PlaySound to loop the sound continuously (or until the next sound is played). This could potentially be used for background music, but because of the large size of WAV files and the inability to play another sound without terminating the music, it is unlikely to be of value.

161

- SND_NOSTOP sounds promising, as it implies that any sound that is already playing should be left active when the new sound starts. What it really means, however, is that any existing sound takes priority over the new sound, so the new sound doesn't play at all.

To play a sound from a file, we simply call PlaySound and pass the path and filename. The function in Listing 7–3 accepts a filename and a flag to indicate whether the sound should be played asynchronously.

Listing 7–3. Using PlaySound to Play a Sound From a File

```
/// <summary>
/// Play a sound contained within an external file
/// </summary>
/// <param name="Filename">The filename of the file to play</param>
/// <param name="ASync">A flag indicating whether to play asynchronously</param>
private void PlaySoundFile(string Filename, bool ASync)
{
    // Playing asynchronously?
    if (ASync)
    {
        // Play the sound asynchronously
        PlaySound(Filename, IntPtr.Zero,
                                SoundFlags.SND_FILENAME | SoundFlags.SND_ASYNC);
    }
    else
    {
        // Play the sound synchronously
        PlaySound(Filename, IntPtr.Zero, SoundFlags.SND_FILENAME | SoundFlags.SND_SYNC);
    }
}
```

Playing a sound from an embedded resource is a little more work, as we need to extract the resource data and store it in a byte array. The function in Listing 7–4 calls PlaySound with the data from an embedded resource.

Listing 7–4. Using PlaySound to Play a sound from an Embedded Resource

```
/// <summary>
/// Play a sound contained within an embedded resource
/// </summary>
/// <param name="Filename">The filename of the resource to play</param>
/// <param name="ASync">A flag indicating whether to play asynchronously</param>
private void PlaySoundEmbedded(string ResourceFilename, bool ASync)
{
    byte[] soundData;

    // Retrieve a stream from our embedded sound resource.
    // The Assembly name is PlaySound, the folder name is Sounds,
    // and the resource filename has been provided as a parameter.
    using (Stream sound =
            Assembly.GetExecutingAssembly().GetManifestResourceStream(ResourceFilename))
    {
        // Make sure we found the resource
```

```
    if (sound != null)
    {
        // Read the resource into a byte array, as this is what we need to pass
        // to the PlaySound function
        soundData = new byte[(int)(sound.Length)];
        sound.Read(soundData, 0, (int)(sound.Length));

        // Playing asynchronously?
        if (ASync)
        {
            // Play the sound asynchronously
            PlaySound(soundData, IntPtr.Zero,
                        SoundFlags.SND_MEMORY | SoundFlags.SND_ASYNC);
        }
        else
        {
            // Play the sound synchronously
            PlaySound(soundData, IntPtr.Zero,
                        SoundFlags.SND_MEMORY | SoundFlags.SND_SYNC);
        }
    }
  }
}
```

The PlaySound project in the accompanying download includes all of the code required to use PlaySound; see Figure 7–1. It contains three embedded WAV files, named EnergySound.wav, MagicSpell.wav, and Motorbike.wav. The Play item in the menu can be used to play the selected item. Additionally, the menu can be used to switch between synchronous and asynchronous playback and to open WAV files from on disk so that they can be played too.

■ **NOTE** The Open File menu item uses an OpenFileDialog to allow a file to be selected. As we discussed back in Chapter 2, this is not available on smart phone devices and will instead display an error. Therefore, this menu item cannot be used in this demonstration on smart phones.

Observe that the project is only able to play one sound at a time. Attempting to start a second sound terminates any sound that is already playing. When the sound is played synchronously, the whole application freezes until playback is finished.

Figure 7–1 *The PlaySound example project*

System.Media.SoundPlayer

As mentioned earlier, the System.Media.SoundPlayer class was added as part of .NET CF 3.5 and is not available in Visual Studio 2005. If you are using Visual Studio 2008 and targeting .NET CF 3.5, this class is superior in every way to the PlaySound function and is well worth using instead.

The SoundPlayer accepts either a Stream (containing the contents of a WAV file, exactly like we retrieve from the GetManifestResourceStream function) or a string (containing the filename of a WAV file) when it is instantiated. With the object created we can then simply call the Play or PlaySync methods to begin playback of the sound. Could it be easier?

Well, as always, there are some minor complexities. Table 7–1 shows that SoundPlayer supports multiple sounds at once, but when we get into the details, we find that each instance actually only supports a single sound. To play multiple sounds together, we must create multiple SoundPlayer instances and play one sound in each.

That, in itself, is not too bad, but then we come to the issue of cleaning up resources when we have finished with them. It's really useful to be able to create as many SoundPlayer objects as we like rather than having to keep a pool of objects, so we need to know when the sound has finished so that we can dispose of it. Without this, we will end up with lots of SoundPlayer objects (and data Streams too if we are using embedded resources) left in memory from all the sounds that have been played.

The SoundPlayer doesn't give us any way to tell when it has finished playing an asynchronous sound. No event is fired, and no property can be interrogated. Using the fire-and-forget approach, we cannot, therefore, clean up SoundPlayer objects that have been used to play asynchronous sounds.

But fear not; there is a workaround. Instead of playing sound asynchronously, we can play it synchronously but launch it in a new thread. This gives exactly the same behavior as asynchronous playback but allows us to tell when the sound has finished (as the play function will return back to the calling code). When the synchronous playback completes we can dispose of the SoundPlayer and the Stream if one is present.

All of this can be wrapped up into a simple class, called SoundPlayerWrapper. The class first declares a private variable _soundPlayer, which is our SoundPlayer instance; see Listing 7–5.

Listing 7–5. The SoundPlayerWrapper's Internal SoundPlayer Instance

```
class SoundPlayerWrapper
{
    // Our local SoundPlayer instance
    private System.Media.SoundPlayer _soundPlayer;

    // [...the rest of the class follows here...]
}
```

Added to this are two functions to allow playback of sounds. The first is for playback from embedded resources and is shown in Listing 7–6.

Listing 7–6. Playing a Sound from an Embedded Resource Using SoundPlayer

```
/// <summary>
/// Play a sound contained within an embedded resource
/// </summary>
/// <param name="ResourceAsm">The assembly containing the resource to play</param>
/// <param name="ResourceName">The name of the resource to play</param>
/// <param name="ASync">A flag indicating whether to play asynchronously</param>
public void PlaySoundEmbedded(Assembly ResourceAsm, string ResourceName, bool ASync)
{
    // Clear up any existing sound that may be playing
    DisposeSoundPlayer();

    // Create and verify the sound stream
    Stream soundStream = ResourceAsm.GetManifestResourceStream(ResourceName);
    if (soundStream != null)
    {
        // Create the SoundPlayer passing the stream to its constructor
        _soundPlayer = new System.Media.SoundPlayer(soundStream);

        // Play the sound
        if (ASync)
        {
            // Play asynchronously by using a separate thread
            Thread playThread = new Thread(PlaySoundAndDispose);
            playThread.Start();
        }
        else
        {
            // Play synchronously
            PlaySoundAndDispose();
        }
    }
}
```

Our parameters include the Assembly inside which the resource is embedded. In our example, this is the same assembly as the wrapper class itself, but it will be useful to be able to place the wrapper into a separate assembly (the game engine, for example) and be able to access resources outside of its containing assembly.

The first thing the code does is release any existing resources that the wrapper class is using. Releasing these resources ensures that if the same instance of the class is used multiple times, the resources allocated earlier on are terminated and released before we continue to avoid them being overwritten.

Next, the resource is retrieved from the provided Assembly and used to instantiate the SoundPlayer object.

The code then checks to see if the sound is to play asynchronously or not. If so, the code creates and starts a new Thread to execute the PlaySoundAndDispose function. Otherwise, it directly calls PlaySoundAndDispose.

The code within the PlaySoundAndDispose function is shown in Listing 7–7.

Listing 7–7. The PlaySoundAndDispose Function

```
/// <summary>
/// Play the loaded sound synchronously and then dispose of the player and release its
/// resources
/// </summary>
private void PlaySoundAndDispose()
{
    _soundPlayer.PlaySync();
    DisposeSoundPlayer();
}
```

The function simply plays the sound synchronously and then calls DisposeSoundPlayer to release all of its resources. The sound is always played synchronously: if the calling code requests asynchronous playback, the Thread will be used to implement this as described previously in this section.

The final function in this chain is DisposeSoundPlayer; see Listing 7–8.

Listing 7–8. Releasing the Resources Used by the SoundPlayer

```
/// <summary>
/// Dispose of the sound player and release its resources
/// </summary>
private void DisposeSoundPlayer()
{
    // Make sure we have a player to dispose
    if (_soundPlayer != null)
    {
        // Stop any current playback
        _soundPlayer.Stop();
        // If we have a stream, dispose of it too
        if (_soundPlayer.Stream != null) _soundPlayer.Stream.Dispose();
        // Dispose of the player
        _soundPlayer.Dispose();
        // Remove the object reference so that we cannot re-use it
        _soundPlayer = null;
    }
}
```

The code first stops any existing sound playback. This prevents problems interrupting playback if a SoundPlayerWrapper instance is re-used. It then calls the Dispose method on the Stream if one is present, and on the SoundPlayer itself. Everything is then ready for the object to be reused.

Just as in the PlaySound example, we also provide a function for playing an external WAV file. The code for this, shown in Listing 7–9, is very similar to that required for playing embedded resources.

Listing 7–9. Wrapping SoundPlayer for Playback of External WAV Files

```
/// <summary>
/// Play a sound contained within an external file
/// </summary>
/// <param name="Filename">The filename of the file to play</param>
/// <param name="ASync">A flag indicating whether to play asynchronously</param>
public void PlaySoundFile(string Filename, bool ASync)
{
    // Clear up any existing sound that may be playing
    DisposeSoundPlayer();

    // Create the SoundPlayer passing the filename to its constructor
    _soundPlayer = new System.Media.SoundPlayer(Filename);

    // Play the sound
    if (ASync)
    {
        // Play asynchronously by using a separate thread
        Thread playThread = new Thread(PlaySoundAndDispose);
        playThread.Start();
    }
    else
    {
        // Play synchronously
        PlaySoundAndDispose();
    }
}
```

The PlaySoundFile code is pretty much identical to that of PlaySoundEmbedded, except that the filename is passed to the SoundPlayer instead of the resource Stream.

All of the preceding code can be found in the SoundPlayer example project in this book's accompanying code download. Note that now it is possible to play as many sound files at the same time as you like, including multiple instances of the same sound. This is much more useful than the PlaySound example you saw before, but you must have Visual Studio 2008 in order to use it.

AygShell Sound Functions

The AygShell sound functions, present in Windows Mobile 6.0 onwards, are accessed using a series of P/Invoke functions, because they are not directly accessible from within the .NET CF. The two main functions that are able to play sounds are SndPlayAsync for asynchronous playback and SndPlaySync for synchronous playbacks.

If we want to play a sound using SndPlayAsync, the sound must first be opened by calling the SndOpen function. This returns a handle for the sound, which can then be passed to SndPlayAsync to begin playback. Once playback completes, the handle is passed into the SndClose function, which releases all of the resources that were used by the sound.

Unfortunately, we run into the same problem we had with the SoundPlayer class: we are unable to tell when the sound has finished playing. There is no event that we can hook into, nor any property or function that will tell us. As a result, the asynchronous playback is impractical for us to use.

We can adopt the same solution we used with SoundPlayer: for asynchronous playback, we launch a new thread and play the sound back synchronously.

The SndPlaySync function is actually simpler to use than SndPlayAsync, simply requiring a filename to be passed with no need to use SndOpen or SndClose. Resources are automatically released once playback has completed.

To simplify using the functions, we can once again wrap them inside a class, AygShellSoundPlayer. Following on from the P/Invoke declarations, we provide a function called PlaySoundFile (see Listing 7–10). This accepts the sound filename and an asynchronous flag as parameters. Just as with the SoundPlayer code, we always play synchronously but launch a separate thread if asynchronous playback was requested.

Listing 7–10. Wrapping the AygShell Sound Functions for Playback of External Sound Files

```
// Declare the P/Invoke functions within AygShell that we use use for playing sounds
[DllImport("aygshell.dll")]
static extern int SndOpen(string pszSoundFile, ref IntPtr phSound);

[DllImport("aygshell.dll")]
static extern int SndPlayAsync(IntPtr hSound, int dwFlags);

[DllImport("aygshell.dll")]
static extern int SndClose(IntPtr hSound);

[DllImport("aygshell.dll")]
static extern int SndStop(int SoundScope, IntPtr hSound);

[DllImport("aygshell.dll")]
static extern int SndPlaySync(string pszSoundFile, int dwFlags);

// The SoundScope value to pass to SndStop
const int SND_SCOPE_PROCESS = 0x1;

// The filename of the sound to play
private string _soundFile;

/// <summary>
/// Play a sound contained within an external file
/// </summary>
/// <param name="Filename">The filename of the file to play</param>
/// <param name="ASync">A flag indicating whether to play asynchronously</param>
public void PlaySoundFile(string Filename, bool ASync)
{
    // Store the sound filename
    _soundFile = Filename;

    // Play the sound
    if (ASync)
    {
        // Play asynchronously by using a separate thread
        Thread playThread = new Thread(PlaySound);
        playThread.Start();
    }
    else
    {
        // Play synchronously
```

```
        PlaySound();
    }
}

/// <summary>
/// Play the specified sound synchronously
/// </summary>
private void PlaySound()
{
    SndPlaySync(_soundFile, 0);
}
```

As was noted previously, the code in Listing 7–10 is capable of playing MP3 and MIDI files in addition to WAV files. The quality of playback of MIDI files will very from one device to another depending on how good the device's built-in MIDI playback support is, so you cannot rely on this producing high-quality sound on all devices even if it sounds good on yours.

Finally, we add a `static` function called `StopAllSounds`. When this is called, it uses the `SndStop` function to terminate all sounds that are currently active (see Listing 7–11). It is a very good idea to call this from your form's `Deactivate` event, so that when another application moves to the foreground, any active sounds stop playing.

Listing 7–11. Stopping Playback of Any Active Sounds

```
/// <summary>
/// Stop all sounds that are currently playing
/// </summary>
public static void StopAllSounds()
{
    SndStop(SND_SCOPE_PROCESS, IntPtr.Zero);
}
```

The AygShell functions have potential, but the limitations of this playback mechanism (for example, lack of support for simultaneous sound playback or embedded resources) unfortunately leave this API disappointing overall.

The AygShell project contains a demonstration of using the wrapper class described in Listing 7–10 to play WAV, MP3, and MIDI files. Note that this project copies all of the files to the device (in the Sounds directory) due to the lack of support for playing from an embedded resource.

BASS.dll

Unlike the other APIs that we have discussed, the functionality provided by BASS is contained within a third-party DLL that you will need to include when distributing your game. Created by Un4Seen Developments (www.un4seen.com), BASS started life as a Windows DLL offering access to a wide selection of sound playback opportunities and has evolved into a rich and powerful sound library.

The DLL can be used free of charge if you are planning to release your game as freeware, but for shareware of commercial use, a license must be purchased. The shareware license is fairly inexpensive and can be used for an unlimited number of applications (though there are restrictions on exactly what qualifies as shareware). Licensing information and pricing can be found on the Un4Seen web site.

BASS was created using C++ and so is not ideal for use by managed .NET languages. To address this issue, developer Bernd Niedergesaess created a managed wrapper around BASS, called BASS.NET. While creating your own wrapper would be possible, a lot of time and effort has gone into BASS.NET, and it provides a very streamlined and simple interface to the underlying functions. BASS.NET can be found online at bass.radio42.com. The wrapper targets .NET CF 2.0 and so is compatible with Visual Studio 2005 and 2008.

BASS.NET also requires a license, with similar terms to those offered by BASS itself. A license must be generated even for freeware use, though this itself is free of charge and just requires an online form to be completed.

This is all very interesting, but how do we use BASS on Windows Mobile? Well, fortunately, both of these DLLs have been compiled to run against Windows Mobile as well as desktop Windows, so we can use the compact versions of BASS and BASS.NET in our games. Visit www.un4seen.com/forum/?topic=9534.0 to find the latest mobile versions of the DLLs.

There is a substantial amount of functionality available through these DLLs, including the ability to stream sound from the Internet and record audio, but we'll concentrate here on the areas that are particularly relevant to our games, namely playing sound effects and music.

Wrapping BASS.NET

BASS provides a degree of management of our sounds that simplifies our work loading and playing them. Unlike the SoundPlayer and AygShell APIs, BASS is able to load the sound just once and then play it multiple times. This means we don't need to worry about releasing resources each time a sound finishes playing; instead, we can leave it loaded in BASS until we want to play it again.

We will, however, still create a wrapper class that keeps track of exactly which sounds have been loaded. We'll use a single instance of the wrapper class per application, rather than an instance per sound as in the previous examples.

If we attempt to load a sound that we have dealt with before, the wrapper will return without doing anything. Each time we ask it to play a sound, it will first ensure it has been loaded and, assuming it has, will instruct BASS to play it.

When BASS loads a sound, it allocates it a unique ID value (or *handle*). We can store just this handle and use it when telling BASS what we want it to play. Any memory that we used to store the sound data can be discarded once BASS has allocated its handle as it keeps a copy of the sound internally.

When loading the sample, we tell BASS how many times we want that particular sound to be able to be played concurrently. Setting this value to 1 will allow only a single instance of the sound to play at a time (though other sounds can still play alongside). If we need to be able to play multiple concurrent instances of the sound, we can set this value higher. We can also instruct BASS to loop the sound when it is played.

When we want to play a sound, we ask BASS to create a *channel*. The channel is initialized with the handle of the sound to be played and results, in turn, in a channel handle being generated. We can then set attributes (such as the volume level) on this channel and initiate playback. The channel handle can be used later on to perform other operations on the sound too, such as pausing or stopping the sound playback for the individual channel.

In our wrapper class, we will put all of this functionality into three main functions: LoadSoundEmbedded will load a sound file from an embedded resource, LoadSoundFile will load from a file, and PlaySound will play a sound that we have loaded. In each case, we will provide the resource or filename of the sound, and this will be used as the key to a Dictionary of sound handles within the wrapper class.

The Dictionary is declared as a private class-level variable. It uses strings for its keys (the sound filename) and integers for its values (the sound handles returned to us by BASS), as shown in Listing 7–12.

Listing 7–12. The Dictionary Containing Sounds That We Have Loaded into Our Wrapper Class

```
private Dictionary<string, int> _sounds = new Dictionary<string, int>();
```

Before we can use BASS.NET, we must initialize it with our license details. These are passed into the BassNet.Registration function. We also need to initialize BASS itself, telling it various pieces of information about how it is to work. All of the values we pass to it can be left at their defaults, which are shown in Listing 7–13.

Listing 7–13. The Wrapper Class Constructor

```
/// <summary>
/// Class constructor. Initialize BASS and BASS.NET ready for use.
/// </summary>
public BassWrapper()
{
    // First pass our license details to BASS.NET
    BassNet.Registration("<license_email_address>", "<license_code>");

    // Now initialize BASS itself and ensure that this succeeds.
    if (!Bass.BASS_Init(-1, 44100, BASSInit.BASS_DEVICE_DEFAULT, IntPtr.Zero))
    {
        throw new Exception("BASS failed to initialize.");
    }
}
```

In Listing 7–13, the call to `BassNet.Registration` has been altered so that no license details are present (the same change has been made within the example project that demonstrates this library, which we'll discuss later in this chapter). You will need to generate your own license from the BASS.NET web site before the code can be executed.

The `LoadSoundEmbedded` function reads a sound file from an embedded resource. Its code is shown in Listing 7–14.

Listing 7–14. Loading a Sound from an Embedded Resource

```
/// <summary>
/// Load a sound contained within an embedded resource
/// </summary>
/// <param name="ResourceAsm">The assembly containing the resource to play</param>
/// <param name="ResourceName">The name of the resource to play</param>
/// <param name="Max">The maximum number of concurrent plays of this sound</param>
/// <param name="Loop">If true, the loaded sound will loop when played.</param>
public void LoadSoundEmbedded(Assembly ResourceAsm, string ResourceName, int Max,
                                                                     bool Loop)
{
    byte[] soundData;
    int soundHandle = 0;
    BASSFlag flags = BASSFlag.BASS_DEFAULT;

    // Do we already have this sound loaded?
    if (!_sounds.ContainsKey(ResourceName.ToLower()))
    {
        // Retrieve a stream from our embedded sound resource.
        using (Stream soundStream =
                Assembly.GetExecutingAssembly().GetManifestResourceStream(ResourceName))
        {
            // Make sure we found the resource
            if (soundStream != null)
            {
```

```
// Read the resource into a byte array, as this is what we need to pass
// to the BASS_SampleLoad function
soundData = new byte[(int)(soundStream.Length)];
soundStream.Read(soundData, 0, (int)(soundStream.Length));

// Load the sound into BASS
// Is it a music file (tracker module)?
if (IsMusic(ResourceName))
{
    // Yes, so use the MusicLoad function
    // Set flags
    if (Loop) flags |= BASSFlag.BASS_MUSIC_LOOP;
    // Load the sound
    soundHandle = Bass.BASS_MusicLoad(soundData, 0, soundData.Length,
                                                  flags, 44100);
}
else
{
    // No, so use the SampleLoad function
    // Set flags
    if (Loop) flags |= BASSFlag.BASS_SAMPLE_LOOP;
    // Load the sound
    soundHandle = Bass.BASS_SampleLoad(soundData, 0, soundData.Length,
                                                  Max, flags);
}

// If we have a valid handle, add it to the dictionary
if (soundHandle != 0)
{
    _sounds.Add(ResourceName.ToLower(), soundHandle);
}
            }
        }
    }
}
```

This code first checks to see that the resource has not already been loaded; if it has, no further action is required. Otherwise, the resource is read into a byte array.

Before passing the sound data to BASS, we determine whether this is a music (tracker) file, as these files are loaded differently. The IsMusic function determines this for us by simply checking the file extension of the sound file being loaded. For music files, the sound is loaded using the Bass.BASS_MusicLoad function, whereas for samples (WAVs, MP3s, OGGs), it is loaded using Bass.BASS_SampleLoad. In both cases, we set an appropriate loop flag if the Loop parameter has been passed as true.

After we check that a valid sound handle was returned, that handle is added to the _sounds dictionary with the resource name as the key. The resource name is converted to lowercase to prevent any case mismatch issues from occurring.

Loading a sound from a file is very similar and results in the same data being added to the _sounds dictionary, except that we use the sound filename as the key this time instead of the resource name; see Listing 7–15.

Listing 7–15. Loading a Sound from a File

```
/// <summary>
/// Load a sound contained within an external file
/// </summary>
/// <param name="Filename">The filename of the file to play</param>
/// <param name="Max">The maximum number of concurrent plays of this sound</param>
/// <param name="Loop">If true, the loaded sound will loop when played.</param>
public void LoadSoundFile(string Filename, int Max, bool Loop)
{
    int soundHandle;
    BASSFlag flags = BASSFlag.BASS_DEFAULT;

    // Convert the filename to lowercase so that we don't have to care
    // about mismatched capitalization on subsequent calls
    Filename = Filename.ToLower();

    // Do we already have this sound loaded?
    if (!_sounds.ContainsKey(Path.GetFileName(Filename)))
    {
        // No, so we need to load it now.
        // Is it a music file (tracker module)?
        if (IsMusic(Filename))
        {
            // Yes, so use the MusicLoad function
            // Set flags
            if (Loop) flags |= BASSFlag.BASS_MUSIC_LOOP;
            // Load the sound
            soundHandle = Bass.BASS_MusicLoad(Filename, 0, 0, flags, 44100);
        }
        else
        {
            // No, so use the SampleLoad function
            // Set flags
            if (Loop) flags |= BASSFlag.BASS_SAMPLE_LOOP;
            // Load the sound
            soundHandle = Bass.BASS_SampleLoad(Filename, 0, 0, 3, flags);
        }
        // If we have a valid handle, add it to the dictionary
        if (soundHandle != 0)
        {
            _sounds.Add(Path.GetFileName(Filename), soundHandle);
        }
    }
}
```

BASS has a function to load a sound from a file, so all we need to do is check that the sound has not already been loaded and then load it either as a music file or as a sample. Once again, the loop flag is set if requested.

To initiate playback of one of our loaded sounds, the PlaySound function is used as shown in Listing 7–16.

Listing 7–16. Playing a Loaded Sound

```
/// <summary>
/// Play a previously loaded sound.
/// </summary>
/// <param name="SoundName">The Filename or ResourceName of the sound to play.</param>
/// <param name="Volume">The volume level for playback (0=silent, 1=full volume)</param>
/// <returns>Returns the activated channel handle if the sound began playing,
/// or zero if the sound could not be started.</returns>
public int PlaySound(string SoundName, float Volume)
{
    int soundHandle = 0;
    int channel = 0;

    // Try to retrieve this using the SoundName as the dictionary key
    if (_sounds.ContainsKey(SoundName.ToLower()))
    {
        // Found it
        soundHandle = _sounds[SoundName.ToLower()];

        // Is this sound for a music track?
        if (IsMusic(SoundName))
        {
            // For music, the channel handle is the same as the sound handle
            channel = soundHandle;
        }
        else
        {
            // Allocate a channel for playback of the sample
            channel = Bass.BASS_SampleGetChannel(soundHandle, false);
        }
        // Check we have a channel...
        if (channel != 0)
        {
            // Play the sample
            if (Volume < 0) Volume = 0;
            if (Volume > 1) Volume = 1;
            Bass.BASS_ChannelSetAttribute(channel,
                                  BASSAttribute.BASS_ATTRIB_VOL, Volume);
            Bass.BASS_ChannelPlay(channel, false);
        }
    }

    // Return the channel number (if we have one, zero if not)
    return channel;
}
```

This function locates the sound handle within the dictionary and then allocates a channel. For music, the sound handle actually is the channel, so there's no need to create a new channel handle for this type of sound. We then set the volume level and begin playback. The channel handle is returned to the calling procedure, which allows the calling code to query or modify the playback of the sound later on if it needs to.

Note that BASS does not offer any synchronous playback functions; all sounds are played asynchronously. It is, however, possible to tell whether playback on a channel has finished or not, and this could be used to provide the behavior of synchronous playback if required. The IsChannelPlaying function in the wrapper class will return a value indicating whether the specified channel handle contains a sound that is still playing, as shown in Listing 7–17.

Listing 7–17. Checking to See Whether a Sound Is Playing on a Specified Channel

```
/// <summary>
/// Check to see whether the specified channel is currently playing a sound.
/// </summary>
/// <param name="Channel">The handle of the channel to check</param>
/// <returns>Returns true if a sound is playing on the channel, or False if the
/// sound has completed or has been paused or stopped.</returns>
public bool IsChannelPlaying(int Channel)
{
    return (Bass.BASS_ChannelIsActive(Channel) == BASSActive.BASS_ACTIVE_PLAYING);
}
```

We also have several other useful functions to allow control over playback. PauseAllSounds will pause playback of all current sounds. After using this function the ResumeAllSounds function can be used to allow all sound playback to carry on from where it was paused. These are perfect for calling in the Deactivate and Activated events of your game form as they ensure that the sound all stops if another application comes to the foreground but allow everything to continue as if nothing had happened when your game comes into focus again.

Along with these is the StopAllSounds function, which fully stops the playback of all active sounds.

Finally, we have the Dispose method, which is responsible for releasing all resources used by the class. This should be called when your game is closing (for example, in the form's Closing event). It loops through all the sounds that have been loaded and frees up the memory used by each, before finally freeing up the memory used by BASS itself, as shown in Listing 7–18.

Listing 7–18. The Wrapper Class Dispose Method

```
/// <summary>
/// Release all resources used by the class
/// </summary>
public void Dispose()
{
    // Release the sounds
    foreach (string soundKey in _sounds.Keys)
    {
        // Is this a music or a sample file?
        if (IsMusic(soundKey))
        {
            Bass.BASS_MusicFree(_sounds[soundKey]);
        }
        else
        {
            Bass.BASS_SampleFree(_sounds[soundKey]);
        }
    }
```

```
      // Close BASS
      Bass.BASS_Free();
  }
```

Using BASS and BASS.NET in Your Projects

The Windows Mobile BASS.dll and Bass.Net.compact.dll can both be downloaded from the URL shown previously, but they come without any documentation. The documentation can be obtained by downloading the Windows desktop versions of the DLLs from the Un4Seen and Radio42 web sites. Each contains a CHM file with full documentation on using the DLLs. BASS.NET's documentation is very comprehensive and is probably all that you need, but the BASS help is available too should you require it. There are minor differences in functionality between the desktop and compact versions of the DLLs, but for the most part, the information will be accurate for Windows Mobile development too.

To use BASS, both Bass.Net.compact.dll and BASS.dll will need to be available to your application. Bass.Net.compact.dll is a managed .NET DLL, so this can be used by your project by simply adding a reference to it within the Solution Explorer.

BASS.dll is not a managed DLL, so you will not be able to reference it. It is still very easy to get it deployed, however. Instead of referencing it, copy the DLL to your project directory and include it in your project using Solution Explorer. Make sure it is added at the root project level and not to a subdirectory. Then, set the properties of the file so that the Build Action is set to Content and the Copy to Output Directory property is "Copy if newer." When your application is deployed, BASS.dll will now be automatically copied to the application directory on the target device.

The BassDLL sample project in the accompanying code download includes all of the code for the BassWrapper class and an example project that uses it. Try playing the included tracker music file (Disillusion.mod), and note how this plays in the background while still allowing other samples to play. All of the samples can be played concurrently, and each individual sound can be played three times at once (though this figure can be increased by changing the values in the PlaySoundEmbedded and PlaySoundFile functions within the example project form's code if required).

You will also see that minimizing the application with the main form "X" button will immediately pause all music and sound playback, and then when the application gains focus again, the sound all continues from the point at which it was paused.

Adding Support for Sounds to the Game Engine

As you have probably gathered by now, there are lots of options for playing sounds, and each one has its advantages and drawbacks. For this reason, we won't be adding support for any of the sound APIs to the game engine within this book.

The only API that we can use across all of the devices that we are covering and across both versions of Visual Studio is the PlaySound function, and it is so simple to use (and basic in function) that there seems little point in adding support for it to the game engine. Instead, we will include sound support directly into the game projects that require it.

When you create your own games, however, it would be worthwhile considering adding support for your sound API of choice directly into your personal copy of the game engine. This will allow you to reuse the code across all of your game projects without having to include the code in each.

One technique that you should adopt regardless of how your sound API is accessed is the use of a single function within your project that is responsible for initiating all sound playback. With all sounds triggered by the same piece of code, it is very easy to implement user preferences to control switching sound on or off, control the volume level, enable background music, or potentially even switch between different sound APIs based on the device capabilities. Using a single piece of code to trigger sound allows your game code to request playback of a sound without needing to care about any of these settings itself.

Choosing a Sound API

The choice of which sound API to use will really depend on your needs and API availability.

If you need flexibility to play lots of sound types across a wide range of devices and can work within the license requirements, BASS is unmatched in terms of flexibility and functionality and will offer excellent results within your games.

If you need to play MP3 files, AygShell is your only other option, though this will exclude users of Windows Mobile 5.0 and earlier.

If you are using Visual Studio 2008 and can manage with just WAV files, the SoundPlayer class will be suitable.

Failing this, falling back to the basic PlaySound function will still give you support for basic sound effects.

Make Some Noise

Sound and music form an important part of a game experience. Carefully crafted sound effects and background music can really bring the game to life and help the player to connect with the action that is taking place on the screen. Carefully choosing the sound that you include with your game is well worth the effort.

Don't overlook the possibility that your player will want to completely disable all of the game sound, however. In many environments (such as in an office), someone may wish to have a quick play of your game but doesn't want to have sound unexpectedly blasting from a device. Be considerate and provide players with an option to switch the sound off quickly and easily should they wish to do so.

In the next chapter, you will see how sound can be included into a real game project.

CHAPTER 8

■ ■ ■

Game in Focus: GemDrops

We've discussed a considerable amount of game technology, graphics, timing, sound and more. It's time now to pull everything you've learned so far together and make a real game.

In this chapter, we'll work from start to finish through an example game called GemDrops. This will be a fully working (and hopefully fun!) game, built using the game engine that we have been constructing.

Designing the Game

Before you create a game, you should always plan what the game will do and how it will work in a "design brief" document. This should explain what the game is about, its mechanics and its objectives. Mock-up screenshots can be included to help demonstrate the design.

If you are working alone, this plan can remain fluid as you progress through the implementation of your game; if you are working in a team then you will have to be much more disciplined when you decide to deviate from the design to ensure that everyone understands the proposed changes and can take them into account within their own role.

The brief may seem superfluous if you are working alone, but it can still be a very useful document to have:

- It can help to identify problems that may occur before you have invested lots of time into writing program code, saving on any potential rework that would result.

- It can help to provide a list of features to implement, which can be useful when working out the sequence of game features to implement when working on the game.

- It can help to inspire you to design new features and spark new ideas before you get bogged down in the complexity of bringing everything to life.

- It can help you communicate the game concept to others quickly and easily.

Let's work through the design brief for GemDrops.

Creating the GemDrops Design Brief

GemDrops is a game based around multiple colored gems. These fall in pairs under player control from the top of the game area towards the bottom. The player can move the gems to the left and to the right, rotate the gems to reorient them relative to one another, and force them to move more quickly to the bottom of the game area to accelerate the flow of the game (see Figure 8–1).

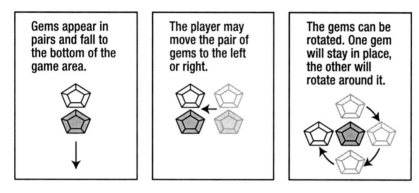

Figure 8–1. The movement of the player-controlled gems

Each time a pair of gems reaches the bottom of the game area, a new pair of gems will be created at the top for the player to continue to control.

The game area itself will be a rectangular region into which the falling gems may be placed. The area will have a width of 7 gems and a height of 15. When gems land at the bottom of the game area, they will be positioned such that they fall within a grid pattern; gems cannot be placed at half positions within the game area. An example of this is shown in Figure 8–2.

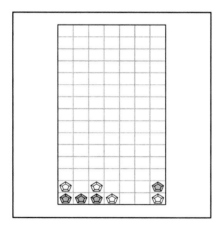

Figure 8–2. The game board with a number of gems dropped in place

The gems under the player's control may not move such that they overlap existing gems. If the player attempts to move the pair of gems sideways into the position of an existing gem, the movement will not be allowed and the player-controlled gems will remain in their existing positions. Similarly, attempts to rotate the gems such that one would end up on top of an existing gem will not be allowed.

If a player-controlled gem is guided so that it lands upon a gem already on the game board, the gem will be considered landed, and control of the pair of gems will terminate.

Gems will not be allowed to float within the board and will always fall as far towards the bottom as possible. If the gems are aligned horizontally as they fall, such that one gem lands on an existing gem and the other is left with space beneath it, the one with space below will fall (without the player being able to control it) until it lands on another gem or reaches the bottom of the board (see Figure 8–3).

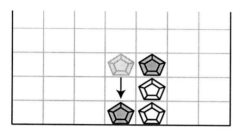

Figure 8–3. A pair of dark colored player-controlled gems landing such that they separate, with one falling away from the other

Once the gems on the board are arranged such that five or more gems of the same color are connected (touching horizontally or vertically but not diagonally), that group of gems will be removed from the board. The gems do not have to all be in a straight line; they just need to be connected (as shown in Figure 8–4). The player will be awarded points based on how large the group of gems was, scoring 10 points for each of the connected gems. Each group of gems removed will therefore be worth at least 50 points.

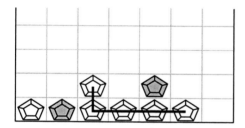

Figure 8–4. A group of five connected gems ready to be removed from the game area

Once a group of gems has been removed, all remaining gems will fall toward the bottom of the game board if there is now space below them. Once they have landed in their final positions, the game board will be checked to see if any further groups of five or more same-colored gems have been formed. If so, these are removed, and the score they provide is multiplied by two, giving a minimum of 100 points per group.

The gems continue to be dropped and their groups checked in this way, and each new generation of groups formed increases the multiplier, so that any third-generation groups have their points multiplied by three, and then the next groups by four, and so on. This continues until no further groups of gems exist on the board.

This game mechanic adds a tactical element to the game play. Instead of simply removing groups as soon as they can be formed, the player can stack up groups so that when one is removed, another will be formed from the falling gems, taking advantage of the score multiplier. Advanced (or lucky) players will be able to stack three of four groups at once, allowing for much higher scores than the individual groups would provide.

Once any and all groups have been eliminated, another pair of gems appears at the top of the board for the player to control, and the game cycle repeats.

Initially, four different colors of gems will be in play. Once 20 pairs of gems have been placed on the board, an additional color will be included to make group formation more difficult. After 40 pairs, a sixth color will be added to increase the difficulty even further.

After 100 pairs have been placed, each new gem that appears under player control will have a 1-in-200 chance of being a special rainbow gem. This gem's color will rapidly fade between those of all the other gems to clearly highlight its unusual status. When the rainbow gem lands, the game will identify the color of gem that it has landed on, and all of the gems of that color on the whole board will be removed. No points will be awarded for this, but it gives the player a chance to remove a large number of gems in order to clear some space or to form more groups from falling gems. Groups that result from other gems falling into the cleared space will be awarded points as normal. If the rainbow gem lands at the very bottom of the game board (rather than on top of another gem), it will disappear without having any special effect.

At all times, the colors of the gems that will *next* be put under user control will be displayed at the top of the screen. This allows the player to plan actions a step ahead of the gems currently in play, which will help when preparing to stack up gem groups.

The speed at which the gems that are under player control move toward the bottom of the game area will very gradually increase as the game progresses. This provides another mechanism for slowly increasing the game's difficulty level.

When the game finds that it cannot add a new pair of player-controlled gems because the space required on the board is already filled with existing gems, the board is declared to be full and the game is over. The player must therefore attempt to clear as many groups as possible to prevent this from happening, and to maximize their score before the game does finally end.

Conceptualizing the Game Controls

The controls that we need the player to be able to use follow:

- Left and right to move the pieces under player control sideways within the game area

- Rotate to change the orientation of the pieces

- Drop to accelerate the movement of the pieces towards the bottom of the game area

For devices with a directional pad, these map nicely to left, right, up, and down respectively. This provides the most straightforward mechanism for controlling the game and will be usable on all smart phones and the majority of touch screen devices too.

However, there are devices available (including a lot of the more recent and popular HTC devices) that have no d-pad to use. How can we support these devices?

We can address this by turning the screen into a virtual control pad. The screen will be split into three horizontal sections. The top section will be used to control rotation. The player can touch the left or right side of this section to rotate counterclockwise or clockwise respectively. The middle section will control movement. The player can press in the left half of this section to move the pieces to the left and in the right half to move right. Finally, the bottom section will allow the player to drop the pieces quickly. Pressing and holding in this section will accelerate the gems' speed.

We can mark out these regions in the background of the game board to clarify where the user can touch the screen in order to use it to control the game pieces, as shown in Figure 8–5.

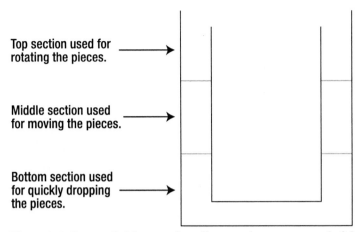

Top section used for rotating the pieces. ⟶

Middle section used for moving the pieces. ⟶

Bottom section used for quickly dropping the pieces. ⟶

Figure 8–5. Screen divisions used to allow touch screen control of the game pieces

This touch screen mechanism is not quite as easy to use as a d-pad, but it becomes natural with a little practice and ensures that all devices are able to play the game.

Choosing the Sound Effects

Sound effects will be provided for the following game actions:

- A new pair of gems appears at the top of the game area.

- A group of gems has been formed and removed. Each new generation of gems will play the sound effect at a higher pitch to indicate that the groups are worth more points. The incremental pitch also provides a pleasant reward to the player for managing to stack groups in this way.

- A rainbow gem has landed.

- The game is finished.

In addition to the sound effects, we will provide background music. BASS will be used to provide all of the audio for the game.

Outlining the Minimum Requirements

The game will not impose any minimum system requirements, working on everything from QVGA to WVGA screens and working with Windows Mobile 2003 SE upwards.

Two different sets of graphics will be provided, one for smaller resolution screens (QVGA) and one for larger screens (VGA). The game will automatically detect which set to use based on the screen size. The small graphics set will also be used on VGA screens if the game is put into landscape mode.

As the board's vertical height is greater than its width, we will use the height of the screen to determine which set of graphics to display. On a QVGA screen running Windows Mobile 6, the ClientSize.Height of the game form returns a value of 268. As we need to display 15 rows of gems within this area, we can divide 268 by 15 to get a height of 17.86 pixels. However, we also need to leave some space for the score, the game board's outline, and so forth, so we will round this down to 16 pixels to allow space for all of this. The height of our small gem graphics will therefore be 16 pixels.

For the larger graphics, the VGA screen returns a `ClientSize.Height` value of 536, which divided by 15 rows gives a height of 35.73 pixels. To simplify the job of creating our graphics, we'll reduce this down to 32 pixels, exactly twice the height of the small graphics.

To determine which graphics set to use, we'll simply see if the screen height is less than 480 pixels. If it is, we're running either on a QVGA-style device in portrait mode, or a VGA-style device in landscape mode. If the screen height is 480 pixels or greater then we have sufficient space to use the large set of graphics.

The screen size can be determined by checking the `Screen.PrimaryScreen.Bounds.Height` property. This returns the actual height of the screen, including the space taken up by the notification bar and the menus. If the screen orientation is changed between portrait and landscape, this property value will update to reflect the resulting new height of the screen.

Writing the Game

With the game design complete, it's time to start putting the code together. All of the source code for the working game can be found in the GemDrops project in the accompanying code download, so everything described here can be examined in detail by opening that within Visual Studio. This section describes exactly how the game was created.

Building a complete game involves a making a lot of iterative modifications to the same pieces of code. We, therefore, need to build up the project piece by piece. As we look at each piece of code within the game, you will notice that the finished code has additional functionality that we won't initially mention. We'll come back to everything important as we progress through, so don't worry about these omissions when you spot them.

The descriptions in the following sections are not intended as a step-by-step guide to how you can re-create the project, so please don't try to follow them in order to rebuild the game from scratch. Instead, they detail the process that the game underwent during its creation and guide you through all the steps that would be necessary for you to create your own games. Not absolutely all of the game code is included in the following sections, as there is a lot of it and you have seen much of it before. Instead, we focus on all the important components of the game and examine how they are built into a finished product.

Creating the Project

First of all, a Windows Mobile application project is created called GemDrops. With this open in Visual Studio, we can add the game engine project to the solution and add a reference from GemDrops to the game engine.

Initially the GemDrops project contains the default form, Form1. We need to add to this some new classes. We will need a game object class to represent each gem that is displayed on the screen and a game class to represent the game itself. We, therefore, add a class named CObjGem that derives from GameEngine.CGameObjectGDIBase and a class named CGemDropsGame that derives from GameEngine.CGameEngine.GDIBase.

We'll come back to these classes in the following sections and start putting code inside them, but they can remain essentially empty for the moment.

Creating the Game Form

The Form1 form is renamed as MainForm and its properties updated so that Text is set to GemDrops and BackColor to Black.

We also add two labels to the top of the form, named lblScore and lblNextPiece. The Text for each is set to "Score: 0" and "Next piece:" respectively. The lblScore label is docked to the top of the form so that there is plenty of space within it to show the player's score. The lblNextPiece label is anchored to the Top and Right, ensuring that if the screen size changes (if the device orientation updates, for example) it will stick to the top-right corner of the screen. lblNextPiece also has its TextAlign property set to TopRight.

The MainMenu control is updated to contain a pause item and a pop-up menu containing items to start a new game and to exit the game. The initial form design is shown in Figure 8–6.

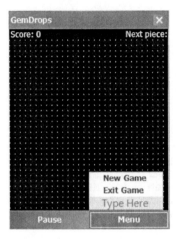

Figure 8–6. The GemDrops form design

In the form code, we declare an instance of CGemDropsGame as a class-level variable named _game. This is instantiated and initialized in our form constructor, as shown in Listing 8–1.

Listing 8–1. Instantiating and Initialising the GemDrops Game Object

```
// Our instance of the GemDrops game
CGemDropsGame _game;

/// <summary>
/// Form constructor
/// </summary>
public MainForm()
{
    InitializeComponent();

    // Instantiate our game and set its game form to be this form
    _game = new CGemDropsGame(this);
    _game.Reset();
}
```

A function called SetScore is added to the form too. This simply accepts an int as a parameter and puts it into the text of the lblScore label. This will be used by the game to display the score to the player each time it changes. The procedure code is shown in Listing 8–2.

Listing 8–2. Function to Display the Player's Score

```
/// <summary>
/// Display the score on the screen
/// </summary>
/// <param name="score">The player's new score</param>
internal void SetScore(int score)
{
    lblScore.Text = "Score: " + score.ToString();
}
```

We then set up the form's OnPaintBackground function and its Load, Paint, and Closing event handlers. These are all exactly the same as we have seen in previous chapters. The RenderLoop function is also added just as in previous examples.

All of this gives us a game that compiles but does nothing more than display an empty black screen. Let's start to develop the game engine.

Preparing the Game

To cope with both QVGA and VGA sized screens, we will use two different sets of graphics. The graphics we need for GemDrops consist of nothing more than a series of different colored gems. As we have already discussed, we will use a height of 16 pixels for the smaller gems, and to get a comfortable object size, we'll set the width at 21 pixels. For the larger gems, we use a height of 32 pixels and a width of 42 pixels.

The gem graphics are contained within two PNG image files, named Gems16.png for the smaller graphics and Gems32.png for the larger. Within each image is a line of six colored gems arranged in a row, each gem occupying exactly 16 × 21 or 32 × 42 pixels as appropriate, as shown in Figure 8–7. We can, therefore, choose which colored gem to display by picking out a rectangle of the appropriate gem size and offsetting the left edge of the rectangle by the color index multiplied by the gem width.

Figure 8–7. The two GemDrops graphic files: Gems16.png on the left and Gems32.png on the right

The first thing we do for our game in the CGemDropsGame.Prepare function is to determine which graphics set we are using. We do this, as already mentioned, by checking the height of the screen. If it is less than 480 pixels, the smaller graphic is used; otherwise, the larger graphic is used. Whichever graphic we select is loaded into the game engine's GameGraphics dictionary, as discussed back in Chapter 4. In addition to loading the graphic file, we also set two fields within the class, _gemWidth and _gemHeight, so that they contain the width and height of each individual gem graphic.

Once we have the size of each gem, we can also calculate the top-left coordinate of the game board on the screen. We want the board to be centered within the window, so we can calculate the left position by taking the form width, subtracting the board area width, and dividing the result by two. We can calculate the board area width by multiplying the number of columns of gems (7) by the width of each gem (as stored in _gemWidth). The exact same calculation is repeated against the heights of the form and the gems to calculate the top position of the board.

All of this can be seen in Listing 8–3.

Listing 8–3. *Preparing the Game Based on the Screen Size*

```
/// <summary>
/// Prepare the game engine for use.
/// </summary>
public override void Prepare()
{
    // Allow the base class to do its work.
    base.Prepare();

    // Get a reference to our assembly
    Assembly asm = Assembly.GetExecutingAssembly();

    // Initialise graphics library
    // Which graphics set are we using?
    if (Screen.PrimaryScreen.Bounds.Height < 480)
    {
        // The screen height is insufficient for the large graphics set,
        // so load the small graphics
        GameGraphics.Clear();
        GameGraphics.Add("Gems",
            new Bitmap(asm.GetManifestResourceStream("GemDrops.Graphics.Gems16.png")));
        _gemWidth = 21;
        _gemHeight = 16;
    }
    else
    {
        // We have enough space to use the large graphics set
        GameGraphics.Clear();
        GameGraphics.Add("Gems",
            new Bitmap(asm.GetManifestResourceStream("GemDrops.Graphics.Gems32.png")));
        _gemWidth = 42;
        _gemHeight = 32;
    }

    // Position the board within the window
    _boardLeft = (GameForm.ClientSize.Width - (GemWidth * BOARD_GEMS_ACROSS)) / 2;
    _boardTop = (GameForm.ClientSize.Height - (GemHeight * BOARD_GEMS_DOWN)) / 2;
}
```

As the final two lines of code show, the board dimensions (7×15 gems) are contained within two constants, BOARD_GEMS_ACROSS and BOARD_GEMS_DOWN (which we will define in Listing 8–8, coming up shortly). Should we wish to change the dimensions of the game board, these constants would allow us to do so very easily.

This code may seem simple, but it has done something very important: it has set up an abstract coordinate system. We can now draw a gem to the screen without caring about our screen resolution or which set of graphics has been loaded. To find the coordinate to draw a gem, we simply take the (_boardLeft, _boardTop) coordinate and offset this by the required x position multiplied by _gemWidth and by the y position multiplied by _gemHeight. This very useful mechanism saves us a lot of complexity elsewhere within the program.

Creating the Gem Game Object

Next, let's shift our attention to the first of two game objects that will be included within GemDrops: the gem. Implemented in the CObjGem class, each instance represents a single gem present within our game. The gem may be settled on the board, under player control or even used for the "Next piece" display, though we'll look at all these different ways of using it a little bit later on.

CObjGem derives from the GameEngine.CGameObjectGDIBase class. We add a number of additional properties to it so that we can configure the gem in the way that we want. The properties we're interested in at the moment are as shown in Listing 8–4.

Listing 8–4. CObjGem Properties

```
// Our reference to the game engine
private CGemDropsGame _game;

// The color of this gem
private int _gemColor = 0;
// The X position within the board (in game units, so from 0 to 6)
private int _boardXPos = 0;
// The Y position within the board (in game units, so from 0 to 14)
private int _boardYPos = 0;
```

These provide some of the fundamental information that we need for the gem: what color is it, and where on the board is it? The x and y coordinate are specified in terms of the position within the board, and not as pixel positions or similar.

We also have a strongly typed reference to the CGemDropsGame object, which allows us to interact with it without having to keep casting it to the appropriate type.

Next are the constructors for the class. In addition to the default constructor, we also allow the gem's position and color to be specified when it is created, as shown in Listing 8–5. Note that this overload calls into our own default constructor, not that of the base class, so we still end up storing the game engine reference in the class-level _game variable.

Listing 8–5. CObjGem Constructors

```
/// <summary>
/// Constructor
/// </summary>
public CObjGem(CGemDropsGame gameEngine)
    : base(gameEngine)
{
    // Store a reference to the game engine as its derived type
    _game = gameEngine;
}

/// <summary>
/// Constructor
/// </summary>
/// <param name="boardX">The x position for the gem</param>
/// <param name="boardY">The y position for the gem</param>
/// <param name="color">The color for the gem</param>
public CObjGem(CGemDropsGame gameEngine, int boardX, int boardY, int color)
    : this(gameEngine)
{
```

```
        _boardXPos = boardX;
        _boardYPos = boardY;
        _gemColor = color;
}
```

One thing to note here is that we are not setting the Width or Height properties in the constructor as we have done in previous examples. We'll see the reason for this when we examine the overrides for those properties in a moment.

The gem naturally needs to be able to render itself. Most of the time, gems will have a simple color applied, and we will render an appropriate section of the gem graphic that we saw in Figure 8–7. The rainbow gem, however, cycles through all of the different colors, providing a pulsating effect on this type of gem that makes it stand out from the normal gems. If this gem's color indicates that it is a rainbow gem (its _gemColor contains the constant GEMCOLOR_RAINBOW), we'll render a different actual gem color each every tenth of a second. The Render function is shown in Listing 8–6.

Listing 8–6. Rendering CObjGem

```
/// <summary>
/// Draw the gem to the screen
/// </summary>
public override void Render(Graphics gfx, float interpFactor)
{
    System.Drawing.Imaging.ImageAttributes imgAttributes;

    base.Render(gfx, interpFactor);

    // Create the transparency key for the gem graphics
    imgAttributes = new System.Drawing.Imaging.ImageAttributes();
    imgAttributes.SetColorKey(Color.Black, Color.Black);

    // If this is not a rainbow gem...
    if (_gemColor != CGemDropsGame.GEMCOLOR_RAINBOW)
    {
        // Then just draw its image
        gfx.DrawImage(_game.GameGraphics["Gems"], GetRenderRectangle(interpFactor),
                _gemColor * (int)Width, 0, (int)Width, (int)Height,
                GraphicsUnit.Pixel, imgAttributes);
    }
    else
    {
        // This is a rainbow gem so we need to cycle its color.
        // Add the elapsed time to our class variable
        _rainbowGemUpdateTime += GameEngine.TimeSinceLastRender;
        // Has 0.1 seconds elapsed?
        if (_rainbowGemUpdateTime > 0.1f)
        {
            // Yes, so advance to the next color
            _rainbowGemUpdateTime = 0;
            _rainbowGemFrame += 1;
            // If we reach the rainbow gem position (pass the final
            // actual gem color), move back to the first
            if (_rainbowGemFrame == CGemDropsGame.GEMCOLOR_RAINBOW) _rainbowGemFrame=0;
        }
```

```
            // Ensure the gem is considered as moved so that it re-renders in its new color.
            // This is important so that it still cycles when in the "next gem"
            // display which isn't otherwise moving.
            HasMoved = true;
            // Draw its image
            gfx.DrawImage(_game.GameGraphics["Gems"], GetRenderRectangle(interpFactor),
                        _rainbowGemFrame * (int)Width, 0, (int)Width, (int)Height,
                        GraphicsUnit.Pixel, imgAttributes);
        }
    }
```

The gem images use a black background for their transparent region, so the code first sets up an ImageAttributes object with this specified as the color key. DrawImage is then called to draw the gem that we are representing in this object. For normal gems, we work out which section of our source image to draw by multiplying the gem color by the width of the gem. This will index into our gem image and retrieve just the color that we are interested in.

For rainbow gems, we accumulate in the _rainbowGemUpdateTime the amount of time that has elapsed since the last call to Render by reading the TimeSinceLastRender property from the game engine. Each time this reaches a total of 0.1 seconds, we increment the _rainbowGemFrame and reset the _rainbowGemUpdateTime to 0. By changing the upper time limit against which we compare _rainbowGemUpdateTime, we can make the rainbow gem cycle faster or slower should we wish to.

CObjGem also overrides some properties from the base class: the get parts of the XPos, YPos, Width, and Height properties are all overridden. This allows us to calculate the values for these properties on demand, rather than having to keep them updated whenever anything within the object changes.

For the XPos and YPos properties, we take advantage of the abstract coordinate system that was set up in the CGemDropsGame.Prepare function. The position is calculated using the BoardLeft and BoardTop values that were calculated when the coordinate system was initialized. The function adds to these values multiples of the gem's width and height. No absolute or hard-coded coordinates need to be included here. This simple approach ensures that the game appears correctly on all supported screen resolutions.

For the Width and Height properties, we simply ask the CGemDropsGame object to tell us the dimensions of the gem. Once again, these values were calculated when the Prepare method was called. If the device orientation changes, resulting in a different graphics set being loaded (and therefore the width and height of the gem changing), this ensures that these two properties always return the correct value without having to be notified about the change.

The overrides of all four of these properties will be observed by the game engine, so they provide a useful simplification for providing these values for game objects where appropriate. The code for these properties within CObjGem is shown in Listing 8–7.

Listing 8–7. CObjGem's Position and Size Property Overrides

```
/// <summary>
/// Override the XPos property to calculate our actual position on demand
/// </summary>
public override float XPos
{
    get
    {
        // Determine the position for the gem from its position within the board
        return _game.BoardLeft + (_boardXPos * Width);
    }
}
```

```
/// <summary>
/// Override the YPos property to calculate our actual position on demand
/// </summary>
public override float YPos
{
    get
    {
        // Determine the position for the gem from its position within the board
        return _game.BoardLeft + (_boardXPos * Width);
    }
}

/// <summary>
/// Return the Width by querying the gem width from the game engine.
/// This means that if the gem width changes (e.g., the screen orientation
/// is changed resulting in new graphics being loaded), we always return
/// the correct value.
/// </summary>
public override int Width
{
    get
    {
        return _game.GemWidth;
    }
}
/// <summary>
/// Return the Width by querying the gem width from the game engine.
/// </summary>
public override int Height
{
    get
    {
        return _game.GemHeight;
    }
}
```

Resetting the Game

Now that we have defined our gem object, let's add some further functionality to the game itself to take advantage of it.

The game is fundamentally based around a grid of gems, so we need to be able to store this grid within the game. We could use various structures to do this, but the easiest is to simply declare an array. Each array element will hold an instance of the CObjGem that is present within that location within the game board, or null if the location is unoccupied.

To specify the dimensions of the array, we also declare two constants, which tell us how many gems across the board is (its width) and how many gems down (its height). Should we decide later on that we want a different size for the game board, we can change these constants and everything else will adjust to match.

The code for this is shown in Listing 8–8.

Listing 8–8. Declaring the Game Board Array

```
// The dimensions of the game board (gems across and gems down)
public const int BOARD_GEMS_ACROSS = 7;
public const int BOARD_GEMS_DOWN = 15;

// Create an array to hold the game board -- all our dropped gems will appear here
private CObjGem[,] _gameBoard = new CObjGem[BOARD_GEMS_ACROSS, BOARD_GEMS_DOWN];
```

We also add some properties for other useful information that the game will need to know. Flags are provided to track whether the game is paused or has finished, and other variables are added for the player's score and to track how many pieces the player has placed into the game, as shown in Listing 8–9.

Listing 8–9. Additional Game State Variables

```
// Track whether the game has finished
private bool _gameOver;
// Track whether the game is paused
private bool _paused;

// The player's current score
private int _playerScore;

// The number of pieces that have dropped into the game.
// We'll use this to gradually increase the game difficulty
private int _piecesDropped;
```

Everything is now in place for us to be able to implement the Reset function, to put our game into its initial state ready to play.

We start off by resetting all the simple game properties back to their initial values. _gameOver is set to false, _playerScore and _piecesDropped are set to 0. As in the previous examples we have looked at, we then clear all of the game objects to reset the game engine to an empty state.

Next, we need to initialize the game board. If we're resetting after a previous game has finished, the game board may contain information that is left over from before. We, therefore, call the ClearBoard function (which we'll look at in a moment) to remove any gems that are present on the board. This leaves the game empty and ready to play. The Reset function's code so far is shown in Listing 8–10.

Listing 8–10. Resetting the Game

```
/// <summary>
/// Reset the game to its detault state
/// </summary>
public override void Reset()
{
    base.Reset();

    // Reset game variables
    _gameOver = false;
    _playerScore = 0;
    _piecesDropped = 0;

    // Clear any existing game objects
    GameObjects.Clear();
```

```
    // Clear the game board
    ClearBoard();

    // Ensure the information displayed on the game form is up to date
    UpdateForm();
}
```

The ClearBoard function called here simply loops through all of the elements within the _gameBoard array and checks to see whether each contains a gem. If it does, the loop instructs the gem to terminate and then clears the gem object from the board. Once this is completed, the board will be entirely empty. The code for ClearBoard is shown in Listing 8–11.

Listing 8–11. Clearing the Game Board

```
/// <summary>
/// Remove all of the gems present on the board.
/// </summary>
private void ClearBoard()
{
    for (int x=0; x<BOARD_GEMS_ACROSS; x++)
    {
        for (int y=0; y<BOARD_GEMS_DOWN; y++)
        {
            // Does this location contain a gem?
            if (_gameBoard[x,y] != null)
            {
                // Yes, so instruct it to terminate and then remove it from the board
                _gameBoard[x, y].Terminate = true;
                _gameBoard[x,y] = null;
            }
        }
    }
}
```

The UpdateForm function copies any required information from the game engine on to the game form. The only thing we need to copy across is the player score, but it's useful to have a centralized function for this in case other things (lives, energy levels, missile reserves) need to be added later. Each time one of the variables in question is modified, we can simply call this function to display the change to the user.

As we have changed the player's score (by resetting it to 0), we must call UpdateForm from the Reset function. The code for UpdateForm is shown in Listing 8–12.

Listing 8–12. Updating the Form with Information from the Game

```
/// <summary>
/// Copy information from the game on to the game form so that it can be
/// seen by the player.
/// </summary>
private void UpdateForm()
{
    // Make sure we have finished initializing and we have a form to update
    if (_gameForm != null)
    {
```

```
            // Set the player score
            _gameForm.SetScore(_playerScore);
        }
    }
```

Pausing the Game

We'll come back to how the _gameOver variable is used a little later, but we can wrap up our processing of the _paused variable very easily. It is exposed outside of the class using a standard public property procedure called Paused. In order to make it actually do something, we override the Advance function as shown in Listing 8–13.

Listing 8–13. Implementing the Pause Functionality

```
/// <summary>
/// Advance the simulation by one frame
/// </summary>
public override void Advance()
{
    // If we are paused then do nothing...
    if (_paused) return;

    // Otherwise get the base class to process as normal
    base.Advance();
}
```

As you will hopefully recall, the game engine's Advance function is where the whole engine is driven forward. Within the base class code, the Update functions are called on the game itself and all of the game objects, keeping everything moving.

We allow the game to be paused by preventing the call to the base class from taking place when the _paused variable is set to true. This prevents any updates taking place to the game or the game objects, preventing any further movement—exactly what we need to pause the game. Once the _paused flag is set back to false, we resume calls to base.Advance and the game starts moving once again.

Displaying the Player Gems

We now have an empty board, so let's allow the player to do something with it. When the game begins, we create a pair of gems at random and place them in the middle of the board at the very top. These will then gradually fall to the bottom of the board under player control.

Enhancing CObjGem

To ensure that the game knows how to handle the movement of the gems, we have to first add some new functionality to the CObjGem class. A gem can exist in three different states: under player control, landed on the board, and forming part of the "Next piece" display showing the player gem colors that will be used next.

We need to process each of these types of gem in a different way. The player-controlled gem gradually moves toward the bottom of the board the whole time. The gem on the board is stationary most of the time but need to fall down fairly quickly if a space is created underneath it. The gem in the "Next piece" display is entirely stationary and so doesn't move at all.

So that each gem instance knows how to behave, we create an enumeration called GemTypes, with an entry for each of these types and a class-level variable to store the type for each object (along with a public property to expose this to the outside world). The enumeration and variable are shown in Listing 8–14.

Listing 8–14. The _gemType Variable and the GemTypes Enumeration

```
// The type of gem represented within this object...
private GemTypes _gemType;
// Possible gem types are:
public enum GemTypes
{
    OnTheBoard,          // A gem that has been placed on to the game board
    PlayerControlled,    // A gem that is moving under player control
    NextGem              // A gem in the "next piece" display
};
```

So that the gems are able to fall smoothly, rather than a whole board coordinate at a time, we add two further variables, _fallDistance and _fallSpeed. _fallDistance stores the distance that this gem has to travel until it lands at its current board position (as stored in the _boardXPos and _boardYPos variables that we have already discussed). A _fallDistance of 0 therefore means that it in directly at its target position; values greater than 0 indicate that it is some distance above its target position.

The distance in this variable is measured in board game units, not in pixels. This continues to fit in with our abstract coordinate system. We can draw a gem half a row upwards by setting its _fallDistance to 0.5, without needing to know how many pixels that actually corresponds to on the screen.

When a player-controlled gem is in motion, it will have its _boardYPos set to the location into which it is falling, and its _fallDistance value initially set to 1. We can get the gem to automatically fall downward by decreasing the _fallDistance value each time the gem's Update method is called.

The faster the gem falls, the more difficult it will be to control. Fast-moving gems give the player less opportunity to position the gem, making mistakes more likely. Increasing the speed is one of the things we can do to make the game more difficult as it progresses.

We set the speed at which it falls in the _fallSpeed variable. The value contained therein will be subtracted from _fallDistance during each update, as shown in Listing 8–15. We only do this for player-controlled gems. "Next piece" gems do not move at all, and we'll come back to the gems on the board later in this chapter.

Listing 8–15. The Gem's Update Function, Decreasing the _fallDistance So That the Gem Moves Downward

```
/// <summary>
/// Update the gem's position
/// </summary>
public override void Update()
{
    // Allow the base class to perform any processing it needs
    base.Update();

    switch (_gemType)
    {
        case GemTypes.NextGem:
            // If this gem is part of the "next piece" display then there
            // is nothing for us to do as these gems don't move
            break;
```

```
        case GemTypes.OnTheBoard:
            // To do...
            break;

        case GemTypes.PlayerControlled:
            // This gem is under player control so allow it to gently drop towards the
            // bottom of the board.
            // We'll let the game itself work out how to deal with it landing, etc.
            _fallDistance -= _fallSpeed;
            break;
    }
}
```

We don't make any provision here for what happens when the gem's fall distance reaches 0. The game itself will have to check for and handle this situation. You'll see how that happens shortly.

In order for the fall distance to have any visible effect, we need to make a change to the YPos property. Instead of calculating the position based only on the _boardYPos, we now take _fallDistance into account too, which will allow the final position to be calculated with support for falling gems.

We also make provision for those gems that form the "Next piece" display. As these are not displayed within the board area, we modify both the XPos and YPos properties so that the gems are displayed at the right edge of the game form, directly underneath the lblNextPiece label that was created when the form was designed. The YPos property still observes the _boardYPos value for this gem type so that we can specify one of the gems to be below the other.

The updated XPos and YPos property code is shown in Listing 8–16.

Listing 8–16. Amended Code for the YPos Property to Take _fallDistance and _gemType into Account

```
/// <summary>
/// Override the XPos property to calculate our actual position on demand
/// </summary>
public override float XPos
{
    get
    {
        switch (_gemType)
        {
            case GemTypes.NextGem:
                // This is a "next piece" gem so determine its position within the form
                return ((MainForm)(_game.GameForm)).ClientRectangle.Width - Width;
            default:
                // This is an "in-board" gem so determine its position within the board
                return _game.BoardLeft + (_boardXPos * Width);
        }
    }
}

/// <summary>
/// Override the YPos property to calculate our actual position on demand
/// </summary>
public override float YPos
{
    get
```

```
    {
        switch (_gemType)
        {
            case GemTypes.NextGem:
                // This is a "next piece" gem so determine its position within the form
                return ((MainForm)(_game.GameForm)).lblNextPiece.ClientRectangle.Bottom
                                                    + (_boardYPos * Height);
            default:
                // This is an "in-board" gem so determine its position within the board
                return _game.BoardTop + ((_boardYPos - _fallDistance) * Height);
        }
    }
}
```

Enhancing the Game Class

The gem class now offers the functionality we need to get it to display the player gems. Let's look at what we need to do next to the CGemDropsGame class.

To create gems for the player to control, we need to be able to randomly generate the gem colors. As stated in the design brief, we will stick to 4 different gem colors for the first 20 pairs of gems dropped into the game, increase this to 5 colors up until 40 pairs have dropped, and then allow 6 colors from there on. Additionally, after 100 pieces, we will offer a small chance of a rainbow gem being generated.

To make it very simple for us to randomly generate a gem color, we wrap this up into a function that does the work for us. The GenerateRandomGemColor function is shown in Listing 8–17.

Listing 8–17. Generating a Random Color for a New Gem

```
/// <summary>
/// Returns a random gem color.
/// </summary>
/// <remarks>The range of colors returned will slowly increase as the
/// game progresses.</remarks>
private int GenerateRandomGemColor()
{
    // We'll generate a gem at random based upon how many pieces the player has dropped.

    // For the first few turns, we'll generate just the first four gem colors
    if (_piecesDropped < 20) return Random.Next(0, 4);

    // For the next few turns, we'll generate the first five gem colors
    if (_piecesDropped < 40) return Random.Next(0, 5);

    // After 100 pieces, we'll have a 1-in-200 chance of generating a "rainbow" gem
    if (_piecesDropped >= 100 && Random.Next(200) == 0) return GEMCOLOR_RAINBOW;

    // Otherwise return any of the available gem colors
    return Random.Next(0, 6);
}
```

This code takes advantage of the _piecesDropped variable to determine the range of gem colors to include in the return value and whether we should occasionally generate a rainbow gem.

To track the movement of the player gems, we declare a two-element array to hold their details. This array is created as a class-level variable and is called _playerGems. Alongside this, we create a second

array that stores the details of the *next* pair of gems that will come into play. This array is called
_playerNextGems. The declaration of both of these arrays can be seen in Listing 8–18

Listing 8–18. The Declaration of the _playerGems and _playerNextGems Arrays

```
// Declare an array to hold the pair of gems that are dropping under player control
private CObjGem[] _playerGems = new CObjGem[2];
// Declare an array to hold the next gems that will be brought into play
private CObjGem[] _playerNextGems = new CObjGem[2];
```

Each time we add a new pair of gems for the player to control, we will copy their colors from
_playerNextGems. This ensures that whatever colors we told the player would come next actually do
come next. To ensure that the next gem details are present right from the start of the game, we initialize
these prior to generating any player gems.

The next gems are initialized by a function called InitNextGems, and its code is shown in Listing 8–
19. A call to this function is added to the game's Reset function.

Listing 8–19. Initializing the "Next Gem" Objects

```
/// <summary>
/// Create the two "next piece" gems to display in the corner of the screen.
/// This should be called just once per game as it is being reset.
/// </summary>
private void InitNextGems()
{
    // Instantiate two new gems.
    // The gems have Y positions of 0 and 1 so that they appear one above the
    // other in the Next Piece display.
    // We also generate initial random colors for the two gems here too.
    _playerNextGems[0] = new CObjGem(this, 0, 0, GenerateRandomGemColor());
    _playerNextGems[1] = new CObjGem(this, 0, 1, GenerateRandomGemColor());

    // These are the 'next' gems -- this affects their position within the screen
    _playerNextGems[0].GemType = CObjGem.GemTypes.NextGem;
    _playerNextGems[1].GemType = CObjGem.GemTypes.NextGem;

    // Add the gems to the game
    GameObjects.Add(_playerNextGems[0]);
    GameObjects.Add(_playerNextGems[1]);
}
```

Now that we know which gem colors to use next, we can finally initialize the player gems. These are
created in a function called InitPlayerGems, shown in Listing 8–20. This is also called from the Reset
function, after InitNextGems. It will also be called each time a new pair of gems is created for the player
once the game is underway; you'll see it being called for this shortly.

Listing 8–20. Initializing a New Pair of Gems for the Player to Control

```
/// <summary>
/// Create two new gems for the player to control.
/// </summary>
private void InitPlayerGems()
{
    // Instantiate and initialize two new gems for the player to control.
```

```
    // Set the gem colors to be those colors stored for the next gems.
    _playerGems[0] = new CObjGem(this, BOARD_GEMS_ACROSS / 2, 0,
                                             _playerNextGems[0].GemColor);
    _playerGems[1] = new CObjGem(this, BOARD_GEMS_ACROSS / 2, 1,
                                             _playerNextGems[1].GemColor);

    // These are the player controlled gems
    _playerGems[0].GemType = CObjGem.GemTypes.PlayerControlled;
    _playerGems[1].GemType = CObjGem.GemTypes.PlayerControlled;

    // Set the gems as falling into the position we have set
    _playerGems[0].FallDistance = 1;
    _playerGems[1].FallDistance = 1;

    // Set the drop speed to increase based on the number of pieces already dropped.
    _playerGems[0].FallSpeed = 0.02f + (_piecesDropped * 0.0004f);
    _playerGems[1].FallSpeed = _playerGems[0].FallSpeed;

    // Add the gems to the game
    GameObjects.Add(_playerGems[0]);
    GameObjects.Add(_playerGems[1]);

    // Check that the board space is actually available.
    // If not, the game is finished.
    CheckGameOver();
    if (GameOver)
    {
        // The game is finished, so no further work is required here
        return;
    }

    // Set two new 'next' gems
    _playerNextGems[0].GemColor = GenerateRandomGemColor();
    _playerNextGems[1].GemColor = GenerateRandomGemColor();
    // Flag the next gems as having moved so that they are re-rendered in their
    // new colors.
    _playerNextGems[0].HasMoved = true;
    _playerNextGems[1].HasMoved = true;

    // Increase the pieces dropped count
    _piecesDropped += 1;
}
```

The code here is mostly straightforward. We first create two new gem objects, setting their x positions to be half the width of the board (putting them into the middle column) and their y positions to be 0 and 1 (arranging them vertically, one above the other). The colors for the gems are read from the next gems that we created earlier.

We then set the GemType property for each of the gems, indicating that they are under player control. The FallDistance is set to 1. As described in the previous section, this will cause each gem to appear one unit higher than the position we have requested, and they will gradually fall down to the actual specified location.

Next, we set the FallSpeed property. For the very first pair of gems, this will be given a value of 0.02. To slowly increase the difficulty of the game, however, we add to this the number of pairs of gems dropped (in the _pieceCount variable) multiplied by 0.0004. If the initial speed of 0.02 is divided by

0.0004, the result is 50, and so after 50 turns, the gem speed will have doubled; after 100 turns it will have tripled, and so on. If we want to make the speed increase happen more or less rapidly, this value of 0.0004 can be tweaked. Its current value makes for a reasonable but noticeable increase in speed as the game progresses.

The gems are now initialized, so the code adds them to the GameObjects collection.

Before we go any further, we call into the CheckGameOver function to make sure that the locations to which we have added the new gems are actually unoccupied. If these locations are already filled, the game finishes. The code for this function can be seen in Listing 8–21.

Listing 8–21. Checking the Game Board to See If the Game Has Finished

```
/// <summary>
/// Check to see whether the player gem board position is occupied by
/// a gem already on the board. If this is the case when the player
/// gems are first added, the board is full and the game is over.
/// </summary>
/// <remarks>If the game is found to be over, the GameOver property
/// will be set to true.</remarks>
private void CheckGameOver()
{
    // Are the positions to which the player gems have been added already occupied?
    if (_gameBoard[_playerGems[1].BoardXPos, _playerGems[1].BoardYPos] != null)
    {
        // They are, so the game is finished...
        // Stop the player gems from moving
        _playerGems[0].FallSpeed = 0;
        _playerGems[1].FallSpeed = 0;

        // Initialize the game over sequence
        GameOver = true;
    }
}
```

Assuming the game is still in action, we generate two new random gem colors for the next gems. After setting the colors, we also set the HasMoved property of each of the next gems so that the game engine knows to redraw them.

After increasing the _piecesDropped variable, the work of initializing the new player gems is finally complete.

CheckGameOver looks to see whether the board is already filled at the position occupied by _playerGems[1]. This particular gem is always placed below the other player gem, and so this is the space we need to check to make sure both gem locations are empty.

If the code finds that the location is occupied, it initiates the game over sequence, which first requires us to set the FallSpeed for the two player gems to 0 to stop them moving any further. The GameOver property is then set to true. Setting this property will cause the rest of the game to cease functioning and will display a message to the user; we'll look at this in more detail later on.

Updating the Player's Gems

At this stage, the game has advanced to the point where we have a pair of gems that slowly fall down the screen. However, nothing is managing the movement of the gems, so they just fall forever, through the bottom of the game board and off the bottom of the screen.

To manage the gems properly, we need to update their positions each time their FallDistance reaches (or falls below) 0. When this happens, the gem has reached its target location as stored within its BoardXPos and BoardYPos properties. What we do at this stage depends on what is happening around the player gems:

- If either of the gems has reached the bottom of the game board, the gems have landed.

- The game checks the two board array elements in the locations below those currently occupied by the player gems. If either location is occupied, the gems have landed.

- Otherwise, the gems are clear to carry on falling downward.

If the gems have landed, they are moved out of player control and placed on to the game board. These can then be checked to see if any gem groups have formed. You'll see how that fits together shortly.

If the gems are found to be still falling, we update their BoardYPos properties to move them down into the next square on the board. This would cause them to jump down a whole grid unit however, which we don't want, so we reset their FallDistance by adding 1 to its value, offsetting the BoardYPos change. The end result is that the gem's BoardYPos changes, but the gem continues to move smoothly down the screen.

The code required to perform all of these steps is placed into the CGemDropsGame.Update function and can be seen in Listing 8–22.

Listing 8–22. Updating the Positions of the Gems As They Fall Down the Screen

```
/// <summary>
/// Update the game
/// </summary>
public override void Update()
{
    bool landed = false;

    // Call into the base class to perform its work
    base.Update();

    // If the game has finished then there's nothing more to do
    if (_gameOver) return;

    // Have the gems reached the bottom of the space they were dropping into?
    if (_playerGems[0] != null && _playerGems[0].FallDistance <= 0)
    {
        // They have...
        // Has either gem landed?
        for (int i = 0; i < 2; i++)
        {
            // See if the gem is at the bottom of the board, or is
            // immediately above a location that is occupied by another gem.
            if (_playerGems[i].BoardYPos == CGemDropsGame.BOARD_GEMS_DOWN - 1
 || _gameBoard[_playerGems[i].BoardXPos, _playerGems[i].BoardYPos + 1] != null)
            {
                landed = true;
            }
```

```
            }
            if (landed)
            {
                // Yes...
                // At this stage we need to make the game become part of the main game board
                MovePlayerGemsToBoard();

                // Get any gems that are left floating to fall to the bottom
                DropGems();

                // We won't Initialize any new player gems at this point, as we want to
                // allow any gems within the board that are dropping to complete their
                // descent first. The gems will be re-Initialized in the next Update loop
                // once all falling gems have landed.
            }
            else
            {
                // We haven't landed. Move the gem to the next row down.
                _playerGems[0].BoardYPos += 1;
                _playerGems[1].BoardYPos += 1;
                // Reset the distance to fall until they reach the bottom of the row.
                _playerGems[0].FallDistance += 1;
                _playerGems[1].FallDistance += 1;
            }
        }

        // Are player gems active at the moment?
        if (_playerGems[0] == null)
        {
            // No...
            // Are there any gems currently dropping?
            if (!GemsAreDropping)
            {
                // No, so we can look for any groups to remove.
                if (RemoveGemGroups())
                {
                    // Gems were removed, so allow the next drop to take place
                }
                else
                {
                    // Everything is up to date so we can Initialize some new player gems
                    InitPlayerGems();
                }
            }
        }
    }
}
```

After calling into the base class to perform any processing it requires, the code then checks the _gameOver variable. If this is set to true, no movement is taking place within the game, so we can exit this function straight away.

We then check the FallDistance of the first of our two gems. As the two gems fall together, the FallDistance will always be identical for both of the player gems, so only one of these needs to be checked. If the value retrieved is 0 or less, we've reached the gem's target location, and we, therefore, need to work out what to do next.

The code then checks whether either gem has landed. If either gem is at the bottom of the board, or has another gem in the location below it, the landed variable is set to true to indicate this. If it finds that this variable has been set, two further functions are called: first MovePlayerGemsToBoard and then DropGems. The first of these moves the gems out of player control and into the board array; the second makes sure that if one of the gems has been left floating, it falls down as far as it can. We'll look at both these functions in a moment.

Note that even though we have detected that a gem has landed, we *don't* call the InitPlayerGems function here. We could do so, but there may be lots of activity within the gems on the board to take care of first: if any groups have formed, these will need to be removed and the positions of all the gems updated. We will create more player gems only once this is all finished.

If the earlier check determined that the gems have not yet landed, we move them a space lower on the board by adding 1 to their BoardYPos properties and update their FallDistance properties too so that visually they continue to fall smoothly.

The movement of the player gems has now been handled, but we need to do a little more work with regard to the gems already placed on the board. The code checks to see whether the player is currently in control of some gems by comparing _playerGems[0] with null. This will only be the case after the player gems have landed and been transferred on to the board. This is the indicator that we need to process updates for the board rather than for the player gems.

Before carrying on we call the GemsAreDropping function to see whether any of the gems on the board are currently falling. If they are, we need to let them finish before we process them any further.

Assuming all the gems have finished falling, we call the RemoveGemGroups function, another piece of code that we will look at shortly. RemoveGemGroups returns true if one or more gem groups was found on the board. This will potentially require the game to move further of the gems on the board, so in this case we do nothing more so that these gems can continue to fall downwards. Only once we find that there are no more groups of gems present do we then call into InitPlayerGems again. This will finally create a new pair of gems for the player to control.

The MovePlayerGemsToBoard function that gets called within Update has the job of transferring the player gems out of player control and into the _gameBoard array. This is actually done by creating two new gems on the board with colors matching those of the player gems and discarding the player gems, as shown in Listing 8–23.

Listing 8–23. *Transferring the Player-Controlled Gems to the Game Board*

```
/// <summary>
/// When the game determines that one of the player gems has landed,
/// this function will move the gems out of player control and place
/// them on to the game board.
/// </summary>
private void MovePlayerGemsToBoard()
{
    CObjGem gem;

    for (int i = 0; i < 2; i++)
    {
        // Create a new gem for the board with the color from the first player gem
        gem = new CObjGem(this, _playerGems[i].BoardXPos, _playerGems[i].BoardYPos,
                                        _playerGems[i].GemColor);
        // Set it as an "on the board" gem
        gem.GemType = CObjGem.GemTypes.OnTheBoard;
        // Put the gem object into the board array
        _gameBoard[gem.BoardXPos, gem.BoardYPos] = gem;
        // Add the gem to the game engine's GameObjects collection
        GameObjects.Add(gem);
```

```
        // Tell the player gem object to terminate itself.
        // This will remove it from the GameObjects collection but ensures
        // that it is properly re-rendered before disappearing
        _playerGems[i].Terminate = true;

        // Clear the reference to the gem so that we know there are no gems
        // under active player control at the moment
        _playerGems[i] = null;
    }
}
```

Once this function completes, both of the _playerGems array elements will be null. This fact is used by the Update code that we have just been looking at to tell that it needs to update the gems on the board rather than the player-controlled gems.

The next function used here that we've not yet examined is DropGems. This is called straight after transferring the player gems to the board. Its job is to ensure that all gems are at their lowest possible positions. If a gem has a space below it, this function will move the gem to the bottom of that space, ensuring that the whole board obeys the law of gravity.

There are two places where this function will need to be used. The first call, which you have already seen in the Update function, is when the player gems have landed. If the player gems are arranged horizontally, it is possible for one gem to land while the other has space below it. DropGems will move the floating gem downward until it too lands on something solid.

We will also use DropGems after a group of gems has been removed from the board. These removed gems will more than likely have been supporting other gems, so we will need to move all of these downward to fill in the space that has been left. You'll see this call being made shortly.

DropGems operates on a simple principal. It works across the board a column at a time from left to right and, within each column, from bottom to top. If it finds any location that is empty but for which the location above is occupied, it moves the gem above to the current location. When the entire board has been processed in this way, it checks to see whether any gems were actually moved. If so, the whole loop is repeated (this is so that gems that have to fall more than one location are moved all the way down rather than by just one row). This is illustrated in Figure 8–8.

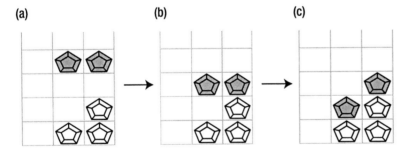

Figure 8–8. Dropping gems on the board to their lowest positions

Figure 8–8(a) shows the board in a state after a group has been removed. The two dark-colored gems have both been left floating on the board. Figure 8–8(b) shows the locations of the floating gems after a single pass through the loop in DropGems. Both of the gems have moved down one position, but the gem on the left has not yet landed. Because gems were moved, the loop is executed again, resulting in Figure

8–8(c). The gems are now in their final locations. The loop is executed one further time to ensure nothing else needs to move, after which it completes. The function is shown in Listing 8–24.

Listing 8–24. Dropping Gems on the Game Board to Their Lowest Possible Positions

```
/// <summary>
/// Scan the board looking for gems that have gaps below them. All of these gems
/// are updated so that they fall as far as they can.
/// </summary>
private void DropGems()
{
    bool gemMoved;

    do
    {
        // Clear the gem moved flag, no gems have been dropped within this iteration yet
        gemMoved = false;

        // Loop for each column of the board
        for (int x = 0; x < BOARD_GEMS_ACROSS; x++)
        {
            // Loop for each cell within the column.
            // Note that we loop from the bottom of the board upwards,
            // and that we don't include the top-most row (as there
            // are no gems above this to drop)
            for (int y = BOARD_GEMS_DOWN - 1; y > 0; y--)
            {
                // If this cell is empty and the one above it is not...
                if (_gameBoard[x, y] == null && _gameBoard[x, y - 1] != null)
                {
                    // ...then drop the gem in the cell above into this cell.
                    // First copy the object to the new array element and remove
                    // it from the original array element
                    _gameBoard[x, y] = _gameBoard[x, y - 1];
                    _gameBoard[x, y - 1] = null;
                    // Update the gem object's position
                    _gameBoard[x, y].BoardYPos = y;
                    // Indicate that it has an (additional) row to fall through
                    _gameBoard[x, y].FallDistance += 1;
                    // Remember that we have moved a gem
                    gemMoved = true;
                }
            }
        }
        // Keep looping around until no more gems movements are found.
    } while (gemMoved);
}
```

If we moved each gem on the screen directly from its start location to its end location, the game wouldn't look very nice. The presentation would be much better if each gem fell smoothly from its start position to its end position.

Fortunately, we can implement that very easily. We already have the FallDistance property in the CObjGem class, which stores how far the gem has to fall to reach its specified coordinate. We can use this to drop the gems smoothly into place. Each time we add 1 to the gem's BoardYPos, we also add 1 to its FallDistance (this is shown in Listing 8–24). The immediate effect of this is that the gem remains in exactly the same place on the screen, even though on the board it has actually been moved to its final position.

Now, we need a little extra code inside CObjGem to make the gem actually fall down. We already looked at its Update function in Listing 8–15 and skipped over the processing for OnTheBoard gems. We'll fill in the missing section now with the code in Listing 8–25.

Listing 8–25. Part of the Gem's Update Function, Updating the Position of OnTheBoard Gems

```
/// <summary>
/// Update the gem's position
/// </summary>
public override void Update()
{
    // Allow the base class to perform any processing it needs
    base.Update();

    switch (_gemType)
    {
        case GemTypes.NextGem:
            // [...] (see Listing 8-15)

        case GemTypes.OnTheBoard:
            // If we have some falling to do, apply gravity now
            if (_fallDistance > 0)
            {
                // Reduce the fall distance
                _fallDistance -= _fallSpeed;
                // Add to the fall speed to simulate gravity
                _fallSpeed += 0.025f;

                // Have we landed?
                if (_fallDistance < 0)
                {
                    // Yes, so ensure we don't pass our landing point,
                    // and cancel any further falling
                    _fallDistance = 0;
                    _fallSpeed = 0;

                }
            }
            break;

        case GemTypes.PlayerControlled:
            // [...](see Listing 8-15)
    }
}
```

The code here uses the same idea that we have used in several other examples already. It simulates gravity by adding a speed value to the object's position and then increasing the speed. In this instance, we store the speed in the _fallSpeed variable and subtract it from the _fallDistance, reducing this toward 0, at which point the gem lands at its destination. When _fallDistance reaches or passes 0, we set it back to 0 and set _fallSpeed to 0 too, to ensure that the gem is positioned correctly. Then no further movement takes place.

Now, our gems smoothly fall whenever they need to. The rest of the game waits until they have finished before it continues; we need to do this to ensure that we have removed all the groups that will form (potentially over multiple iterations of groups forming and being removed). How can we tell if the gems have finished falling?

This question is answered by the GemsAreDropping function. We can tell if a gem is dropping by simply checking its FallDistance property. If this is greater than 0, the gem is falling. GemsAreDropping returns true if any gem on the board is in this state or false if FallDistance is 0 for every gem, as shown in Listing 8–26.

Listing 8–26. Checking to See Whether All Gems on the Board Have Finished Dropping to Their Final Locations

```
/// <summary>
/// Determines whether any of the gems contained within the board and currently
/// dropping towards their resting positions. Returns true if any gem is still
/// falling, or false once all gems on the board have landed.
/// </summary>
private bool GemsAreDropping
{
    get
    {
        // Loop for each column of the board
        for (int x = 0; x < BOARD_GEMS_ACROSS; x++)
        {
            // Loop for each cell within the column.
            for (int y = 0; y < BOARD_GEMS_DOWN; y++)
            {
                // Is there a gem in this location?
                if (_gameBoard[x, y] != null)
                {
                    // Is the gem dropping?
                    if (_gameBoard[x, y].FallDistance > 0)
                    {
                        // This gem is dropping so return true
                        return true;
                    }
                }
            }
        }

        // None of the gems are dropping so return false
        return false;
    }
}
```

As you saw in Listing 8–22, if no player gems are active, the game's Update function will continuously check to see whether the board's gems are falling. As soon as it detects that all gems have landed, it will look for further groups to remove. If groups are found, they are removed, and the DropGems function is called once again to move everything to where it needs to go.

Once everything is finally settled and no more groups are formed, we make the call to InitPlayerGems so that the next gems appear for the player to move.

Adding Player Control

The game is starting to come together and meet the design that we set out for it. An important aspect that is still missing however is the ability for the player to control the gems.

There are two sides to adding this control: we need functions within the game class that will cause the player gems to move, and we need code in the user interface that calls into those functions. Let's look at the game class functions first.

Moving the Gems to the Side

The first type of movement that the player can request is sideways movement. Before we can move the player's gems to the side, we first need to ensure that the locations to which they would be moved are empty—attempting to move into existing gems is now allowed. We also need to ensure that the gems are not moving off the side of the game board.

To help us check the availability of the new locations, we use a function called GetGemColor. We provide it with an x and a y coordinate within the board, and it will look at the board location to see what is present. We will get back either a value of GEMCOLOR_NONE if the specified location is empty, GEMCOLOR_OUTOFBOUNDS if the location is outside of the board area (e.g., an x coordinate of –1), or the color of the gem at the location.

This function is handy, because it saves us having to check whether the coordinates we will be moving to are actually valid. We can simply pass the coordinate for each of the player gems and make sure we get back GEMCOLOR_NONE. Any other value means that we are unable to complete the requested movement. GetGemColor is shown in Listing 8–27.

Listing 8–27. Finding the Contents of the Board at Any Specified Board Coordinate

```
// The GetGemColor can return some special values to indicate
// that the requested element is empty or off the edge of the board.
public const int GEMCOLOR_NONE = -1;
public const int GEMCOLOR_OUTOFBOUNDS = -2;

[...]

/// <summary>
/// Determine the color of gem on the board at the specified location.
/// </summary>
/// <param name="x">The x coordinate to check</param>
/// <param name="y">The y coordinate to check</param>
/// <returns>Returns GEMCOLOR_NONE if the location is empty,
/// GEMCOLOR_OUTOFBOUNDS if it is out-of-bounds, otherwise the
/// gem color</returns>
private int GetGemColor(int x, int y)
{
    // Is the specified location valid?
    if (x < 0 || x >= BOARD_GEMS_ACROSS || y < 0 || y >= BOARD_GEMS_DOWN)
    {
        // This cell is out of bounds, so return the out of bounds value
        return GEMCOLOR_OUTOFBOUNDS;
    }

    // Is there a gem at the specified location?
    if (_gameBoard[x, y] == null)
```

```
    {
        // No, so return the "no gem" value
        return GEMCOLOR_NONE;
    }

    // Return the color of gem at the specified location
    return _gameBoard[x, y].GemColor;
}
```

With this function at our disposal, now we can process the request to move the player gems. This is handled within the MovePlayerGems function, shown in Listing 8–28.

Listing 8–28. Moving the Player's Gems to the Side

```
/// <summary>
/// Move the player's gems left or right
/// </summary>
/// <param name="direction">-1 for left, 1 for right</param>
public void MovePlayerGems(int direction)
{
    // Don't allow any interaction if the game is finished or paused
    if (_gameOver || _paused) return;
    // Make sure we have some player gems in action
    if (_playerGems[0] == null) return;

    // Make sure direction only contains a value of -1 or 1.
    if (direction < 0) direction = -1;
    if (direction >= 0) direction = 1;

    // Make sure the board is clear to the left...
    if (GetGemColor(_playerGems[0].BoardXPos + direction, _playerGems[0].BoardYPos)
                == GEMCOLOR_NONE
        && GetGemColor(_playerGems[1].BoardXPos + direction, _playerGems[1].BoardYPos)
                == GEMCOLOR_NONE)
    {
        // The board is empty in the requested direction so move the player gems
        _playerGems[0].BoardXPos += direction;
        _playerGems[1].BoardXPos += direction;
    }
}
```

MovePlayerGems expects a value of –1 to be passed to move left and 1 to move right. After checking that the game is not finished and that player gems are currently active, it ensures that the direction parameter definitely does contain one of these two values.

The GetGemColor function is then called, once for each of the player gems, to ensure that when the direction offset is added to the current position, the resulting board element is GEMCOLOR_NONE, which will only be returned for empty elements. If the element is already occupied or is off the edge of the board, different values will be returned.

Assuming both gems are able to move in the specified direction, the direction value is added to their BoardXPos values in order to actually move them.

Rotating the Gems

The next movement type is rotation. The player is able to rotate the position of one gem around the other, as shown back in Figure 8–1. We'll implement this by rotating _playerGems[1] around _playerGems[0]. _playerGems[0] will, therefore, always remain stationary during a rotation.

To simplify the rotation, an enumeration named gemPosition is created with each of the possible positions that the rotating gem may occupy relative to the static gem. This enumeration is shown in Listing 8–29.

Listing 8–29. The gemPosition Enumeration

```
/// <summary>
/// An enumeration to allow us to identify the location of the "rotating" gem
/// relative to the "static" gem around which it rotates.
/// </summary>
private enum gemPosition
{
    Above,
    Left,
    Below,
    Right
};
```

Note that the enumeration items are specified in clockwise order. If we can determine which position the rotating gem currently occupies relative to the static gem, we can then move to the next gem enumeration value to rotate clockwise or the previous value to move counterclockwise. In both cases, if we move past the first or last enumeration value, we will loop back to the other end.

The code to perform this is contained within the RotatePlayerGems function, shown in Listing 8–30.

Listing 8–30. Rotating the Player's Gems

```
/// <summary>
/// Rotate the player's gems
/// </summary>
/// <param name="clockwise">true to rotate clockwise, false for anti-clockwise</param>
public void RotatePlayerGems(bool clockwise)
{
    gemPosition position = gemPosition.Above;
    int newXPos;
    int newYPos;

    // Don't allow any interaction if the game is finished or paused
    if (_gameOver || _paused) return;
    // Make sure we have some player gems in action
    if (_playerGems[0] == null) return;

    // We will rotate gem[1] around gem[0], leaving the position of gem[0] unchanged
    // Determine the current position of gem[1] relative to gem[0].
    if (_playerGems[1].BoardYPos > _playerGems[0].BoardYPos)
                        position = gemPosition.Below;
    if (_playerGems[1].BoardYPos < _playerGems[0].BoardYPos)
                        position = gemPosition.Above;
    if (_playerGems[1].BoardXPos > _playerGems[0].BoardXPos)
```

```
                              position = gemPosition.Right;
        if (_playerGems[1].BoardXPos < _playerGems[0].BoardXPos)
                              position = gemPosition.Left;

        // Add to the position to rotate the gem
        position += (clockwise ? 1 : -1);
        // Loop around if we have gone out of bounds
        if (position > gemPosition.Left) position = gemPosition.Above;
        if (position < gemPosition.Above) position = gemPosition.Left;

        // Determine the new gem location. Start at the static gem's location...
        newXPos = _playerGems[0].BoardXPos;
        newYPos = _playerGems[0].BoardYPos;
        // And apply an offset based upon the rotating gem's position
        switch (position)
        {
            case gemPosition.Above:
                newYPos -= 1;
                break;
            case gemPosition.Below:
                newYPos += 1;
                break;
            case gemPosition.Left:
                newXPos -= 1;
                break;
            case gemPosition.Right:
                newXPos += 1;
                break;
        }

        // Is the newly requested gem position valid and unoccupied?
        if (GetGemColor(newXPos, newYPos) == GEMCOLOR_NONE)
        {
            // It is, so the rotation is OK to proceed.
            // Set the new position of the rotated gem
            _playerGems[1].BoardXPos = newXPos;
            _playerGems[1].BoardYPos = newYPos;
        }
    }
}
```

After checking once again that the game has not finished and player gems are active, the code first determines the current position of the rotating gem relative to the static gem. The appropriate enumeration value is placed into the position variable.

Once this is determined, we either add 1 to this value to rotate clockwise or subtract 1 to rotate counterclockwise. This calculation will give us the position that the rotating gem needs to be moved into relative to the static gem. If we pass the final enumeration value (gemPosition.Left) we loop back to the first value (gemPosition.Above). Similarly, if we move back past the first enumeration value, we loop back to the last.

Now that we know where we want to put the rotating gem, we work out its location by first looking at that of the static gem and then adding to the x or y coordinate based on the direction in our position variable. Once the location has been determined, we use the GetGemColor function once again to ensure that the new position is valid and unoccupied. If this turns out to be the case, the rotating gem's position is updated to the location we have calculated.

Quickly Dropping the Gems

Once the player has worked out where the gems are to go, we provide an option to quickly move them down the game board until they land. Without this, waiting for the gems to land can be very tedious: the player just wants to get on with the next piece rather than waiting aimlessly for this one to finish moving.

We therefore provide a key that can be pressed to provide this acceleration. When the key is held down, the player gems will move quickly. When it is released, they will return to normal speed.

The implementation of this is very simple. A function called DropQuickly is added to the game; it accepts a parameter indicating whether to activate or remove the fast movement of the gems. After checking that the game is not finished and the player gems are active, DropQuickly simply passes the parameter value to a new CObjGem property, IsDroppingQuickly. The function is shown in Listing 8–31.

Listing 8–31. Allowing the Player to Drop Gems More Quickly

```
/// <summary>
/// Sets a value indicating whether the player gems are to drop
/// 'quickly' (i.e., the player is pressing the Down button to speed their descent).
/// </summary>
public void DropQuickly(bool beQuick)
{
    // Don't allow any interaction if the game is finished or paused
    if (_gameOver || _paused) return;
    // Make sure we have some player gems in action
    if (_playerGems[0] == null) return;

    // Tell the gems how we want them to move
    _playerGems[0].IsDroppingQuickly = beQuick;
    _playerGems[1].IsDroppingQuickly = beQuick;
}
```

CObjGem.IsDroppingQuickly is implemented as a simple bool property. We use this within the gem's Update method to force faster movement when the property is set, as shown in Listing 8–32.

Listing 8–32. Making the Player Gem Move Faster If Its IsDroppingQuickly Property Is true

```
/// <summary>
/// Update the gem's position
/// </summary>
public override void Update()
{
    // Allow the base class to perform any processing it needs
    base.Update();

    switch (_gemType)
    {
        case GemTypes.NextGem:
            // [...] (see Listing 8-15)

        case GemTypes.OnTheBoard:
            // [...] (see Listing 8-25)

        case GemTypes.PlayerControlled:
            // This gem is under player control so allow it to gently drop towards the
```

```
        // bottom of the board.
        // We'll let the game itself work out how to deal with it landing, etc.

        // Are we dropping quickly or at normal speed?
        if (_isFallingQuickly)
        {
            // Quickly, subtract a fairly fast constant value from _fallDistance.
            _fallDistance -= 0.4f;
        }
        else
        {
            // Normal speed, subtract the gem's _fallSpeed from _fallDistance.
            _fallDistance -= _fallSpeed;
        }
        break;
    }
}
```

When the gem's _isFallingQuickly variable is true, we subtract a fixed value (0.4) from its _fallDistance to move it fairly rapidly. Otherwise, we subtract _fallSpeed to observe the gem's natural vertical speed.

Implementing Control in the User Interface

On devices with d-pads, calling the game class's methods is very easy. We simply hook into the form's KeyDown and KeyUp events, calling the movement functions as required based on the key that has been pressed. The code required for this is in Listing 8–33.

Listing 8–33. Controlling the Player Gems Using a D-pad

```
/// <summary>
/// Process the player pressing a key
/// </summary>
private void GameForm_KeyDown(object sender, KeyEventArgs e)
{
    switch (e.KeyCode)
    {
        case Keys.Up:
            // Rotate the gems when Up is pressed
            _game.RotatePlayerGems(true);
            break;
        case Keys.Left:
            // Move to the left with Left is pressed
            _game.MovePlayerGems(-1);
            break;
        case Keys.Right:
            // Move to the right with Left is pressed
            _game.MovePlayerGems(1);
            break;
        case Keys.Down:
            // Set the DropQuickly flag when down is pressed
            _game.DropQuickly(true);
            break;
```

```
        }
    }

    /// <summary>
    /// Process the user releasing a key
    /// </summary>
    private void GameForm_KeyUp(object sender, KeyEventArgs e)
    {
        switch (e.KeyCode)
        {
            case Keys.Down:
                // Clear the DropQuickly flag to return the gem to its normal speed
                _game.DropQuickly(false);
                break;
        }
    }
```

▨ **NOTE** The game uses the KeyDown and KeyUp events here rather than GetAsyncKeyState. As noted in Chapter 6, this input mechanism's key repeat delay is advantageous for this style of game.

The touch screen control code is very similar. The code works out which horizontal section of the screen was touched (top, middle ,or bottom) and which side of the screen (left or right). The same game functions are called in the MouseDown event based on the results of these checks. In MouseUp, the code simply calls the _game.DropQuickly(false) to cancel any quick dropping that is in effect. The two event handlers are shown in Listing 8–34.

Listing 8–34. Controlling the Player Gems Using a Touch Screen

```
    /// <summary>
    /// Process the player making contact with the screen
    /// </summary>
    private void GameForm_MouseDown(object sender, MouseEventArgs e)
    {
        // Which segment of the screen has the user pressed in?
        // - The top third will be used for rotating the piece
        // - The middle third will be used for moving the piece left and right
        // - The bottom third will be used to drop the piece quickly

        switch ((int)(e.Y * 3 / this.ClientRectangle.Height))
        {
            case 0:
                // Top third, so we will deal with rotating the player's gems
                // Did the user tap the left or right side of the window?
                if (e.X < this.ClientRectangle.Width / 2)
                {
                    // Left side, rotate anticlockwise
                    _game.RotatePlayerGems(false);
                }
```

```
            else
            {
                // Right side, rotate clockwise
                _game.RotatePlayerGems(true);
            }
            break;

        case 1:
            // Middle third, so we will deal with moving the player's gems
            // Did the user tap the left or right side of the window?
            if (e.X < this.ClientRectangle.Width / 2)
            {
                // Left side, move left
                _game.MovePlayerGems(-1);
            }
            else
            {
                // Right side, move right
                _game.MovePlayerGems(1);
            }
            break;

        case 2:
            // Bottom third, so we will deal with dropping the gem more quickly
            _game.DropQuickly(true);
            break;

    }

}

/// <summary>
/// Process the player releasing contact with the screen.
/// </summary>
private void GameForm_MouseUp(object sender, MouseEventArgs e)
{
    // Cancel any "drop quickly" that may be in operation
    _game.DropQuickly(false);
}
```

Removing Gems from the Board

The game is functionally nearly complete now. Gems appear under player control, can be fully manipulated, and interact with existing gems on the board. All that is missing is to detect the gems that need to be removed from the game board as the game progresses.

The function with overall responsibility for this is the RemoveGems function. It looks after the process of looking for gems to be suitable for removal, and its code can be seen in Listing 8–35.

Listing 8–35. Removing Gems from the Game Board

```
/// <summary>
/// Locate and remove gems that are ready to be removed from the board.
```

```
/// Add to the player's score as appropriate.
/// </summary>
/// <returns>Returns true if any gems were removed, false if not.</returns>
private bool RemoveGems()
{
    bool gemsRemoved = false;

    // See if we can remove any linked groups of gems.
    gemsRemoved = RemoveGemGroups();

    // See if we can remove any rainbow gems
    gemsRemoved |= RemoveRainbowGems();

    // If any gems were removed then instruct those remaining gems to fall
    // into their lowest positions.
    if (gemsRemoved)
    {
        // Drop any gems that are now floating in space
        DropGems();
        // Increase the multiplier in case any more groups are formed
        _scoreMultiplier += 1;
        // Update the form to show the player's new score
        UpdateForm();
    }

    // Return a value indicating whether anything happened
    return gemsRemoved;
}
```

Two different scenarios can result in gems being removed: a group of five or more connected gems is formed, or a rainbow gem lands. The code calls into a function for each of these scenarios and stores true in the gemsRemoved variable if either function indicates that it actually removed some gems. We'll look at these two functions in a moment.

If gems were removed, we once again call DropGems so that any gems that are now floating fall downward. We also increase the _scoreMultiplier variable by 1. This variable allows second- and third-generation groups to score double and triple points and so on for each subsequent generation of gem groups. _scoreMultiplier is set back to 1 in the InitPlayerGems function and is used to multiply up the score awarded for removing gem groups in the RemoveGemGroups function.

With everything else done, the UpdateForm function is called to update the player's score display on the game form.

Removing Gem Groups

Let's look at how the groups of connected gems are found and removed. The RemoveGemGroups function takes care of this, as shown in Listing 8–36.

Listing 8–36. Removing Groups of Connected Gems from the Board

```
/// <summary>
/// Look for groups of connected gems and remove them.
/// </summary>
/// <returns>Returns true if gems were removed, false if not.</returns>
```

```
private bool RemoveGemGroups()
{
    List<Point> connectedGems;
    Rectangle connectedRect;
    bool gemsRemoved = false;
    int groupScore;

    // Loop for each gem on the board
    for (int x = 0; x < BOARD_GEMS_ACROSS; x++)
    {
        for (int y = 0; y < BOARD_GEMS_DOWN; y++)
        {
            // Is there a gem here?
            if (_gameBoard[x, y] != null)
            {
                // Initialize a list to store the connected gem positions
                connectedGems = new List<Point>();
                // See if we have a group at this location
                RemoveGemGroups_FindGroup(x, y, connectedGems);
                // Is the group large enough?
                if (connectedGems.Count >= 5)
                {
                    // Remove all of the gems within the group.
                    // Retrieve a rectangle whose dimensions encompass the removed group
                    // (The rectangle will be in board coordinates, not in pixels)
                    connectedRect = RemoveGemGroups_RemoveGroup(connectedGems);
                    // Indicate that gems have been removed from the board
                    gemsRemoved = true;
                    // Add to the player's score
                    groupScore = connectedGems.Count * 10;
                    _playerScore += groupScore * _scoreMultiplier;
                    // Add a score object so that the score "floats" up from the removed
                    // group. Use the rectangle that we got back earlier to position
                    // it in the position that the group had occupied.
                    AddScoreObject(
                            (float)(connectedRect.Left + connectedRect.Right) / 2,
                            (float)(connectedRect.Top + connectedRect.Bottom) / 2,
                            groupScore, _scoreMultiplier);
                }
            }
        }
    }

    return gemsRemoved;
}
```

The function loops through each element in the board array, and for each gem it finds, it calls the RemoveGemGroups_FindGroup function. It passes as parameters the board coordinate that is being scanned and an empty list of Point objects. The called function will count how many gems of the same type are in the group at the provided location and return each of their board positions within the list.

If the list contains five or more points, the group is large enough to be removed. The RemoveGemGroups_RemoveGroup function will eliminate all of the gems and returns a Rectangle that encompasses the board locations that the group occupied. We'll use this in a moment.

Now, we can add some points to the player's score. Ten points are awarded for each gem removed, but we also multiply by the _scoreMultiplier variable we discussed earlier, so stacked gem groups score more points for each subsequent generation.

To clarify exactly how many points the player has gained, we also create a score object, a number displayed on the screen that floats away from the removed group showing how many points the player earned. You'll see the implementation of this object in the "Creating the Score Objects" section later on, but for now, we will call a function called AddScoreObject, passing in the x and y position (again as a board coordinate) at which the object should be displayed. We calculate this by finding the midpoint between the left and right and the top and bottom edges of the Rectangle we retrieved from RemoveGemGroups_RemoveGroup.

Let's look now at the RemoveGemGroups_FindGroup function, in Listing 8–37.

Listing 8–37. Finding All the Gems in a Group

```
/// <summary>
/// Finds all gems on the board connected to the one specified in the x and y parameters
/// </summary>
/// <param name="x">The x position on the board of a gem within a possible group</param>
/// <param name="y">The y position on the board of a gem within a possible group</param>
/// <param name="gemGroup">An empty List of Points into which all connected gem
/// positions will be added</param>
private void RemoveGemGroups_FindGroup(int x, int y, List<Point> gemGroup)
{
    int gemColor;

    // Do we already have an item at this position in the groupGems list?
    foreach (Point pt in gemGroup)
    {
        if (pt.X == x && pt.Y == y)
        {
            // The gem at this position is already present so don't add it again.
            return;
        }
    }

    // Add this gem to the list
    gemGroup.Add(new Point(x, y));

    // Read the color of gem at this location
    gemColor = _gameBoard[x, y].GemColor;

    // Are any of the connected gems of the same color?
    // If so, recurse into RemoveGems_RemoveGroup and add their gems to the group.
    if (GetGemColor(x + 1, y) == gemColor)
                        RemoveGemGroups_FindGroup(x + 1, y, gemGroup);
    if (GetGemColor(x - 1, y) == gemColor)
                        RemoveGemGroups_FindGroup(x - 1, y, gemGroup);
    if (GetGemColor(x, y + 1) == gemColor)
                        RemoveGemGroups_FindGroup(x, y + 1, gemGroup);
    if (GetGemColor(x, y - 1) == gemColor)
                        RemoveGemGroups_FindGroup(x, y - 1, gemGroup);
}
```

This code uses a recursive algorithm to find the extent of each group. Throughout the whole operation, the List<Point> object gemGroup is passed. The first thing we do is check that the coordinate we're looking at is not present in the list. If it is, we've already included it within the gem group, so we don't need to look at it again. When the function is called for the first time for a potential group, this list will be empty, so we'll always continue past here. The location of the current gem is then added to the gemGroup list so that we know it has now been examined.

Having got this far, we check the gems above, below, to the left, and to the right of the current gem. Every time we find that the connected gem is of the same color, we call into RemoveGemGroups_FindGroup again to continue scanning the group in that direction.

Once the entire group has been exhausted, the procedure will finish its recursion and return back to the calling procedure. The locations of all the connected gems will be stored in the gemGroup list.

Actually removing the gems is very straightforward, as shown in Listing 8–38.

Listing 8–38. Removing All the Gems in a Gem Group

```
/// <summary>
/// Remove all of the gems in the provided list of Points
/// </summary>
/// <param name="gemGroup">A list of Points, each of which contains the coordinate of
/// one of the gems to be removed</param>
/// <returns>Returns a rectangle whose bounds encompass the group removed.</returns>
private Rectangle RemoveGemGroups_RemoveGroup(List<Point> gemGroup)
{
    int groupLeft, groupTop, groupRight, groupBottom;

    // Set the group boundaries to match the position of the first gem in the group
    groupLeft = gemGroup[0].X;
    groupTop = gemGroup[0].Y;
    groupRight = gemGroup[0].X;
    groupBottom = gemGroup[0].Y;

    // Do we already have an item at this position in the groupGems list?
    foreach (Point pt in gemGroup)
    {
        // Instruct this gem to terminate and then remove it from the board
        _gameBoard[pt.X, pt.Y].Terminate = true;
        _gameBoard[pt.X, pt.Y] = null;

        // If this position is outside of our group boundary, extend the boundary
        if (pt.X < groupLeft) groupLeft = pt.X;
        if (pt.X > groupRight) groupRight = pt.X;
        if (pt.Y < groupTop) groupTop = pt.Y;
        if (pt.Y > groupBottom) groupBottom = pt.Y;
    }

    // Return a rectangle whose size encompasses the group boundary
    return Rectangle.FromLTRB(groupLeft, groupTop, groupRight, groupBottom);
}
```

We are passed the same gemGroup list that was built when the group was identified, and each gem within it is simply terminated and removed from the board.

Along the way, we maintain the positions of the left, right, top, and bottom edges of the group. These are initialized to all contain the position of the first gem in the list, and every subsequent gem will extend the positions if they are found to lie outside the area we have already seen. Once the loop is complete, these are built into a Rectangle using the static Rectangle.FromLTRB (i.e., the "from left, top, right, bottom") function. This is returned to the calling procedure, which uses it to position the score object over the top of the removed group.

Removing Rainbow Gems

Processing for the rainbow gems is much easier. The RemoveRainbowGems function is shown in Listing 8–39.

Listing 8–39. Removing Rainbow Gems

```
/// <summary>
/// Remove any rainbow gems and all gems of the type that they have landed on.
/// </summary>
/// <returns>Returns true if gems were removed, false if not.</returns>
private bool RemoveRainbowGems()
{
    bool gemsRemoved = false;
    int gemColor;

    // Now look for landed rainbow gems. These need to be removed, and we'll
    // also remove any matching gems of the color found beneath them.
    // Loop for each gem on the board
    for (int x = 0; x < BOARD_GEMS_ACROSS; x++)
    {
        for (int y = 0; y < BOARD_GEMS_DOWN; y++)
        {
            // Is this a rainbow gem?
            if (_gameBoard[x, y] != null &&
                        _gameBoard[x, y].GemColor == GEMCOLOR_RAINBOW)
            {
                // It is, so remove the gem from the game...
                _gameBoard[x, y].Terminate = true;
                _gameBoard[x, y] = null;
                // Find the color of gem in the location below this one
                gemColor = GetGemColor(x, y + 1);
                // Is this a valid gem?
                if (gemColor >= 0)
                {
                    // Yes, so remove all gems of this color
                    RemoveGemGroups_RemoveColor(gemColor);
                }
                // Gems were removed -- the rainbow gem itself was at the very least
                gemsRemoved = true;
            }
        }
    }

    return gemsRemoved;
}
```

The code once again makes a simple loop across the board, looking for gems whose color is GEMCOLOR_RAINBOW. Each one that is found is terminated and removed from the board. The color of the gem directly below the rainbow gem position is then retrieved, and assuming that an actual gem was found (and not an out of bounds location), the RemoveGemGroups_RemoveColor function is called to eliminate all gems of that color. All gems of the color the rainbow gem landed upon are therefore removed.

RemoveGemGroups_RemoveColor contains another simple loop across the board, looking for all and removing all gems of the specified color, as shown in Listing 8–40.

Listing 8–40. Removing All of the Gems Eliminated by the Rainbow Gem

```
/// <summary>
/// Remove all of the gems of the specified color from the board.
/// This is used to implement the Rainbow gem.
/// </summary>
/// <param name="gemColor">The color of gem to be removed</param>
private int RemoveGemGroups_RemoveColor(int gemColor)
{
    int x,y;
    int removed = 0;

    for (x = 0; x < BOARD_GEMS_ACROSS; x++)
    {
        for (y = 0; y < BOARD_GEMS_DOWN; y++)
        {
            // Does this gem match the specified color?
            if (GetGemColor(x, y) == gemColor)
            {
                // It does, so remove the gem from the game...
                _gameBoard[x, y].Terminate = true;
                _gameBoard[x, y] = null;
                removed += 1;
            }
        }
    }

    // Return the number of gems we removed
    return removed;
}
```

Creating Score Objects

As mentioned in the Removing Gem Groups section, each group that is removed is replaced with a score indicator that floats off up the screen to highlight the points awarded. These are implemented using our final class, another game object class named CObjScore.

The implementation of this is very straightforward. It maintains _boardXPos and _boardYPos variables to store its location in board coordinates, just like the CObjGem class. It also keeps track of the text being displayed in the _scoreText variable and the distance that it has floated upward from its initial position in the _floatDistance variable.

All of these are initialized in the class constructor. The constructor requires and board x and y positions, the basic score, and the multiplier to be provided. The variables are all then given their values, with _scoreText being set to just the score value if the multiplier is 1 (e.g., 50) or the score and multiple values if the multiplier is greater than 1 (e.g., 50 × 2). The object's Width and Height are calculated using the Graphics.MeasureString function that we looked at back in Chapter 3. The constructor and class variables are shown in Listing 8–41.

Listing 8–41. Initializing the CObjScore Object

```
// The x and y position (measured in game units) within the game board
private float _boardXPos = 0;
private float _boardYPos = 0;
// The text to display within the score object
private String _scoreText;
// The distance (in board units) that we have floated up from our original position
private float _floatDistance = 0;

/// <summary>
/// Constructor
/// </summary>
/// <param name="gameEngine">The GameEngine object instance</param>
/// <param name="boardXPos">The x position for the score</param>
/// <param name="boardYPos">The y position for the score</param>
/// <param name="score">The score that was achieved</param>
/// <param name="multiplier">The score multiplier</param>
public CObjScore(CGemDropsGame gameEngine, float boardXPos, float boardYPos,
                                            int score, int multiplier)
    : base(gameEngine)
{
    SizeF textSize;

    // Store a reference to the game engine as its derived type
    _myGameEngine = gameEngine;

    // Store the parameter values
    _boardXPos = boardXPos;
    _boardYPos = boardYPos;

    // Store the score text
    if (multiplier == 1)
    {
        _scoreText = score.ToString();
    }
    else
    {
        _scoreText = score.ToString() + " x " + multiplier.ToString();
    }

    // Determine the pixel size of the supplied text
    using (Graphics g = _myGameEngine.GameForm.CreateGraphics())
    {
        textSize = g.MeasureString(_scoreText, _myGameEngine.GameForm.Font);
    }
    // Set the game object's dimensions
    Width = (int)(textSize.Width * 1.2f);
    Height = (int)(textSize.Height * 1.2f);
}
```

To render the score, we just call the Graphics.DrawString function. To update it, we add a small amount to the _floatDistance variable, causing it to move upwards on the screen. Once the _floatDistance value reaches 2, the object is terminated so that it disappears after a brief period. These two procedures are shown in Listing 8–42.

Listing 8–42. Rendering and Updating the CObjScore Object

```
/// <summary>
/// Render the object to the screen
/// </summary>
public override void Render(Graphics gfx, float interpFactor)
{
    base.Render(gfx, interpFactor);

    // Create a brush to write our text with
    using (Brush br = new SolidBrush(Color.White))
    {
        // Render the text at the appropriate location
        gfx.DrawString(_scoreText, _myGameEngine.GameForm.Font, br,
            new RectangleF((float)XPos, (float)YPos, (float)Width, (float)Height));
    }
}

/// <summary>
/// Move the object
/// </summary>
public override void Update()
{
    // Allow the base class to perform any processing it needs
    base.Update();

    // Float upwards
    _floatDistance += 0.02f;

    // If we have floated far enough then terminate the object
    if (_floatDistance >= 2)
    {
        Terminate = true;
    }
}
```

Finally, the XPos and YPos properties are overridden just as they were for CObjGem to calculate the on-screen position for the score. When calculating the x position, half the Width of the object is subtracted from the calculated location to center the score at the specified location. When calculating the y position, the _floatDistance value is subtracted from the calculated position to make the score value actually move. These properties are shown in Listing 8–43.

Listing 8–43. Rendering and Updating the CObjScore Object

```
/// <summary>
/// Override the XPos property to calculate our actual position on demand
/// </summary>
public override float XPos
```

223

```
{
    get
    {
        return _myGameEngine.BoardLeft + (_boardXPos*_myGameEngine.GemWidth) - Width/2;
    }
}

/// <summary>
/// Override the YPos property to calculate our actual position on demand
/// </summary>
public override float YPos
{
    get
    {
        return _myGameEngine.BoardTop +
                        ((_boardYPos - _floatDistance) * _myGameEngine.GemHeight);
    }
}
```

Finishing Up

We've looked at a substantial amount of code and functionality here for what essentially forms a simple game. It takes a lot of effort to finish a game, and the steps we've looked at here are still not quite complete. Additional code is still required for implementing music, sound effects, menus, and a variety of other small tasks.

These items are all fairly trivial to implement, so the details of these aren't included in this chapter. They are all present in the GemDrops code in the accompanying download, however. Please do spend some time with this code, and familiarize yourself with how it all fits together.

Feel free to tweak the game play and see how it feels. Here are some things that you might want to try:

- Change the size of the board so that it's different from the 7 × 15 board used in the original source code. After simply changing the BOARD_GEMS_ACROSS and BOARD_GEMS_DOWN constants, observe how the entire game readjusts to fit the new coordinates without any other changes needing to be made.

- Change the speed at which the gems drop into the board.

- Change the number of gems required in order for a group to be removed. Values greater than 5 can make for a much more difficult game.

Hopefully seeing all of the techniques and ideas that we've discussed so far in the book brought together into a working example like this helps to show you the potential for Windows Mobile games and inspires you to begin thinking about and writing the design briefs for the games that you want to write yourself.

■■■

CHAPTER 9

Common Game Components

There are many different styles and varieties of games, and they can be diverse in the ways that they play and function. Some game features are useful in many different games though, and in this chapter, we'll examine some useful pieces of functionality that fall into this category. These game components will be created in such a way as to be easily reusable so that they can be quickly and easily dropped into any game that would benefit from them.

The components that we will create are as follows:

- A settings class, allowing us to easily set and retrieve configuration values and save these to files so that they can be retrieved the next time the game is executed

- A message box replacement that resolves some problems with the .NET CF `MessageBox`

- A high score table, providing a very easy mechanism for adding and displaying scores that the player has achieved

- An About screen, with a very simple interface to allow information about the game to be presented to the player

Each of these components will be created within the game engine and can be easily accessed by calling into the methods of the appropriate class.

Let's take a look at what each of these components does in more detail, how they are used, and how they work internally. The internal workings are only discussed fairly briefly here, as these are intended as end user components but are described in case you wish to make any changes to how they work or to lift any of the code out for use in other projects. The full source code is, of course, available in the `GameEngine` project in the accompanying download.

Managing Game Settings

Most games and applications will want to offer the user control over how some of the features of the program function. In a game, these will include things such as settings for the game itself (difficulty level and different game modes), settings for the game environment (sound effect and music volume levels and graphic options) or settings that are controlled by the application itself (such as remembering the date the game was last played or the name that the player last entered into a high score table).

There is nothing particularly difficult about managing this information, but as with everything else we have done with the game engine, our objective is to make this as simple to manage as possible. To look after all of this for us, we will add a new class, `CSettings`, to the game engine project.

Using the Settings Class

An instance of CSettings is accessed using the CGameEngineBase class's Settings property. We use this instance for all interaction with the game settings rather than creating separate instances within the game. That way, we ensure that all parts of the game see the same settings without having to pass instance of the class around between functions.

The first thing that the game can choose to do is set the filename within which the settings will be loaded and saved, which is accessed via the FileName property. This can be either a fully qualified path and filename, or just a filename with no path specified (in which case, the settings will be stored in the same directory as the game engine DLL). If a path is specified, the application must ensure that the path is for a valid directory. If no filename is specified at all, the class defaults to using a name of Settings.dat in the game engine's directory.

Once the settings file has been identified, the LoadSettings method can be called to retrieve any previously stored settings and store them in the object. If the settings file doesn't exist (for example, if the game is being launched for the first time), LoadSettings will return without doing anything; this is not considered an error.

Once the settings are initialized, the game can, at any stage, set or retrieve a setting value using the SetValue or GetValue methods. A number of different overloads of these two functions are provided for different datatypes, with versions available for string, int, float, bool, and DateTime types. Internally these are all stored as strings, but the overloads ensure that the values are encoded and decoded properly such that this internal storage mechanism is transparent to the calling code.

Whenever a value is retrieved using one of the GetValue methods, a DefaultValue parameter is provided. This serves two purposes. First, it allows for a sensible value to be returned if the requested setting is unknown and doesn't exist within the object. This simplifies the use of the class as shown in Listing 9–1. If we try to retrieve the sound effects volume level and it hasn't already been set, we default it to 100 so that its initial setting is at full volume, even though no setting value actually exists within the object.

Listing 9–1. Retrieving a Setting Value from the CSettings Object

```
int volumeLevel;

// Retrieve the volume level from the game settings
volumeLevel = Settings.GetValue("SoundEffectsVolume", 100);
```

The second function that the DefaultValue parameter provides is identifying the expected return type of the GetValue function. If the DefaultValue is passed as an int, the return value will be an int too. This provides a convenient variable type mechanism, avoiding the need to cast and convert values to the appropriate types.

In addition to setting and getting values, the class also allows existing settings to be deleted. The DeleteValue function will remove a setting from the class, causing any subsequent calls to GetValue to return the provided default once again.

Whenever the settings are modified, they can be stored back to the device by calling the SaveSettings method. This uses exactly the same file as LoadSettings and stores all of the setting names and values into the storage file, ready to be retrieved the next time the game is started. Typically, LoadSettings will be called when the game is initializing, and SaveSettings either when the game is closing or whenever one of the settings contained in the object is modified.

A simple example of this in action can be found in the Settings project in the accompanying download. This project contains a form with a number of fields showing possible configuration options that the user may want to use. When the application first runs, each of these is given a default value in the form's Load event, as shown in Listing 9–2.

Listing 9–2. Loading and Displaying the Game Settings

```
private void Form1_Load(object sender, EventArgs e)
{
    DateTime lastRun;

    // Load the settings
    _game.Settings.LoadSettings();

    // Put the settings values on to the form
    txtName.Text = _game.Settings.GetValue("Name", "");
    cboDifficulty.SelectedIndex = _game.Settings.GetValue("Difficulty", 0);
    trackVolume.Value = _game.Settings.GetValue("Volume", 75);
    chkAutoStart.Checked = _game.Settings.GetValue("AutoStart", true);

    // Find the last run date, too
    lastRun = _game.Settings.GetValue("LastRun", DateTime.MinValue);
    if (lastRun == DateTime.MinValue)
    {
        lblLastRun.Text = "This is the first time this game has been started.";
    }
    else
    {
        lblLastRun.Text = "This game was last used at " + lastRun.ToString();
    }
}
```

When the game form is closing, the settings are retrieved from the form and saved back to the settings file, as shown in Listing 9–3.

Listing 9–3. Updating and Saving the Game Settings

```
private void Form1_Closing(object sender, System.ComponentModel.CancelEventArgs e)
{
    // The game is closing, ensure all the settings are up to date.
    _game.Settings.SetValue("Name", txtName.Text);
    _game.Settings.SetValue("Difficulty", cboDifficulty.SelectedIndex);
    _game.Settings.SetValue("Volume", trackVolume.Value);
    _game.Settings.SetValue("AutoStart", chkAutoStart.Checked);
    _game.Settings.SetValue("LastRun", DateTime.Now);

    // Save the settings
    _game.Settings.SaveSettings();
}
```

Try launching and closing this application a few times and note how the settings are retained each time the application restarts. The form used in the example is shown in Figure 9–1.

Figure 9–1. The Settings example project

Understanding How the CSettings Class Works

Let's take a quick look at what is going on inside the CSettings class.

Accessing the Settings Object

A single instance of CSettings is created within the CGameEngineBase constructor. This is stored in a class-level variable and made accessible to the outside world via the Settings property.

The constructor of the CSettings class itself has internal scope, so it cannot be instantiated outside of the game engine assembly.

Setting and Retrieving Values

Inside the class is a private Dictionary object containing the setting names and values. Each item in the dictionary is keyed by the setting name and stores the corresponding value. The key and value are both stored as strings, and the key is always converted to lowercase to make it case insensitive.

The SetValue function first looks to see whether the specified setting key exists within the dictionary. If it does, the existing item is updated with the new value; otherwise, a new item is added with the provided key and value.

A number of different overloads for the SetValue function follow on from this initial method, one for each of the supported datatypes. As the dictionary values are always stored as strings, the methods ultimately all call into the first version of the function, which takes its parameter as a string.

These overloads will convert the provided typed value into a string so that it can be safely decoded again later on. Mostly, this consists of just calling the ToString method on the provided value, but the overload that takes a DateTime as a parameter formats the date to a string using the following string format:

```
yyyy-MM-ddTHH:mm:ss
```

This is the ISO 8601 date format and is the only safe and unambiguous method for storing dates as text. There is no possibility here for the year, month, or day values to become confused (unlike other date formats where the sequence of these elements can be swapped around), nor for any system language problems to occur, which might be a problem if we stored the month name ("January" might be easily understood by systems using the English language but may fail to be parsed in systems running in French or Spanish, for example).

GetValue also has an overload for each supported datatype, and each one correspondingly converts the stored string back to the required type. Just as before, all of the overloads initially obtain the value as string and convert that back to the appropriate type.

Finally, the DeleteValue simply removes the specified item from the dictionary. If no such item actually exists, it returns without doing anything.

Loading and Saving Settings

The settings are stored in an XML file with a very simple structure. The top-level element is named settings, and underneath this is an element for each setting key, containing the value as its text. An example of the content saved from the Settings example project is shown in Listing 9–4.

Listing 9–4. The Contents of the Storage File from the Settings Example Project

```
<settings>
 <name>Adam</name>
 <difficulty>1</difficulty>
 <volume>50</volume>
 <autostart>False</autostart>
 <lastrun>2010-01-01T12:34:56</lastrun>
</settings>
```

The SaveSettings function uses an XmlTextWriter to build the content of the file and then simply loops through all of the items within the settings dictionary. Once the XML has been built, it is written to the file identified using the FileName property.

■ **NOTE** There are various different ways we could store this information, including using alternative types of files or writing to the registry. In terms of file storage, XML offers a great degree of flexibility with little effort and allows us to extend the file content very easily. Writing to the registry is a possible option, but using a file on disk makes it much easier to back up or copy settings files and keeps the game and all of its resources self-contained.

Loading the settings is a very similar process, but in reverse. The SaveSettings function first clears the settings dictionary and then loads the XML file. If the file does not exist or contains non-XML content, it exits without performing any further work, resulting in all the setting values resetting to their defaults when next queried.

If the XML was loaded successfully, the function loops through each of the elements contained within the root settings element, adding their names and values back into the dictionary. Once this is complete, all of the settings will have been restored.

Replacing the MessageBox

The .NET CF MessageBox is a very useful method for asking the user a question. It suffers from an irritating problem in our games however: when the message box is displayed, the game form loses focus. This loss of focus results in all of the logic we have put into the Deactivate event triggering: any music playback is suspended, and the game may switch into pause mode. We need a similar simple method of asking the user a question that doesn't suffer from these issues.

A solution is provided by the CMessageBox class within the game engine. An instance of this can be obtained from the CGameEngineBase.MessageBox property, providing a similar single line of code call for our custom message box to that provided by the .NET CF MessageBox.Show function.

Additionally, the customized message box allows us to use our own game-specific color scheme. It's also consistent in appearance between touch screen and smart phone devices, while the .NET CF MessageBox is not.

Using the MessageBox Class

The CMessageBox class first provides a number of properties to allow its appearance to be customized. BackColor sets the main background color for the dialog. TitleBackColory and TitleTextColory allow the title area of the dialog to be set. Finally, MessageTextColory provides a color for the text of the main dialog message. The area of effect of each of these is shown in Figure 9–2.

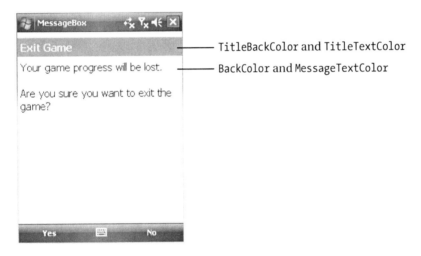

Figure 9–2. The MessageBox dialog

These properties can be set just once when the game initializes and will then be retained for the lifetime of the application.

To display a message, call the CMessageBox.ShowDialog method. The dialog will be displayed on the screen, but the application form will not lose focus.

The ShowDialog method has two overloads. The first of these expects parameters to be passed to identify the target form over which the dialog will be displayed, to specify the dialog title and message, and to provide the caption of the button to display in the menu in order to close the dialog. The call is synchronous and will not return control to the calling function until the dialog is closed by the user.

The second overload accepts a further parameter, providing the text to place on to the second top-level menu item (on the right side of the menu). When a second button caption is provided, the dialog allows a question to be asked, with the two possible answers displayed within the menu. ShowDialog will return a value of 0 if the left menu item was selected to close the dialog or 1 if the right item was selected.

One other property that interacts with the dialog is added to CGameEngineBase, called IsModalPanelDisplayed. This function checks to see whether a modal dialog (such as the message box described here or the high score table coming up in the next section) is currently open. It can be useful to know this to help control the automatic pause feature when the game form's Deactivate event fires; if a modal dialog is open, there is no need to pause the game, because the dialog has effectively paused it already.

An example of the message box is contained within the MessageBox project in the accompanying code download. This shows two message boxes, one on each of the menu buttons. The left button shows an exit confirmation box and will close the application only if the Yes option is selected. The right button shows a simple message.

Understanding How the CMessageBox Class Works

Let's see how the CMessageBox class is implemented.

Accessing the Message Box Object

A single instance of CMessageBox is created within the CGameEngineBase constructor. This is stored in a class-level variable and made accessible to the outside world via the MessageBox property.

The constructor of the CMessageBox class itself has internal scope, so it cannot be instantiated outside of the game engine assembly.

Displaying the Message

The message box code relies on a UserControl named CMessageBoxControl contained within the game engine assembly. This control class has internal scope, so it cannot be accessed from external code.

CMessageBoxControl contains a Panel and a Label that together form the title section of the dialog, as well as a Textbox that displays the dialog message. The Textbox is configured such that it has no visible border, but if enough text is displayed to require a vertical scrollbar to appear, one will be added so that the entire message can be read.

When the CMessageBox.ShowDialog method is called, an instance of the user control is created and sized so that it completely fills the game form's client area. The user control is configured so that it contains the requested text and the configured color scheme and is then added to the game form so that it can be seen by the player.

Next, the form's menu control is swapped out for one provided by the message box. A new MainMenu object is created containing the requested item (or items if two have been specified), and this is set into the game form's Menu property. Before setting this, the game form's original menu is retrieved and stored in a local variable.

The code waits in a loop until the user control's Visible property changes to false. This will happen when the user selects one of the menu items, as set in the menu item Click events.

Finally, the game form's original menu is restored, and all of the message box objects are tidied up.

Control returns back to the calling procedure so that it can continue doing whatever it needs to do in response to the dialog. The index of the selected menu item is returned, so the calling code knows the answer to whatever question it asked, if appropriate.

Creating a High Score Table

Another common requirement across many games is the ability to keep track of the highest scores that players have achieved. .NET CF provides some useful features to implement high scores (such as sortable collections into which we can place all of our scores), but actually implementing the feature into a game requires a little effort, most of which is fairly unexciting—not what we want to be spending time addressing when we could be being creative instead.

To reduce the amount of work required, we can build support for high scores into the game engine. We won't make things too complicated, but our implementation will have the facility for keeping track of multiple tables at once if the game requires such a feature (for different difficulty levels, for example) and a very simple API so that the game doesn't require very much code to interact with the high scores.

One final feature that we will add is the ability to encrypt the scores when we save them. Game players can be fairly competitive with their high scores, and if we leave the score file in plain text so that anyone can hack in their own fabricated scores, it takes all the challenge away. While the encryption will be far from military grade, it will be sufficient to stop the average player from being able to manipulate their score file.

Using the High Score Class

The high scores are implemented using another new class in the game engine, CHighScores. This provides all of the functionality required to configure, display, save and restore all of the high scores. Let's take a look at the functionality that it offers.

Setting the Dialog Presentation Properties

Just as with CMessageBox, a number of properties are available to allow the presentation of the high score table to be controlled, allowing it to be configured to match the color scheme of your game. The available properties are BackColor to control the main background of the dialog, TextColor to control the text displayed at the top of the dialog, TableBackColor for the background area of the table itself, TableTextColor1 and TableTextColor2 for the scores within the table (the dialog will fade the color of the entries between the two colors provided), NewEntryBackColor and NewEntryTextColor to allow newly-added entries to be highlighted, and ShowTableBorder to control whether a border is displayed around the table. The area of effect of each of these properties is shown in Figure 9–3.

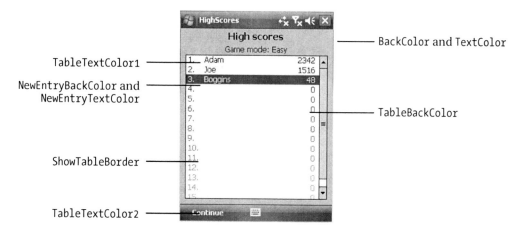

Figure 9–3. The High Score dialog

The presentation of the dialog can be set once when the game is initializing and will remain for the lifetime of the application.

Initializing the High Score Table

Before the high scores can be used, the game must first add one or more tables into which scores will be added. If the game only has one set of scores, just one table will be added. If multiple sets of scores are required (for different difficulty levels or game modes), add as many as are required. Each table must be given a unique name so that it can be identified within the high score system.

High score tables are initialized by calling the CHighScores.InitializeTable method. This must be supplied with the unique name for the table and the number of entries to store in the table. A third parameter may be optionally supplied that contains a description for the table. If present, the description will appear above the scores whenever the table is viewed (the description used in the example in Figure 9–3 is "Game mode: Easy.")

Before any further work is done with the high scores, the storage filename and encryption key must be considered. Filenames may be specified either as full paths or as local filenames, just as we discussed previously for the CSettings class. By default, scores will be saved to a file named Scores.dat, stored in the game's directory.

If you wish to encrypt the scores, set the CHighScores.EncryptionKey property before carrying on any further. This can be set to any string, and this string will be used as part of the encryption to increase the difficulty of altering the stored scores. To disable encryption, set an empty string or leave this property at its default value.

■ **NOTE** If you ever decide to change the encryption key used for your high score file, the code will be unable to read any scores created with the original key. You should, therefore, ensure that the key is set once within your game source code and never modified. Do not use anything sensitive that you wouldn't want others to be able to see, in case someone should attempt to decompile your program code.

Once the tables have been initialized, any existing stored scores can be loaded by calling the LoadScores method. Scores will only be loaded for high score tables that have been initialized; any scores in unknown tables will be discarded. If the number of high scores entries in the file exceeds the number of entries that the table has been configured to hold, the excess entries will be discarded.

With the scores loaded, everything is set up and ready for action.

Displaying the High Scores Dialog

The dialog can be displayed by calling its ShowDialog method. There are two different ways in which the dialog may be used: to simply display the scores that are already in one of the tables (when the user requests to see them) and to add a new entry to a table (when the player has finished a game and achieved a potential new high score).

To view the existing scores, call ShowDialog passing just a reference to the game form and the name of the table to be displayed. The high score dialog will appear as shown in Figure 9–3. If a description for the table was provided when it was initialized, this will appear above the scores; otherwise, the score table will expand to fill the area that this would have occupied.

To add a new score to the table, the score and a default player name are additionally passed to ShowDialog. The score will be retrieved from the game itself, and the player name can be either an empty string or the name that was previously entered the last time a high score was added. The CHighScores.LastEnteredName property will return this after a score has been added, and used in combination with the CSettings class, this can also be stored and used the next time the game is launched.

If the player's score is high enough to rank on the table, another window will appear into which the player can enter his or her name, as shown in Figure 9–4. The default player name will be initially populated here, so if this is the same player as when the last score was added, the Continue menu item can be pressed without having to enter any text at all, speeding up the operation.

Figure 9–4. Adding a new entry to the high score table

Once the Continue menu item is clicked or the Enter key is pressed, the high score table will be displayed just as when viewing scores, with the new entry highlighted.

All high scores are date stamped, so if there is a collision between the new score and an existing score, the existing score will be given precedence and will appear higher in the list than the new entry.

If a new score is added, the call to ShowDialog will automatically save the scores to the defined storage file, so there is no need to save it from within your game code. Should you wish to manually save the scores however, the SaveScores method is available to perform this task.

The existing scores may be cleared by calling the CHighScores.Clear method. This will completely erase all of the stored scores. To erase the scores for a single table, retrieve the table by calling the GetTable method, and call Clear on the table object that is returned. The scores will need to be saved by using the SaveScores method after being cleared, as they do not save automatically.

An example of the high score class can be found in the HighScores project in the accompanying download. This contains three different high score tables (named Easy, Medium, and Hard), which can be selected using the drop-down list on the main form. Once a table is selected, the existing scores can be seen by selecting the View Scores menu item, or a randomly generated new score can be added with the Add Score button. Note how the code uses the CSettings class to remember the name that was added between executions of the program.

Understanding How the CHighScores Class Works

Let's see how the CHighScores class is implemented.

Accessing the HighScores Objects

A single instance of CHighScores is created within the CGameEngineBase constructor. This is stored in a class-level variable and made accessible to the outside world via the HighScores property.

The constructor of the CHighScores class itself has internal scope, so it cannot be instantiated outside of the game engine assembly.

Understanding the Data Structure

The scores are represented using three different classes. CHighScores itself contains a collection of CHighScoreTable objects, each of which contains information about the individual table (including its name, description, and the number of score entries to hold). The tables, in turn, contain collections of CHighScoreEntry objects, each of which stores the name, score, and achieved date for the individual score. The score entry class also implements the IComparer interface, allowing a collection of these objects to be easily sorted by score and achieved date.

The relationship between these classes is shown in the class diagram in Figure 9–5.

Figure 9–5. Relationships between the high score classes

The CHighScores._highscoreTables collection is a Dictionary of CHighScoreTable objects, keyed by the unique table name. Each call to CHighScores.InitializeTable adds a new CHighScoreTable object to this collection.

The CHighScoreTable._scoreEntries collection is a List of CHighScoreEntry objects. The IComparer interface within CHighScoreEntry allows the entries to be sorted by simply calling _scoreEntries.Sort. The CHighScoreTable class contains an AddEntry method, which appends a new entry to this list and sorts it. If the number of items in the list exceeds the defined table size, the additional element is removed from the list.

These classes together provide a simple and efficient representation of the tables and scores that are present within the game.

Presenting High Scores

Just as with the message box control, the high score table is presented using a UserControl named CHighScoreControl hidden away inside the game engine. The main elements of the control are a ListView inside which the scores are displayed and a Panel containing fields to allow the user to enter their name.

The class contains all of the code required to populate the scores into the ListView (in the ShowScores function) and ensure that the layout is updated when the control resizes.

If the player has achieved enough points to add a new score, the pnlEnterName panel is displayed. This contains a message informing the user of the new high score and allowing that person to enter a name. Pressing the Enter key within the txtName Textbox contained within this panel, or clicking the Continue menu item, will cause this panel to be made invisible, signaling to the ShowDialog function that a name has been entered. The score is added to the table and saved, and the table within the ListView updated to include the new score.

When Continue is selected with the main table displayed, the user control itself is hidden, signaling ShowDialog to return control back to the calling procedure.

Storing Data

The scores are stored in XML format, which is easy to create and parse. The SaveScores method uses an XmlTextWriter to build up the score information ready to be saved.

The XML document consists of a root element named HighScores. Within here are a number of Table elements, each of which contains a Name and Entries child elements. Each Entries element in turn contains a series of Entry elements, with the Score, Name, and Date stored within them. This exactly matches the structure that the data is stored in within the high score classes we have already described.

An example of the XML produced by this function is shown in Listing 9–5. This example contains three tables named Easy, Medium, and Hard. Only the Easy table actually has any scores stored within it.

Listing 9–5. The Generated XML for a Set of High Score Tables

```
<HighScores>
 <Table>
  <Name>Easy</Name>
  <Entries>
   <Entry>
    <Score>2342</Score>
    <Name>Adam</Name>
    <Date>2010-01-01T12:34:54</Date>
   </Entry>
   <Entry>
    <Score>1516</Score>
    <Name>Joe</Name>
    <Date>2010-01-01T12:34:55</Date>
   </Entry>
```

```
  <Entry>
   <Score>48</Score>
   <Name>Boggins</Name>
   <Date>2010-01-01T12:34:56</Date>
  </Entry>
 </Entries>
</Table>
<Table>
 <Name>Medium</Name>
 <Entries />
</Table>
<Table>
 <Name>Hard</Name>
 <Entries />
</Table>
</HighScores>
```

Note that we only store the information that is actually required; blank entries are omitted from the table. The score achieved dates are stored in ISO 8601 format, as were the dates in the CSettings class.

With the XML generated, the function is now ready to store the information to a file for later use. However, at this stage, it needs to see whether it has been asked to encrypt the data. This is simply a matter of checking the EncryptionKey length: if it's greater than 0, encryption is indeed required.

We will perform this encryption using a lightweight piece of code called the Tiny Encryption Algorithm (TEA). This widely known algorithm has implementations in many languages and, while not highly secure, it will render a file that cannot be easily decoded without some effort. The algorithm is fast to execute and produces output that is never more than a few bytes larger than the input. While .NET CF does offer other more complex encryption algorithms, this is a simple and unobtrusive way of protecting our data from prying eyes. The encryption code is contained within the game engine's CEncryption class.

Once the XML has been encrypted, if needed, the final score data is written to the file identified by the FileName property.

Loading the scores back into the set of objects is handled by the LoadScores function. This opens the file that was created when the scores were saved and decrypts its contents if required. The XML is then loaded into an XmlDocument object.

The function next loops through the known high score tables (previously initialized with calls to InitializeTable) and attempts to locate a Table element within the XML for each. The element is located very easily using an XPath expression, as shown in Listing 9–6. For each matching Table element, the score entries are read into the required collections to repopulate the high score objects.

Listing 9–6. Locating an XML Table Element for Each Known High Score Table

```
// Loop for each known highscore table
foreach (string tableName in _highscoreTables.Keys)
{
    // See if we can find the element for this table
    xmlTable = (XmlElement)xmlDoc.SelectSingleNode
                        ("HighScores/Table[Name='" + tableName + "']");
    // Did we find one?
    if (xmlTable != null)
    {
        // Yes, so load its data into the table object
        LoadScores_LoadTable(_highscoreTables[tableName], xmlTable);
    }
}
```

The SelectSingleNode call shows some of the power of XPath: it looks for the first node it can find whose element type is Table contained within the top-level HighScores element, where the Table contains a child element called Name whose value is the specified tableName. This simple instruction saves what would be a considerable amount of manual looping and XML interrogation to perform this without using XPath.

Once the Table element is located, its scores are loaded into the appropriate CHighScoreTable object by the LoadScores_LoadTable function, shown in Listing 9–7. This also uses XPath to easily obtain all of the Entry elements contained within the Entries collection inside the Table.

Listing 9–7. Loading Scores from a Table XML Element into a CHighScoreTable Object

```
/// <summary>
/// Load the scores from an individual table within the provided
/// XML definition.
/// </summary>
/// <param name="table">The table to load</param>
/// <param name="xmlTable">The XML score entries to load</param>
private void LoadScores_LoadTable(CHighScoreTable table, XmlElement xmlTable)
{
    int score;
    string name;
    DateTime date;

    // Loop for each entry
    foreach (XmlElement xmlEntry in xmlTable.SelectNodes("Entries/Entry"))
    {
        // Retrieve the entry information
        score = int.Parse(xmlEntry.SelectSingleNode("Score").InnerText);
        name = xmlEntry.SelectSingleNode("Name").InnerText;
        date = DateTime.Parse(xmlEntry.SelectSingleNode("Date").InnerText);
        // Add the entry to the table.
        table.AddEntry(name, score, date);
    }
}
```

If any errors occur during loading, the code empties all of the high score tables by calling the Clear method, and returns without rethrowing the exception. Any errors retrieving the high scores are therefore ignored. So if a problem occurs (such as the high score file becoming corrupted), the scores are simply lost rather than the entire game failing to initialize—annoying, but better than having to instruct users how to delete the high score file manually.

Creating an About Box

The final component we will look at in this chapter is a general-purpose About box. Most games and applications have such a feature, which displays information about the program, including the following:

- The application name and version

- The name of the author

- Author contact details (web site and e-mail address)

These screens are not particularly difficult to make, but once all the intricacies of different screen sizes and device rotation are taken into consideration, writing these for each game can become frustrating. We will, therefore, create a reusable component within the game engine to take care of everything for us automatically.

Using the About Box Class

The About box is implemented using a new game engine class, CAboutBox. To display information within the box, we first obtain a reference from the CGameEngineBase.AboutBox property, and then add a series of items that to the box so that it can display them.

Items can be either a piece of text or a picture. Both types of item will appear centered within the about box. Text can be customized with different text and background colors, font sizes, and text styles (bold, italic, and so on). Text and picture items can also both specify an amount of empty space to appear below them, allowing sections of content to be grouped together.

The About box releases all of its resources when it is closed so that it doesn't waste any memory, so it must be fully initialized each time it is to be displayed. The CAboutBox class has two properties to set: BackColor and TextColor. These control the overall background color of the dialog and the default color for text items added to the dialog.

Text and picture items are then added by repeatedly calling the AddItem method. Passing a string to this method will add a text item; passing a Bitmap will add a picture. AddItem returns the added item (whose type is another new game engine class named CAboutItem) so that it can be further customized if required.

For text items, the BackColor and TextColor properties of this CAboutItem object may be set to alter the item colors, FontSize to increase or reduce the text size (the default size is 9), and FontStyle to change the font style. The SpaceAfter property allows extra space to be added below the item, set in pixels.

For picture items, the only property that will have any effect is SpaceAfter.

Text items also support two tokens that can be placed within the display text. Passing the string {AssemblyName} will cause the game assembly name to appear in place of the token. Passing {AssemblyVersion} will cause the game assembly version to appear. These provide a simple way of ensuring that the about box is up to date even when things in your project change. These tokens can be placed alongside other strings in the same item if required and are case sensitive.

Listing 9–8 shows some sample code to set up the About box, with the results of the code shown in Figure 9–6.

Listing 9–8. *Setting Up the Contents of an About Box*

```
private void mnuMain_About_Click(object sender, EventArgs e)
{
    GameEngine.CAboutItem item;
    Bitmap logo;

    // Get a reference to our assembly
    Assembly asm = Assembly.GetExecutingAssembly();
    // Load the AboutBox logo
    logo = new Bitmap(asm.GetManifestResourceStream("AboutBox.Graphics.Logo.png"));

    // Set the AboutBox properties
    _game.AboutBox.BackColor = Color.PaleGoldenrod;
    _game.AboutBox.TextColor = Color.Black;

    // Add the AboutBox items
```

```
        item = _game.AboutBox.AddItem("{AssemblyName}");
        item.FontSize = 14;
        item.FontStyle = FontStyle.Bold;
        item.BackColor = Color.SlateBlue;
        item.TextColor = Color.Yellow;

        item = _game.AboutBox.AddItem("version {AssemblyVersion}");
        item.FontSize = 7;

        item = _game.AboutBox.AddItem(logo);
        item.SpaceAfter = 20;

        item = _game.AboutBox.AddItem("By Adam Dawes");
        item.SpaceAfter = 30;

        item = _game.AboutBox.AddItem("For updates and other games,");
        item = _game.AboutBox.AddItem("visit my web site at");
        item = _game.AboutBox.AddItem("www.adamdawes.com");
        item.TextColor = Color.DarkBlue;
        item.FontStyle = FontStyle.Bold;
        item.SpaceAfter = 10;

        item = _game.AboutBox.AddItem("Email me at");
        item = _game.AboutBox.AddItem("adam@adamdawes.com");
        item.TextColor = Color.DarkBlue;
        item.FontStyle = FontStyle.Bold;

        // Display the dialog
        _game.AboutBox.ShowDialog(this);
    }
```

Figure 9–6. The output from an about box dialog

The dialog will do its best to position everything nicely on the screen. If there is surplus vertical space available, it will increase the spacing between the items a little to fill it. If there is insufficient vertical space, a scrollbar will be displayed so that the content is still accessible. Changing the screen orientation will automatically reposition the items to ensure they are still displayed correctly.

This About box example can be seen in the AboutBox project in the accompanying code download.

Understanding How the CAboutBox Class Works

Let's look at the CAboutBox implementation.

Accessing the About Box Objects

A single instance of CAboutBox is created within the CGameEngineBase constructor. This is stored in a class-level variable and made accessible to the outside world via the AboutBox property.

The constructor of the CAboutBox class itself has internal scope, so it cannot be instantiated outside of the game engine assembly.

The CAboutItem class, used to add text and picture items into the dialog, also has a constructor with internal scope. Instances can be created by external assemblies only by using the CAboutBox.AddItem functions.

Displaying the About Box

The approach to displaying the box is just the same as that used by the message box and high score table, except that no predefined UserControl is present for the About box. As the entire content of the box is generated dynamically, there is no need to such a control class; everything is placed into a Panel control that is itself generated at runtime.

All of the added CAboutItem objects are stored in a private collection named _items. Along with the public item properties that can be set by the game class are two further internal properties: ItemControl and TopPosition.

When the dialog is being prepared for display in the CAboutBox.ShowDialog method, a form control is created for each item: a Label for text items and a PictureBox for picture items. References to these controls are stored within the ItemControl property of each item, allowing the controls to be easily retrieved again later on. This takes place in the CAboutBox.CreateAboutItems function.

The TopPosition is used to calculate the vertical position of each of the items. A first pass is made to calculate this position by simply taking the control heights and item spacing into account. If the total height is found to be less than the form height, a second pass recalculates this by adding further spacing to each item so that the spread of controls extends further towards the bottom of the form. The CAboutBox.CalculatePositions and CAboutBox.LayoutControls procedures take care of this functionality.

The About box is then ready for display, which is handled in just the same way as the other components we have looked at. When the Continue menu item is selected by the user, all of the controls are disposed and destroyed; the About box Panel is removed from the form, and control is returned back to the calling procedure.

Using Common Game Components

It is very easy to find yourself rewriting sections of code over and over again as you develop games, and each time you write things slightly differently or change how things work. Creating reusable components such as those in this chapter can save you the effort of reinventing these same concepts in each new project that you create.

Even though writing reusable components such as this may require a little extra work, you'll be pleased that you made the effort when you plug them into your future projects, as the overall amount of development time will be decreased, plus you'll get a consistency in the appearance and functionality of your games. We have so far covered a lot of game development subjects in this book, but now, it is time to start a journey into a brand new area: the OpenGL ES graphics library.

PART 3

OpenGL ES Graphics

■ ■ ■

CHAPTER 10

A New Window on the World with OpenGL ES

It is time now to take a major step forward in graphical technology. GDI is supported on a wide range of devices and as we have seen it is quite possible to create enjoyable games with it. To really move your games into the next dimension, however, a different graphics API is required. For the next few chapters, we will look at such an API: Open Graphics Library for Embedded Systems (OpenGL ES).

The main OpenGL library is powerful and an industry-standard platform for creating 2D and 3D computer graphics. It is supported on all modern PCs and graphics hardware. OpenGL ES is a cut down version of this library, with some functionality removed but a substantial amount still left in place. OpenGL ES will allow us to create graphical effects that we couldn't get close to achieving using GDI.

■ **NOTE** In the context of this book, we will refer to OpenGL ES as simply "OpenGL" from this point onward. Any references to the full OpenGL implementation found on desktop PCs will be clarified within the text.

Preparing to Use OpenGL

Before we dive into working with OpenGL, let's take a look at some of its abilities and features and see which devices are able to support OpenGL games and applications.

Hardware Support

Before we go any further, it is important to stress that OpenGL requires *hardware acceleration* to perform at an acceptable speed. Many new Windows Mobile devices (including most of the HTC models from the Touch Diamond and Touch Pro onward, the Samsung Omnia 2 and the Sony Ericsson Xperia X1 and X2) have such hardware acceleration. Other devices, including virtually everything running Windows Mobile 5.0 or older, are lacking such hardware acceleration.

Without acceleration, OpenGL applications will run at an extremely slow speed, much too slow to be usable for games. While this graphics API unleashes a huge amount of power for capable devices, it unfortunately excludes other devices completely. It is important to take this into account when you decide to use OpenGL to power your games.

The Windows Mobile emulators do not have support for hardware accelerated OpenGL. While it is possible to install a software-based OpenGL renderer (just as it is with nonaccelerated devices), the performance will be so slow that the renderer will be of almost no value. When we move into the realm of OpenGL, it is essential to develop your application on a real device. Please check the device that you are using is able to provide hardware accelerated OpenGL graphics; a Google search should be able to provide this information if you are unsure.

We will write some code shortly that will check whether OpenGL is supported on a device and retrieve information about the implementation that is available.

Language Support

Everything we have looked at so far has been written in C# but could also have been developed in Visual Basic .NET if required. Some of the features required for OpenGL, however, are not supported within VB.NET, while others are somewhat awkward to use compared to their equivalents in C#.

This doesn't mean that VB.NET developers cannot use OpenGL, but certain functions will need to be placed into a C# project that is then called from the VB.NET project.

Those areas of functionality that are not directly supported in VB.NET will be highlighted as we encounter them.

Understanding the OpenGL Features

Let's look at some of the features that OpenGL offers.

Performance

When we use OpenGL on an accelerated device, we are able to provide significantly greater levels of performance that we would be able to get using an unaccelerated technology such as GDI. This means we can display more graphics on the screen without our frame rate dropping.

Scaling and Rotation

While GDI was able to scale graphics, displaying them at larger or smaller sizes than the original graphic image, but there is a significant performance cost involved in this. In addition, graphics scaling is handled in a rather unattractive manner, with graphical artifacts appearing on the scaled images.

OpenGL is able to scale very much more easily, with no noticeable performance impact (although the hardware capabilities of many Windows Mobile devices do actually suffer when graphics are rendered at sizes very much larger sizes than the originals). This allows us to perform all sorts of interesting graphical effects, enlarging and shrinking graphics as we see fit.

Another option that was not available at all in GDI is the ability to rotate graphics, allowing images to be displayed at any angle. This makes it possible to display graphical objects that follow paths around the screen and face one another very easily.

Transparency and Alpha Blending

You saw that the GDI renderer is able to use a color key to make certain area of graphics transparent when they are displayed to the screen. OpenGL is able to do this too, but it uses an actual alpha channel contained within the image to determine whether pixels are transparent or opaque.

OpenGL is also able to perform *alpha blending* when drawing graphics to the screen. This allows graphics to be rendered semitransparently, so any existing content on the screen can show through the graphic being drawn. The level of transparency can be smoothly faded from fully opaque to fully transparent.

Rendering in 3D

One of the major features that OpenGL offers is the ability to render 3D graphics. OpenGL is able to display graphics with perspective, so that objects further away from the player appear smaller than those that are nearer. It can also display with *depth buffering* so that objects can appear behind other objects.

Our discussions of OpenGL will remain in just two dimensions for the moment, but we will look at 3D rendering in much more detail in Chapter 12.

Abstract Coordinate System

OpenGL uses an abstract coordinate system rather than a pixel-based coordinate system like the one used by GDI, meaning that we are not concerned with pixels. While this may sound like a disadvantage at first, freeing ourselves from pixel coordinates actually turns out to be rather useful. When we initialize OpenGL, we can tell it the dimensions of the screen and the coordinate system will scale to match. Moving a graphic object a certain distance to the right, therefore, moves the same distance regardless of the screen size.

After all the time we have spent with GDI, getting to grips with the OpenGL coordinate system requires a slight twist of the brain. First, the coordinate (0, 0) is generally right in the center of the screen, rather than in the top-left corner. Second, movement along the positive y axis will travel up the screen in OpenGL, as opposed to down in GDI. It can be a nuisance having to keep these two conflicting coordinate systems in your brain, but once you are in the frame of mind for one API over the other, it should be easy to remember which way is up.

As OpenGL provides a 3D graphical environment, we actually need to add a third element to our coordinates. The coordinate values we have looked at in the past have been in the form of (x, y), representing the specified distances along the x and y axes. OpenGL coordinates are in the form (x, y, z), providing values in the z axis as well as the x and y axes. The z axis represents movement into or out of the screen—literally the third dimension. Positive values on the z axis result in movement toward the player, negative values result in movement into the screen.

Color Specification

When we specify a color to OpenGL, we still use the red, green, blue (RGB) model that we have used throughout our work with GDI. However, the way in which the values are specified is slightly different for OpenGL.

Instead of int values from 0 (no intensity) to 255 (full intensity), OpenGL instead uses float values between 0 (no intensity) and 1 (full intensity). White is therefore represented by the values (1, 1, 1), red by (1, 0, 0), and grey by (0.5, 0.5, 0.5).

OpenGL will *clamp* colors to this range. In other words, values less than 0 will be treated as 0, and any values greater than 1 will be treated as 1. This is in contrast to the GDI approach, which threw an exception of the color values were outside the expected range.

Drawing Primitives

When it comes to drawing graphics, OpenGL is actually not able to draw anything more complex than triangles. This may at seem very restrictive, but in fact, it is not as you will see when we start to use it in some example projects.

The reason we are able to create more complex scenes is partly because much more complex shapes can be created by putting lots of triangles together (for example, a rectangle is just two triangles joined along their long edge) and partly because we can put graphic images on to the triangles. As a simple example, we can create a 2-D sprite that works along very similar lines to the ones we used with the GDI DrawImage function by simply rendering a rectangle with a graphic displayed across it.

When we are drawing, we refer to each triangle as a *surface*. The points that form the triangle are called *vertices*. Figure 10–1 shows two triangular surfaces created using four vertices. Two of the vertices are shared between the triangles.

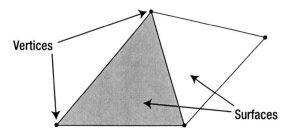

Figure 10–1. Vertices and surfaces used in OpenGL rendering

The vertices are not actually drawn by OpenGL, just the surfaces that they define; the vertices are shown in Figure 10–1 just to clarify what they are.

The only primitives available other than triangles are lines and points (individual pixels).

Textures

Whenever we take a bitmap and use this to fill the triangles that we are rendering, this bitmap is known as a *texture*. We have a lot of flexibility to use textures within our OpenGL applications. We can take small rectangular sections just as we did in GDI, or we can stretch textures in a variety of different ways across the shapes that we draw. We'll look at some of the tricks and techniques that we can use when texturing in the "Using Texture Mapping" section later in this chapter.

Using OpenGL in Visual Studio.NET

Unfortunately, using OpenGL as is not as simple as using GDI. Let's look at what is required to use OpenGL in our game code.

Calling OpenGL from Managed Languages

The OpenGL functionality is implemented in a DLL called libgles_cm.dll. With devices that have accelerated OpenGL support, this DLL should be present in ROM inside the \Windows\ directory.

The DLL is a native Windows Mobile DLL, however, and is not a managed DLL such as we would use in a .NET application. In order for us to be able to utilize it, we need to define all of its functions using P/Invoke.

Fortunately, developer Koushik Dutta (www.koushikdutta.com) came to the rescue and provided a complete set of P/Invoke functions and all of the related constants, allowing us to make full use of OpenGL in .NET applications. These and a series of supporting classes are wrapped up into a convenient class library that we can reference and use without any pain or inconvenience.

■ **NOTE** The normal names for OpenGL functions all begin with a prefix of gl. Function names include glClear, glLoadIdentity, and glRotatef (we'll look at the purpose of these later on, so don't worry about what they do for now). When using the managed wrapper around OpenGL, the functions are defined within a class named gl and have the prefix removed. These same functions will, therefore, be accessed as gl.Clear, gl.LoadIdentity, and gl.Rotatef in our projects. This change is small but is very important if you use example OpenGL code from the Internet that is not written with the managed wrapper in mind or if you are searching the Internet for help.

We will be using a version of this for all of our OpenGL applications throughout the rest of this book. The DLL is called OpenGLES and its source code can be found in the accompanying download if you wish to look through it. There is no need to understand what is going on within this project however, as it will simply operate as a black box to provide access to the underlying OpenGL functionality.

Understanding OpenGL's Rendering Approach

We spent a lot of time and effort when developing GDI games making sure that we updated only those areas of the screen that had changed, which provided a substantial boost to performance. OpenGL approaches this very differently however. In an OpenGL application, the whole window is entirely discarded and redrawn every time the game graphics are updated.

This approach might seem very inefficient, but because we have hardware acceleration on our side, it is actually much better than it appears. Rendering graphics in this way makes it very much simpler for OpenGL to draw to the screen, as it doesn't have to keep track of what was rendered in each of the previous frames.

The full frame redraw also makes it possible for us to create very rich and active graphical displays. If the entire window is being redrawn every frame anyway, we may as well take advantage of that and offer all of our content on the screen the opportunity to move should it wish to. The need to keep most of our graphics static that we encountered with GDI is not present at all using OpenGL.

Considering the Hardware Capabilities and Limitations

The capabilities of the graphics hardware in different devices can vary substantially. Many newer devices can be found with very fast CPUs and graphics hardware, but older and midrange devices will not be able to display graphics as quickly, even assuming that they do have hardware acceleration available.

For this reason, it is important to try testing your game out on a range of devices to ensure that the performance is acceptable on each. If you experience performance problems, you may be able to offer configuration options that reduce the volume of graphic rendering operations that take place each frame.

In the next chapter, we will integrate OpenGL functionality into the game engine, and once that is done, we can take advantage of the timing features that we built back in Chapter 5. This will ensure that your games run at the same speed on all devices, but devices that suffer from poor rendering performance will display very jerky graphics which may ultimately render the game unplayable.

Closing OpenGL Applications

We take advantage of lots of unmanaged functionality when using OpenGL, and when our form closes, we include code to release all of the resources that have been allocated during the execution of the game.

Unfortunately, when an application running from within Visual Studio is closed by clicking the Stop Debugging button, it is closed without having an opportunity to execute this cleanup code. It is therefore advisable to add an Exit option to your game (which simply closes the game form) and to always close your application using this instead of from Visual Studio. It can take a little while to get in the habit of doing this however!

If you find that your OpenGL games unexpectedly begin to fail with an error message when launching, try closing any running applications and soft resetting your device (by pressing the hardware reset button on most devices).

■ **NOTE** The presence of an Exit menu option used to be frowned upon by Microsoft, who preferred to allow the device to manage the lifetime of its applications automatically. This situation has changed now, and many applications, including those from Microsoft, support an option to close an application on demand. Including an Exit menu item is generally worth considering in your finished product, regardless of its implications when developing.

Creating an OpenGL Program

That's enough theory and background information, now let's fire up Visual Studio and create our first OpenGL application. The program we are about to build can be found in the ColoredQuad project in the accompanying code download. If you wish to experiment with the program, please open this project rather than attempting to build it from scratch from the instructions here, as we will skip over some of the program code that you have already seen in previous chapters.

Configuring the Project

An important step in our project is to indicate to Visual Studio that we are going to be using *unsafe code*, which relies on memory pointers. We need to use memory pointers in order to communicate with the OpenGL DLL, but the code is considered unsafe because incorrect manipulation of these pointers could result in memory being unexpectedly modified, leading to your application crashing.

By default, Visual Studio will raise a compiler error if we attempt to use unsafe code. To prevent this, we must set a switch in the Project Properties window.

Open the Project Properties window for the project that will be interacting with OpenGL by double-clicking the Properties node in the Solution Explorer tree and navigating to the Build tab. The check box labeled "Allow unsafe code" must be checked in order for unsafe code to compile. This setting is shown in Figure 10–2.

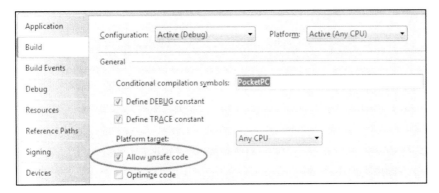

Figure 10–2. *Setting the "Allow unsafe code" configuration option*

NOTE There is no equivalent to the "Allow unsafe code" configuration option in VB.NET. Access to unsafe code is one of the few functional differences between C# and VB.NET, so the unsafe functions we look at in the next few chapters cannot be translated into VB. All is not lost however: only the functions that directly interact with OpenGL need to use unsafe code, and we can (and will) place these into the game engine project where they can then be used from VB without needing to include any unsafe code in the VB project itself.

All we need to do in addition now is add a reference to the OpenGLES project, as shown in Figure 10–3.

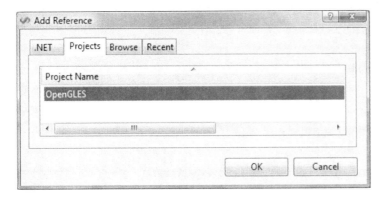

Figure 10–3. *Adding a reference to the OpenGLES project*

Creating the OpenGL Environment

Before we can use OpenGL, we need to perform some initialization steps. The first set of these is performed in the CreateGL function. This function is responsible for creating and initializing the OpenGL environment so that we can begin rendering to it. Let's walk through the code inside to see what is actually happening. Note that the way we are configuring OpenGL here is for displaying 2D graphics. We will look at how to use it for 3D graphics in Chapter 12.

The basic operations required to prepare OpenGL for use can be summarized as follows:

1. Create and initialize the *display* for OpenGL.

2. Set the display *attributes* so that OpenGL knows how to interact with it.

3. Create a *surface* for OpenGL to draw on.

4. Create a *context* to bind together the display and the surface.

5. Activate the display, surface, and context so that OpenGL is ready to draw to the screen.

Let's look at how each of these steps is performed in detail.

OpenGL on Windows Mobile uses a library called Embedded-System Graphics Library (EGL). This in itself doesn't offer any of the kind of graphics functions that OpenGL does, but instead it provides an interface between OpenGL and the mobile device. It is responsible to wiring up the OpenGL renderer to our game form, for example. The first thing that we need to do when initializing OpenGL is to create an EGLDisplay object connected to our form.

We do this by first calling egl.GetDisplay, passing in an EGLNativeDisplayType object that contains a reference to our game form. The function returns back to us an EGLDisplay object, which we will use later in the function to tell EGL about our form.

We then need to initialize the display, which is achieved by calling the egl.Initialize method and passing in the display to be initialized (the EGLDisplay object that we just created). The egl.Initialize function also returns the major and minor version numbers of EGL itself, though we have no need for these at present. The code for the function so far can be seen in Listing 10–1. Note that the _eglDisplay variable is defined as a class-level variable within the form and is not shown in the listing.

Listing 10–1. Creating and Initializing the EGLDisplay Object

```
/// <summary>
/// Create the OpenGL environment
/// </summary>
/// <returns></returns>
private void CreateGL()
{
    // Try to create an EGL display for our game form
    try
    {
        _eglDisplay = egl.GetDisplay(new EGLNativeDisplayType(this));
    }
    catch
    {
        throw new ApplicationException("Unable to initialise an OpenGL display");
    }

    // Initialize EGL for the display that we have created
    int major, minor;
```

```
egl.Initialize(_eglDisplay, out major, out minor);
```

The egl.GetDisplay function will fail on devices that do not have OpenGL support, as this is the first time we call into the libgles_cm.dll. We will add a proper capabilities check for OpenGL when we integrate it into the game engine so that this problem can be found in a more proactive fashion.

The next step is to tell EGL about the configuration parameters we want it to run with. A number of different parameters can be set, but all we need concern ourselves with for the moment is specifying the number of data bits to assign to the color display.

As we discussed back in Chapter 3, Windows Mobile displays generally use 5 bits for specifying the red intensity level, 6 bits for green, and 5 bits for blue. To tell EGL to use the same color range, we add these specifications into the configuration. The application will still work without these values, but providing the information ensures that we will have at least the color depth specified. If greater color depth is available, it will be used.

The configuration is built as an array of integers. Each parameter consists of a pair of integers, the first identifies the parameter that is to be set, and the second provides a value for the parameter. These parameter specifications are terminated with the parameter type EGL_NONE.

Once the configuration array is constructed, it is passed to the egl.ChooseConfig function to locate a frame buffer configuration that matches the requested parameters. There may be multiple matching configurations, so they are returned in an array. The array is sorted, however, so that the one that best matches the configuration parameters provided will be the first item in the array. We, therefore, need to simply check that ChooseConfig doesn't return a failure value and that it returns at least one array item. If all is well, we store the first array element into the config variable; otherwise, an exception is thrown to indicate that OpenGL initialization has failed. The configuration code is shown in Listing 10–2.

Listing 10–2. Obtaining an EGLConfig Object Within the CreateGL Function

```
// Set the attributes that we wish to use for our OpenGL configuration
int[] attribList = new int[]
{
    egl.EGL_RED_SIZE, 4,
    egl.EGL_GREEN_SIZE, 5,
    egl.EGL_BLUE_SIZE, 4,
    egl.EGL_NONE
};

// Declare an array to hold configuration details for the matching attributes
EGLConfig[] configs = new EGLConfig[1];
int numConfig;
// Ensure that we are able to find a configuration for the requested attributes
if (!egl.ChooseConfig(_eglDisplay, attribList,
                      configs, configs.Length, out numConfig) || numConfig < 1)
{
    throw new InvalidOperationException("Unable to choose config.");
}
// Retrieve the first returned configuration
EGLConfig config = configs[0];
```

We are now ready to create an EGLSurface object. This provides the area into which OpenGL will actually render. It automatically provides a front and back buffer, mirroring the double buffering approach that we used for our GDI games. The surface hides all of this functionality away from us, however, so we don't need to expend any extra effort to use this for OpenGL rendering.

The surface is created by calling the egl.CreateWindowSurface function, providing the EGLDisplay and EGLConfig objects that we have created, and the Handle of the target form into which we will render.

A further parameter allows for an attribute list to be provided, but this is currently unused in EGL, so we just pass null. The call can be seen in Listing 10–3.

Listing 10–3. Creating an EGL Surface Object in the CreateGL Function

```
// Create a surface from the config.
_eglSurface = egl.CreateWindowSurface(_eglDisplay, config, this.Handle, null);
```

Next, we need to create an EGLContext object. This provides all the information that OpenGL needs to connect it up to the display that we have created. The context is created with the egl.CreateContext function, passing in the EGLDisplay object once again as well as the EGLConfig object that we created earlier. We also have the possibility of sharing textures with other contexts (which we will not use) and specifying context attributes (which we also won't use), so empty values are provided for both of these parameters. The context is created in Listing 10–4.

Listing 10–4. Creating an EGL Context Object in the CreateGL Function

```
// Create a context from the config
_eglContext = egl.CreateContext(_eglDisplay, config, EGLContext.None, null);
```

Finally, we take the objects that we have created and activate them all within EGL, using the egl.MakeCurrent method. This sets all future calls to render and configure OpenGL so that they work within the objects we have created. We need to pass four parameters to egl.MakeCurrent: the EGLDisplay object, the EGLSurface to use for drawing, the EGLSurface to use for reading pixels, and the EGLContext. As we use the same EGLSurface for drawing and reading, the function call it as shown in Listing 10–5, in which we also finally finish the CreateGL function.

Listing 10–5. Activating the EGL Objects in the CreateGL Function

```
// Activate the display, surface and context that has been created so that
// we can render to the window.
egl.MakeCurrent(_eglDisplay, _eglSurface, _eglSurface, _eglContext);

// At this stage the OpenGL environment itself has been created.
}
```

If the program execution got to the end of this function without any errors, the OpenGL environment is created and ready to use.

Initializing OpenGL

OpenGL is implemented as a *state machine*. In simple terms, this means that it has lots of different properties, each of which can be set to a value depending on how we want it to work. The properties will retain their state until further code asks them to change again. This is very similar to how a .NET class is implemented so the concept should not be unfamiliar.

All of the state properties will be set to initial values, but in order for us to know that OpenGL is prepared in the way that we want, we explicitly set some of these to our own values. Many of the OpenGL properties will be constantly updated as our game runs; others will be set just once and then left for the duration of the game. This latter set of properties is set within the InitGL function.

The code for the whole InitGL function can be seen in Listing 10–6.

Listing 10–6. The InitGL Function

```
/// <summary>
/// Initialize the OpenGL environment ready for us to start rendering
/// </summary>
private void InitGL()
{
    // We can now configure OpenGL ready for rendering.

    // Set the background color for the window
    gl.ClearColor(0.0f, 0.0f, 0.25f, 0.0f);

    // Enable smooth shading so that colors are interpolated across the
    // surface of our rendered shapes.
    gl.ShadeModel(gl.GL_SMOOTH);

    // Disable depth testing
    gl.Disable(gl.GL_DEPTH_TEST);

    // Initialize the OpenGL viewport
    InitGLViewport();

    // All done
}
```

Let's take a look at what is going on within this function.

First of all, we call ClearColor to set the background color for the game form. The parameters passed in are red, green, blue, and alpha respectively. In this example, we specify a dark blue background by providing 25 percent intensity for the blue color component.

The following instructions set various operating states for OpenGL. The ShadeModel call instructs OpenGL to smoothly fade colors between different points within our rendered graphics. It can alternatively be set to GL_FLAT, but for most projects, GL_SMOOTH will be the desired setting, so this is the one that we choose here. The effect of this property will be very clear when we execute the project in a moment.

Next, we call the Disable function, which switches off one of the OpenGL states. In this case, we are switching off the depth test, using the GL_DEPTH_TEST flag. Depth testing is very important to use in 3D rendering, as it allows OpenGL to know which objects are in front of or behind other objects, allowing it to tell which should actually be drawn. As we are only using 2D rendering in our example for the moment, we can switch this off to reduce the amount of work OpenGL needs to do.

Finally, we call into another function, InitGLViewPort. This sets up OpenGL's abstract coordinate system (giving it the dimensions of the form) and tells it the region of the form into which it will render. For our example, we use the entire form client area for this, as shown in Listing 10–7.

Listing 10–7. Initializing the OpenGL Viewport

```
/// <summary>
/// Set up OpenGL's viewport
/// </summary>
private void InitGLViewport()
{
    // Set the viewport that we are rendering to
    gl.Viewport(this.ClientRectangle.Left, this.ClientRectangle.Top,
                        this.ClientRectangle.Width, this.ClientRectangle.Height);
```

```
// Switch OpenGL into Projection mode so that we can set the projection matrix.
gl.MatrixMode(gl.GL_PROJECTION);
// Load the identity matrix
gl.LoadIdentity();
// Apply a perspective projection
glu.Perspective(45,
        (float)this.ClientRectangle.Width / (float)this.ClientRectangle.Height,
        .1f, 100);
// Translate the viewpoint a little way back, out of the screen
gl.Translatef(0, 0, -3);

// Switch OpenGL back to ModelView mode so that we can transform objects rather than
// the projection matrix.
gl.MatrixMode(gl.GL_MODELVIEW);
// Load the identity matrix.
gl.LoadIdentity();
}
```

Some of the code in this function will be examined in more detail when we look at 3D graphics in Chapter 12, so we'll skip some of it for the moment. The important parts are the call to the Viewport function, which tells OpenGL the area of the form into which we want it to render, and the call to glu.Perspective, which sets up the abstract coordinate system. Both of these calls use the form's ClientRectangle dimensions to tell OpenGL the size of the game form.

■ **NOTE** The glu class, short for GL utility, is another class contained within OpenGL that provides useful helper functions that run alongside OpenGL. The Perspective function is an example of such a function, which is not provided by the core OpenGL library but will still be widely useful in a large number of projects.

The reason for initializing the viewport separately from the rest of the OpenGL is that we need to reset the viewport if our window resizes. This ensures that changing the device orientation will keep everything in the appropriate place. Because OpenGL has its own abstract coordinate system, we don't need to do any extra work to support this functionality ourselves.

Another really useful feature of this abstract coordinate system is that OpenGL will automatically resize everything that it draws to match the height of the game window. This means that if a device is switched from portrait to landscape mode, the graphics displayed will all shrink to match the new reduced form height. We do not need to provide different sets of graphics as we did in GDI (such as in the GemDrops project), as our existing graphics will be automatically scaled to fit.

These functions complete the initialization of OpenGL; it is now completely ready for us to start drawing our graphics.

Rendering Graphics in OpenGL

The rendering of graphics to the screen is performed in our example project's Render function. The first thing that Render does is to clear the background. We don't tell it the color to clear to, as this has already been specified in the call to ClearColor back in the InitGL function. The clear color can of course be changed any time you want by calling ClearColor again. The beginning of Render is shown in Listing 10–8.

Listing 10–8. Clearing the Window in the Render Function

```
/// <summary>
/// Render the OpenGL scene
/// </summary>
void Render()
{
    // Clear the color and depth buffers
    gl.Clear(gl.GL_COLOR_BUFFER_BIT);
```

You will note that when we call Clear, we tell OpenGL exactly what we want to clear by providing, in this case, GL_COLOR_BUFFER_BIT as a parameter; this relates the drawing buffer, so the screen is cleared. There are other things that we can clear as well as or instead of the drawing buffer, notably the depth buffer. We will examine that in more detail when we discuss 3D rendering in Chapter 12.

In a moment, we will draw a square on the screen (the quadrilateral implied from the project's title). Instead of drawing it in a single color, we'll use a spread of different colors. This takes advantage of the ShadeModel property that we set in the InitGL function. So that we can tell OpenGL how to color the square, we will define a color for each of its corners.

The colors are defined as an array of float values. Each color requires three floats, one each for the red, green and blue intensity, each specified in the range of 0 to 1. As we have four corners on our square, we need to define four colors, and so we have a total of 12 different values in the array. We put a line break in the source code after each complete color definition to aid the readability of the array content. The color array can be seen in Listing 10–9.

Listing 10–9. The Four-Color Array Definition in the Render Function

```
// Generate an array of colors for our quad.
// Each triplet contains the red, green and blue values
// for one of the vertices of the quads, specified from
// 0 (no intensity) to 1 (full intensity).
float[] quadColors = new float[]    {   1.0f, 0.0f, 0.0f,     // red
                                        0.0f, 1.0f, 0.0f,     // green
                                        0.0f, 0.0f, 1.0f,     // blue
                                        1.0f, 1.0f, 1.0f};    // white
```

■ **NOTE** We are not supplying any alpha components to the colors in Listing 10–9, which would allow us to render with semitransparency. We will look at how to use alpha in our colors in the "Using Transparency and Alpha Blending" section later in this chapter.

The next step is to position the quadrilateral on the screen. We will look at the purpose and operation of the functions shown here in more detail in the "Using Matrix Transformations" section later in this chapter, but as a brief summary of their purpose, the three commands reset the drawing position to the centre of the screen, moves it a short distance into the screen (which makes rendered objects look smaller due to the perspective projection that is in use) and then rotates it by the angle specified in variable _rotation around the z axis.

■ **NOTE** The z axis runs forward to backward, into and out of the screen. Rotating around this axis, therefore, causes an object to spin like the blades of a fan viewed face on.

The code required to perform these movements is shown in Listing 10–10.

Listing 10–10. Setting the Drawing Position in the Render Function

```
// Load the identity matrix
gl.LoadIdentity();
// Rotate by the angle required for this frame
gl.Rotatef(_rotation, 0.0f, 0.0f, 1.0f);
```

Two instructions remain to look at in the Render code. The first calls into another function, RenderColorQuad. We'll look at this in a moment. After this, we simply add to the _rotation variable so that our shape is drawn at a different angle each time the scene is rendered. The final part of Render is shown in Listing 10–11.

Listing 10–11. Rendering the Quadrilateral and Updating the Rotation Angle in the Render Function

```
// Render the quad using the colors provided
RenderColorQuad(quadColors);

// Increase the rotation angle for the next render
_rotation += 1f;
}
```

The actual drawing of the shape is performed by RenderColorQuad. We name the function in this way because we want it to draw just using solid color. Later on, we will create a similar function called RenderTextureQuad that will allow us to draw quadrilaterals with images draw on them.

The code for RenderColorQuad is shown in Listing 10–12.

Listing 10–12. Drawing a Colored Quadrilateral to the Screen

```
/// <summary>
/// Render a quad at the current location using the provided colors
/// for the bottom-left, bottom-right, top-left and top-right
/// corners respectively.
/// </summary>
/// <param name="quadColors">An array of four sets of Red, Green and Blue
/// floats.</param>
unsafe private void RenderColorQuad(float[] quadColors)
{
    // The vertex positions for a flat unit-size square
    float[] quadVertices = new float[]  {   -0.5f, -0.5f, 0.0f,
                                             0.5f, -0.5f, 0.0f,
                                            -0.5f,  0.5f, 0.0f,
                                             0.5f,  0.5f, 0.0f};

    // Fix a pointer to the quad vertices and the quad colors
    fixed (float* quadPointer = &quadVertices[0], colorPointer = &quadColors[0])
```

```
    {
        // Enable processing of the vertex and color arrays
        gl.EnableClientState(gl.GL_VERTEX_ARRAY);
        gl.EnableClientState(gl.GL_COLOR_ARRAY);

        // Provide a reference to the vertex array and color arrays
        gl.VertexPointer(3, gl.GL_FLOAT, 0, (IntPtr)quadPointer);
        gl.ColorPointer(3, gl.GL_FLOAT, 0, (IntPtr)colorPointer);

        // Draw the quad. We draw a strip of triangles, considering
        // four vertices within the vertex array.
        gl.DrawArrays(gl.GL_TRIANGLE_STRIP, 0, 4);

        // Disable processing of the vertex and color arrays now that we
        // have used them.
        gl.DisableClientState(gl.GL_VERTEX_ARRAY);
        gl.DisableClientState(gl.GL_COLOR_ARRAY);
    }
}
```

The first thing to note about this procedure is that it is declared with the unsafe keyword. This is the first procedure we have looked at that needs this flag, and the reason for this is that it uses memory pointers, which is not normally permitted in C# (and is not supported at all in VB.NET). We specify this keyword to tell Visual Studio to relax this restriction for our function and permit us to use pointers even though they are not normally allowed.

The function requires a single parameter, a float array containing the colors for each corner of the quad. This will receive the quadColors array that we declared in the Render function.

Inside the function, the first thing that happens is that another array of float values is defined. This time, they are not colors but coordinates. We again have four sets of coordinates (one for each point of the square), and the values here define x, y, and z positions respectively. As negative values on the y axis are toward the bottom of the screen, the points represent the bottom-left, bottom-right, top-left, and top-right corners of a square respectively.

The extent of the coordinates is from –0.5 to 0.5 across the x and y axes, giving the square a total width and height of 1 and centering it on the coordinate (0, 0, 0). The z coordinate is unused in these positions and is left at 0 for each point.

In order for us to pass the coordinate and color arrays to OpenGL, we need to obtain a pointer to their locations within the system memory. To obtain this pointer, we must use the fixed statement, which will return a pointer to the variables that we specify and—crucially—*pins* the memory used by these variables so that they will not be moved by .NET CF. Without this, a garbage collection operation could occur while we are using the pointer, moving the underlying data elsewhere in memory and leaving our pointer invalid; this would result in memory corruption and a crashed or malfunctioning application.

With our two pointers obtained, we tell OpenGL that we want to draw from a vertex array (an array of points, as we defined in the quadVertices variable) and that we want to draw using colors (from the quadColors array). This is achieved using the two calls to EnableClientState.

Next, we tell OpenGL the memory locations where it can find the vertex and color data that we have told it we are going to use. The VertexPointer and ColorPointer functions both take essentially the same parameters. First of all, we tell them how many data elements make up each vertex or color. As we are using three coordinates for the vertices and three elements for the colors, we pass the value 3 for the parameter to both function calls.

Next, we specify the data type contained within our data arrays. We are using float values, so we pass the constant GL_FLOAT to reflect this.

The third parameter is the *stride*. This is the number of bytes that appears between each set of float values and the next. If we were using a structure to store multiple pieces of data about each vertex such that additional pieces of information existed between the values for each vertex or color, we would set this to be the number of bytes that data occupied. As there is no gap between each vertex or color, we provide the value 0 for this parameter.

Finally, we provide the pointer to the vertices or colors that we wish to use.

Everything is ready to actually draw the quadrilateral now. This is achieved by calling the DrawArrays function and telling it that we want to draw a strip of triangles via the GL_TRIANGLE_STRIP parameter—this will be discussed in more detail in the "Drawing Functions" section later in this chapter. The next parameter states that we want to start drawing from the first vertex in the array, vertex 0. Finally we specify to draw four vertices: the first three form the first triangle and the final vertex concludes the last triangle. If this second triangle doesn't make sense, it, too, will be discussed in the "Drawing Functions" section.

The quadrilateral has now been drawn to the back buffer. We reset OpenGL to its previous state by disabling the vertex and color processing states that were set up earlier on and end the fixed block, releasing the pins on the vertex and color arrays.

Adding Form Functions

The next piece of wiring required to hook everything together is in the form functions. We need to hook into various events to initialize and drive the simulation.

First, we have the Load event. This calls into our CreateGL and InitGL functions to create and configure the environment. If everything is successful, the class-level _glInitialized flag is set to indicate that OpenGL is ready for action. Otherwise, an error message is displayed to the user and the form (and the application) closes. The event code can be seen in Listing 10–13.

Listing 10–13. The Form's Load Event Handler

```
/// <summary>
/// Process the form load
/// </summary>
private void MainForm_Load(object sender, EventArgs e)
{
    try
    {
        // Create and initialize the OpenGL environment
        CreateGL();
        InitGL();
        // Indicate that initialization was successful
        _glInitialized = true;
    }
    catch (Exception ex)
    {
        // Something went wrong
        MessageBox.Show(ex.Message);
        // Close the application
        this.Close();
    }
}
```

Now, we deal with the form painting. The first requirement here is to override the OnPaintBackground function to prevent the background from painting, exactly as we did in our GDI examples.

Then, we come to the Paint event. We can do something interesting with OpenGL to simplify the rendering and painting loop compared to the one we used with GDI. As OpenGL requires the entire form to be repainted for every frame, we can get the Paint event to render to the back buffer, swap the back buffer to the front, and then simply Invalidate the whole form. Because the form was invalidated, another paint will be immediately triggered, causing the render/invalidate cycle to loop endlessly.

However, should the application lose focus, the Paint event will stop firing (the form only needs to be painted when it is visible). Minimizing the form, therefore, automatically pauses the render/invalidate cycle. When the form comes to the front again, Windows Mobile automatically invalidates it and so the loop restarts. This is a very neat (and most importantly, fast) mechanism for keeping our game content moving.

The code for the form's Paint event is shown in Listing 10–14.

Listing 10–14. The Form's Paint Event Handler

```
/// <summary>
/// Paint the form
/// </summary>
private void MainForm_Paint(object sender, PaintEventArgs e)
{
    // Make sure OpenGL is initialized -- we cannot
    // render if it is not.
    if (_glInitialized)
    {
        // Render to the back buffer
        Render();
        // Swap the buffers so that our updated frame is displayed
        egl.SwapBuffers(_eglDisplay, _eglSurface);
    }

    // Invalidate the whole form to force another immediate repaint
    Invalidate();
}
```

The code first ensures that OpenGL has been initialized by checking the _glInitialized flag. If this is set, it calls into Render so that OpenGL can perform all of its drawing to the surface back buffer. The egl.SwapBuffers function is then called, instructing EGL to switch the front and back buffers so that we can see what has just been rendered. Finally, the form is invalidated to trigger the next call to the Paint event.

The remaining form events are all self-explanatory: the Exit menu item closes the form when clicked, the form's Resize event calls into the InitGLViewport function as we discussed back in the "Initializing OpenGL" section, and the Closing event terminates OpenGL, as discussed in the next section.

Terminating OpenGL

When our application finishes and closes down, it is important that it releases all of the resources that have been allocation during its operation. As our OpenGL interface uses a number of unmanaged resources, it is even more important that these are released properly so as to avoid memory leaks within the device.

The resources are released very easily, by instructing EGL to release the surface, context, and display objects that we created in the CreateGL function. The code required to do this is contained in the DestroyGL function, shown in Listing 10–15.

Listing 10–15. Terminating Our Connection with OpenGL

```
/// <summary>
/// Destroy the EGL objects and release their resources
/// </summary>
private void DestroyGL()
{
    egl.DestroySurface(_eglDisplay, _eglSurface);
    egl.DestroyContext(_eglDisplay, _eglContext);
    egl.Terminate(_eglDisplay);
}
```

Running the Program

That's it—we're all ready to run! Ensure that Visual Studio is set to deploy to your Windows Mobile device, and start the program running. If all is well, a smooth spinning colored square should appear, as shown in Figure 10–4.

Figure 10–4. The output from the ColoredQuad project

It should be apparent even from this simple example that OpenGL has a considerable amount of graphical power, especially when compared to GDI.

The colors within the quadrilateral are generated by OpenGL with the same interpolation technique that we used for smooth object movement in the game engine. It smoothly fades the colors across the surface of the rendered graphics, providing a very attractive set of colors within the square. By tailoring the colors used, all sorts of attractive color fade effects can be achieved.

Adding Some Sparkle

This spinning quadrilateral only scratches the surface of what OpenGL is able to do for us. Let's make a simple change to the project that results in a dramatic and attractive enhancement to the displayed graphics.

Simply changing the call to RenderColorQuad within the Render function to the loop shown in Listing 10–16 has a significant effect on the graphics that are displayed on the screen, as shown in Figure 10–5. This code can be found in the NestedQuads project in the accompanying download.

Listing 10–16. Rendering the Quadrilaterals in the NestedQuads Project

```
// Draw a series of quads, each at a slightly smaller size
for (int i = 0; i < 20; i++)
{
    // Scale the size down by 5%
    gl.Scalef(0.95f, 0.95f, 1);
    // Rotate by our rotation angle
    gl.Rotatef(_rotation, 0.0f, 0.0f, 1.0f);
    // Render the colored quad
    RenderColorQuad(quadColors);
}
```

Figure 10–5. Some example screen shots from the NestedQuad project

The screen shots sadly don't do justice to the NestedQuad project in operation; it is much better in motion than in still images, but this gives an idea of the patterns that this tiny piece of code is able to generate.

All that the loop is doing is drawing 20 shapes instead of one, each of which is slightly smaller than the last and rotated to a different angle. The scale and rotate operations are cumulative, meaning that while the first (largest) square is rotated by the angle specified in _rotation, the second square is rotated by double this angle, the third by three times the angle, and so on.

Using Matrix Transformations

Let's take a closer look at what is happening when we move the shape that we are drawing.

Within OpenGL, the position at which we are going to draw graphics is tracked using a *matrix*. This is a set of values, arranged in rows or columns, which can be applied to the coordinates of our vertices in order to move them around on the screen.

By combining multiple matrices, movement operations can be grouped together. For example, we may want to move an object 1 unit to the right and then rotate it by 45 degrees. To do this, we start with an empty matrix, apply the movement matrix, and then the rotation matrix. The resulting matrix can be used to transform any vertex coordinate so that it moves 1 unit to the right and rotates by 45 degrees. There is no need to apply the movement and rotation individually to each vertex.

This allows for transformations to be built up into greater and greater levels of complexity but doesn't make calculating the point on screen at which each vertex will be drawn any more difficult.

Exactly how these matrices are created, manipulated, and applied is not something that we will cover in any detail in this book. There are plenty of online references that will explain this subject in further detail; for example, see http://en.wikipedia.org/wiki/Matrix_(mathematics) for information on what a matrix is, how matrices and constructed, and how arithmetic operations are performed, and http://tinyurl.com/matrixtransform to read about how matrix transformations work at a mathematical level.

We will discuss how matrix transformations are actually used in practical terms. Though the numerical representations of transformations may be somewhat abstract, visualizing what each transformation is going to do is somewhat easier.

Setting the Identity Matrix

We have already discussed the fact that OpenGL maintains state for lots of properties that affect how it will render to the screen. One of these properties is the matrix that will be used to transform vertices for rendering that we discussed in the previous few paragraphs. This is known as the *model-view* matrix.

In order to reset this matrix to its initial state, we set the matrix to a preset set of values called the *identity matrix*. This ensures that any rendering that takes place will initially be centered at the origin, that is, at coordinate (0, 0, 0), and will not be rotated or scaled at all.

We can load the identity matrix at any time by calling the LoadIdentity function. We will almost always call this at the beginning of our rendering code, as the model-view matrix will have been left in an unknown state by the previous rendering operation. You can see this being called at the beginning of the example project's Render function back in Listing 10–10.

A square with a width and height of 1 unit can be seen in Figure 10–6 after the identity matrix has been loaded. It is directly centered on the origin of the coordinate system.

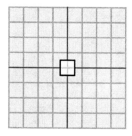

Figure 10–6. A unit square rendered after a call to LoadIdentity

Applying Translation Transformations

In the terminology of matrix transformations, moving an object along one or more of the axes is called a *translation*. The shape, size, and angle of the object are entirely unchanged, the object is just moved sideways, up, or down and in or out of the world to a new position.

Figure 10–7 shows the effect of a translation matrix. The image on the left shows the unit square in position after the identity matrix has been loaded, whereas the image on the right shows the same square after it has been translated 3 units in the x axis and –2 units in the y axis.

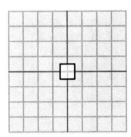 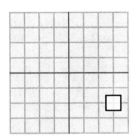

Figure 10–7. Translation of a square along the x and y axes

To apply a translation to the model-view matrix, call the Translatef function. This function requires three parameters: the translation distance for the x, y, and z axes respectively.

■ **NOTE** The reason for the letter *f* on the end of the Translatef function name is to indicate that we are passing float values as parameters. The full OpenGL implementation allows other data types to be passed; for example, the Translated function expects double values instead of floats. For the most part, we will use float values in all of our OpenGL ES code.

Applying Rotation Transformations

We are also able to rotate the objects that we draw. Objects can be rotated around any of the three available axes, as shown in Figure 10–8.

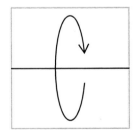 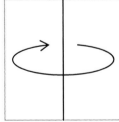 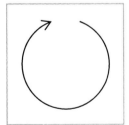

Figure 10–8. Rotations around the x, y, and z axes

Rotation around the x axis rotates around a horizontal line drawn across the screen. If you held a sheet of paper in front of you so that you were looking directly at the flat face of the paper, rotation on the x axis would rotate the paper such that the bottom edge was brought toward you and the top edge away, resulting in you looking at the paper's edge.

Rotation on the y axis is exactly the same but rotating around a vertical line.

It is z axis rotation that will be of primary use when developing a 2D game using OpenGL. This rotates around a line that traces a path into and out of the screen. Rotation on the z axis is what we used to rotate the quads in the ColoredQuad and NestedQuads example projects.

Rotation is performed by calling the Rotatef function. This expects four parameters to be passed. The first is the angle of rotation. Angles in OpenGL are always specified in degrees.

The remaining parameters identify the axis around which the rotation is to be performed. We can specify the x, y, or z axes by passing a 1 for that axis and a 0 for the others. For example, Listing 10–17 shows a rotation of 45 degrees around the z axis.

Listing 10–17. Rotating Around the z Axis

```
// Rotate by 45 degrees around the z axis
gl.Rotatef(45, 0.0f, 0.0f, 1.0f);
```

■ **NOTE** Rotating around the z axis will result in counterclockwise rotation. To rotate clockwise, either the angle can be negated or the rotation axis can be specified with –1 for the z value instead of 1.

Rotation around other axes can also be achieved by specifying the direction of the axis within the x, y, and z values. For example, to rotate around an axis that is at a 45-degree angle up and to the right, pass values of 1.0f for x, 1.0f for y and 0.0f for z. The line formed by drawing from coordinate (0, 0, 0) to (1, 1, 0) is at a 45 degree angle, and so this is the line around which rotation will be performed.

Applying Scaling Transformations

The final transformation that OpenGL offers is for *scaling*, or changing the size of the objects that we render. Scaling can be either *uniform*, in which case the object scales by the same amount on all axes, or *non-uniform* in which case each axis scales by a different amount.

Figure 10–9 shows an object in its identity location on the left, with a uniform scale of 2.0 in the middle, and then on the right with a scale of 4.0 on the x axis and 0.5 on the y axis.

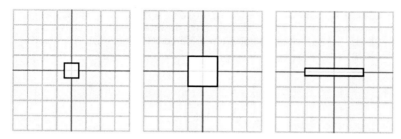

Figure 10–9. Scaling transformations.

To scale your objects, call the Scale function, passing the scaling amount for the x, y, and z axes for its three parameters.

Passing a scale value of 0 for any of the axes will squash the shape on that axis so that it is completely flat. For any axis that you wish to leave unchanged when scaling, pass a value of 1.

Negative scale values are also permitted. These will cause the object to flip over so that the vertices appear on the opposite side of the negatively scaled axis.

Applying Multiple Transformations

All of the transformations we have described are cumulative: each transformation that is applied will add to the previous translations, not replace it. If we translate 2 units to the right and then translate 3 units to the right, our overall transformation is 5 units, not just the 3 from the most recent translation.

■ **NOTE** The exception to this is loading the identify matrix. This is not itself a transformation, but rather it replaces any existing transformations, resetting everything back to an initial state.

The different types of translation can have an effect on each other that may not at first be obvious. Let's look at some examples of this.

Rotating Objects

When we rotate an object, we actually rotate its entire coordinate system. This is because we are operating on what is called the *local coordinate system* for the object. Initially, when the identity matrix is loaded, the local coordinate system exactly matches the *world coordinate system*, which describes the location of objects within the world as a whole. After we perform a rotation, the local coordinate system is no longer at the same angle as the world itself.

Objects always move relative to their local coordinate system, not the world coordinate system. This means that if we rotate an object by 45 degrees around the z axis and then translate it along the y axis, it will actually move diagonally on the screen rather than vertically. The rotation has changed the direction of the axes within the object's local coordinate system.

The effects of this rotation can be seen in Figure 10–10. On the left is our usual unit square at the identity position. In the middle, we rotate it by 45 degrees around the z axis (counterclockwise). The pale lines show the x and y axes in the world coordinate system, while the darker diagonal lines show the x and y axes for the rotated local coordinate system. On the right, we translate it along its y axis. Observe how it has moved diagonally relative to world coordinates, though it has followed its own local y axis. Also note that the local coordinate system follows the translation, too. The coordinate (0, 0, 0) is always at the centre of an object's local coordinate system.

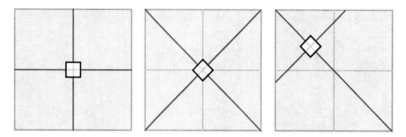

Figure 10–10. Rotation and translation in the local coordinate system

This sequence of updates brings us to another important feature of matrix transformations: the order in which they are applied is significant. In Figure 10–10, we first rotated and then translated our object. If we instead translate and then rotate it, the local coordinate system for the translation would still be aligned with the world coordinate system, so the movement on the screen would be vertical. This is shown in Figure 10–11, which contains exactly the same transformations but performed with the translation before the rotation.

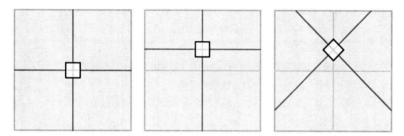

Figure 10–11. Translation before rotation

As you can see, the object ends up in a different place if we translate it first.

This is actually very easy to visualize. Imagine that you are standing in place of the square object in these diagrams. You are initially standing at the origin of the world coordinate system, looking along the positive y axis (up the screen).

You then decide to rotate 45 degrees counterclockwise, just as we did in Figure 10–10. You are still facing straight ahead of your body, but relative to the world, you are now looking diagonally. If you now take a few paces forward, you are walking diagonally in terms of the world but straight ahead in terms of your own position within the world.

If you hold your arms out to the sides, these will be pointing along the x axis relative to your position but are once again at a diagonal angle relative to the world.

At any time when you want to visualize the transformations that you are applying, think of this same scenario and apply each transformation in sequence to yourself in the world. It should then be easy to see the sequence of transformations that you need to apply to get from one place to another.

Hopefully, this makes the relationship between the local and world coordinate systems clear. Always remember that when you transform an object, the transformation will be relative to its local coordinates and not to those of the world.

Scaling Objects

When we scale an object, the transformation once again has an effect on the object's local coordinate system. If we scale an object such that its size doubles, a movement of 1 unit in the x axis in the local coordinate system will correspond to a movement of 2 units in the world coordinate system.

If you simply want to draw an object at a different size but without affecting its position, remember to perform the scale transformation after all of the translations and rotations have been completed.

Specifying Vertex Positions

You may recall that when we looked at the RenderColorQuad function back in Listing 10–12, the code defined a unit square by specifying four vertices with coordinates at (–0.5, –0.5, 0), (0.5, –0.5, 0), (–0.5, 0.5, 0), (0.5, 0.5, 0). These coordinates are, of course, specified within the local coordinate system too, not the world coordinate system.

When we use transformations to manipulate the local coordinate system, these transformations are applied to each individual vertex when rendering, which causes the object to actually move on the screen. Because the local origin has been moved, rotated, and scaled relative to the world, all of the vertex positions transformed in exactly the same way. We can, therefore, define any shape we like using these vertex coordinates, and it will move around the screen as specified by our matrix transformations.

Pushing and Popping the Matrix

Sometimes, when the transformation matrix is being manipulated, it can be useful to be able to store its current state so that you can return to it again later. For example, if you wish to draw an object at various different positions around a central location, it can be useful to translate away from the center point, draw the object, return back to the center point, rotate for the next object, translate away again, draw the second object, and so on.

To tell OpenGL to remember your transformation matrix at any stage, you can call the PushMatrix function. This puts the current matrix on to a *stack*. The transformation matrix itself it not affected by this call.

At a later point in time, you can call the PopMatrix function to retrieve the matrix on the top of the stack and make it the active transformation matrix once again. This retrieves the stored matrix.

It is important to ensure that each and every PushMatrix call is matched with a corresponding PopMatrix call. You should ensure that there are never any surplus matrices left on the stack.

Practicing Matrix Transformations with Example Projects

Two example projects demonstrating matrix transformations are provided in the accompanying download for this chapter. Let's take a quick look at each of them.

The Orbits Project

Orbits demonstrates a very simple simulation of a solar system. In the center of the screen is a yellow sun object. Around this orbits a blue planet, and a gray moon orbits around the planet.

The Render function that displays these objects is shown in Listing 10–18.

Listing 10–18. Orbiting Planets

```
/// <summary>
/// Render the OpenGL scene
/// </summary>
void Render()
{
    // Clear the color and depth buffers
    gl.Clear(gl.GL_COLOR_BUFFER_BIT);

    // Reset the model-view matrix so that we can draw the tree
    gl.LoadIdentity();
    // Scale down so that the shapes are not too large
    gl.Scalef(0.1f, 0.1f, 0.1f);

    // Draw the sun
    RenderColorQuad(Color.Yellow);

    // Rotate for the the orbiting planet
    gl.Rotatef(_rotation, 0, 0, 1);
    // Translate into position for the planet
    gl.Translatef(0, 6, 0);
    // Draw the planet
    RenderColorQuad(Color.MediumBlue);

    // Rotate for the moon
    gl.Rotatef(_rotation * 4, 0, 0, 1);
    // Translate into position for the moon
    gl.Translatef(0, 3, 0);
    // Draw the moon
    RenderColorQuad(Color.Gray);

    // Advance the simulation
    _rotation += 1;
}
```

First, we draw a yellow box in the middle of the screen to represent the sun. This is completely stationary; it doesn't move or rotate.

Next, we draw the planet. To do this, we first rotate our viewpoint so that we are looking toward the planet's current position, and then we translate along the rotated y axis to reach the planet's location. The planet is then drawn as a blue box.

Continuing on from our current position and angle, we rotate again for the moon's angle (multiplying _rotation by 4 so that the moon orbits faster than the planet). Next, we translate to the planet's final position and render it as a gray box.

Because we rotate and translate from the planet's position into the moon's position, the moon orbits around the planet rather than around the sun. The movement paths are shown in Figure 10–12 as the dashed circles, and the translations are shown as black lines.

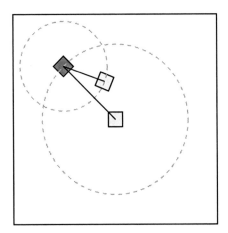

Figure 10–12. The movement paths of the objects in the Orbits example

This movement pattern could easily translate into any of a variety of different scenarios. For example, the box that is being drawn to represent the sun could instead represent a robot's shoulder, the planet the robot's elbow, and the moon the robot's hand. Combined with some limitations in the angles to which each element is allowed to rotate, this would simulate the ability of the robot to move its arm.

The FractalTrees project

The second example is slightly more complex but again demonstrates the principles of repeated rotation and translation. It also uses the PushMatrix and PopMatrix functions to remember and recall the current transformation matrix.

The concept behind the project is simple. First, draw a thin vertical box to form the trunk of the tree. At the top of the box, rotate a little to the left and draw another box for the left part of a branch on the tree; then, rotate a little to the right and draw a third box for the right part of the tree branch. This results in the shape shown in Figure 10–13.

Figure 10–13. The base of the fractal tree

Each of the two rotated branches repeats the same process: it draws itself (as shown in Figure 10–13) and then draws two further rotated branches at its own end point. The result of this is shown in Figure 10–14.

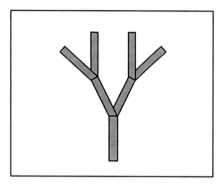

Figure 10–14. Growing the fractal tree

This pattern is repeated again and again to grow the whole tree. In addition to the steps shown here, the project also reduces the size of each subsequent generation of branches a little (just as a real tree does) and introduces an extra rotation to each child branch based on a sine wave, which allows us to make the tree sway as if in the breeze. The output of this project can be seen in Figure 10–15.

Figure 10–15. The FractalTrees project in action

The code to generate the tree is still fairly simple, but it uses a concept called *recursion*, which may seem a little complex if you've not used it before. Recursion is where a function calls back into itself to repeat a task over and over again. Uncontrolled, this self-calling would end up in an infinite loop, so recursive algorithms always have an *exit condition* under which the recursion returns without doing any further work instead of calling into itself again.

Our recursive function is called RenderBranch, and it takes a single parameter called recursionLevel. Each time the function calls back into itself, it adds 1 to the parameter value, and when it detects that a sufficient level of recursion has been reached, it doesn't call into itself any further. This allows execution to return back to the calling procedure so that it can continue to execute.

RenderBranch sets up the position for the new branch before calling into itself to draw each of the child branches, it. It first rotates a little to the left so that the left branch can be drawn, and then it rotates a little to the right for the right branch. The child branches render in whatever position they find themselves, as the parent has already set the position that is required.

As each branch is drawn along with its two child branches, and those child branches each draw their own child branches and so on, the whole tree is formed as shown in Figure 10–15.

The code for RenderBranch is shown in Listing 10–19.

Listing 10–19. The Recursive DrawBranch Function

```
/// <summary>
/// Draw a branch of the tree, and then any sub-branches higher up the tree
/// </summary>
/// <param name="recursionLevel">The current recursion level.</param>
private void RenderBranch(int recursionLevel)
{
    // Generate an array of colors for the branch.
    float[] branchColors = new float[] {   0.8f, 0.6f, 0.0f,    // light-brown
                                           0.2f, 0.1f, 0.0f,    // dark-brown
                                           0.8f, 0.6f, 0.0f,    // light-brown
                                           0.2f, 0.1f, 0.0f};   // dark-brown

    // The number of levels of recursion that we will follow.
    const int MAX_RECURSION = 6;
    // The angle for each branch relative to its parent
    const float BRANCH_ANGLE = 15;

    // Push the matrix so that we can "undo" the scaling
    gl.PushMatrix();
    // Scale down on the x axis and up on the y axis so that our
    // quad forms a vertical bar
    gl.Scalef(0.4f, 2.0f, 1.0f);
    // Draw this element of the branch
    RenderColorQuad(branchColors);
    // Restore the unscaled matrix
    gl.PopMatrix();

    // Do we want to recurse into sub-branches?
    if (recursionLevel < MAX_RECURSION)
    {
        // Yes.
        // First translate to the top of the current branch
        gl.Translatef(0, 1, 0);

        // Push the matrix so that we can get back to it later
        gl.PushMatrix();
        // Rotate a little for the left branch
        gl.Rotatef(BRANCH_ANGLE + (float)Math.Sin(_treeSway / 10) * 10, 0, 0, 1);
        // Scale down slightly so that each sub-branch gets smaller
```

```
          gl.Scalef(0.9f, 0.9f, 0.9f);
          // Translate to the mid-point of the left branch
          gl.Translatef(0, 1, 0);
          // Render the branch
          RenderBranch(recursionLevel + 1);
          // Pop the matrix so that we return to the end of this branch
          gl.PopMatrix();

          // Push the matrix so that we can get back to it later
          gl.PushMatrix();
          // Rotate a little for the right branch
          gl.Rotatef(-BRANCH_ANGLE - (float)Math.Sin(_treeSway / 15) * 10, 0, 0, 1);
          // Scale down slightly so that each sub-branch gets smaller
          gl.Scalef(0.9f, 0.9f, 0.9f);
          // Translate to the mid-point of the right branch
          gl.Translatef(0, 1, 0);
          // Render the branch
          RenderBranch(recursionLevel + 1);
          // Pop the matrix so that we return to the end of this branch
          gl.PopMatrix();
     }
}
```

Drawing Functions

All of the actual drawing in our examples has been handled by the RenderColorQuad function, which we looked at back in Listing 10–12. The procedure first sets up pointers to an array of vertices and vertex colors, and then draws it with a call to the OpenGL DrawArrays function.

The first parameter passed to the DrawArrays function, the mode parameter, was the constant GL_TRIANGLE_STRIP. There are several values that we can pass here, so let's take a look at each and discuss how they are used.

Drawing Points

If we pass the constant GL_POINTS for the mode parameter when calling DrawArrays, the vertices within the vertex array will be rendered as individual pixels. Each pixel will be colored according to the color specified for that vertex.

Drawing Lines

A few different drawing modes can be used for lines: GL_LINES, GL_LINE_LOOP, and GL_LINE_STRIP.

GL_LINES will work through the supplied vertices, taking each pair as the beginning and end coordinate of a line. The lines do not need to be connected (and indeed, if they are it may be more efficient to use one of the other line drawing modes). Any surplus vertex at the end of the array will be ignored.

Figure 10–16 shows the lines drawn between four vertices using the GL_LINES mode.

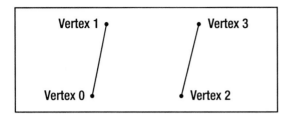

Figure 10–16. *Drawing lines in GL_LINES mode*

GL_LINE_STRIP is similar, but instead of working through pairs of vertices, it takes each new vertex and draws a line between it and the previous vertex. The result is a line drawn between all of the specified vertices, as shown in Figure 10–17.

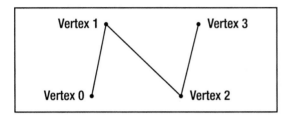

Figure 10–17. *Drawing lines in GL_LINE_STRIP mode*

The final line mode, GL_LINE_LOOP, is exactly the same as GL_LINE_STRIP except that it automatically joins the final vertex back to the first vertex to create a closed shape.

Drawing Triangles

The final group of drawing modes covers different methods for creating triangles. The available triangle modes are GL_TRIANGLES, GL_TRIANGLE_STRIP, and GL_TRIANGLE_FAN.

The GL_TRIANGLES mode takes each set of three vertices as an individual triangle. This allows multiple isolated triangles to be drawn. Figure 10–18 shows how six vertices are used to build two triangles using this mode. Any surplus vertices at the end of the array will be ignored.

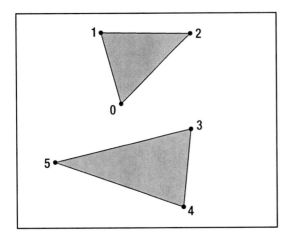

Figure 10–18. Drawing triangles in GL_TRIANGLES mode

GL_TRIANGLE_STRIP reuses vertices within the vertex array to create multiple triangles, each of which shares an edge with the previous triangle. The first three vertices are used to create the first triangle, and after that, the next triangle is formed by removing the earliest vertex in the triangle and replacing it with the next vertex. The second triangle is, therefore, formed from vertices 1, 2, and 3, the third triangle from vertices 2, 3, and 4, and so on.

As long as you want all of your triangles to share their edges, this is a very efficient way of drawing, as the shared vertices only need to be transformed once even though they are used by as many as three different triangles.

Figure 10–19 shows an example using GL_TRIANGLE_STRIP to join a series of vertices.

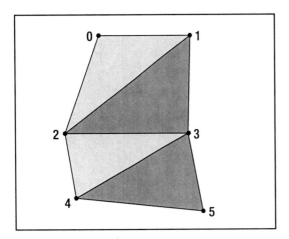

Figure 10–19. Drawing triangles in GL_TRIANGLE_STRIP mode.

The final mode, `GL_TRIANGLE_FAN`, allows a series of triangles to be drawn that all share one single point. The uses of this are more limited than the other triangle modes, but can be useful in particular when drawing ellipses or elliptical segments.

The first vertex specified is shared by all of the triangles. OpenGL then takes the next two vertices to complete the first triangle. It then works through the remaining vertices one at a time, combining each one with the previous vertex and the first vertex to construct the next triangle. Each triangle, therefore, also shares an edge with the previous triangle.

Figure 10–20 shows an example of a series of vertices rendered with this mode.

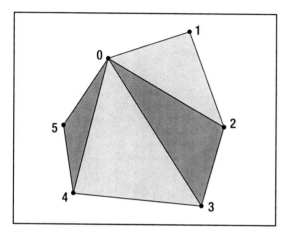

Figure 10–20. *Drawing triangles in GL_TRIANGLE_FAN mode*

Using Texture Mapping

Colored shapes are all very nice, but they're not generally what we need when we are creating a game. For our games, we want to be able to display graphics on the screen. How do we do this with OpenGL?

Fortunately, it is very easy to do so. First, we need to load a graphic file, and then we tell OpenGL to display that as a texture on the triangles that it draws. Look and see how this is done in the following sections.

Loading Graphics

Contained within the OpenGLES project is a class called Texture, which manages the loading of graphics that we want to display inside OpenGL.

To load a graphic, we call its static LoadStream method, passing in a Stream object that contains an image file (in PNG, JPG, or GIF format). If you plan to use embedded resources, this Stream can be obtained using the Assembly.GetManifestResourceStream function, the same function we used for GDI graphics. To load from a file, simply open a FileStream to the file and load from there.

The Texture.LoadStream function returns to us a Texture object, which we store away for when we are ready to render.

The code required to load a graphic can be seen in Listing 10–20. This has been added to the InitGL function and can be found in the Textures project in the accompanying download.

Listing 10–20. Loading a Texture from an Embedded Resource

```
// Load our textures
Assembly asm = Assembly.GetExecutingAssembly();
_texture = Texture.LoadStream(
        asm.GetManifestResourceStream("Textures.Graphics.Grapes.png"), true);
```

The Boolean value that is passed to the LoadStream method indicates whether the image contains transparency information. The value is passed as true in this example, but as you will see, there is no transparency visible when the image is rendered. We will address the reason for this in the "Using Transparency and Alpha Blending" section later in this chapter.

Rendering with Textures

When we are ready to render with our texture, we first need to instruct OpenGL to use the texture. Just as with the other properties, it will remember the specified texture until we tell it to use a different texture. The code in Listing 10–21 tells OpenGL to use our loaded texture and then renders a quadrilateral with the texture displayed on it.

Listing 10–21. Rendering with a Texture

```
/// <summary>
/// Render the OpenGL scene
/// </summary>
void Render()
{
    // Clear the color and depth buffers
    gl.Clear(gl.GL_COLOR_BUFFER_BIT);

    // Bind to the texture we want to render with
    gl.BindTexture(gl.GL_TEXTURE_2D, _texture.Name);

    // Load the identity matrix
    gl.LoadIdentity();
    // Draw the rotating image.
    // First translate a little way up the screen
    gl.Translatef(0, 0.5f, 0);
    // Rotate by the angle required for this frame
    gl.Rotatef(_rotation, 0.0f, 0.0f, 1.0f);
    // Render the quad using the bound texture
    RenderTextureQuad();

    // Increase the rotation angle for the next render
    _rotation += 1f;
}
```

The first thing the code does here in to tell OpenGL the texture to use by calling the BindTexture function. We pass the value returned by the Name property of our texture object. This Name is actually generated by OpenGL and is just an int rather than a readable name.

Just as we called the RenderColorQuad function in our earlier examples, we now call the RenderTextureQuad to use a texture rather than colors. RenderTextureQuad has two overloads: The first takes no parameters and displays the entire texture on the quad. The second overload allows a texture coordinate array to be passed, allowing just a section of the texture to be displayed on the shape. We'll discuss texture coordinates in the next section.

The code for the two overloads of RenderTextureQuad is shown in Listing 10–22.

Listing 10–22. Rendering a Quadrilateral with Texture Mapping Enabled

```
/// <summary>
/// Render a quad at the current location using with the current
/// bound texture mapped across it.
/// </summary>
private void RenderTextureQuad()
{
    // Build the default set of texture coordinates for the quad
    float[] texCoords = new float[] {   0.0f, 1.0f,
                                        1.0f, 1.0f,
                                        0.0f, 0.0f,
                                        1.0f, 0.0f };

    // Render the quad
    RenderTextureQuad(texCoords);
}
/// <summary>
/// Render a quad at the current location using the provided texture
/// coordinates for the bottom-left, bottom-right, top-left and top-right
/// corners respectively.
/// </summary>
/// <param name="texCoords">An array of texture coordinates</param>
unsafe private void RenderTextureQuad(float[] texCoords)
{
    // The vertex positions for a flat unit-size square
    float[] quadVertices = new float[] {    -0.5f, -0.5f, 0.0f,
                                             0.5f, -0.5f, 0.0f,
                                            -0.5f,  0.5f, 0.0f,
                                             0.5f,  0.5f, 0.0f};

    // Fix a pointer to the quad vertices and the texture coordinates
    fixed (float* quadPointer = &quadVertices[0], texPointer = &texCoords[0])
    {
        // Enable textures
        gl.Enable(gl.GL_TEXTURE_2D);

        // Enable processing of the vertex and texture arrays
        gl.EnableClientState(gl.GL_VERTEX_ARRAY);
        gl.EnableClientState(gl.GL_TEXTURE_COORD_ARRAY);

        // Provide a reference to the vertex and texture arrays
        gl.VertexPointer(3, gl.GL_FLOAT, 0, (IntPtr)quadPointer);
        gl.TexCoordPointer(2, gl.GL_FLOAT, 0, (IntPtr)texPointer);

        // Draw the quad. We draw a strip of triangles, considering
        // four vertices within the vertex array.
        gl.DrawArrays(gl.GL_TRIANGLE_STRIP, 0, 4);

        // Disable processing of the vertex and texture arrays now that we
```

```
        // have used them.
        gl.DisableClientState(gl.GL_VERTEX_ARRAY);
        gl.DisableClientState(gl.GL_TEXTURE_COORD_ARRAY);

        // Disable textures
        gl.Disable(gl.GL_TEXTURE_2D);
    }
}
```

The first overload builds a default set of texture coordinates, mapping the entire texture onto the quadrilateral, and then calls the second overload.

The second overload is very similar to the RenderColorQuad function, except that it works with textures instead of colors. First, the GL_TEXTURE_2D flag is passed to the Enable function to enable texture mapping. There is no point having this flag enabled if texture mapping is not in use, so it is kept switched off until then.

The GL_TEXTURE_COORD_ARRAY client state is enabled, and the TexCoordPointer function called with the location of the texture coordinates. Note that texture coordinates are specified in two dimensions, as our images are only 2D. They can still be mapped onto 3D objects however.

After the quadrilateral has been drawn with the DrawArrays function, all of the texture mapping features that we have enabled are disabled again so that everything is put back to a known state.

Specifying Texture Coordinates

Just as coordinates on the screen are measured using axes called x and y, textures have axes called s and t. The s axis covers the distance across the width of a texture, while the t axis covers the distance across its height.

Regardless of the resolution of the graphic that has been loaded, the s and t coordinates will scale from 0 to 1, where 0 represents the left edge of the s axis and the top edge of the t axis, and 1 represents the right edge of the s axis and the bottom edge of the t axis, as shown in Figure 10–21.

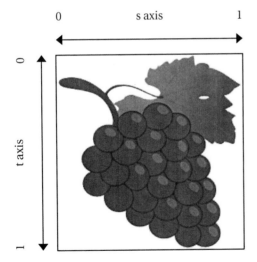

Figure 10–21. The s and t axes for texture coordinates

When we want to draw using texture mapping, we set up an array of values that indicate the texture coordinates to use for each vertex. Although the vertices are specified in three dimensions and contain three values per vertex, texture coordinates are reading from a 2D image, so we provide just two values per vertex, the s and t coordinates for that vertex to use.

To draw a quadrilateral so that it contains the entire texture mapped on it, we specify s and t coordinates of (0, 1) for the bottom-left corner, (1, 1) for the bottom-right corner, (0, 0) for the top-left corner and (1, 0) for the top-right corner. This is the array that you can see being constructed in the first overload of RenderTextureQuad in Listing 10–22.

Alternatively, we can specify just a section of the texture that we want to map. Remember that the physical vertex coordinates are completely unaffected by this; all we are doing is specifying the area of the texture that will be applied to the quadrilateral. If we provide texture coordinates that cover only a smaller portion of the texture image, this portion will be stretched to fit the shape being drawn.

Figure 10–22 shows an example of using a subsection of the texture in this way. The texture coordinates span from 0 to 0.5 along the both the s and t axes.

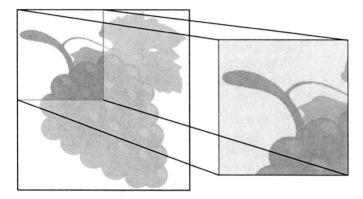

Figure 10–22. Mapping a section of the source texture into a rendered quadrilateral

Another feature of the texture coordinates is that they are not restricted to staying within the range of 0 to 1. If we specify coordinates outside of this range, we can get the texture to repeat within out rendered graphics. Figure 10–23 shows a quadrilateral rendered with values from 0 to 3 on the s axis and 0 to 2 on the t axis.

The Textures project in the accompanying download shows examples of all of the techniques we have discussed in this section. A variety of interesting effects can be achieved by moving the texture coordinates around within the image when rendering. Please do take some time to experiment with how texture coordinates work so that you feel comfortable using them.

Figure 10–23. Wrapping the texture

Cleaning Up

Textures are yet another unmanaged resource, so it is important that we clean them up when we have finished. The Texture object has a Dispose method, so we simply need to call that for each texture when terminating the rest of our OpenGL objects.

Using Transparency and Alpha Blending

OpenGL offers us some mechanisms for dealing with transparency when we render our graphics. The first is to allow parts of a texture to be made transparent, while the second allows semitransparent rendering to be performed. Let's take a look at how we can use these.

Applying Transparency

As already noted, the background of the image in the Textures project was rendered as solid color. It would be very useful to be able to make it transparent so that any graphics already on the screen showed through.

Fortunately, this is easy to implement. The first step is to tell OpenGL how to determine whether a pixel is transparent or not. We can tell it, whenever a pixel's alpha value is 1.0, to consider this pixel transparent and not draw it to the window. The second step is to enable the alpha test, without which the alpha check will be ignored.

These steps are performed using the instructions shown in Listing 10–23.

Listing 10–23. Enabling the Alpha Test for Transparent Backgrounds

```
// Enable the alpha test
gl.Enable(gl.GL_ALPHA_TEST);
// Set the alpha function to treat pixels whose alpha value
// is 1.0 as transparent.
gl.AlphaFunc(gl.GL_EQUAL, 1.0f);
```

If you add these lines to the Textures project, you will see that the background does indeed become transparent. The code can be added to the InitGL function if it will be left active for all rendering operations, or it can be updated, enabled, and disabled as required during the rendering code.

Unlike GDI, we actually use the alpha channel contained within the image to determine whether each pixel in the texture is to be rendered transparent or opaque. This means that whatever paint package you use to create textures needs to be able to create images that use the alpha channel for transparency. Many paint packages (including Paint.NET, Paint Shop Pro, and Photoshop) are capable of creating images with alpha channels – consult your documentation for further details. Make sure you save your graphics in PNG format so that the alpha channel is retained, as not all graphic formats support them.

Alpha Blending

In addition to rendering textures with transparent backgrounds, we can also render quads with different degrees of transparency. This is known as *alpha blending*, as it uses an alpha value (for example, the one contained within each color definition which up until this point we haven't used at all) to blend the objects being drawn in with the existing colors that have already been drawn.

Just as with the other OpenGL effects, alpha blending must first be enabled. If part or all of your rendering doesn't need alpha blending, disabling it will improve performance as the graphics hardware will have less work to do.

Once blending is enabled, it needs to be told exactly how to blend colors in the objects you are rendering with the colors already present on the screen. Essentially, the mechanism involves providing a source color and a source *factor*, which controls how that color is manipulated for display. OpenGL then uses the destination color (the color that is already on the screen) and a destination factor controlling how it is manipulated. The colors and their factors are then multiplied for both source and destination, and the results are added together to produce the final output color.

The code required to enable alpha blending and select the blending factors is shown in Listing 10–24.

Listing 10–24. *Enabling and Configuring Alpha Blending*

```
// Enable alpha blending
gl.Enable(gl.GL_BLEND);
// Set the blending function
//gl.BlendFunc(gl.GL_SRC_ALPHA, gl.GL_ONE_MINUS_SRC_ALPHA);
```

Let's take a look at the blending factors in more detail and gain some insight into what they do.

One of the factors available for the source color is defined by the constant GL_ONE. This provides the value 1 for each of the color's red, green, blue, and alpha color elements. Another factor is GL_ZERO, which provides the value 0 for each color component. If we use GL_ONE as the source factor and GL_ZERO as the destination factor, the color for each pixel is calculated as follows:

```
OutputRed = (SourceRed * 1) + (DestinationRed * 0)
OutputGreen = (SourceGreen * 1) + (DestinationGreen * 0)
OutputBlue = (SourceBlue * 1) + (DestinationBlue * 0)
OutputAlpha = (SourceAlpha * 1) + (DestinationAlpha * 0)
```

As you can see, the end result if this pair of blending factors is that the object is rendered absolutely opaque; no blending takes place at all. The output colors calculated are exactly the same as the source colors, with the existing destination color completely ignored.

Let's take a look at a different pair of blending functions. We will use the GL_SRC_ALPHA factor for the source, and GL_ONE_MINUS_SRC_ALPHA for the destination. GL_SRC_ALPHA provides the alpha component for the source color, and GL_ONE_MINUS_SRC_ALPHA provides, as you might expect, the source color's alpha subtracted from 1. The output color of each pixel is therefore calculated as follows:

```
OutputRed = (SourceRed * SourceAlpha) + (DestinationRed * (1 - SourceAlpha))
OutputGreen = (SourceGreen * SourceAlpha) + (DestinationGreen * (1 - SourceAlpha))
OutputBlue = (SourceBlue * SourceAlpha) + (DestinationBlue * (1 - SourceAlpha))
OutputAlpha = (SourceAlpha * SourceAlpha) + (DestinationAlpha * (1 - SourceAlpha))
```

Do these calculations look familiar? They are exactly the same calculation that we used for interpolation when calculating the positions of our game objects between updates. If SourceAlpha is 1.0, the color will be taken entirely from the source red, green, blue, and alpha (as it was in the previous set of calculations), resulting in the object being rendered entirely opaque. If SourceAlpha is 0.0, the color will be taken entirely from the destination red, green, blue, and alpha, resulting in the object being rendered entirely transparent (and therefore invisible). Values between 1 and 0 will gradually fade the object from opaque to transparent.

Another useful pairing of factors is to use GL_SRC_ALPHA for the source factor and GL_ONE for the destination. This creates an *additive blend*: objects will never be entirely opaque as the destination color is being retained in full; instead, the source color adds to the color that is already present. Overlapping regions of color will mix together, so that blue and red will become purple, green and red will become yellow, and so on.

The AlphaBlending project included in the accompanying download contains a simple example with three colored quadrilaterals rendered in the screen so that they all partially overlap. The code gradually fades the level of alpha for each quadrilateral between 0 and 1, at a slightly different speed for each shape, so the blending interaction can be easily seen.

Take a look at the project and try experimenting with different blending functions in the InitGL function. A list of all the available blending functions (and a description of each) can be found in the "Knowing the Available Blending Factors" section coming up soon.

The example's new RenderColorAlphaQuad takes care of passing the alpha values to OpenGL. Note that colors are now specified with four elements instead of three (red, green, blue, and alpha) and that the call to the ColorPointer function tells OpenGL about this extra element by specifying 4 as its first parameter value, rather than 3 as in the RenderColorQuad function earlier.

Alpha Blending with Textures

Alpha blending has some very useful functions when we are using texture mapping too, as shown in the following sections. The AlphaBlending example project has a demonstration using textured quadrilaterals too; select the Use Textures option from the menu to enable this.

Textures with Alpha Channels

First of all, we can use the alpha channel within a texture to give us controlled transparency across the texture when rendering. If a texture is created that is opaque around the outside and fades to transparent in the middle, the rendered texture can observe the same faded transparency levels in the rendered object. Another useful technique for this is to use the alpha channel to provide smoothing around the edge of the graphic within the texture. When rendered, the edges of the graphic will blend in with whatever color is already present on the screen.

The blend factors required to draw textures in this way are GL_SRC_ALPHA for the source factor and GL_ONE_MINUS_SRC_ALPHA for the destination factor—exactly the same as one of the color blend pairs that we looked at a moment ago.

Additive Texture Blending

Another useful function is the ability to leave black areas of the texture entirely unchanged when rendered on the screen but allow colored areas of the texture to still appear. This is particularly useful for *particle effects*, where we want to display stars, sparks or flames on top of existing graphics.

This blending effect can be achieved using GL_ONE for both the source and destination. The source color and the destination color are both retained and added together. This is another additive blend.

Controlled Transparency of Textures

The final scenario we will examine here is fading a texture between opaque and transparent. Everything you have seen so far uses an alpha channel from either a color or a texture. The alpha channel of a texture is completely static: we cannot change it in order to change the texture's transparency level. When we are using a texture, we are not using vertex colors, so we have no opportunity to specify an alpha level within the color.

So how can we fade textured objects?

The answer is to use both textures and colors at the same time. This actually has other uses too, allowing a texture to be colored based on the vertex colors specified. At the moment, however, we will make every vertex color white, so that the colors of the texture are not disturbed. The alpha value can then be placed into the vertex colors to fade the texture between opaque and transparent.

All we need to do to implement this is make another call to EnableClientState to enable the color array as well as the vertex and texture arrays. This can be seen in the RenderColorAlphaTextureQuad function in the AlphaBlending example project.

Knowing the Available Blending Factors

Table 10–1 shows the blending factors that can be used in OpenGL ES, the places they can be used (as source or destination factors), and a brief description of what each factor does.

In Table 10–1, the Src calculation items represent the source red, green, blue or alpha values being blended. The Dest calculation items represent the destination red, green, blue or alpha values being blended. The Min calculations take the minimum of the two values – for example, if SrcAlpha is 0.5 and 1 – DestAlpha is 0.25, the value 0.25 will be used.

Table 10–1. Blending Factors

Factor	Used For	Calculation
GL_ZERO	Source and destination	(0, 0, 0, 0)
GL_ONE	Source and destination	(1, 1, 1, 1)
GL_SRC_ALPHA	Source and destination	(SrcAlpha, SrcAlpha, SrcAlpha, SrcAlpha)
GL_ONE_MINUS_SRC_ALPHA	Source and destination	(1 – SrcAlpha, 1 – SrcAlpha, 1 – SrcAlpha, 1 – SrcAlpha)
GL_DST_ALPHA	Source and destination	(DestAlpha, DestAlpha, DestAlpha, DestAlpha)
GL_ONE_MINUS_DST_ALPHA	Source and destination	(1 – DestAlpha, 1 – DestAlpha, 1 – DestAlpha, 1 – DestAlpha)
GL_SRC_COLOR	Destination	(SrcRed, SrcGreen, SrcBlue, SrcAlpha)
GL_ONE_MINUS_SRC_COLOR	Destination	(1 – SrcRed, 1 – SrcGreen, 1 – SrcBlue, 1 – SrcAlpha)
GL_DST_COLOR	Source	(DestRed, DestGreen, DestBlue, DestAlpha)
GL_ONE_MINUS_DST_COLOR	Source	(1 – DestRed, 1 – DestGreen, 1 – DestBlue, 1 – DestAlpha)
GL_SRC_ALPHA_SATURATE	Source	(Min(SrcAlpha, 1 – DestAlpha)) for all four values

Understanding Orthographic Coordinate Systems

The one last area that I want to discuss to wrap up this overview of OpenGL is an alternative coordinate system that is available for use.

As mentioned back in the "Abstract Coordinate System" section near the start of this chapter, OpenGL normally uses an abstract coordinate system whose origin is in the center of the screen. All transformation operations work within this system.

This system is useful in many ways, as it separates the rendering of graphics from the actual device resolution. The image is always scaled to match the height of the window, meaning that no additional work is required to draw objects at different sizes for different devices.

On some occasions, particularly when developing 2D games, it can be useful to revert to a pixel-based coordinate system. You don't have to use it all the time and can switch back and forth between a pixel-based system and the perspective-based system we have used throughout the rest of this chapter within the same rendering operation if you wish.

Pixel-based coordinates are accessed by setting OpenGL up with an *orthographic* coordinate system, which allows us to specify the direct coordinates of the left, right, bottom, and top of the viewable area of the coordinate system by passing in these values to the Orthof function. By providing (0, 0) for the bottom and left positions and (this.Width, this.Height) for the right and top positions, the coordinate system will switch to being pixel based.

The modified InitGLViewport function that sets up this coordinate system is shown in Listing 10–25.

Listing 10–25. Setting Up a Pixel-Based Orthographic Projection

```
/// <summary>
/// Set up OpenGL's viewport
/// </summary>
private void InitGLViewport()
{
    // Set the viewport that we are rendering to
    gl.Viewport(this.ClientRectangle.Left, this.ClientRectangle.Top,
                    this.ClientRectangle.Width, this.ClientRectangle.Height);

    // Switch OpenGL into Projection mode so that we can set the projection matrix.
    gl.MatrixMode(gl.GL_PROJECTION);
    // Load the identity matrix
    gl.LoadIdentity();
    // Apply an orthographic projection
    gl.Orthof(0, this.Width, 0, this.Height, -1, 1);

    // Switch OpenGL back to ModelView mode so that we can transform objects rather than
    // the projection matrix.
    gl.MatrixMode(gl.GL_MODELVIEW);
    // Load the identity matrix.
    gl.LoadIdentity();
}
```

Remember that the unit square quadrilateral we have been rendering will now be just a single pixel in size, so you will need to scale it up to see it. Also remember that this puts the origin in the bottom-left corner of the window rather than in the center, so you will need to translate your objects differently to position them where you want.

Of course, you can provide any values you wish to Orthof for the left, bottom, right, and top values. Listing 10–26 shows a coordinate system with the same scale but with the origin in the center of the screen instead of the bottom-left.

Listing 10–26. Setting Up a Pixel-Based Orthographic Projection with the Origin at the Screen's Center

```
/// <summary>
/// Set up OpenGL's viewport
/// </summary>
private void InitGLViewport()
{
    [...]
    // Apply an orthographic projection
    gl.Orthof(-this.Width / 2, this.Width / 2, -this.Height / 2, this.Height / 2, -1,1);
    [...]
}
```

You could also set up your own custom abstract coordinate system. Listing 10–27 shows another call to Orthof, this time setting up a coordinate system that runs from 0 to 10 across both the x and y axes. This coordinate system will almost certainly have a different physical scale on the x and y axes, as the screen width and height are not the same.

Listing 10–27. Setting Up a Custom Abstract Coordinate System

```
/// <summary>
/// Set up OpenGL's viewport
/// </summary>
private void InitGLViewport()
{
    [...]
    // Apply an orthographic projection
    gl.Orthof(0, 10, 0, 10, -1,1);
    [...]
}
```

Taking Control of OpenGL

I hope that this chapter has given you an idea of what OpenGL is capable of. Providing your player's device has the capability to use it, the amount of graphical power and flexibility available to you as a developer is vast compared to what we have seen with GDI.

In the following chapters, we will put OpenGL to work for us in a gaming environment, starting with implementing it into the game engine.

Please take some time to experiment with what you have learned so far, as there is a lot to see and do here! The example projects should provide a gateway into familiarizing yourself with what OpenGL can do.

If you would like to read more about the OpenGL functions that are available, take a look at http://www.khronos.org/opengles/sdk/1.1/docs/man/ where the full OpenGL ES documentation can be found.

■ ■ ■

CHAPTER 11

Creating 2D Games with OpenGL

Now that you know the basics of 2D rendering with OpenGL, let's combine those concepts with the game engine that we've been developing throughout this book. Together, they will give us all of the benefits that you've already seen regarding timing, object, and graphic management and lots more.

The good news is that OpenGL is actually a lot easier to work with than GDI. All of the complexity we used to have to deal with calculating which areas of the form had been updated and which objects had moved all disappears with OpenGL. As we redraw the screen entirely each frame, all we need to concern ourselves with is which objects are active and whereabouts they need to be drawn.

Let's start by integrating the OpenGL code into the game engine project.

Adding OpenGL to the Game Engine

When we added support for GDI to the game engine, we implemented it using two derived classes. The first, CGameEngineGDIBase, is derived from the underlying CGameEngineBase and adds lots of additional functionality that was required for GDI. The second, CGameObjectGDIBase, is derived from CGameObjectBase and also adds GDI-specific object-processing code.

You won't be surprised to see that we adopt exactly the same approach for OpenGL, adding new classes named CGameEngineOpenGLBase and CGameObjectOpenGLBase. The information about what these classes do and how they work is contained within the following sections.

The class diagram in Figure 11–1 shows all of the engine and object classes within the project.

Figure 11–1. The class diagram showing all related engine and object classes

Understanding the CGameEngineOpenGLBase Class

An overview of the CGameEngineOpenGLBase class is as follows:

- *Purpose*: An implementation of CGameEngineBase with functionality required for OpenGL graphics

- *Type*: Abstract base class

- *Derived from*: CGameEngineBase

- *Inherited by*: Individual games created in separate assemblies

- *Main functionality*:

    - CreateGL: Creates the OpenGL environment

    - Dispose: Terminates the OpenGL environment and releases all allocated resources

    - InitGL: Sets up the OpenGL environment ready for rendering

    - InitGLViewport: Sets up the OpenGL viewport for the current window

    - Render: Draws the game

The preparation and initialization of OpenGL is all performed in this abstract base class. Individual games can derive from CGameEngineOpenGLBase to access this functionality and set up everything that is needed to display the game.

Initializing OpenGL

The example projects in the previous chapter used a single form in which all of the OpenGL initialization, rendering, and update code was present. When we move into the game engine, the functionality is split between the CGameEngineOpenGLBase and CGameObjectOpenGLBase classes.

All of the code required to create and initialize the OpenGL environment is placed into CGameEngineOpenGLBase. The CreateGL and InitGL functions are present here and are essentially unchanged from before. However, the functions are now declared with private scope, so they cannot be called from outside of the class itself.

Instead, a single public-facing function named InitializeOpenGL has been added, which creates and initializes the environment. This function must be able to be called directly from the game (rather than as part of the class constructor, for example) so that the capabilities check may be carried out first. We'll discuss this in the section entitled "Performing the Capabilities Check," coming up shortly.

InitGLViewport is also to be found here in the CGameEngineOpenGLBase class and is automatically called from InitGL just as you saw before. This is now a virtual function, however, allowing derived classes to override this and initialize the viewport differently. In particular, this function allows for different projection matrices (perspective or orthographic) to be set by the game, as discussed in Chapter 10.

In addition to calling InitGLViewport from within the InitGL function, the class constructor also adds an event handler to the game form's Resize event. Each time this event fires, InitGLViewport is automatically called again to allow the viewport to be reconfigured as appropriate for the new window size.

The clean-up code that releases all of the allocated OpenGL resources is now contained within the standard Dispose method.

Rendering Game Objects

The Render function is still responsible for telling each game object to render itself. The code required for OpenGL is very simple, essentially just checking that each object is not terminated prior to rendering. The full Render function is shown in Listing 11–1.

Listing 11–1. Rendering Game Objects in the OpenGL Game Engine

```
/// <summary>
/// Render all required graphics in order to update the game display.
/// </summary>
/// <param name="interpFactor">The interpolation factor for the current update</param>
public override void Render(float interpFactor)
{
    // Allow the base class to perform any processing it needs to do
    base.Render(interpFactor);

    // Make sure OpenGL has been initialized
    if (!_glInitialized)
                throw new Exception("Cannot Render: OpenGL has not been initialized");

    // Clear the background.
    gl.Clear(gl.GL_COLOR_BUFFER_BIT);

    // Render all game objects
    foreach (CGameObjectOpenGLBase gameObject in GameObjects)
    {
        // Is this object terminated? Don't draw if it is
        if (!gameObject.Terminate)
        {
            gameObject.Render(null, interpFactor);
        }
    }
}
```

Note that we pass null to each object for its gfx parameter when calling each object's Render method. As OpenGL takes care of getting the graphics on to the screen for us, there is no need for us to create a Graphics object to provide it to the game objects.

Accessing the Graphics Library

In CGameEngineGDIBase, we provide a Dictionary of Bitmap objects into which each of our graphics can be loaded, and it is accessed via the GameGraphics property.

CGameEngineOpenGLBase provides a very similar facility, accessed via the same property name. For OpenGL, we have a Dictionary of Texture objects instead of Bitmap objects. The Texture object was discussed in Chapter 10.

Calling Utility Functions

A small selection of utility functions is also present to assist with some common tasks. For the moment, these consist of color conversion functions. OpenGL colors, defined as arrays of floats, are easy enough to use, but it's much simpler to be able to refer to colors using the Color object that we used with GDI. These functions will translate between GDI-style colors and OpenGL-style colors.

ColorToFloat3 converts a GDI color to an array of three floats (no alpha component is included). ColorToFloat4 performs the same task but includes the alpha component (which will always be set to 1). Finally, FloatToColor converts an array of floats back to a GDI color.

Understanding the CGameObjectOpenGLBase Class

An overview of the CGameObjectOpenGLBase class is as follows:

- *Purpose*: An implementation of CGameObjectBase with functionality required for OpenGL graphics

- *Type*: Abstract base class

- *Derived from*: CGameObjectBase

- *Inherited by*: Game objects within individual games, created in separate assemblies

- *Main functionality*:

    - XScale, YScale, *and* ZScale: Scaling properties

    - XAngle, YAngle, *and* ZAngle: Rotation properties

    - RenderColorQuad, RenderTextureQuad, *and* RenderColorTextureQuad: Utility functions to simplify drawing rectangular quadrilaterals

None of the code in this class should look unfamiliar, as it is all based on code and ideas we have discussed in previous chapters. Let's take a quick look at what you can find in this class.

Setting the Object State for OpenGL

The GDI version of this class tracked Width and Height properties of each object. These were critical to the GDI engine so that it knew exactly where the object would render on the screen. In OpenGL, we have no concern about this; objects can render wherever they want. In fact, game objects in OpenGL games can actually be much more complex than a simple graphic if required—a whole solar system could be represented by a single game object if necessary.

Instead of these size properties, we instead offer a series of properties that may or may not be useful to the derived object classes. If they have a use for them, the classes simply hook into the provided functionality; if not, these properties can be ignored.

We provide support for scaling on each axis via the XScale, YScale, and ZScale properties. The previous values are accessible via the LastXScale, LastYScale, and LastZScale properties. To calculate the value for rendering (taking interpolation into account), the GetDisplayXScale, GetDisplayYScale, and GetDisplayZScale functions may be used.

Along exactly the same lines are properties to access the rotation of an object (using XAngle, YAngle, ZAngle and so on, just as with the scaling properties and functions). Note that these only track rotation directly around the x, y, and z axes; if rotation is required around any other axis, this will need to be implemented using custom properties within the derived class.

The UpdatePreviousPosition function is overridden so that, in addition to updating the position properties of the object (via the base class), the scale and angle properties are all updated too, as shown in Listing 11–2.

Listing 11–2. Updating the Previous Object Positions for OpenGL Objects

```
/// <summary>
/// In addition to the positions maintained by the base class, update
/// the previous positions maintained by this class too (scale
/// and rotation for each axis)
/// </summary>
internal override void UpdatePreviousPosition()
{
    // Let the base class do its work
    base.UpdatePreviousPosition();

    // Update OpenGL-specific values
    LastXScale = XScale;
    LastYScale = YScale;
    LastZScale = ZScale;

    LastXAngle = XAngle;
    LastYAngle = YAngle;
    LastZAngle = ZAngle;
}
```

Any derived class can create its own state properties should this be required. For example, if an object needed to smoothly fade between different colors, it could implement this effect by adding properties to store the current and previous red, green, and blue values. The previous values can be updated by overriding UpdatePreviousPosition, and functions can be added to interpolate between the previous and current values just as the base classes do for position, scale, and angle.

Rendering Quadrilaterals

To simplify the rendering of basic rectangular quadrilaterals for derived classes, we retain versions of the quadrilateral rendering functions that we used in the previous chapter. These are slightly reduced in number to form three basic functions: RenderColorQuad, RenderTextureQuad, and RenderColorTextureQuad.

RenderColorQuad now automatically detects whether the alpha component is being supplied in the provided color array by checking the array length. 12 items (3 per vertex) means that no alpha is present, whereas 16 items (4 per vertex) indicates that it is. If any other array size is detected, an exception is thrown, as the content cannot be identified.

After checking the color array, a unit square is drawn just as you saw before. The code for RenderColorQuad is shown in Listing 11–3.

Listing 11–3. Rendering a Colored Quadrilateral

```
/// <summary>
/// Render a quad at the current location using the provided colors
/// for the bottom-left, bottom-right, top-left and top-right
/// corners respectively.
/// </summary>
/// <param name="quadColors">An array of four sets of red, green blue
/// (and optionally alpha) floats.</param>
unsafe protected void RenderColorQuad(float[] quadColors)
{
```

```
    int elementsPerColor;

    // The vertex positions for a flat unit-size square
    float[] quadVertices = new float[] {   -0.5f, -0.5f, 0.0f,
                                            0.5f, -0.5f, 0.0f,
                                           -0.5f,  0.5f, 0.0f,
                                            0.5f,  0.5f, 0.0f};

    // Determine how many elements were provided for each color
    switch (quadColors.Length)
    {
        case 12: elementsPerColor = 3; break;   // no alpha
        case 16: elementsPerColor = 4; break;   // alpha present
        default: throw new Exception("Unknown content for quadColors");
    }

    // Fix a pointer to the quad vertices and the quad colors
    fixed (float* quadPointer = &quadVertices[0], colorPointer = &quadColors[0])
    {
        // Enable processing of the vertex and color arrays
        gl.EnableClientState(gl.GL_VERTEX_ARRAY);
        gl.EnableClientState(gl.GL_COLOR_ARRAY);

        // Provide a reference to the vertex array and color arrays
        gl.VertexPointer(3, gl.GL_FLOAT, 0, (IntPtr)quadPointer);
        gl.ColorPointer(elementsPerColor, gl.GL_FLOAT, 0, (IntPtr)colorPointer);

        // Draw the quad. We draw a strip of triangles, considering
        // four vertices within the vertex array.
        gl.DrawArrays(gl.GL_TRIANGLE_STRIP, 0, 4);

        // Disable processing of the vertex and color arrays now that we
        // have used them.
        gl.DisableClientState(gl.GL_VERTEX_ARRAY);
        gl.DisableClientState(gl.GL_COLOR_ARRAY);
    }
}
```

RenderTextureQuad is identical to the code you saw in Chapter 10, with the exception of another array length check, this time on the texCoords array. If any value other than 8 is found (a value for the s and t axes for each of the four vertices), an exception is thrown.

Finally, the RenderColorTextureQuad function is again virtually identical to the last chapter, except once more, for the addition of the color array length check.

Performing the Capabilities Check

To provide informative feedback to the user if the game is started on a device that does not support OpenGL, we will add to the capabilities check that we first developed back in Chapter 4.

The first requirement for this is to add a new item to the Capabilities enumeration, defined in CGameEngineBase. The next power-of-two value available is 2,048, so we add this value to the existing enumeration as shown in Listing 11–4.

Listing 11–4. The New OpenGL Element in the Capabilities Enumeration

```
/// <summary>
/// Capabilities flags for the CheckCapabilities and ReportMissingCapabilities functions
/// </summary>
[Flags()]
public enum Capabilities
{
    [...]
    OpenGL = 2048
}
```

The CheckCapabilities function is then modified by the addition of the code shown in Listing 11–5. This looks to see whether the OpenGL enumeration item has been specified as a required capability and, if so, calls into the CheckCapabilities_CheckForOpenGL function to perform the check.

Listing 11–5. Checking Whether to Test the OpenGL Capability

```
// Check hardware capabilities
if ((requiredCaps & Capabilities.OpenGL) > 0 && !CheckCapabilities_CheckForOpenGL())
                                    missingCaps |= Capabilities.OpenGL;
```

The CheckCapabilities_CheckForOpenGL function simply accesses one of the EGL functions contained within libgles_cm.dll. If the function operates correctly, it returns true to indicate that OpenGL support is present; otherwise, it returns false to indicate that it is not. The test is shown in Listing 11–6.

Listing 11–6. Checking for OpenGL Support

```
/// <summary>
/// Detect whether OpenGL support is available in this device
/// </summary>
/// <returns>Returns true if OpenGL support is found, false if not.</returns>
/// <remarks>This function uses the OpenGLES DLL to perform its check.
/// Note however that unless this function is called, there is no dependency
/// on the OpenGLES DLL being deployed with the application.</remarks>
private bool CheckCapabilities_CheckForOpenGL()
{
    OpenGLES.EGLDisplay eglDisplay;
    // Try to create an EGL display for our game form
    try
    {
        // Attempt to create an EGL display object
        eglDisplay = OpenGLES.egl.GetDisplay(
                            new OpenGLES.EGLNativeDisplayType(GameForm));
        // Destroy the object that we created -- we were just testing
        // whether the call succeed and don't actually need the object.
        OpenGLES.egl.Terminate(eglDisplay);
        // The capability is present
        return true;
    }
    catch
    {
```

295

```
        // OpenGL not supported
        return false;
    }
}
```

Having this check present in a separate function means that OpenGLES.dll does not need to be installed along with the game unless this function is actually called. Structuring the check in this way means that GDI games, which have no use for OpenGLES.dll, can be deployed without the DLL having to be included too, reducing the size and complexity of the installation.

Finally, a message to report the missing OpenGL capability is added to the ReportMissingCapabilities function, as shown in Listing 11–7.

Listing 11–7. Reporting the Lack of OpenGL Capability

```
// Check hardware capabilities
if ((missingCaps & Capabilities.OpenGL) > 0)
    ret.Append("- requires accelerated OpenGL support, which was not found.\n");
```

When we create a project using the OpenGL capabilities check (see the section entitled "Using the OpenGL Game Engine" coming up shortly), we can test running against devices that have OpenGL support available and device that do not (for example, the emulators) to see this working as expected.

Creating the Game Form

Finally, we have the game form itself. As you have seen, most of the functionality in our examples in the previous chapter has moved into the game engine, but we still have a little bit of work to do in the game form.

In the form's Load event, we perform the capabilities check, and assuming all is OK, we initialize OpenGL. The code for a typical Load event is shown in Listing 11–8.

Listing 11–8. Initializing a Game in the Form's Load Event

```
private void Form1_Load(object sender, EventArgs e)
{
    try
    {
        // Create the game object
        _game = new CBalloonsGame(this);

        // Check capabilities...
        GameEngine.CGameEngineBase.Capabilities missingCaps;
        // Check game capabilities -- OR each required capability together
        missingCaps = _game.CheckCapabilities(
                            GameEngine.CGameEngineBase.Capabilities.OpenGL);
        // Are any required capabilities missing?
        if (missingCaps > 0)
        {
            // Yes, so report the problem to the user
            MessageBox.Show("Unable to launch the game as your device does not meet "
                + "all of the hardware requirements:\n\n"
                + _game.ReportMissingCapabilities(missingCaps), "Unable to launch");
            // Close the form and exit
            this.Close();
```

```
            return;
        }

        // Initialize OpenGL now that we know it is available
        _game.InitializeOpenGL();
    }
    catch (Exception ex)
    {
        // Something went wrong
        _game = null;
        MessageBox.Show(ex.Message);
        // Close the application
        this.Close();
    }
}
```

The form needs to prevent the background painting using the OnPaintBackground override, just as in all the other examples we have looked at.

In the Paint event, we advance the game and validate the form. The game engine's Advance function automatically swaps the OpenGL render buffers so there is no need for the form to do this itself. A Paint event handler is shown in Listing 11–9.

Listing 11–9. Painting the Game Form

```
private void Form1_Paint(object sender, PaintEventArgs e)
{
    // Make sure the game is initialized -- we cannot render if it is not.
    if (_game != null)
    {
        // Advance the game and render all of the game objects
        _game.Advance();
    }

    // Invalidate the whole form to force another immediate repaint
    Invalidate();
}
```

The final requirement is to tidy up everything and release all of our unmanaged resources when the game is closing. This is handled via the Closing event; we are simply required to call into the game engine's Dispose method as shown in Listing 11–10.

Listing 11–10. Closing the Form and Releasing All Allocated Resources

```
private void Form1_Closing(object sender, CancelEventArgs e)
{
    // Make sure the game is initialized
    if (_game != null)
    {
        // Dispose of all resources that have been allocated by the game
        _game.Dispose();
    }
}
```

Using the OpenGL Game Engine

Let's now create a very simple game using OpenGL. In addition to displaying graphics, we'll also add interactivity to the program and see how we can map user input back into the game. The full source code for the game can be found in the Balloons project in the accompanying code download.

Preparing the Balloons Game

Our example game will display a cloud of colorful balloons that slowly drift up from the bottom of the screen to the top. The balloons will be shown at different sizes to simulate some being further away than others. The larger balloons will therefore rise more quickly, as they are nearer to the player.

When the player touches one of the balloons, it will pop. While we won't actually do it here, we could easily turn this into a fairly enjoyable game where the player has to burst all of the balloons before they reach the top of the screen. A point could be scored for each balloon burst, and the game would end when a certain number of balloons escape unpopped. The balloons could gradually increase in number and in speed.

Although the balloon will be displayed in a variety of colors, we will actually include only a single graphic in our game. We can use OpenGL's rendering features to display it in whatever color we want when rendering. This ability is in sharp contrast to your experience in GDI—the GemDrops game, for example, had to include each of the different colored gems prerendered in its graphics file.

Using a single graphic for multiple render colors not only simplifies the preparation for the game but also makes fading between different colors much easier. If we wanted we could also use color interpolation (as we did in the ColoredQuad example in the last chapter) to fade colors across the graphic.

To allow the balloon to be rendered in different colors, the single graphic that we do add to our game is in grayscale rather than any particular balloon color. This is the easiest way to get OpenGL to render in whatever color we want. The balloon graphic file (Balloon.png) is included as an embedded resource.

The game itself is created in a new project, inside a class named CBalloonsGame. The first thing we need to do in the game class is to load our balloon graphic. Just as we did with the GDI engine, we load the graphic in the game's Prepare function. The code is shown in Listing 11–11.

Listing 11–11. Preparing the Game

```
/// <summary>
/// Prepare the game
/// </summary>
public override void Prepare()
{
    // Allow the base class to do its work
    base.Prepare();

    // Make sure OpenGL is initialized before we interact with it
    if (OpenGLInitialized)
    {
        // Set properties
        BackgroundColor = Color.SkyBlue;

        // Load the graphics if not already loaded
        if (GameGraphics.Count == 0)
        {
            // Load our textures
```

```
            Assembly asm = Assembly.GetExecutingAssembly();
            Texture tex = Texture.LoadStream(
                    asm.GetManifestResourceStream("Balloons.Graphics.Balloon.png"), true);
            GameGraphics.Add("Balloon", tex);
        }
    }
}
```

The game's Reset function does very little; it simply clears any objects that have been added to the GameObjects collection.

The Update function is also very simple. It checks to see if there are 20 balloons active in the game, and if not, it adds one. When the game first begins, this function will be repeated over and over again until the full set of balloons is present. As the game continues to run, it will replenish any balloons that are terminated. The function code is in Listing 11–12.

Listing 11–12. Updating the Game

```
/// <summary>
/// Update the game
/// </summary>
public override void Update()
{
    // Allow the base class to do its work
    base.Update();

    // Do we have less then 20 balloons active at the moment?
    if (GameObjects.Count < 20)
    {
        // Yes, so add a new balloon to the game engine
        GameObjects.Add(new CObjBalloon(this));
        // Sort the objects. The balloons have an override of CompareTo
        // which will sort those with the smallest size to the beginning
        // of the list, so that they render first and so appears to be
        // at the back.
        GameObjects.Sort();
    }
}
```

You will notice that the code sorts the GameObjects collection each time a new balloon is added. The reason we do this and the mechanism by which the sort is performed are discussed in the "Sorting the Balloons" section coming up shortly.

Setting up the Projection Matrix

To simplify the layout of the game objects in the project, the Balloons game class sets up an orthographic projection. We looked at this type of projection at the end of the previous chapter.

This projection gives us accurate control over exactly where our objects appear on the screen. Perspective projections give the advantage of making things look smaller when they move into the distance (and we'll look at this more closely in the next chapter), but in our game, we can simulate this by just scaling the balloons to smaller sizes.

Instead of setting the orthographic projection to exactly match the screen coordinates, we will instead set it up so that its x coordinates range from –2 on the left edge of the screen to 2 on the right edge. The x coordinate of 0 will therefore form a line down the center of the screen. The width of the screen in game coordinates is 4 (from –2 to 2).

To calculate the y coordinate, we will find the aspect ratio of the screen and scale the width to match. For example, if the screen height were twice the width, we would use a range of –4 to 4 for the y coordinate.

We can find the aspect ratio by dividing the screen height by the width. We then multiply this by 4 (the width of the game coordinate system), and the result is the height of the game coordinate system. This can be seen in Figure 11–2.

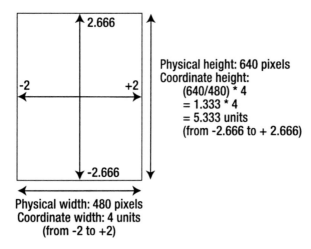

Figure 11–2. The orthographic coordinate system set up for the Balloons game on a VGA screen

Choosing an appropriate orthographic coordinate system can greatly simplify the layout of your objects. Getting the coordinate system set up correctly before you develop your game too far will save you time, because changing it later will require all of your game objects to be repositioned for them to appear in the same locations on the screen.

The projection matrix described here is set up by overriding the InitGLViewport function in the CBalloonsGame class. The code is shown in Listing 11–13.

Listing 11–13. Setting Up the Orthographic Coordinate System

```
/// <summary>
/// Override the viewport initialization function to set our own viewport.
/// We will use an orthographic projection instead of a perspective projection.
/// This simplifies the positioning of our graphics.
/// </summary>
protected override void InitGLViewport()
{
    float orthoWidth;
    float orthoHeight;

    // Let the base class do anything it needs.
    // This will create the OpenGL viewport and a default projection matrix.
    base.InitGLViewport();
```

```
    // Switch OpenGL into Projection mode so that we can set our own projection matrix.
    gl.MatrixMode(gl.GL_PROJECTION);
    // Load the identity matrix
    gl.LoadIdentity();

    // Set the width to be whatever we want
    orthoWidth = 4;
    // Set the height to be the appropriate value based on the aspect
    // ratio of the screen.
    orthoHeight = (float)GameForm.Height / (float)GameForm.Width * orthoWidth;

    // Set the orthoCoords rectangle. This can be retrieved by other
    // code in the game to determine the coordinate that are in use.
    _orthoCoords = new RectangleF(-orthoWidth / 2, orthoHeight / 2,
                                                orthoWidth, -orthoHeight);

    // Apply an orthographic projection. Keep (0, 0) in the center of the screen.
    // The x axis will range from -2 to +2, the y axis from whatever values have
    // been calculated based on the screen dimensions.
    gl.Orthof(-orthoWidth / 2, orthoWidth / 2, -orthoHeight / 2, orthoHeight / 2,
                                                -1, 1);

    // Switch OpenGL back to ModelView mode so that we can transform objects rather than
    // the projection matrix.
    gl.MatrixMode(gl.GL_MODELVIEW);
    // Load the identity matrix.
    gl.LoadIdentity();
}
```

In addition to providing the coordinates for the projection to OpenGL, the function also stores them in a class-level Rectangle variable named _orthoCoords. This can be accessed via the rest of the game using the OrthoCoords property in order for the dimensions of the coordinate system to be queried.

Rendering the Balloons

The balloons are implemented in a class named CObjBalloon, derived from the game engine's CGameObjectOpenGLBase class. Most of the code is self-explanatory, so let's focus on a few of the areas of interest.

First, in the constructor, we set a random position and size for the balloon. These values use a simple function contained later within the class named RandomFloat to return a float value within the requested range, as the .NET CF Random object doesn't contain a function for this directly.

The XPos variable is set so that the balloon appears anywhere along the width of the orthographic coordinate system. The width is queried from the game by calling the OrthoCoords property as mentioned in the previous section.

The YPos variable is first calculated to put the balloon immediately off the bottom of the window and then has a random value subtracted so that the balloon takes a little extra time before it appears. This delay allows the balloons to be vertically distributed rather than having them all appear on the screen at the same moment.

The color is then set and stored in a standard GDI Color variable for later use when rendering. A small set of possible colors is provided, but of course, this could easily be extended to cover whatever colors were required.

The rendering of the balloon is handled within the Render function. The code for this function is shown in Listing 11–14.

Listing 11–14. Rendering a Balloon to the Screen

```
/// <summary>
/// Render the balloon
/// </summary>
public override void Render(Graphics gfx, float interpFactor)
{
    base.Render(gfx, interpFactor);

    // Bind to the texture we want to render with
    gl.BindTexture(gl.GL_TEXTURE_2D, _myGameEngine.GameGraphics["Balloon"].Name);

    // Load the identity matrix
    gl.LoadIdentity();

    // Translate into position
    gl.Translatef(GetDisplayXPos(interpFactor), GetDisplayYPos(interpFactor), 0);

    // Rotate as required
    gl.Rotatef(GetDisplayZAngle(interpFactor), 0, 0, 1);

    // Scale according to our size
    gl.Scalef(_size, _size, 1);

    // Enable alpha blending
    gl.Enable(gl.GL_BLEND);
    gl.BlendFunc(gl.GL_SRC_ALPHA, gl.GL_ONE_MINUS_SRC_ALPHA);

    // Generate an array of colors for the balloon.
    // The alpha component is included but set to 1 for each vertex.
    float[] color3 = _myGameEngine.ColorToFloat3(_color);
    float[] balloonColors = new float[] { color3[0], color3[1], color3[2], 1,
                                          color3[0], color3[1], color3[2], 1,
                                          color3[0], color3[1], color3[2], 1,
                                          color3[0], color3[1], color3[2], 1 };

    // Render the balloon
    RenderColorTextureQuad(balloonColors);

    // Disable alpha blending
    gl.Disable(gl.GL_BLEND);
}
```

After binding to the balloon texture so that the correct graphic is drawn, the rendering code loads the identity matrix so that the object coordinate system is reset to the origin with all rotation and scaling removed.

The position of the balloon is then translated to the position stored in the XPos and YPos variables. Just as in our GDI games, we use the GetDisplayXPos and GetDisplayYPos functions to interpolate between the previous and current position, ensuring that motion is smooth and governed by our game engine's timing feature. The balloon is also rotated slightly around the z axis (to make it gently rock back and forth) and scaled according to its size. As the size is constant, there is no need to use the GetDisplayXScale or GetDisplayYScale functions, though these would be used were the size to be variable during the object's lifetime.

The balloon is now transformed into position and ready for rendering. We will use alpha blending to ensure that the balloon quadrilateral doesn't obstruct anything else already drawn on the screen. The balloon image contains an alpha channel, which we can take advantage of to make the balloon appear very slightly transparent. Alpha blending is enabled using the Enable function, and the blend function set up as described in Chapter 10.

We're almost ready to actually render, but the last step is to set the balloon colors. We use the game engine's ColorToFloat3 function to transform the stored _color value into a float array whose values can be passed to OpenGL. These values are then placed into a larger array with colors for each of the four vertices of the quadrilateral. The colors will apply to the grayscale balloon image, painting it in whatever color has been specified.

With everything now set up as required, we call into the RenderColorTexture function to render a colored and textured quadrilateral. We provide the color array and allow the function to use the default texture coordinates, which will paint the whole image on to the shape.

Finally, alpha blending is disabled once again. It is good practice to disable rendering states that your code has enabled in case the next object to render doesn't want to use that state. This keeps the behavior of the renderer predictable from one object to the next.

Sorting the Balloons

To ensure that our balloons render correctly, we need to draw them in the correct order. The smallest balloons (those which we are simulating being further away) need to be drawn first so that the larger balloons (which are nearer to the player) are then drawn on top of them. Otherwise, the smaller balloons can appear in front, which spoils the illusion.

This sorting could be implemented in various ways, but the easiest is to add support for sorting the entire collection of game objects. The objects are implemented in a List<CGameObjectBase> collection, which is capable of sorting its content, but the objects themselves do not support being sorted. To provide this support, we modify CGameObjectBase so that it implements the IComparable interface. This just requires a modification to the class declaration, as shown in Listing 11–15.

Listing 11–15. Adding Support for Sorting Game Objects

```
public abstract class CGameObjectBase : IComparable<CGameObjectBase>
{
```

Once this interface has been added to our class, we need to ensure that we implement all of its members. Without all members implemented, the code will no longer compile. The interface has a single method named CompareTo.

The CompareTo method is passed another object to which the current instance is to be compared. If the current instance is deemed to be less than the other object, a value less than 0 is returned. If the current instance is greater than the other object, a value greater than 0 is returned. If the two objects are equal, 0 is returned.

The base object class, however, has no idea how a game might want its objects to be sorted, so we simply return 0 from CompareTo. The function is, however, marked as being virtual, so derived object classes may override this and provide their own implementation. The code for the base class CompareTo method is shown in Listing 11–16.

Listing 11–16. The CompareTo Function in CGameObjectBase

```
/// <summary>
/// Allow the game object list to be sorted.
/// </summary>
public virtual int CompareTo(CGameObjectBase other)
{
    // We don't know how the game will want to sort its objects,
    // so just return 0 to indicate that the two objects are
    // equal. Individual objects can override this to provide
    // their own sorting mechanism.
    return 0;
}
```

In CGameObjectOpenGLBase, we guess that the required behavior of sorting the objects might be to sort by the objects' z positions. This may or may not be what is required (and, in fact, in our Balloons sample it is not what we need), but it may be useful in some instances so it's useful as a default. The CompareTo code in this class is shown in Listing 11–17.

Listing 11–17. The CompareTo Function in CGameObjectOpenGLBase

```
/// <summary>
/// Provide default sorting for OpenGL objects so that they
/// are ordered from those with the highest z position first
/// (furthest away) to those with the lowest z position last
/// (nearest).
/// </summary>
/// <param name="other"></param>
/// <returns></returns>
public override int CompareTo(CGameObjectBase other)
{
    // Sort by z position
    return ((CGameObjectOpenGLBase)other).ZPos.CompareTo(ZPos);
}
```

In the CObjBalloon class, we provide the implementation that is actually needed for our game. The class overrides the CompareTo method and uses the _size variable to determine the order in which the balloons should be sorted. First, the code ensures that the other object actually is a balloon. If other types of object are added to the GameObjects list, these will all be included in the sort operation too, so we need to make sure we are definitely comparing two balloons. Once this has been checked, the size of the current balloon is compared to the size of the other balloon using the int.CompareTo method. As int also implements CompareTo, this is a quick and easy way to perform the comparison. The code for the balloon's CompareTo method is shown in Listing 11–18.

Listing 11–18. The CompareTo Function in CObjBalloon

```
/// <summary>
/// Allow the balloons to be sorted by their size, so that the smallest
/// balloons come first in the object list
/// </summary>
public override int CompareTo(GameEngine.CGameObjectBase other)
{
    // Are we comparing with another balloon?
```

```
    if (other is CObjBalloon)
    {
        // Yes, so compare the sizes
        return -((CObjBalloon)other)._size.CompareTo(_size);
    }
    else
    {
        // No, so let the base class handle the comparison
        return base.CompareTo(other);
    }
}
```

With support for sorting the objects added to the GameObjects list, performing the sort is now just a matter of calling GameObjects.Sort each time a balloon is added in the CBalloonsGame.Update function. The balloons will then be rendered from the back to the front exactly as we need.

Note also that the CGameObjectOpenGL class implements the MoveToFront and MoveToBack methods that we first created for GDI game objects, so individual objects can be repositioned within the object list using these methods if necessary.

With sorting in place, all of the balloons appear as required when the game is running. Figure 11–3 shows the game in action. Note that the balloons are slightly transparent and show through one another and that the smaller balloons all appear to be behind the larger balloons.

Figure 11–3. An image taken from the Balloons example project

Playing the Game

To add some interactivity to the game, we will make the balloons burst when they are touched by the player. The input will be triggered from the form's MouseDown event.

Before we can work out which balloon the user has touched, we have a bit of a problem to solve. The game is using an abstract coordinate system, so we cannot test whether a balloon has been touched by simply comparing the touch position with the balloon position. The touch has its (0, 0) coordinate in the top-left corner of the screen and is measured in pixels, whereas the balloon positions have (0, 0) in the center of the screen and are measured based on the units we set in the InitGLViewport function back in Listing 11–13. To find the balloon that has been selected, we need to perform some form of mapping from the touch point back into OpenGL's coordinate system.

In our example, we could calculate this manually if we wanted. We know for example that the x coordinate 0 maps to a game coordinate of –2 and that the x coordinate 480 (assuming a WVGA screen) maps to a game coordinate of 2. So we could simply divide the x coordinate by 120 and subtract 2.

While this approach would certainly work, there is a better way of achieving this mapping. When we render a game object, OpenGL uses a *projection* calculation to project its game coordinates on to the screen using the matrix that we set inside InitGLViewport. With a little bit of work, we can use the projection matrix, the viewport, and the touch position to get the screen coordinate back into the game coordinate system.

There are two advantages of mapping the point from the screen into the game coordinate system in this way. First, if we decide to change the coordinate system in any way, the mapping function will automatically take this into account; we don't need to remember to update our calculations separately. Second, when the projection matrix is more complicated (and it will become so in the next chapter when 3D projection is introduced), the approach for returning screen coordinates will still work, whereas calculating positions in 3D space in our code would become much more complex.

OpenGL doesn't directly support the backward projection calculation, but the OpenGL Utility (GLU) library does. A partial implementation of the GLU code can be found inside the OpenGLES project contained within the glu.cs source file.

The GLU function we need to call is called UnProject. It requires a number of pieces of information to be provided, as follows:

- The x and y position of the screen coordinate to be unprojected (winx and winy)

- The z coordinate at the touch position (winz)

- The current model matrix (modelMatrix)

- The current projection matrix (projMatrix)

- The current viewport (viewport)

It then returns the mapped coordinate in 3D space in the output parameters objx, objy, and objz.

The winx and winy values are easy to obtain, as these are the screen coordinates that we retrieved from the MouseDown event. How do we find the winz coordinate? Well, as we are using an orthographic coordinate system, the z position of each object doesn't actually have any effect on where it is rendered. We can, therefore, simply pass 0 for this parameter.

The model matrix, projection matrix, and viewport can all be retrieved by querying OpenGL. However, the functions we need to call require a pointer to an array to be provided, so we need to declare our function as unsafe once again and use the fixed statement to retrieve an array pointer. To wrap up all of this and keep it neat and tidy, we create a function inside CGameEngineOpenGLBase called UnProject that wraps around the glu.UnProject function. The code for this wrapper function is shown in Listing 11–19.

Listing 11–19. The UnProject Function Inside CGameEngineOpenGLBase

```
/// <summary>
/// "Unproject" the provided screen coordinates back into OpenGL's projection
/// coordinates.
/// </summary>
/// <param name="x">The screen x coordinate to unproject</param>
/// <param name="y">The screen y coordinate to unproject</param>
/// <param name="z">The game world z coordinate to unproject</param>
/// <param name="xPos">Returns the x position in game world coordinates</param>
/// <param name="yPos">Returns the y position in game world coordinates</param>
/// <param name="zPos">Returns the z position in game world coordinates</param>
unsafe public bool UnProject(int x, int y, float z,
                                        out float objx, out float objy, out float objz)
{
    int[] viewport = new int[4];
    float[] modelview = new float[16];
    float[] projection = new float[16];
    float winX, winY, winZ;

    // Load the identity matrix so that the coordinates are reset rather than calculated
    // against any existing transformation that has been left in place.
    gl.LoadIdentity();

    // Retrieve the modelview and projection matrices
    fixed (float* modelviewPointer = &modelview[0], projectionPointer = &projection[0])
    {
        gl.GetFloatv(gl.GL_MODELVIEW_MATRIX, modelviewPointer);
        gl.GetFloatv(gl.GL_PROJECTION_MATRIX, projectionPointer);
    }
    // Retrieve the viewport dimensions
    fixed (int* viewportPointer = &viewport[0])
    {
        gl.GetIntegerv(gl.GL_VIEWPORT, viewportPointer);
    }

    // Prepare the coordinates to be passed to glu.UnProject
    winX = (float)x;
    winY = (float)viewport[3] - (float)y;
    winZ = z;

    // Call UnProject with the values we have calculated. The unprojected values will be
    // returned in the xPos, yPos and zPos variables, and in turn returned back to the
    // calling procedure.
    return glu.UnProject(winX, winY, winZ, modelview, projection, viewport,
                                        out objx, out objy, out objz);
}
```

As the code shows, we still pass in the screen coordinate and receive back the game world coordinate, but all of the complexity of retrieving array data from OpenGL is handled internally within the class.

With this function available, we can add a function to CBalloonsGame that takes a screen coordinate and determines whether this is within the area occupied by any of the balloons. If it is, the balloon is terminated, and a popping sound effect is played. The function is named TestHit and is shown in Listing 11–20.

Listing 11–20. Testing Whether Any of the Balloons Contains the Touch Coordinate

```
/// <summary>
/// Test whether the supplied x and y screen coordinate is within one of the balloons
/// </summary>
/// <param name="x">The x coordinate to test</param>
/// <param name="y">The y coordinate to test</param>
unsafe public void TestHit(int x, int y)
{
    float posX, posY, posZ;
    CObjBalloon balloon;

    // Convert the screen coordinate into a coordinate within OpenGL's
    // coordinate system.
    if (UnProject(x, y, 0, out posX, out posY, out posZ))
    {
        // Loop for each game object.
        // Note that we loop backwards so that objects at the front
        // are considered before those behind.
        for (int i = GameObjects.Count - 1; i >= 0; i--)
        {
            // Is this object a balloon?
            if (GameObjects[i] is CObjBalloon)
            {
                // Cast the object as a balloon
                balloon = (CObjBalloon)GameObjects[i];
                // See if the balloon registers this position as a hit
                if (balloon.TestHit(posX, posY))
                {
                    // It does. Terminate the balloon so that it disappears
                    balloon.Terminate = true;
                    PlayPopSound();
                    // Stop looping so that we only pop the frontmost balloon
                    // at this location.
                    break;
                }
            }
        }
    }
}
```

The code first calls the UnProject function to translate the screen coordinate into a game coordinate. It then checks to see whether the mapped coordinate is inside any of the balloons, looping backward so that the balloons at the front are considered first. After verifying that each game object actually is a balloon, it asks the balloon whether the game coordinate falls within its space by calling its own TestHit function (which we will look at in a moment). If this call returns true, the balloon is terminated and the sound triggered (we just use the simple PlaySound function for this, as we don't need anything more sophisticated).

To find which balloon (if any) has been hit, the `CObjBalloon.TestHit` function compares the provided coordinate against its position, taking its own location and the balloon size into account. The code to check this is very simple and is shown in Listing 11–21.

Listing 11–21. Comparing the Touch Coordinate Against the Location of an Individual Balloon

```
/// <summary>
/// Test whether the supplied coordinate (provided in the game's
/// coordinate system) is within the boundary of this balloon.
/// </summary>
/// <returns></returns>
internal bool TestHit(float x, float y)
{
    // Calculate the bounds of the balloon
    float left, right, bottom, top;
    left = XPos - _size / 2;
    right = XPos + _size / 2; ;
    bottom = YPos - _size / 2;
    top = YPos + _size / 2;

    // Return true if the x and y positions both fall between
    // the calculated coordinates
    return (left < x && right > x && bottom < y && top > y);
}
```

2D Possibilities with OpenGL

The very simple example in this chapter hopefully demonstrates some of the graphical power and flexibility that is available to us as game developers when we use OpenGL. The techniques we have used in this chapter, including flexible alpha blending, texture coloring, rotation, scaling, and unprojection, bring a huge number of opportunities for exciting and attractive games. OpenGL is clearly able to smoothly display much greater numbers of moving objects than we were able to use when developing against GDI.

At the time of this writing, OpenGL games are very much in the minority for Windows Mobile. I strongly suspect that many users of OpenGL-capable devices are actually unaware of the type of graphics that their hardware is able to display. Let your imagination flow, and show the world what you and Windows Mobile are capable of!

Many types of game work very well in two dimensions, but OpenGL is fully capable of creating 3D graphics too, and these are what we will explore in the next chapter.

■ ■ ■

CHAPTER 12

The Ins and Outs of the Third Dimension

3D graphics have completely revolutionized computer games over the last decade. For some time before this, it had been obvious that 3D games were going to be big, with games such as DOOM creating moving images the likes of which had never been seen before.

When dedicated 3D graphics hardware began to appear back in the late 1990s, graphics were transformed further still, moving away from the blocky and grainy images that players had become accustomed to and replacing them with smooth textures, dynamic lighting, and enormous levels of detail. Game words really started to look like real worlds.

Mobile graphics hardware, even in dedicated devices such as Sony's PlayStation Portable, are trailing a fair distance behind the power of modern PC graphics hardware. The OpenGL capabilities of current Windows Mobile devices are fairly modest but steadily improving as newer and faster hardware is released. While we may not be able to replicate the vistas of desktop computing, we can still use the hardware to create impressive 3D scenes and games.

In this chapter, we will examine how to bring the third dimension to life.

Understanding Perspective Projection

The vast majority of 3D games use a *perspective projection* to display their graphics. Just as in the real world, this simulates the application of perspective to objects rendered within the game, so that objects that are further away appear smaller than objects that are nearer.

In addition to this obvious size effect, more subtle effects of perspective are picked up intuitively by the brain and add a substantial feeling of depth to the rendered scene. The sides of a cube will seem to narrow slightly as they increase in distance from the viewer, allowing the brain to automatically determine the exact position in which the cube is situated.

Understanding the Viewing Frustum

When we use a perspective projection in OpenGL, we create as part of the viewport initialization a 3D volume known as a *viewing frustum*. The shape of the frustum is that of a rectangular cone with its tip cut off, as shown in Figure 12–1.

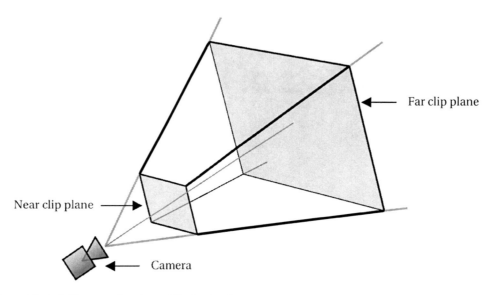

Figure 12–1. A diagram showing a 3D viewing frustum

The frustum can be visualized in the real world by imagining yourself looking through a window. Outside the window, you can see the ground and various objects. The further away into the distance you look, the wider the area that you can see. Objects that are too far to the side of you, or too far above or below you, will be hidden by the window frame.

Objects that fall inside the volume described by the frustum are visible to the camera (they would be visible through the window). Objects that fall outside the frustum volume are hidden from the camera (and would not be able to be seen through the window).

The *near and far clip planes* are also taken into account when deciding whether objects are visible. Objects nearer to the camera than the near clip plane are deemed to be too close and are excluded from rendering. Similarly, objects further than the far clip plane are too far away to be seen and are once again excluded.

■ **NOTE** When we specify an object's z position (its distance into the screen), the negative z axis represents movement away from the player and into the screen: as an object's z coordinate decreases, it moves further away. However, when we specify the distance of the near and far clip planes, these are specified purely as distances from the camera and are therefore positive values.

When OpenGL transforms the objects that fall inside the frustum from the 3D space in which we have defined our world into the 2D space that is actually presented on the screen, it takes into account how much of the width and height of the frustum is filled by any particular object. An object will occupy a greater proportion of the frustum when it is positioned toward the near clip plane than it will at the far clip plane, as shown in Figures 12–2 and 12–3. Figure 12–2 shows two identically sized objects within the viewing frustum. Figure 12–3 shows the same scene after the perspective projection has taken place to transform the scene into two dimensions for display on the screen. Note that the object at the near clip plane appears substantially larger than the one at the far clip plane.

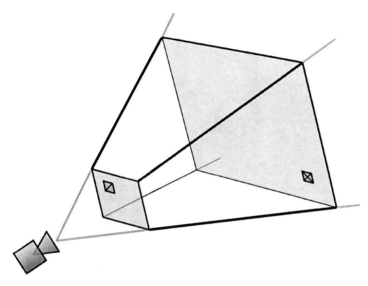

Figure 12–2. Two identically sizes objects in the viewing frustum shown in 3D space

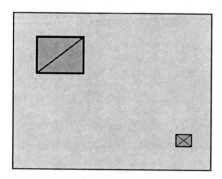

Figure 12–3. The same two objects after perspective projection into 2D

In addition to the clip planes, the frustum is defined by two further pieces of information: the viewing angle and the aspect ratio. The *viewing angle* defines the angle, in degrees, between the camera and the upper edge of the frustum (the angle on the y axis). Changing this will cause the overall shape of the frustum to expand or compress, causing the apparent reduction in size of objects further away to be increased or decreased.

Figure 12–4 shows two viewing frustums side on, the first with a viewing angle of 45 degrees, the second with 22.5 degrees. The distance of the near and far clip planes is the same in both cases.

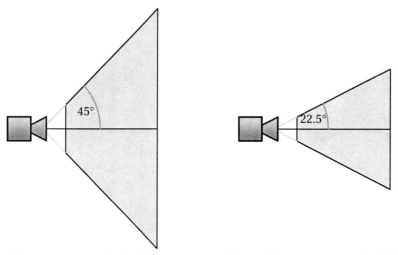

Figure 12–4. Two viewing frustums, one with a 45-degree viewing angle (left) and one with a 22.5-degree angle (right)

Consider how objects that fall into these two frustums will be projected. On the left, objects can deviate further from the center of the frustum and still be seen by the camera. Objects that are further away will become rapidly smaller as their size relative to the extent of the frustum becomes less and less. On the right, objects further from the center will leave the frustum more quickly and disappear off the edge of the screen. Distant objects will appear larger than with the first frustum, as they occupy a greater proportion of the frustum's area.

Exactly what you should specify for the viewing angle will potentially vary from one game to the next. An angle of 45 degrees is usually a safe value. Setting the angle too low can make everything appear closer to the player than it really is, which can result in the game feeling uncomfortable to play.

■ **TIP** Some interesting effects can be achieved by varying the viewing angle at strategic times within the game. For example, you could provide a transition between two scenes by rapidly decreasing the viewing angle down to 0, switching scenes, and increasing the angle back to its original value. This will cause everything in the center of the screen to appear to zoom toward the player and then zoom back again after the scene change. Slow motion effects can often be accentuated by slightly reducing the viewing angle while they are active.

The second piece of information that the viewing frustum requires is the aspect ratio. This is calculated by dividing the frustum's width by its height. The aspect ratio allows the viewing angle on the x axis to be calculated by OpenGL. The aspect ratio together with the viewing angle and the distance of the clip planes provides everything that is needed to fully describe the frustum.

Defining the Viewing Frustum in OpenGL

OpenGL actually performs the perspective transformation with the use of another matrix. You may recall that in the CGameEngineOpenGLBase.InitGLViewport function that we looked at in the last chapter; the code shown in Listing 12–1 is present to set up the default projection matrix.

Listing 12–1. Setting the Perspective Projection Inside InitGLViewport

```
// Switch OpenGL into Projection mode so that we can set the projection matrix.
gl.MatrixMode(gl.GL_PROJECTION);
// Load the identity matrix
gl.LoadIdentity();
// Apply a perspective projection
glu.Perspective(45,
    (float)GameForm.ClientRectangle.Width / (float)GameForm.ClientRectangle.Height,
    .1f, 100);
```

The call to glu.Perspective is provided with everything we have discussed for the viewing frustum. In order, we pass the viewing angle (45), the aspect ratio (the game form's width divided by its height), the distance to the near clip plane (0.1), and the distance to the far clip plane (100). This information allows glu.Perspective to create the projection matrix for the requested frustum.

When rendering, OpenGL first calculates the positions of all of the object vertices in 3D space and then uses the projection matrix to transform them into 2D coordinates to display on the screen.

If you wish to change the viewing angle (or any of the other properties of the frustum), you can override InitGLViewport to apply the required glu.Perspective parameters and then call this from your rendering code. Alternatively, just reset the projection matrix directly in your render code using the same code shown in Listing 12–1. Don't forget to switch the MatrixMode back to GL_MODELVIEW once you have reconfigured the projection matrix so that further transformations affect the objects within the game rather than the projection matrix itself.

The Perspective example project in this chapter's accompanying download shows how objects move when a perspective projection is applied. The code is very simple; it creates a number of objects with random x, y, and z coordinates. Each time the objects update, they add to their ZPos and move closer to the screen. When they get to a value of 0, they add 100 to move back into the distance. A screenshot from the demonstration is shown in Figure 12–5.

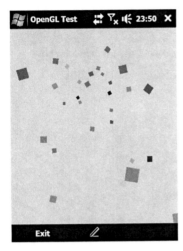

Figure 12–5. The perspective projection of multiple identically sized objects in the Perspective example

Understanding the Depth Buffer

Something you may have observed in the Perspective example is that the objects nearer the camera all appear in front of the objects further away. When we displayed our graphics in the last chapter's Balloons project, we had to sort all of the objects by their size to achieve this. There is no equivalent functionality in the Perspective project, yet the objects still all appear in the right places. Why does this happen?

The answer is that OpenGL has a built-in mechanism for ensuring that objects in the front of the scene automatically hide any objects that fall behind them. This happens regardless of the order in which objects are drawn: objects drawn behind existing objects can still be partially (or totally) obscured even though they may be rendered after the object in front.

OpenGL achieves this using a feature known as the *depth buffer*. This buffer can be enabled or disabled, and for performance reasons, we didn't use this in the 2D examples in the previous chapter. In 3D scenes, it is almost certain to be required.

Just as the color of each rendered pixel is written into a graphical buffer, so the distance into the screen of each rendered pixel is written into a corresponding depth buffer when the buffer is enabled. For each individual pixel that it is about to render, OpenGL checks the depth of the pixel against the depth already stored in the buffer. If it finds that the new pixel is further away than the pixel already in the buffer, the new pixel is not rendered to the screen; otherwise the pixel is rendered and the depth buffer updated to remember the new depth of the pixel.

Enabling the Depth Buffer

There are two things we need to do so that we can use the depth buffer. First, we need to tell OpenGL to enable it. Second, we need to remember to clear the depth buffer each time we start rendering a new frame. Just as we need to clear the color buffer to prevent old graphic imagery from appearing in our new frame, we must clear the depth buffer to prevent old depth information from affecting the new frame.

Support for the depth buffer is added to CGameEngineOpenGLBase. A new function is added called InitGLDepthBuffer, as shown in Listing 12–2.

Listing 12–2. Enabling the OpenGL Depth Buffer

```
/// <summary>
/// Initialise the depth buffer
/// </summary>
private void InitGLDepthBuffer()
{
    // Set the clear depth to be 1 (the back edge of the buffer)
    gl.ClearDepthf(1.0f);
    // Set the depth function to render values less than or equal to the current depth
    gl.DepthFunc(gl.GL_LEQUAL);
    // Enable the depth test
    gl.Enable(gl.GL_DEPTH_TEST);

    // Remember that the depth buffer is enabled
    _depthBufferEnabled = true;
}
```

InitGLDepthBuffer first uses the ClearDepth function to tell OpenGL the initial depth that should be put into the depth buffer when it is cleared. This is similar in concept to setting the background color for the color buffer, except that we are configuring depths instead of colors. The depth buffer stores values in the range of 0 to 1, where 0 represents a depth on the near clip plane and 1 a depth on the far clip plane. Setting the clear depth to 1, therefore, ensures that all objects rendered within the viewing frustum will be initially in front of the values in the depth buffer.

The next statement sets the depth function. The value GL_LEQUAL tells OpenGL that any depth value it calculates that is less than or equal to the stored depth (that is, at the same position or nearer to the viewer) should result in the pixel being drawn.

Finally, the depth buffer is enabled by calling Enable with the GL_DEPTH_TEST function.

A class-level variable named _depthBufferEnabled is also set when the depth buffer is switched on. This is used by the Render function so that the depth buffer is cleared prior to each frame being rendered. The code that was previously clearing just the color buffer in the Render function is modified to take this into account as shown in Listing 12–3.

Listing 12–3. Clearing the Color and Depth Buffers

```
// Clear the rendering buffers
if (_depthBufferEnabled)
{
    // Clear the color and the depth buffer
    gl.Clear(gl.GL_COLOR_BUFFER_BIT | gl.GL_DEPTH_BUFFER_BIT);
}
else
{
    // Clear just the color buffer
    gl.Clear(gl.GL_COLOR_BUFFER_BIT);
}
```

So that our games can tell the game engine whether to use the depth buffer, we add an overloaded version of the CGameEngineOpenGLBase.InitializeOpenGL function with a Boolean parameter, enableDepthBuffer. If this is passed as true, the InitGLDepthBuffer function shown in Listing 12–2 is called during initialization. The InitializeOpenGL function is otherwise unchanged.

The effects of the depth buffer can be clearly seen in the DepthBuffer example project. With the depth buffer enabled (calling _game.InitialiseOpenGL(true) in the form's Load event), each of the rendered quadrilaterals is prioritized according to its position in 3D space, appearing in front or behind the others, depending on their distances into the screen. If you change the Load event code so that it instead calls _game.InitialiseOpenGL(false), you will see that we return back to the last-drawn object always appearing in the front, just as you saw in the previous chapter.

Rendering Transparent Objects with the Depth Buffer

The depth buffer may not work exactly as you expect when it comes to drawing semitransparent objects. While OpenGL's alpha blending feature is able to merge together objects that are being drawn with those already on the screen, the depth buffer is only able to store a single depth for each pixel. This means that if you draw a semitransparent object and then draw a further object behind it, the object behind will be completely eliminated by the depth buffer, even though the first object was transparent.

There are two approaches that can be employed to handle this. The first is to draw all of your transparent object so that those in the back of your scene are rendered first. This will ensure that objects in the front do not obscure those behind.

The second approach is to draw all of your opaque objects first and then disable the depth buffer before drawing the transparent objects. This way, objects will not obscure anything subsequently drawn behind them.

Exactly which of these approaches is best will depend on what your game is drawing. Bear this limitation in mind when creating transparent objects in 3D space.

Rendering 3D Objects

Moving objects around our 3D game world is great, but we need to be able to create 3D objects too. So far, we've just worked with flat quadrilaterals. In this section, we'll discuss how solid objects can be created.

The quadrilaterals that we have been drawing up to this point have defined four vertices (all with a z values of 0) and used a triangle strip to combine these into the rendered shape. When we move into 3D objects, we are unlikely to be able to use triangle strips. Every triangle of a triangle strip shares an edge with the previous triangle, and with 3D objects, you will very quickly find that you are unable to draw objects in this way. Instead, we will use list of individual triangles, which gives us the flexibility to draw whatever triangle we need wherever we need it.

Defining a 3D Object

To start with, we will define our 3D object by manually providing all of its vertex coordinates. This is fairly straightforward for simple shapes but does quickly become impractical once we want to move on to more complicated objects. We'll use a simple cube for the time being and will look at how complicated geometry can be constructed in the "Importing Geometry" section in the next chapter.

A cube consists of six square faces and eight vertices. As each square needs to be rendered as two triangles, we end up with a total of 12 triangles to draw, as shown in Figure 12–6.

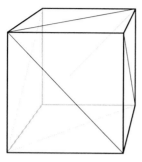

Figure 12–6. The triangles required to build a 3D cube

Since we are going to draw individual triangles rather than use a triangle strip, we actually need to specify each triangle coordinate individually. This means that when two triangles share a single coordinate, we actually need to specify the coordinate twice, once for each of the triangles. As a result we have to provide a total of 36 vertices, three for each triangle. As there are actually only eight distinct vertices forming the cube, this is quite wasteful, requiring OpenGL to perform the same calculations over and over again. We will look at a more efficient rendering method in the "Using Indexed Triangles" section coming up shortly.

To build the vertices of the cube, we simply declare an array of floats and add to it sets of three values, representing the x, y, and z coordinates. The coordinates for the front face of a unit-size cube is shown in Listing 12–4. Note that the z coordinate in each coordinate is 0.5, meaning that it extends half a unit toward the viewpoint.

Listing 12–4. Defining the Front Face of the Cube

```
// Define the vertices for the cube
float[] vertices = new float[]
{
    // Front face vertices
    -0.5f, -0.5f,  0.5f,     // vertex 0
     0.5f, -0.5f,  0.5f,     // vertex 1
    -0.5f,  0.5f,  0.5f,     // vertex 2
     0.5f, -0.5f,  0.5f,     // vertex 3
     0.5f,  0.5f,  0.5f,     // vertex 4
    -0.5f,  0.5f,  0.5f,     // vertex 5
    // [... and so on for the other faces...]
}
```

Plotting out these coordinates shows that we have indeed formed a square that will form the front face of the cube; see Figure 12–7.

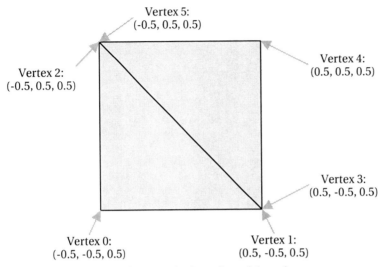

Figure 12–7. *The vertices forming the front face of the cube*

The array is extended to cover all of the faces of the cube, extending into the 3D space by using positive and negative values for the z positions. The full array is not included in the text here as it is fairly large and not particularly interesting, but it is shown in full inside the `CObjCube.Render` function in the ColoredCubes example project.

To provide colors for the faces of the cube, we build a second array of floats. We will still provide three array elements per vertex, but this time, they will be red, green, and blue values (we could of course add a fourth color element per vertex and include alpha values if we needed them).

The color array for the cube (which has its front face colored red) begins as shown in Listing 12–5. Once again the full array is not included here but can be found in the ColoredCubes project.

Listing 12–5. *Setting the Color Values for the Front Face of the Cube*

```
// Define the colors for the cube
float[] colors = new float[]
{
    // Front face colors
    1.0f, 0.0f, 0.0f,      // vertex 0
    1.0f, 0.0f, 0.0f,      // vertex 1
    1.0f, 0.0f, 0.0f,      // vertex 2
    1.0f, 0.0f, 0.0f,      // vertex 3
    1.0f, 0.0f, 0.0f,      // vertex 4
    1.0f, 0.0f, 0.0f,      // vertex 5
    // [... and so on for the other faces...]
}
```

With the vertices and colors prepared, we are now ready to render the cube. But how do we do that? The functions we have provided in `CGameObjectOpenGLBase` so far are only capable of drawing quadrilaterals, not 3D objects. We need a new function, and the function is called `RenderTriangles`.

To cut down on the combinations of ways in which the function can be called, we provide a single version of the function, accepting four array parameters to provide the vertices, colors, texture coordinates, and vertex normals (we will discuss vertex normals in the "Lighting Your Project" section later in this chapter.)

While the vertices array is always required, colors, textures and normals are optional and may be passed as null to indicate that they are not being used. The RenderTriangles code begins as shown in Listing 12–6.

Listing 12–6. Interrogating the vertices Array in RenderTriangles

```
unsafe protected void RenderTriangles(float[] vertices, float[] colors,
                                      float[] texCoords, float[] normals)
{
    int vertexCount = 0;
    int triangleCount = 0;
    int texCoordCount = 0;
    int elementsPerColor = 0;
    int normalCount = 0;

    // Make sure we have some coordinates
    if (vertices == null || vertices.Length == 0)
                throw new Exception("No vertices provided to RenderTriangles");
    // Find the number of vertices (3 floats per vertex for x, y and z)
    vertexCount = (int)(vertices.Length / 3);
    // Find the number of triangles (3 vertices per triangle)
    triangleCount = (int)(vertexCount / 3);
```

As the code shows, RenderTriangles first examines the vertices array. If it is empty, an exception is thrown. Otherwise, the number of vertices and triangles are determined from the array length.

Next, the code looks at the colors array, as shown in Listing 12–7.

Listing 12–7. Interrogating the colors Array in RenderTriangles

```
    // Do we have color values?
    if (colors == null)
    {
        // No, so create an empty single-element array instead.
        // We need this so that we can fix a pointer to it in a moment.
        colors = new float[1];
    }
    else
    {
        // Find the number of colors specified.
        // We have either three or four (including alpha) per vertex...
        if (colors.Length == vertexCount * 3)
        {
            elementsPerColor = 3;   // no alpha
        }
        else if (colors.Length == vertexCount * 4)
        {
            elementsPerColor = 4;   // alpha
        }
        else
```

```
    {
        throw new Exception("Colors count does not match vertex count");
    }
}
```

The code first checks to see if the colors array is null. If it is, a single item array is created (this is required for the fixed statement coming up shortly), and the elementsPerColor value is left with its initial value of 0. Otherwise, the array length is compared to the vertex count to see if we have been provided with three elements per color (no alpha) or four (alpha included). If the array size doesn't match either of these color definitions, an exception is thrown.

Very similar processing is then performed on the texCoords array, as is shown in Listing 12–8.

Listing 12–8. Interrogating the texCoords Array in RenderTriangles

```
// Do we have texture coordinates?
if (texCoords == null)
{
    // No, so create an empty single-element array instead.
    // We need this so that we can fix a pointer to it in a moment.
    texCoords = new float[1];
}
else
{
    // Find the number of texture coordinates. We have two per vertex.
    texCoordCount = (int)(texCoords.Length / 2);
    // Check the tex coord length matches that of the vertices
    if (texCoordCount > 0 && texCoordCount != vertexCount)
    {
        throw new Exception("Texture coordinate count does not match vertex count");
    }
}
```

Following on from processing the texture coordinate, we perform another very similar piece of processing for vertex normals. As we haven't yet covered these, we'll skip over this code for the moment.

The remainder of the function, shown in Listing 12–9, obtains pointers to the three arrays (of vertices, colors, and texture coordinates), checks whether colors and textures are in use, enables the required features in OpenGL as appropriate, and then renders the triangles. Note that the call to DrawArrays specifies GL_TRIANGLES as the primitive type instead of GL_TRIANGLE_STRIP as we used when rendering quadrilaterals earlier on. Once the triangles are drawn, any color or texture features that were enabled are disabled once again.

Listing 12–9. Rendering the Triangles in RenderTriangles

```
// Fix pointers to the vertices, colors and texture coordinates
fixed (float* verticesPointer = &vertices[0], colorPointer = &colors[0],
                                            texPointer = &texCoords[0])
{
    // Are we using vertex colors?
    if (elementsPerColor > 0)
    {
        // Enable colors
        gl.EnableClientState(gl.GL_COLOR_ARRAY);
        // Provide a reference to the color array
        gl.ColorPointer(elementsPerColor, gl.GL_FLOAT, 0, (IntPtr)colorPointer);
```

```
        }

        // Are we using texture coordinates
        if (texCoordCount > 0)
        {
            // Enable textures
            gl.Enable(gl.GL_TEXTURE_2D);
            // Enable processing of the texture array
            gl.EnableClientState(gl.GL_TEXTURE_COORD_ARRAY);
            // Provide a reference to the texture array
            gl.TexCoordPointer(2, gl.GL_FLOAT, 0, (IntPtr)texPointer);
        }

        // Enable processing of the vertex array
        gl.EnableClientState(gl.GL_VERTEX_ARRAY);
        // Provide a reference to the vertex array
        gl.VertexPointer(3, gl.GL_FLOAT, 0, (IntPtr)verticesPointer);

        // Draw the triangles
        gl.DrawArrays(gl.GL_TRIANGLES, 0, vertexCount);

        // Disable processing of the vertex array
        gl.DisableClientState(gl.GL_VERTEX_ARRAY);

        // Disable processing of the texture, color and normal arrays if we used them
        if (normalCount > 0)
        {
            gl.DisableClientState(gl.GL_NORMAL_ARRAY);
        }
        if (texCoordCount > 0)
        {
            gl.DisableClientState(gl.GL_TEXTURE_COORD_ARRAY);
            gl.Disable(gl.GL_TEXTURE_2D);
        }
        if (elementsPerColor > 0)
        {
            gl.DisableClientState(gl.GL_COLOR_ARRAY);
        }
    }
}
```

Using this code to draw the cube is then a simple matter of calling RenderTriangles as shown in Listing 12–10. Array data is passed for the vertices and colors, but as we are not using textures coordinates or normals in this example, we pass null for both of these.

Listing 12–01. Rendering a Cube Using RenderTriangles

```
// Render the cube
RenderTriangles(vertices, colors, null, null);
```

The ColoredCubes example project shows all of this in action. A single cube is added to the game initially, but further cubes can be added by selecting the Add Cube menu item. This example clearly demonstrates 3D objects, movement in 3D space, and the function of the depth buffer. An image from the program is shown in Figure 12–8.

Figure 12–8. *The ColoredCubes example project*

Removing Hidden Surfaces

When we draw solid, opaque objects such as cubes, the inside of the cube is completely obscured from view. OpenGL is unaware of this, however, and continues drawing the inside faces of the cube. This wastes processing power, as it unnecessarily compares and updates the inside faces with the depth buffer, and if the faces toward the back are rendered before those at the front, it also actually renders them, only to subsequently draw over them completely with the outer faces of the cube.

You probably won't be surprised to hear that OpenGL has a solution for this—and it's nice and easy to use too.

OpenGL is able to work out whether each triangle is facing toward us (as the front face of the cube is) or away from us (as the back face of the cube is). It does this based on how the triangle is actually rendered, not just how its vertices were defined, so that as a triangle rotates the direction in which it is facing will change. Those triangles that are found to be facing away from us are *culled* and are not considered for inclusion in the depth or color buffers, saving all of the work that would otherwise have been involved in checking and updating these.

In order for OpenGL to be able to determine the direction the triangles are facing, we need to give our triangle vertices to it in a slightly special way. When we define the triangles, we ensure that when the front of the triangle is facing toward us, the vertices are provided such that they appear in a counterclockwise direction. Figure 12–9 shows two triangles, one whose vertices are defined in counterclockwise order (on the left) and the other in clockwise order.

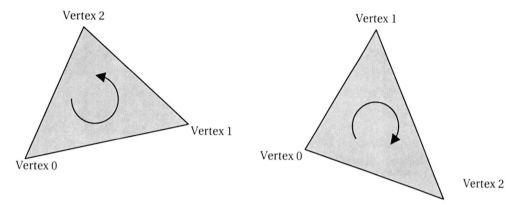

Figure 12–9. Triangles with vertices defined in counterclockwise (left) and clockwise (right) order

---

■ **NOTE** It is important to remember that the vertices must appear in counterclockwise order *when the triangle is facing you.* When we define a cube, the rear face is initially facing away from us, so the triangles would appear to be in clockwise order instead. If the cube were rotated around so that the back face was oriented toward us, the vertices would then appear to be counterclockwise as we need them to be.

If you look back at the vertices defined for the front face of the cube in Figure 12–7, you will see that both of the triangles have their vertices defined in counterclockwise order. This is, of course, by design.

With our triangles specified correctly, we can tell OpenGL to ignore those triangles that face away from us by enabling the GL_CULL_FACE state as shown in Listing 12–11.

Listing 12–11. Enabling Hidden Surface Removal

```
// Enable hidden surface removal
gl.Enable(gl.GL_CULL_FACE);
```

If you apply this to the ColoredCubes project, you will see that it has no visible effect at all, as you would expect. The overall performance of the project will improve, however, allowing more cubes to be added before the simulation begins to slow down.

To see hidden surface removal actually having an effect, execute the HiddenSurfaceRemoval example project. This displays a cube similar to the one in the previous example, but with one of its faces missing so that you can see inside the box. When the project first begins, hidden surface removal is disabled, and the interior of the box is rendered. Switching hidden surface remove on from the menu will cause the box interior to vanish.

Figure 12–10 shows two identical views from this example, the one of the left with hidden surface removal disabled and on the right with it enabled. If the surface that has been cut away was still being rendered, the missing interior would not be noticeable at all.

■ **NOTE** Although OpenGL's standard behavior is to cull clockwise faces and show counterclockwise, this can be reversed if required. Call `gl.CullFace(gl.GL_FRONT)` to switch OpenGL so that it culls counterclockwise faces and draws those that are clockwise. Or call `gl.CullFace(gl.GL_BACK)` to switch back to the original behavior. This flexibility can be particularly useful when reading object geometry from external files (as we will look at in the "Importing Geometry" section in the next chapter), which may define triangles in the opposite order to OpenGL's default requirement.

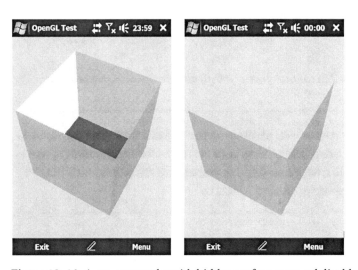

Figure 12–10. A cut-away cube with hidden surface removal disabled (left) and enabled (right)

Using Indexed Triangles

To draw the cube shown in the previous examples, we have had to provide the same vertex coordinates to OpenGL multiple times. As we discussed earlier, a cube has eight vertices, yet in our examples we are creating our vertex array with 36 vertices in it, six for each face (consisting of three vertices for each of the two triangles used to draw the face).

This is, of course, quite wasteful in terms of processing resources, because we are calculating the exact same vertex position many times.

OpenGL provides an alternative mechanism for providing vertex coordinates that allows the number of repeated identical coordinates to be reduced. Instead of creating each vertex independently of the others, we can instead provide a list of just the unique vertices and then separately tell OpenGL how to join them together to make the triangles that it is to render. The list of vertex numbers that specifies how to join the vertices is called an *index list*.

Consider again the front face of the cube in Figure 12–7. If we specify just the unique vertices, the vertex count will be reduced from the previous six to four. The four vertices are shown in Figure 12–11.

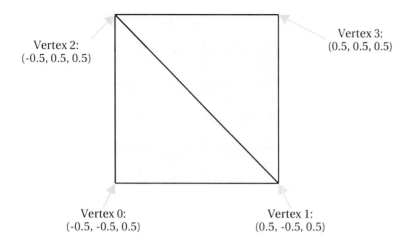

Figure 12–11. *Specifying just the unique coordinates for the front face of the cube*

While this allows the vertices to be defined, we no longer have the information required to join them together to form the rendered triangles. This is where the index list appears. To draw the front face, we need two triangles, and the vertex indices for each are as follows:

- *First triangle*: 0, 1, 2

- *Second triangle*: 1, 3, 2

Just as before, the triangle is formed by specifying its vertices in counterclockwise order so that hidden surface removal can cull the triangles facing away from the viewer.

That takes care of the vertex coordinates, but what about the vertex colors and texture coordinates? These are specified in exactly the same method as the vertices themselves: colors are formed from an array with a color for each defined vertex, and texture coordinates from another array with a texture coordinate for each defined vertex. When OpenGL is rendering, it reads the indices required for each triangle and uses these to access all of the arrays that are in use, reading vertex position, color, and texture coordinates from the specified location within each.

Rendering of indexed vertices is provided by the game engine in the CGameEngineOpenGLBase.RenderIndexedTriangles function. This is virtually identical to RenderTriangles, except that it takes an extra parameter, indices, to provide the vertex indices for the triangles. This parameter is passed as an array of short integers. To actually render the graphics, the new function calls OpenGL's DrawElements function (instead of the DrawArray function that is used by RenderTriangles), passing a pointer to the array of indices.

The cube vertices and colors can now be defined as shown in Listing 12–12.

Listing 12–12. *Declaring the Unique Indices for the Cube*

```
// Define the vertices for the cube
float[] vertices = new float[]
{
    -0.5f, -0.5f,  0.5f,    // front bottom left
     0.5f, -0.5f,  0.5f,    // front bottom right
```

```
        -0.5f,  0.5f,  0.5f,    // front top left
         0.5f,  0.5f,  0.5f,    // front top right

         0.5f, -0.5f, -0.5f,    // back bottom right
        -0.5f, -0.5f, -0.5f,    // back bottom left
         0.5f,  0.5f, -0.5f,    // back top right
        -0.5f,  0.5f, -0.5f,    // back top left
};

// Define the colors for the cube
float[] colors = new float[]
{
    0.0f, 0.0f, 0.0f,
    1.0f, 0.0f, 0.0f,
    0.0f, 1.0f, 0.0f,
    1.0f, 1.0f, 0.0f,
    0.0f, 0.0f, 1.0f,
    1.0f, 0.0f, 1.0f,
    0.0f, 1.0f, 1.0f,
    1.0f, 1.0f, 1.0f,
};
```

Note that we provide exactly the same number of vertices and colors, as each color in the colors array relates to the corresponding vertex in the vertices array.

Finally, we have the array of indices used to form the triangles that make up the cube. As each vertex is specified by just a single number now (its vertex index), we can place each triangle's three indices on to a single line of code, which makes the array easier to read. The array of indices for the cube is shown in Listing 12–13.

Listing 12–13. The Array of Indices Used to Form the Triangles of the Cube

```
// Define the indices for the cube
short[] indices = new short[]
{
    // Front face
    0, 1, 2,
    1, 3, 2,
    // Right face
    4, 6, 1,
    6, 3, 1,
    // Back face
    4, 5, 6,
    5, 7, 6,
    // Left face
    0, 2, 5,
    2, 7, 5,
    // Top face
    2, 3, 7,
    3, 6, 7,
    // Bottom face
    1, 0, 4,
    0, 5, 4,
};
```

The cube is then rendered by calling `RenderIndexedTriangles`, as shown in Listing 12–15.

Listing 12–14. Rendering the Cube from the Defined Vertices, Colors, and Indices

```
// Render the cube
RenderIndexedTriangles(vertices, colors, null, null, indices);
```

The only downside to this indexed rendering approach is that each vertex can have only a single color and a single texture coordinate. If you wish to have two vertices at the same location but with different colors (as I have used for our cubes so far, where the corner points are shared between different vertices but yet have different colors on each face) or with different textures, these must be defined as separate vertices. Even taking this into account, we could reduce the number of vertices in our cube from 36 to 24 (four per face), a reduction of one third.

An example of rendering a cube using an index array can be found in the `IndexedTriangles` project in the accompanying code download.

Lighting Your Projects

Up to this point, all of the colors used in our examples have been directly specified within our program code. This gives us a high level of control over the appearance of the graphics but leads to a flat and cartoony look to the graphics. To add a further degree of realism to the objects that we render, we can use OpenGL's lighting features.

In this section, we will examine the lighting capabilities and explore how they can be used within our games.

Introducing the Lights and Materials

OpenGL offers the facility to place up to eight different lights into our game world and use these to illuminate the objects that we render. When lighting is switched on, the way in which our objects are colored is altered from the behavior you have seen so far. OpenGL applies lighting to our objects by calculating the amount and color of light that falls on to each vertex and actually adjusts the vertex colors based on the result of this.

The outcome of this is that we can generate highly dynamic and realistic-looking shading on our objects. The downside is that as OpenGL has taken control of coloring the vertices itself, any vertex colors that we specify are entirely ignored. We can still apply textures to our objects just as before, but there is no point in passing vertex color information when lighting is enabled.

While we are no longer able to color vertices, we can still use different colors within a texture to provide coloring to different sections of our objects, so this problem is not necessarily as big as it might first sound.

The loss of ability to control the colors of individual vertices is offset by a new color control mechanism: object material. We are able to control how much light and the color of light our objects reflect. This provides a fair degree of flexibility with regard to how our objects are lit.

The following sections will discuss how lights and materials can be used within our game worlds.

Exploring the Types of Illumination

A number of different types of illumination are available to shine on to our objects. Any or all of the illumination types may be applied to an OpenGL light source, and the color of each type of illumination may also be specified independently.

Let's take a look at each of the illumination types that a light may use.

Ambient Light

The simplest type of light is ambient light. Ambient light is light that comes from all directions at once and falls on to all parts of each object rendered. It is completely flat in intensity, leaving no bright or dark areas on the objects that it illuminates.

In the real world, the closest analogy to ambient light is the light that is reflected from all the objects in the environment. If you are in a room with a single light source, a light bulb in the ceiling, those areas of the room that are not in direct line of sight from the bulb still receive some light from their surroundings. Ambient light seeks to replicate this illumination.

When ambient light is present, all vertices will be equally lit by the appropriate ambient light level.

An example object illuminated with ambient light is shown in Figure 12–12. The figure shows a 3D cylinder with a medium-intensity ambient light and no other lighting. Note how the object appears just as a silhouette: no variation of light intensity can be seen anywhere within the object.

Figure 12–12. A cylinder illuminated with an ambient light source

Diffuse Light

Diffuse light is reflected by an object based on how the object is rotated toward the light source. If an object is rotated so that its faces are angled directly toward the light source, the faces will radiate the light with a high intensity. As they rotate away from the light, the intensity fades.

The light is radiated equally in all directions, so the viewpoint from which the object is seen has no effect on the intensity of the lit surfaces.

An example object illuminated with diffuse light is shown in Figure 12–13. The figure shows the same cylinder with a bright diffuse light situated directly to its right. Note how the object illumination increases as the object surface becomes more directly angled toward the light source.

Figure 12–13. A cylinder illuminated with a diffuse light source

Specular Light

Specular light is also reflected by an object based on its angle with regard to the light source, but this type of illumination radiates light more like a mirror: light is reflected from the surface based on the angle of the surface relative to the viewer and light source.

If the light source is in the same location as the viewpoint and a surface also faces directly toward the viewpoint, the specular light will radiate intensely. As soon as the surface rotates away from the viewpoint, the specular light will rapidly fall away. If the viewpoint and light source are in different locations, those faces that are angled directly between the two will radiate light most brightly, just as a mirror would.

This behavior allows objects to be given a shine or highlight that can make them very realistic looking.

An example object illuminated with diffuse light is shown in Figure 12–14. The figure shows the same cylinder with a bright specular light situated directly to its right. Note that the object illumination increases as the angle of the cylinder reflects our viewpoint toward the light, where the surface of the cylinder is at about a 45-degree angle from the viewpoint. As the surface deviates from this angle, the light intensity rapidly drops away.

Figure 12–14. A cylinder illuminated with a specular light source

Using Material Properties

Just as lights emit different types and intensities of light, objects can reflect different types of light in different colors. For example, a red object in the real world is red because it reflects any red light that falls on it and absorbs the green and blue light.

In OpenGL, we can set the color and intensity of light reflected from each individual object by setting the object *material*. Just as we can set different colors for ambient, diffuse, and specular light, we can define the intensity and color that objects reflect for each different type of light.

Let's take a look at the different material properties, and then we will examine exactly how lights and materials interact with each other.

Ambient Material

The ambient material defines how much ambient light is reflected by the object. Setting this to black will result in all ambient light being completely absorbed by the object; none of it will be reflected at all. Setting it to white will result in all ambient light being reflected.

Varying the intensity levels of the ambient red, green, and blue within the material will cause it to reflect just the color and intensity of light specified. For example, setting the ambient material color to a red value of 1, a green of 0.5, and a blue of 0 will cause it to reflect the red component of the ambient light in full, half of the green component, and none of the blue.

Diffuse Material

A material's diffuse property controls the amount of diffuse light reflected. This need not be the same as the ambient color (or indeed any of the other material colors), which allows the material to respond differently to each of the different types of incoming light.

Specular Material

The material's specular property controls the amount of specular light that is reflected from the object. Setting this to 0 will completely disable the specular element of the light, preventing any shine effects from displaying on the object. The material shininess can also be used to control how specular light reflects from an object, as discussed next.

Material Shininess

When specular light is being used, a useful material property is its *shininess*. This is not a color, like the other properties we have looked at, but rather an integer value in the range of 0 to 128.

Setting a high shininess value makes the object shine more: the specular light will become more focused on the object. Lower values make the object less shiny: the specular light will be scattered more, making it look closer in appearance to a diffuse light.

Emissive Material

The final material property allows us to set an *emissive color*. This property is used to specify a color that is simulated as originating from the object itself, allowing it to have its own illumination independently of that of the lights around it.

It should be noted however that rendering an object with an emissive color set does not make the object into a light source itself. It will not add any light to the rest of the scene or cause any other objects to be illuminated in any way.

Exploring Light and Material Interaction

Now that you know how to add light into a 3D scene and how to make light reflect from game objects, you need to know how these lights and materials actually interact.

A fairly simple calculation is used to determine the level of light for each vertex that is rendered. The engine first calculates the amount of ambient light to apply to the object by multiplying each of the red, green, and blue ambient values for the light (which each range from 0 to 1) by the corresponding red, green, and blue ambient values for the material (also ranging from 0 to 1). The resulting values are used to form the final ambient color level for the object.

Let's take an example of this. If we have a midlevel gray ambient light with (red, green, blue) values of (0.5, 0.5, 0.5), and an object that has a blue ambient material with color (0.7, 0.2, 0.2), the color components are multiplied as follows:

- Red: $0.5 \times 0.7 = 0.35$

- Green: $0.5 \times 0.2 = 0.1$

- Blue: $0.5 \times 0.2 = 0.1$

The resulting ambient color for the object is (0.35, 0.1, 0.1).

Consider another example where we have a pure red ambient light with color (1, 0, 0) and a pure green ambient material with color (0, 1, 0). The calculation for this would be as follows:

- Red: $1 \times 0 = 0$

- Green: $0 \times 1 = 0$

- Blue: $0 \times 0 = 0$

The resulting color is therefore (0, 0, 0)—black. Shining a green light on to a red object results in all of the green light being absorbed, so the object is not illuminated at all.

Once the final ambient light has been calculated as shown, the same calculation is repeated for the diffuse and specular light. This gives us three calculated colors. The object's emissive color is then taken into account in isolation of any lights in the scene to provide a forth color.

Next, the red, green, and blue components of these four colors are simply added together to produce the final color of light that will be applied to the object. If any of the color components exceed their upper limit of 1, they are *clamped* at this value and treated as being equal to 1.

Using Multiple Lights

We are not limited to having a single light active within our rendered scene. Any or all of the eight available lights may be switched on when an object is rendered to provide light of different color and in different directions.

If our object is rendered with more than one light active, the final color for the object is calculated as explained in the previous section for each individual light. The color components for the individual lights are then all added together to provide a final color for the object being rendered.

This behavior means that colors can become oversaturated if lots of different lights are present at once. Some thought and attention may be required to ensure that light sources don't cause objects to be flooded with so much light that they are overwhelmed by it.

Reusing Lights

An important feature to remember when using lights is that they are only observed at the moment at which an object is rendered. After an object render has been called, the lights that were active can be reconfigured, moved, enabled or disabled in whatever way you wish for the next object, and these changes will have no effect at all on those objects already rendered.

Lights do not therefore need to necessarily affect all objects in the game world, as lights in the real world would, but can be configured to only apply to specific game objects if needed.

■ **TIP** Also remember that you can switch the entire lighting feature on and off partway through rendering if you wish. It is quite acceptable to draw a series of objects with lighting enabled, then disable lighting, and draw further objects without any lighting effects at all so that vertex colors can be used.

Exploring the Types of Light Source

In addition to the different types of illumination that are available, there are also several different types of light source that can be added: directional lights, point lights, and spotlights. Let's take a look at each of these.

Directional Lights

Directional lights shine light in a single direction equally across an entire scene. They do not have a position and are treated as being infinitely far away from the scene. The rays of light are parallel to each other.

The closest analogy that we can get to this in the real world is sunlight. While the sun clearly does actually have a position, it is so far away that the light it emits is, for all intents and purposes, coming from the entire sky rather than from a single point.

Figure 12–15 shows the way in which a directional light shines on objects rendered within a 3D scene. Note how the light has direction but does not have a position: the rays shown are all parallel and do not converge on any specific location.

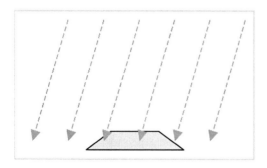

Figure 12–15. Light rays from a directional light source

Point Lights

Point lights, on the other hand, have a position instead of a direction. Light is emitted from the position in all directions, illuminating everything around. As objects move around the light source, they will be illuminated on different sides depending on the position of the light relative to that of the object. An analogy to a point light in the real world is a light bulb hanging from the ceiling or in a lamp.

Figure 12–16 shows the light rays emitted by a point light. Notice that the light has a defined position (shown by the light bulb image within the figure) but does not have a direction; it shines equally in all directions.

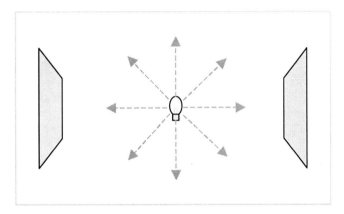

Figure 12–16. Light rays from a point light source

Spotlights

The final type of light that we can use is a spotlight. Spotlights combine features of both the directional and position lights: they have positions defined within the game world, but they also shine in a defined direction.

As well as defining a spotlight's position and direction, we can also define two further properties: the *cutoff* angle and the *exponent*.

The cutoff angle defines the spread of light from the spotlight. It is specified as the angle between the center direction line of the light and the outer edge of the generated light beam. This is measured as a value between 0 and 90, where 0 represents an infinitely thin beam of light and 90 represents a spread of light that completely floods the direction specified. The only value allowed outside of this range is the special value 180 (the default value), which switches the light back to being a directional or point light.

The exponent defines how tightly focused the light is along its center point. The light gradually falls off outside of this area of focus toward the cutoff angle. A spotlight's exponent is set as a value between 0 and 128. Setting it to 0 provides completely uniform distribution of light within the defined cutoff angle, whereas higher values concentrate the light towards the center of its directional beam.

Figure 12–17 shows an example of a spotlight.

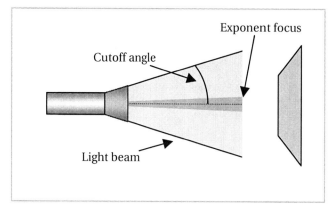

Figure 12–17. The light beam from a spotlight

Calculating Light Reflections in OpenGL

The explanations we have looked at for each light revolve to a significant degree around determining whether each triangle in a rendered object is facing toward or away from a light. Triangles that are at the appropriate angle relative to the light will be illuminated brightly, whereas triangles facing away from the light will be darker or not illuminated at all.

How does OpenGL tell whether a triangle is facing toward a light or not? There's nothing magical about this. In fact, the answer is rather basic: we have to tell OpenGL the direction in which each triangle is facing.

We do this just once when we create our object. When the object is rotating or moving in the game world, OpenGL will use this information to apply all of the object transformations to it, just as it does to the position of the vertices. The object lighting will, therefore, be automatically and dynamically calculated as each object or light moves within the scene.

Describing a Triangle's Face Direction

To tell OpenGL the direction in which each triangle is facing, we provide a set of values known as a *normal*. A normal describes a line that is pointing in a direction perpendicular to the front of the triangle. Figure 12–18 shows a single triangle with its normal. The triangle itself is completely flat with its surface pointing directly upward. The normal, represented by a dashed arrow, therefore points upward too.

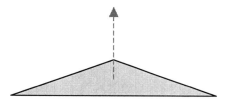

Figure 12–18. A triangle and its normal

In Figure 12–19, a solid shape is shown with its normals. Each side of the cube faces in a different direction, and once again, dashed arrows are used to indicate the direction of the normal from each side.

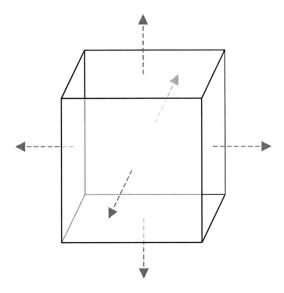

Figure 12–19. A cube and the normals of each of its faces

To describe each normal, we provide OpenGL with a 3D *vector*. The vector consists of three different values (for the x, y, and z axis) and describes the distance along each axis that would need to be traveled to move along the line of the normal.

■ **NOTE** A vector is written down in the same way as a coordinate, with its x, y, and z distances in parentheses separated by commas.

For the triangles on top of the cube whose faces point directly upward, the normal vector would be (0, 1, 0). This shows that to travel along the line of the normal, we would move 0 units along the x and z axes, and 1 unit along the positive y axis—in other words, we would move directly upward. The opposite face that points downward would have a normal vector of (0, –1, 0). Moving in the direction of this vector would move us along the negative y axis.

Similarly, the triangles on the right edge of the cube have a normal vector of (1, 0, 0), and the triangles at the back of the cube (facing away from us) have a normal vector of (0, 0, –1).

We need to provide these normal vectors to OpenGL when our object is being rendered. We only need to provide the vectors for when the object is in its default, untransformed position. As the object is moved around the scene, OpenGL will recalculate its resulting normal vectors automatically.

Notice that the normals we have discussed all have a length of 1 unit. This is important, because OpenGL takes the normal length into account when performing its lighting calculations, and normal vectors that are longer or shorter than this will cause the reflected light to become brighter or darker.

Vectors with a length of 1 unit are known as *normalized* vectors, whereas those with longer or shorter lengths are *unnormalized*.

Once OpenGL knows the direction each triangle is facing, it can work out whether they face towards or away from the scene's lights and so determine how much light to provide for the triangle.

Calculating Normals

While working out normal vectors is easy when they are aligned directly along the x, y, or z axis, they can be much more difficult to work out in your head when the triangle faces in a direction away from these axes. Calculating the normals manually for these triangles would be both tedious and error prone.

Fortunately, we are using a computer (albeit a small one), so we can get it to calculate the normals for us automatically. It can also normalize them easily ,saving us from having to do that job too.

There are all sorts of mathematical operations that can be calculated on vectors (and there are lots of books and online references that will cover this subject in immense detail if you wish to investigate it further), and we can use one of these called a *cross product* to calculate the normal for us.

To perform a cross product calculation, we need to find two vectors that lay along the surface of our triangle. These are easy to calculate, because we can simply find the difference in position between the vertices of the triangle. We will call these vectors a and b.

Consider the triangle shown in Figure 12–20. It is orientated so that its surface points directly upward (to keep the example simple!) and has vertex coordinates as shown.

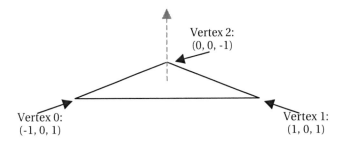

Figure 12–20. *The vertices of a triangle ready for normal calculation*

Note that the triangle vertices are as always defined in counterclockwise order. This is important to our calculation; if they were defined in clockwise order, the normal we calculate would be facing in the opposite direction (downwards in this case).

To calculate the two vectors that we need, we subtract the coordinates of vertex 1 from vertex 0 for the first vector, and subtract the coordinates of vertex 2 from vertex 1 for the second vector, as follows:

- Vector a: $(-1 - 1, 0 - 0, 1 - 1) = (-2, 0, 0)$

- Vector b: $(1 - 0, 0 - 0, 1 - -1) = (1, 0, 2)$

As you can see, these do indeed represent the distances from each vertex to the next. To move from vertex 1 to vertex 0, we would need to move –2 units along the x axis and 0 units on the y and z axes. To move from vertex 2 to vertex 1, we would need to move 1 unit on the x axis, 0 units on the y axis, and 2 units along the z axis.

To perform the cross product operation, we need to perform the following calculations on the vectors a and b. These will produce the normal vector n.

- $n.x = (a.y \times b.z) - (a.z \times b.y)$

- n.y = (a.z × b.x) – (a.x × b.z)
- n.z = (a.x × b.y) – (a.y × b.x)

Let's substitute in the values for our vectors and see the results:

- n.x = (0 × 2) – (0 × 0) = 0 – 0 = 0
- n.y = (0 × 1) – (-2 × 2) = 0 – -4 = 4
- n.z = (-2 × 0) – (0 × 1) = 0 – 0 = 0

The resulting vector n is, therefore, calculated as (0, 4, 0). This does indeed describe a line in the positive y axis, directly upward, exactly as we had hoped. The same calculation can be performed for any triangle regardless of its vertex locations.

The vector we have calculated is not normalized however. To normalize it, we apply a 3D version of the Pythagorean theorem. Fortunately, this is not really any more complex than the 2D calculation that we looked at back in Chapter 6. The current length of the vector is found as follows:

$$\text{Vector length} = \sqrt{x^2 + y^2 + z^2}$$

Once the length is found, we can divide each element of the vector by this length. This will reduce or increase the vector length as required in order to make it exactly 1 unit in length.

Applying this to our vector results in the following calculations:

$$\text{Vector length} = \sqrt{0 + 16 + 0} = \sqrt{16} = 4$$
$$\text{n.x} = 0 / 4 = 0$$
$$\text{n.y} = 4 / 4 = 1$$
$$\text{n.z} = 0 / 4 = 0$$

The resulting vector is therefore (0, 1, 0)—a normalized vector pointing directly upward. Perfect.

We will look at implementing all of this in our program code in the section entitled "Calculating Normals Programmatically," which is coming up shortly.

Using Surface Normals and Vertex Normals

We have so far considered normals as applying to each face in our 3D object. In actual fact, it is not the faces that we apply normals to but the individual vertices that form the face. OpenGL calculates the color for the vertices based on its lighting equations, and it then applies this to the whole triangle by interpolating the colors between the vertices, just as we have manually interpolated colors ourselves by providing vertex colors.

This gives us an opportunity to perform a very useful lighting trick. We can provide different normals for the vertices of a single triangle. OpenGL will then consider each vertex to be facing in a different direction and will effectively interpolate the light directions across the surface of the triangle.

Consider the triangles in Figure 12–21; these are shown as thick lines, representing the triangles viewed edge-on. The long dashed arrows show the normals that have been applied for each of the vertices within the triangles. Note that, for each triangle, the normals are pointing in different directions (they point away from one another).

The shorter dashed arrows show the effective normals within the interior of the triangles due to interpolation. These smoothly transition from one normal to the next, giving the impression that the surface of the object when viewed face on is perfectly smooth, although, in fact, it is created from just five flat faces.

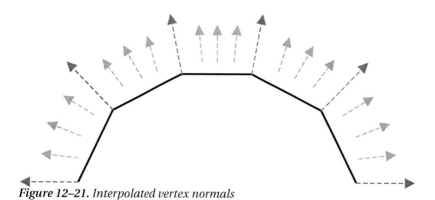

Figure 12–21. *Interpolated vertex normals*

An example of this in practice is shown in Figure 12–22. The two images shown are both of the same cylinder, rendered using a number of flat surfaces. The individual surfaces can be clearly seen in the image on the left, which uses the same normals for all vertices within each face. On the right, the vertex normals are modified so that they differ from one side of the face to the other (exactly as we did in Figure 12–21). Note that the appearance of this cylinder is entirely smooth, even though it is formed from the exact same faces as the image on the left.

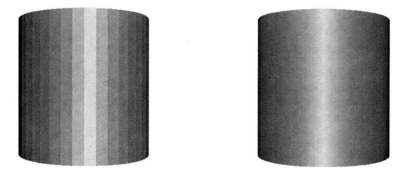

Figure 12–22. *A cylinder with normals applied to each whole face (left) and to individual vertices (right)*

Adding Light to the Game Engine

That's plenty of theory. Let's now see how we can add support for lighting into the game engine. All of the code that we will look at in this section can be found within the Lighting project in this chapter's accompanying download.

Enabling Lighting

To switch on lighting, we simply tell OpenGL to use it by calling the Enable function. Listing 12–15 shows the code required for this.

Listing 12–15. Enabling Lighting in OpenGL

```
// Enable lighting
gl.Enable(gl.GL_LIGHTING);
```

To disable lighting, make the same call to the Disable function instead. In the Lighting example project, you will see that lighting is enabled inside the CLightingGame.InitLight function.

Once the lighting model has been switched on, each of the available lights must be individually enabled to cast light into the rendered scene. As has already been discussed, OpenGL provides eight separate lights that can be individually configured. These lights are identified by using one of the GL_LIGHT*n* constants: GL_LIGHT0 specifies the first light for example, whereas GL_LIGHT7 specifies the eighth light.

To enable a light, call the Enable function once again and pass in the constant for the light that is to be switched on. To disable a light, pass the same constant to the Disable function. Listing 12–17 shows some code that switches on light 0 and switches off light 1.

Listing 12–16. Enabling and Disabling Individual Lights

```
gl.Enable(gl.GL_LIGHT0);
gl.Disable(gl.GL_LIGHT1);
```

In the Lighting example project, you will see that while the lights are configured inside the InitLight function, they are not actually switched on. When the project starts up, all the lights are disabled, resulting in the 3D objects rendering as black silhouettes. The lights are instead enabled and disabled in the menu selection events contained within the game form.

Adding the Game Engine Light Functions

The lights have various parameters to define their illumination colors, position, direction, and so on. The parameters are set by calling one of two OpenGL functions: Lightf (if passing a single value) or Lightfv (if passing an array of values). In both cases, the call tells OpenGL which light to update, which parameter to set, and the parameter value to apply.

Most of the OpenGL light parameters require a pointer to an array to be provided. This array will contain a color, a direction, or a position, depending on which light parameter is being set. To pass this pointer to OpenGL, we once again need to use the fixed statement to retrieve a pointer to the array. An example of setting the diffuse color of light 0 to red is shown in Listing 12–17.

Listing 12–17. Setting a Light's Diffuse Color

```
// Declare the color -- full red intensity, no green or blue
float[] diffuseColor = new float { 1, 0, 0, 1 };
// Get a pointer to the color array
fixed (float* colorPointer = &diffuseColor[0])
{
    // Pass the pointer into OpenGL to configure the light
    gl.Lightfv(gl.GL_LIGHT0, gl.GL_DIFFUSE, colorPointer);
}
```

Setting the color in this way is slightly awkward however:

- It requires our project and function to both be configured to allow unsafe code. Using unsafe code also prevents us from making these function calls from VB.NET, which does not support it at all.

- The code is fairly long-winded, requiring multiple lines of code for a simple color change. Once this is expanded to set multiple different types of illumination across different lights, a lot of code is required, which reduces the readability of the program.

To eliminate both of these problems, we add some new functions to CGameEngineOpenGLBase. The SetLightParameter function accepts as its parameters the light that we wish to modify, the parameter to set, and the array of float values that form the parameter value.

We add to this a second overload, which takes a single float rather than an array (some light parameters, such as the spotlight cutoff angle, require just a simple value instead of an array). For these light parameters, we have no need to obtain a pointer. In that case, the need to have a game engine function is reduced, but it allows us to make consistent calls into the game engine for both array and single-value parameters, which increases the readability of our game code.

The implementations of both overloads of SetLightParameter can be seen in Listing 12–18.

Listing 12–18. The Game Engine's Implementations of the SetLightParameter Functions

```
/// <summary>
/// Set a light parameter to the provided value
/// </summary>
public void SetLightParameter(uint light, uint parameter, float value)
{
    gl.Lightf(light, parameter, value);
}

/// <summary>
/// Set a light parameter to the provided value array
/// </summary>
unsafe public void SetLightParameter(uint light, uint parameter, float[] value)
{
    fixed (float* valuePointer = &value[0])
    {
        gl.Lightfv(light, parameter, valuePointer);
    }
}
```

Now, if we want to set the diffuse color for light 0, the code is reduced from that in Listing 12–17 to the much shorter code in Listing 12–19.

Listing 12–19. Setting a Light's Diffuse Color Using the Game Engine's SetLightParameter Function

```
// Set the diffuse color of light 0 to red
SetLightParameter(gl.GL_LIGHT0, gl.GL_DIFFUSE, new float[] {1, 0, 0, 1});
```

The parameters and expected values that can be passed when configuring lights are shown in Table 12–1.

Table 12–1. Light parameters and expected values.

Parameter	Expected Value
GL_AMBIENT	An array of four floats defining the red, green, blue and alpha components of the ambient light color
GL_DIFFUSE	An array of four floats defining the diffuse light color
GL_SPECULAR	An array of four floats defining the specular light color
GL_POSITION	An array of four floats defining either the position or the direction of the light (this will be explained in more detail in the "Creating Directional Lights" and "Creating Point Lights" sections)
GL_SPOT_DIRECTION	An array of three float defining the direction of the spotlight
GL_SPOT_EXPONENT	A float value in the range of 0 to 128 defining the spotlight's exponent
GL_SPOT_CUTOFF	A float value in the range of 0 to 90 (or the special value 180) defining the spotlight's cutoff angle

Creating Directional Lights

To create a directional light, we configure its color as required and then set its GL_POSITION property. The first three elements define the direction in which the light will shine, such that one of the light rays will pass through this position and also through the original coordinate (0, 0, 0).

This means that if we specify the position as (0, 0, 1), the light direction will be a line between coordinates (0, 0, 1) and (0, 0, 0). In other words, the light will shine directly along the negative z axis. If we provided the position as (0, 1, 0), the light would shine down from above, along the negative y axis.

The fourth and final value that we pass when setting the GL_POSITION property for a directional light is simply the value 0. This identifies to OpenGL that the type of light we are using is a directional light.

Listing 12–20 shows the code used within the Lighting example project to configure light 0 as a directional light with position (1, 0, 0).

Listing 12–2o. Configuring a Directional Light

```
// Configure light 0.
// This is a green directional light at (1, 0, 0)
SetLightParameter(gl.GL_LIGHT0, gl.GL_DIFFUSE, new float[] { 1, 1, 0, 1 });
SetLightParameter(gl.GL_LIGHT0, gl.GL_SPECULAR, new float[] { 0, 0, 0, 1 });
SetLightParameter(gl.GL_LIGHT0, gl.GL_POSITION, new float[] { 1, 0, 0, 0 });
```

Creating Point Lights

To create a point light, we perform the same steps as for the directional light but pass the value 1 in the fourth element of the GL_POSITION array. This tells OpenGL to treat the light as a point light rather than as a directional light.

For point lights, the provided position coordinate is significant as an actual location within the world, rather than just used to determine a direction. Providing a coordinate of (2, 0, 0) as the position will result in the light being placed differently to a light at coordinate (4, 0, 0), whereas for a directional light, these would have been equivalent.

Listing 12–21 shows some code from the Lighting example that configures light 1 as a red point light. This light also has white a specular illumination element.

Listing 12–21. Configuring a Point Light

```
// Configure light 1.
// This is a red point light at (0, 0, 2) with white specular color
SetLightParameter(gl.GL_LIGHT1, gl.GL_DIFFUSE, new float[] {1, 0, 0, 1});
SetLightParameter(gl.GL_LIGHT1, gl.GL_SPECULAR, new float[] { 1, 1, 1, 1 });
SetLightParameter(gl.GL_LIGHT1, gl.GL_POSITION, new float[] { 0, 0, 2, 1 });
```

Creating Spotlights

Spotlights are created in just the same way as point lights, except that they additionally have a GL_SPOT_CUTOFF angle specified. In most cases, the GL_SPOT_DIRECTION will also be set (this defaults to a direction of (0, 0, –1) if not specifically configured) and possibly the exponent too.

Listing 12–22 contains some example code that creates a yellow spotlight at position (0, 10, 0), shining directly downward with a cutoff angle of 22 degrees.

Listing 12–22. Configuring a Spotlight

```
// Configure a yellow spotlight positioned at (0, 10, 0) and shining downwards
SetLightParameter(gl.GL_LIGHT2, gl.GL_DIFFUSE, new float[] {1, 1, 0, 1});
SetLightParameter(gl.GL_LIGHT2, gl.GL_SPECULAR, new float[] { 0, 0, 0, 0 });
SetLightParameter(gl.GL_LIGHT2, gl.GL_POSITION, new float[] { 0, 10, 0, 1 });
SetLightParameter(gl.GL_LIGHT2, gl.GL_SPOT_DIRECTION, new float[] { 0, -1, 0 });
SetLightParameter(gl.GL_LIGHT2, gl.GL_SPOT_CUTOFF, 22);
```

■ **CAUTION** As lights actually only affect vertex colors, spotlights that shine into the center of a triangle and don't reach its vertices will have no visible effect whatsoever. As objects with large triangles are transformed such that their vertices move into and out of the beam of the spotlight, unexpected lighting effects may be experienced as those vertices are individually affected by the light. To make a spotlight cast its spot of light on to a flat plane, the plane must be divided up into lots of smaller triangles so that the vertices are closer together and thus able to more accurately reflect the incoming light.

Setting the Scene's Ambient Light

Although ambient light may be added as a component to any of the individual lights, it is also possible to set an ambient light that independently affects the entire rendered scene. In fact, this ambient light is enabled by default with a color of (0.2, 0.2, 0.2, 1), so it may, instead, be a requirement to set this to black so it has no impact on objects rendered within the scene.

The scene's ambient light is set using a very similar call to the one to the Lightfv parameter described earlier but instead calls the LightModelfv function. We wrap this up inside CGameEngineOpenGLBase in a function called SetAmbientLight. The code for this function is shown in Listing 12–23.

Listing 12–23. The SetAmbientLight Function

```
/// <summary>
/// Set the scene ambient light to the provided four-element color array
/// </summary>
unsafe public void SetAmbientLight(float[] color)
{
    fixed (float* colorPointer = &color[0])
    {
        gl.LightModelfv(gl.GL_LIGHT_MODEL_AMBIENT, colorPointer);
    }
}
```

This function can then be easily called to set the scene's ambient light level. For example, the code in Listing 12–24 uses the function to switch off ambient light completely.

Listing 12–24. Using the SetAmbientLight Function to Disable Ambient Light

```
// Default the ambient light color to black (i.e., no light)
SetAmbientLight(new float[] { 0, 0, 0, 1 });
```

Setting Material Properties

Material properties are set in a very similar way to light properties. Instead of the Lightf and Lightfv functions, we use the Materialf and Materialfv functions, again expecting a single value and a value array respectively.

We create wrapper functions around these for exactly the same reasons as we created them around the light functions. The wrapper functions are named SetMaterialParameter and, once again, have two versions: one that accepts an array and one that accepts a single float. The code for these functions is shown in Listing 12–25.

Listing 12–25. The Game Engine's Implementations of the SetMaterialParameter Functions

```
/// <summary>
/// Set a material parameter to the provided value
/// </summary>
public void SetMaterialParameter(uint face, uint parameter, float value)
{
    gl.Materialf(face, parameter, value);
}

/// <summary>
/// Set a material parameter to the provided value array
/// </summary>
unsafe public void SetMaterialParameter(uint face, uint parameter, float[] value)
{
    fixed (float* valuePointer = &value[0])
    {
        gl.Materialfv(face, parameter, valuePointer);
    }
}
```

Instead of passing in a light number, we pass in the type of object face that we want to set the material for, which can be GL_FRONT to affect the front side of each triangle, GL_BACK to affect the back side of each triangle, or GL_FRONT_AND_BACK to affect both sides. Of course, this is only useful if hidden surface culling is disabled, as the back of each triangle would otherwise not be rendered regardless of any material that has been set.

Note that, when we set of a material, we are not applying that material to any specific object. Just like everything else in OpenGL, the material is a state and will stay in place until it is subsequently modified. A single material can thus be configured once for the entire game if required, or once per object rendered if different materials are needed.

The parameters and expected values that can be passed when configuring materials are shown in Table 12–2.

Table 12–2. Material Parameters and Expected Values

Parameter	Expected Value
GL_AMBIENT	An array of four floats defining the red, green, blue and alpha components of the ambient material reflectance
GL_DIFFUSE	An array of four floats defining the diffuse material reflectance
GL_SPECULAR	An array of four floats defining the specular material reflectance
GL_EMISSION	An array of four float defining the emission color for the material
GL_SHININESS	A value in the range of 0 to 128 defining the shininess of the material where 0 is extremely shiny and 128 is not shiny at all

Listing 12–26 shows some code from the Lighting example project that sets up a material to fully reflect all ambient, diffuse, and specular light, as well as configuring its shininess.

Listing 12–26. Configuring Material Properties

```
// Set the material color to fully reflect ambient, diffuse and specular light
SetMaterialParameter(gl.GL_FRONT_AND_BACK, gl.GL_AMBIENT, new float[] { 1, 1, 1, 1 });
SetMaterialParameter(gl.GL_FRONT_AND_BACK, gl.GL_SPECULAR, new float[] { 1, 1, 1, 1 });
SetMaterialParameter(gl.GL_FRONT_AND_BACK, gl.GL_DIFFUSE, new float[] { 1, 1, 1, 1 });
// Set the material shininess (0 = extremely shiny, 128 = not at all shiny)
SetMaterialParameter(gl.GL_FRONT_AND_BACK, gl.GL_SHININESS, 20);
```

OpenGL Lighting in Action

The Lighting example project that has been mentioned several times already contains a demonstration of most of the lighting features that we have discussed in this chapter. Some screenshots of the program are shown in Figure 12–23.

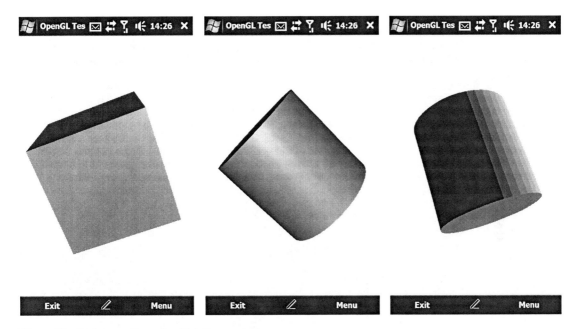

Figure 12–23. Images from the Lighting project

The example is able to display either a cube or a cylinder; the object can be selected from the menu. The cylinder can be displayed with normals that are the same for all vertices on each face or that interpolate across each face (smooth), but note that the vertex positions of the two versions of the cylinder are identical.

Three light options can be switched on and off within the project. The Ambient Light menu option will apply a dark blue light across the entire scene. Light 0 will switch on a green directional light shining from right to left. Light 1 will switch on a red point light in front of the object, which also has a white specular component. The effect of the specular light can be seen very clearly on the cylinder.

The cube and cylinder are created within the CObjCube and CObjCylinder classes respectively. The cube is simple enough in structure that the code is able to provide the vertices and their normals just as hard-coded arrays. The cylinder has more complexity, so both the vertices and normals are calculated in a loop using simple trigonometric functions. This calculation is performed just once when the cylinder object is instantiated and the vertices and normals are stored in class-level arrays, so the calculations do not need to be repeated each time the cylinder is rendered.

Spend some time looking at this example to familiarize yourself with the concepts we have been looking at. Feel free to modify the existing lights, create new light sources, and experiment with your own object and normal calculations.

Calculating Normals Programmatically

As you saw earlier, it is straightforward to programmatically calculate the normals for a triangle, but doing so manually can be a long-winded exercise. To simplify the task, we can add some code to the game engine to automatically calculate normals for us.

As we have two different ways of rendering triangles (using a simple list of triangles or vertex indices), we will create two corresponding functions that process data in these same two formats. To

347

reduce the amount of code, we will set up the two functions so that one simply calls into the other, allowing all of the calculation to be put into just a single function.

The easiest way to implement this is to get the version that takes a simple list of triangles (without vertex indices) to build a corresponding index array. Once this is done, the vertices and the indices can be passed into the other function to calculate on its behalf.

The indices for a triangle list are very simple: each triangle is formed from the next three vertices in the list, so the indices are just a sequence of incremental numbers. The first triangle is formed from indices 0, 1 and 2; the second triangle from indices 3, 4 and 5; the third from indices 6, 7 and 8, and so on.

The code for this function, named GenerateTriangleNormals and added to the game engine's CGameObjectOpenGLBase class, can be seen in Listing 12–27. It creates an array for the indices whose length is equal to the number of vertices (the size of the vertices array divided by three as each vertex consists of three coordinate values). This array is then filled with sequential numbers starting from 0, and the vertices and constructed indices array are passed into the GenerateIndexedTriangleNormals function, which we will examine in a moment.

Listing 12–27. Calculating Normals for Unindexed Triangles

```
/// <summary>
/// Builds an array of vertex normals for the array of provided triangle vertices.
/// </summary>
/// <param name="vertices">An array of vertices forming the triangles to render. Each
/// set of threevertices will be treated as the next triangle in the object.</param>
/// <returns>Returns an array of vertex normals, one normal for each of the provided
/// vertices. The normals will be normalized.</returns>
protected float[] GenerateTriangleNormals(float[] vertices)
{
    int[] indices;

    // Build an array that allows us to treat the vertices as if they were indexed.
    // As the triangles are drawn sequentially, the indexes are actually just
    // an increasing sequence of numbers: the first triangle is formed from
    // vertices 0, 1 and 2, the second triangle from vertices 3, 4 and 5, etc.

    // First create the array with an element for each vertex
    indices = new int[vertices.Length / 3];

    // Then set the elements within the array so that each contains
    // the next sequential vertex index
    for (int i = 0; i < indices.Length; i++)
    {
        indices[i] = i;
    }

    // Finally use the indexed normal calculation function to do the work.
    return GenerateIndexedTriangleNormals(vertices, indices);
}
```

The GenerateIndexedTriangleNormals function is where the actual calculation takes place. You may wish to refer to the "Calculating Normals" section earlier in this chapter, because the steps the function undertakes are exactly the same as the steps described there.

The function begins by declaring a number of arrays. The three vertex arrays will store the coordinates of the vertices that form the triangle that we are calculating the normal for. The va and vb arrays store the two vectors that are retrieved from the triangle, and the vn array stores the calculated normal vector. Finally, the normals array is the array of vertex normals that we will build as the code progresses. The beginning of the function is shown in Listing 12–28.

Listing 12–28. Preparing to Calculate Normals in the GenerateIndexedTriangleNormals Function

```
/// <summary>
/// Builds an array of vertex normals for the array of provided vertices and triangle
/// vertex indices.
/// </summary>
/// <param name="vertices">An array of vertices that are used to form the rendered
/// object.</param>
/// <param name="indices">An array of vertex indices describing the triangles to render.
/// Each set of three indices will be treated as the next triangle in the
/// object.</param>
/// <returns>Returns an array of vertex normals, one normal for each of the provided
/// vertices. The normals will be normalized.</returns>
protected float[] GenerateIndexedTriangleNormals(float[] vertices, int[] indices)
{
    // Three arrays to hold the vertices of the triangle we are working with
    float[] vertex0 = new float[3];
    float[] vertex1 = new float[3];
    float[] vertex2 = new float[3];

    // The two vectors that run along the edges of the triangle and a third
    // vector to store the calculated triangle normal
    float[] va = new float[3];
    float[] vb = new float[3];
    float[] vn = new float[3];
    float vnLength;

    // The array of normals. As each vertex has a corresponding normal
    // and both vertices and normals consist of three floats, the normal
    // array will be the same size as the vertex array.
    float[] normals = new float[vertices.Length];
```

Next, the code begins a loop through the triangles. We use the indices array to determine which three vertices form the next triangle are to be processed. For each vertex, the three coordinates are copied into one of the vertex arrays (vertex0, vertex1, and vertex2).

Once the coordinates are obtained, we subtract vertex1 from vertex0 to form the va vector and subtract vertex2 from vertex1 to form the vb vector. The code for these steps is shown in Listing 12–29.

Listing 12–29. Retrieving Two Vectors from a Triangle in the GenerateIndexedTriangleNormals Function

```
    // Loop for each triangle (each triangle uses three indices)
    for (int index = 0; index < indices.Length; index += 3)
    {
        // Copy the coordinates for the three vertices of this triangle
        // into our vertex arrays
        Array.Copy(vertices, indices[index] * 3, vertex0, 0, 3);
        Array.Copy(vertices, indices[index+1] * 3, vertex1, 0, 3);
        Array.Copy(vertices, indices[index+2] * 3, vertex2, 0, 3);

        // Create the a and b vectors from the vertices
```

```
// First the a vector from vertices 0 and 1
va[0] = vertex0[0] - vertex1[0];
va[1] = vertex0[1] - vertex1[1];
va[2] = vertex0[2] - vertex1[2];
// Then the b vector from vertices 1 and 2
vb[0] = vertex1[0] - vertex2[0];
vb[1] = vertex1[1] - vertex2[1];
vb[2] = vertex1[2] - vertex2[2];
```

With our two vectors calculated, the code is now ready to perform the cross product operation on them. The result is used to build the normal vector, vn. Because we need to ensure that the normal is normalized, the code then determines the length of the vector. If it is not 0 (which means that two or more of the triangle vertices were in exactly the same position) and not 1 (which means that the vector already is normalized), the elements of the vector are divided by its length to give an overall length of 1 unit. The code for this part of the function is shown in Listing 12–30.

Listing 12–30. Calculating and Normalizing the Normal Vector in the GenerateIndexedTriangleNormals Function

```
// Now perform a cross product operation on the two vectors
// to generate the normal vector.
vn[0] = (va[1] * vb[2]) - (va[2] * vb[1]);
vn[1] = (va[2] * vb[0]) - (va[0] * vb[2]);
vn[2] = (va[0] * vb[1]) - (va[1] * vb[0]);

// Now we have the normal vector but it is not normalized.
// Find its length...
vnLength = (float)Math.Sqrt((vn[0]*vn[0]) + (vn[1]*vn[1]) + (vn[2]*vn[2]));
// Make sure the length isn't 0 (and if its length is 1 it's already normalized)
if (vnLength > 0 && vnLength != 1)
{
    // Scale the normal vector by its length
    vn[0] /= vnLength;
    vn[1] /= vnLength;
    vn[2] /= vnLength;
}
```

This then leaves the finished normal contained within vn. The final part of the loop writes the normals to the appropriate positions in the normals array (positioned so that the normals correspond to the vertices that formed the triangle in the first place). When the loop completes, the entire normals array is populated and can be returned back to the calling procedure. These steps are shown in Listing 12–31.

Listing 12–31. Building and Returning the Normals Array in the GenerateIndexedTriangleNormals Function

```
// The normal for this triangle has been calculated.
// Write it to the normal array for all three vertices
Array.Copy(vn, 0, normals, indices[index] * 3, 3);
Array.Copy(vn, 0, normals, indices[index + 1] * 3, 3);
Array.Copy(vn, 0, normals, indices[index + 2] * 3, 3);
}

// Finished, return back the generated array
```

```
    return normals;
}
```

Try changing the code in the `Lighting` project's `CObjCube` and `CObjCylinder` classes so that they use this function instead of the current methods that are implemented. Note that values returned are exactly the same as those previously calculated specifically for the objects, except for those of the smooth cylinder. To create smooth vertex normals such as this, the code would need to be modified to look for vertices that share the same position and average their normals. Enhancing the function in this way is left as an exercise for you.

Using Normals with Scaled Objects

Here's a final note regarding vertex normals: they are affected by the `gl.Scale` function just as all other aspects of the rendered object are. This means that, as soon as a scale transformation is applied to an object, the normals will no longer be normalized, resulting in brighter or darker light reflection than may have been expected.

OpenGL provides a simple solution to this issue if it should cause any problems. One of the options that can be enabled switches on automatic normalization of all vertex normals. When a scale transformation is used, this normalization feature will ensure that all vertex normals are renormalized before they are used for light calculation.

To enable automatic normalization, call the `gl.Enable` function as shown in Listing 12–32. To disable it, call into OpenGL again using the `gl.Disable` function.

Listing 12–32. Enabling Automatic Normalization

```
// Switch on automatic normalization
gl.Enable(gl.GL_NORMALIZE)
```

Of course, there is a reason why we have discussed manually normalizing our vertex normals rather than just switching on this feature in the first place: OpenGL has to perform a number of additional steps to normalize a vertex normal, which increases the amount of processing required when rendering. If automatic normalization is not needed, switch it off to remove this processing overhead. Automatic normalization is unavoidable only when rendering objects with dynamic scaling, where a single, precalculated, normalized vector cannot be provided.

Mastering the 3D World

Moving out of the realm of flat 2D graphics and into the depths of 3D is undeniably a big step. All sorts of additional challenges appear both in terms of code complexity and graphical modeling. However, OpenGL provides a sound and flexible technology base to build on, and the rewards of 3D game programming can be great for players and developers alike.

Once you are happy and comfortable with the concepts and the code that we have discussed in this chapter, the next chapter will introduce you to a number of additional techniques that we can use in OpenGL to help bring our games to life.

■ ■ ■

CHAPTER 13

Further OpenGL Features and Techniques

In this chapter, you will extend your knowledge of OpenGL and take the features and capabilities of your code up to the next level. When you finish working through this chapter, you will be able to import 3D models from an external modeling application and use a number of additional OpenGL features to add life to your games.

Importing Geometry

In Chapter 12, we used two different methods for defining 3D objects in our OpenGL programs. The first required us to manually define a big array of vertex coordinates. This may be workable for simple objects such as cubes (though it is fairly tedious even for that!), but when we move on to more complex objects such as treasure chests or spaceships, it quickly becomes unrealistic. The second approach used mathematical formulas to create shapes for us (the cylinder from the Lighting example project). This is useful for regular geometric shapes, but once again is unlikely to be of value for real-world game objects.

The solution to this is to use a 3D modeling application. Modeling applications are third party software products that provide a rich (and often rather complex) user interface that is specifically designed to allow 3D models to be constructed.

In addition to creating the geometry itself, most modeling applications also allow textures to be mapped on to the objects that they build and will provide the resulting texture coordinates. They may also allow vertex normals to be calculated and stored as part of the object too.

All of this sounds wonderful, but unfortunately there is a bewildering array of formats into which 3D object definitions can be saved, and not all of them are easy to read.

The good news is that there is a modeling application available that is free to download, relatively easy to use, and (with a bit of creative tweaking) as able to save to a file format that we can easily read. The application is Google SketchUp.

Introducing SketchUp

SketchUp was originally created by a company called @Last Software, with the design goal of creating a 3D modeling application that was just as easy to use as a pen and paper. As such, its user interface was considerably easier to learn than that of many other applications.

Some years later, @Last Software enhanced SketchUp so that it was able to create 3D building models for Google Earth. Shortly after this, Google acquired the company and rebranded SketchUp as one of their own applications. You can visit www.sketchup.com to download a copy for yourself.

The new Google SketchUp is available in two different versions: SketchUp and SketchUp Pro. The basic SketchUp version is freely available and contains a huge amount of functionality. The Pro version adds even more features, including a larger range of 3D file formats.

Unfortunately, the free version doesn't export to a file format that we can easily use within our OpenGL applications. There is a clever workaround for this, however, which we will look at shortly.

Creating 3D Objects in SketchUp

Even the easiest of 3D modeling applications can be complex to use. The challenge of interactively describing a 3D world using the 2D input and output devices that we have available to use (the mouse, keyboard, and monitor) is always going to make this requirement difficult to fulfill.

Despite SketchUp's relative ease of use, there is still a lot to learn to become proficient in using it, and a full guide to how to use it is beyond the scope of this book. Don't let this discourage you though, because SketchUp also has an immense amount of help and guidance available online, including manuals, tutorials, walkthroughs, and video guides. All of these can be accessed from the links presented when SketchUp is first launched.

To work with imported geometry in this chapter, we will create a simple object in SketchUp that will be subsequently read into an example project by the game engine. The following paragraphs define how a very simple model of a house was created. They are not intended as a step-by-step guide to using SketchUp but merely provide information about the sequence of operations that could be used to create such a model.

When SketchUp is launched, it prompts you to select a Template. Select one of the two Simple Template options, and click "Start using SketchUp" to launch its main user interface. By default, SketchUp adds an image of a person to the empty scene to help put the scene's scale into perspective. The figure can be deleted to make way for our 3D object.

Our object can now be constructed in the empty scene. The first few steps toward this are shown in Figure 13–1. A rectangle is first drawn along the x/z plane to form the base of the house, as shown Figure 13–1(a). The rectangle is then extruded using the Push/Pull tool to form a box, as shown in Figure 13–1(b). The Line tool is then used to create a line across the centre of the top face of the box, as shown in Figure 13–1(c).

Once the top face has been divided in two, the line that was drawn can be moved around, and all of the faces connected to it will move accordingly. Moving the line directly upward, therefore, creates a satisfactory roof shape; see Figure 13–1(d). The basic geometry of the house is complete at this point.

Of course, we will almost certainly want to apply textures to our objects to complement the structure that we have created, and we will do just that now to make the house look more realistic. SketchUp has some simple but effective tools for adding textures to objects, and its online help will provide everything you need to know to get familiar with this tool.

In Figure 13–1(e), a texture has been applied to the front face of the house. Figure 13–1(f) shows the finished house object, with textures applied to all of the faces in the object.

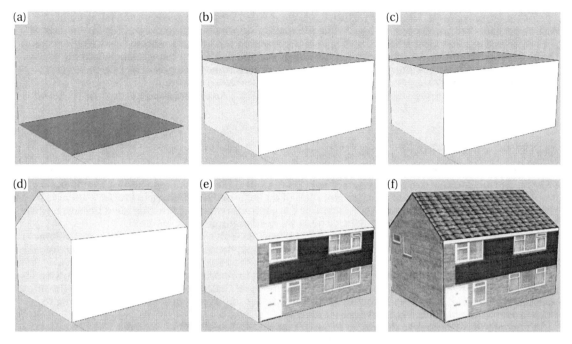

Figure 13–1. The steps required to build a simple 3D house object in Google SketchUp.

An important detail to remember when texturing objects is that we can only use a single texture image at a time when rendering. If we need to render an object using multiple textures, we must perform three individual renders, switching the active texture between each.

A much simpler approach is to place all of the graphics for your object into a single image, and apply subsections of the image to the model's faces rather than the entire image. This is the approach that has been taken with the house shown here: the front, sides, and roof are all contained within a single texture image, as shown in Figure 13–2.

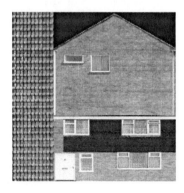

Figure 13–2. The texture graphic used for the 3D house object

As the graphic shows, the house texture has been divided into three sections: the left third of the texture contains the graphic for the roof, while the remaining area is split into a graphic for the side of the house and another for the front. Putting all of the required texture information into a single graphic file in this way simplifies both the design of the object and the rendering. Using a single graphic makes rendering more efficient, as the graphics hardware can process the whole object in a single step and doesn't need to move as many textures around inside the device's memory.

With the object completed, it can be saved to a SketchUp .skp file in case it needs to be retrieved later on.

Exporting 3D Geometry

Unfortunately, the free version of SketchUp has very limited options when it comes to exporting its objects. The two formats natively supported are Collada (.dae) files and Google Earth (.kmz) files.

Collada files are an XML-based representation of the exported file. SketchUp is able to include the texture coordinates in the file and also *triangulate* the geometry (making sure that all of the surfaces are broken down into triangles), which is exactly what we need to import.

Importing from Collada files would definitely be feasible with a little effort. However, we will not actually be importing these into the game engine in this book; there is a simpler alternative that we will look at in just a moment.

Google Earth files are not ideally suited for subsequent importing into our games. They are actually zip archives containing various files including the geometry in Collada format. Having to go to the effort of unzipping the content (either manually or in code) makes this a long-winded way of retrieving the Collada file that could have exported directly anyway.

So what will we do to save the model in a way that we can import it?

One of the many 3D model file formats that has become established over the years is the .obj format. This rather generic file extension was originally developed in the 1980s by Wavefront Technologies to store geometry for their Advanced Visualizer modeling and animation application. While the application may have faded into history, the file format is still useful to us.

The main reason it is useful is because it is extremely simple to decode. It contains simple lists of vertex positions, texture coordinates and vertex normals, followed by a list of triangle definitions that join everything together to make a 3D shape.

The problem with .obj files is that they are only supported as an export format in the Pro version of SketchUp. If you have purchased this full version, you will be able to use the built-in exporter, but anyone without it will be unable to save objects in this format.

Not wanting to leave developers on a budget out in the cold, enterprising programmers on the Internet have managed to persuade the free version of SketchUp to save its objects in .obj format too. SketchUp provides a programming interface, accessed using the Ruby programming language and able to query all the information about the object that is currently being worked on. A Ruby script has been created that takes advantage of this to create .obj files from the free version of SketchUp. You can visit http://www.idevgames.com/forum/showthread.php?t=13513 to download the script, or find it in the downloadable content for this chapter in the file ExportObj.rb.

To install the exporter into SketchUp, close the application, and copy ExportObj.rb into SketchUp's PlugIns directory (which can be found by default at C:\Program Files\Google\Google SketchUp 7\Plugins). Restart SketchUp, and two new menu items should appear under its PlugIns menu: ExportOBJ and ExportTexturedOBJ, as shown in Figure 13–3. These two plug-in options can be used to save the current object as an .obj file, excluding or including texture coordinates respectively.

Figure 13–3. The ExportOBJ and ExportTexturedOBJ Plugins inside SketchUp

When one of the plug-ins is selected from the menu, it will prompt you to save your model as an OBJ file.

■ **CAUTION** Don't forget to save your objects into SketchUp's native .skp file format too. An exported .obj file is ideal for loading into your game, but SketchUp itself won't be able to read data back from it.

Using the .0bj File Format

The content of an .obj file is very easy to read and process. Each line contains multiple data items separated by spaces. The first item on each line identifies the purpose of the remaining data on that line.

Vertex coordinates are specified with a first item containing the letter v (short for "vertex"). Following this are three floating point values, which are the x, y, and z coordinate for the vertex. Each vertex found within the file is implicitly given a numerical index, starting with 1. The first v element is, therefore, vertex 1; the second v element is vertex 2, and so on. Listing 13–1 shows a vertex definition.

Listing 13–1. A Line From an .obj file Containing a Vertex Definition

```
v 0.0 0.0 37.0
```

If a texture is included within the object export, its coordinates are stored with a first item containing the characters vt (vertex texture). These will be followed by two floating point numbers, representing the s and t coordinate within the texture. Just as with vertices, each texture coordinate is given an implicit numerical index starting from 1. Listing 13–2 shows a texture coordinate definition.

Listing 13–2. A Line from an .obj File Containing a Texture Coordinate

```
vt 0.25 0.5
```

If vertex normals are included within the export, these are specified with a first item containing vn (for vertex normal). This will be followed by the normal vector, as x, y, and z values. The normal is not guaranteed to be normalized, so may need to be normalized when the object file is being processed. Once again, normals are numbered starting from 1. An example vertex normal can be seen in Listing 13–3.

Listing 13–3. A Line from an .obj File Containing a Vertex Normals

```
vn 1.0 0.0 0.0
```

The final type of data that we are interested in is the triangles that form the object. These are stored on lines whose first element is f (face). Although the file specification does not require these to be triangles, the SketchUp exporter plug-in will always render each face as a triangle. The remaining values within the line will specify the indices of the three vertices, texture coordinates, and normals that form the triangle.

Each of these face elements will consist as a minimum of a vertex index. If texture coordinates and normals are present, these will follow each vertex index, separated by slashes. If any of these elements are missing or blank, the feature they represent (texture coordinate or vertex normal) is not supported by the current object definition. Note that the SketchUp exporter plug-in does not provide vertex normals.

An example triangular face definition (referencing vertices and texture coordinates but not vertex normals) is shown in Listing 13–4.

Listing 13–4. A Line from an .obj file Containing a Face Definitio.

```
f 1/1 2/2 3/3
```

Various other pieces of data may also be stored in .obj files, but we will be ignoring these in our .obj file import code.

■ **NOTE** The importer function that we will add to the game engine will be relatively basic. While it should cope quite satisfactorily for all .obj files created from the SketchUp plug-ins, other .obj files found on the Internet may contain information that it does not know how to process. If such objects are to be included within your game code, you will need to enhance the provided importer class to handle whatever extra features the file requires.

Listing 13–5 shows a complete extract from a simple .obj file. The data shown represents an untextured, unit-sized cube centered at point (0, 0, 0). Note that the definition first specifies the positions of each of the eight vertices required to form the cube, and then uses these to construct the 12 triangles that form the faces of the cube.

Listing 13–5. The .obj Definition for a Simple Cube

```
v 0.5 0.5 -0.5
v -0.5 -0.5 -0.5
v -0.5 0.5 -0.5
v 0.5 -0.5 -0.5
v 0.5 -0.5 0.5
v -0.5 0.5 0.5
v -0.5 -0.5 0.5
v 0.5 0.5 0.5
f 1 2 3
f 2 1 4
f 5 6 7
f 6 5 8
f 6 2 7
f 2 6 3
f 6 1 3
f 1 6 8
f 1 5 4
f 5 1 8
f 5 2 4
f 2 5 7
```

Note that the vertex indices specified by each face are all one-based, so the first vertex is specified as 1 rather than 0. Also notice that the vertices for each face are already specified in counterclockwise order, just as we need them to be for use in OpenGL.

Importing Geometry into the Game Engine

Now that we have our 3D model exported as an .obj file, it is time to look at the code that will read this into our game engine.

To perform the import of the data, we will create a new geometry loader class inside the game engine. This will be set up so that it can load geometry from a file, a stream (such as an embedded resource) or even from just a string containing the geometry data.

To make it easy to extend geometry support to other file formats (such as Collada .dae files), we will construct the import using an abstract base class called CGeomLoaderBase that provides certain core geometry functions and will then create a derived class specifically for loading .obj files. If in the future we want to add support for other files, we can once again derive from the base class without needing to repeat the tasks that it performs. Note that we will not be adding support for any other geometry file types in this book, however.

The base class provides three basic pieces of functionality: It declares float arrays that can be used to store the vertices, texture coordinates, and normals. It provides functions to simplify retrieving the geometry data from a file, stream, or string. And it provides functions for manipulating the geometry once it has been loaded.

Retrieving Geometry Data

The geometry base class assumes that the object data will ultimately be read from a string. Three functions are provided to allow the geometry data to be retrieved: LoadFromFile, LoadFromStream, and LoadFromString. Internally, the first two of these functions read the specified file or stream into a string and then pass control to LoadFromString. LoadFromString itself is an abstract function and must, therefore, be overridden in the derived class.

The code for these three functions is shown in Listing 13–6.

Listing 13–6. Preparing to Load Geometry Data from a File, Stream, or String

```
/// <summary>
/// Load geometry from a file
/// </summary>
public virtual void LoadFromFile(string filename)
{
    string content;

    // Load the file into a string
    using (StreamReader file = new StreamReader(filename))
    {
        content = file.ReadToEnd();
    }

    // Call LoadFromString to process the string
    LoadFromString(content);
}

/// <summary>
```

```
/// Load geometry from a stream
/// </summary>
public virtual void LoadFromStream(Stream stream)
{
    string content;
    byte[] contentBytes;

    // Create space to read the stream
    contentBytes = new byte[stream.Length];
    // Seek to the beginning of the stream
    stream.Seek(0, SeekOrigin.Begin);
    // Read the string into the byte array
    stream.Read(contentBytes, 0, (int)stream.Length);

    // Convert the byte array into text
    content = Encoding.ASCII.GetString(contentBytes, 0, contentBytes.Length);

    // Call LoadFromString to process the string
    LoadFromString(content);
}

/// <summary>
/// Load geometry from a string
/// </summary>
public abstract void LoadFromString(string content);
```

■ **NOTE** While it is the case that .obj files (and .dae files) are stored as strings, this is not necessarily true for other types of file. For example, the common .3ds file produced by Autodesk's 3ds Max application is a binary file that shouldn't be stored in a string variable. LoadFromFile and LoadFromStream are declared as virtual, so that these files can be handled by derived geometry loader classes. A derived class could modify these so that they loaded the file or stream data into a byte array and then process that instead of a string.

Once the object file has been loaded by a derived class, its details are stored in the _vertices, _texcoords and _normals arrays. These can then be read by external code through the corresponding properties or may be updated by the geometry manipulation functions described next. If no texture coordinate or normal data is available within the imported geometry, the arrays corresponding to these should be left with a null value so that this can be detected by the calling code.

We will look at how the geometry is actually read from .obj files in just a moment.

Manipulating Geometry Data

Once a 3D model has been loaded into the geometry class, there is a reasonable chance that the game will want to manipulate it in some way before it uses it for rendering. Two common tasks that may be required are the abilities to center the object so that its center point is at coordinate (0, 0, 0) and to scale the object.

The object can be centered by calling into the class's CenterObject function, which works by scanning all of the vertices to determine the minimum and maximum value along the x, y, and z axes. Once these values have been determined, the midpoint is identified by averaging the minimum and maximum values for each axis. This midpoint is then subtracted from the position of each vertex to center the object at the coordinate (0, 0, 0). The code for CenterObject is shown in Listing 13–7.

Listing 13–7. The CenterObject Function

```
/// <summary>
/// Adjust the vertex positions so that the object is centered around
/// the coordinate (0, 0, 0).
/// </summary>
public void CenterObject()
{
    // Make sure we have some vertices to work with
    if (_vertices == null || _vertices.Length == 0) return;

    float minx = float.MaxValue, miny = float.MaxValue, minz = float.MaxValue;
    float maxx = float.MinValue, maxy = float.MinValue, maxz = float.MinValue;
    float xcenter, ycenter, zcenter;

    // Loop through the vertices getting the minimum and maximum values
    // in each axis
    for (int i = 0; i < _vertices.Length; i += 3)
    {
        if (_vertices[i] < minx) minx = _vertices[i];
        if (_vertices[i] > maxx) maxx = _vertices[i];
        if (_vertices[i + 1] < miny) miny = _vertices[i + 1];
        if (_vertices[i + 1] > maxy) maxy = _vertices[i + 1];
        if (_vertices[i + 2] < minz) minz = _vertices[i + 2];
        if (_vertices[i + 2] > maxz) maxz = _vertices[i + 2];
    }

    // Now we know the box inside which the object resides,
    // subtract the object's current center point from each
    // vertex. This will put the center point at (0, 0, 0)
    xcenter = (minx + maxx) / 2;
    ycenter = (miny + maxy) / 2;
    zcenter = (minz + maxz) / 2;
    // Apply the offset to the vertex coordinates
    for (int i = 0; i < _vertices.Length; i += 3)
    {
        _vertices[i] -= xcenter;
        _vertices[i + 1] -= ycenter;
        _vertices[i + 2] -= zcenter;
    }
}
```

The object can be scaled by calling the ScaleObject function. If the object will always be rendered at the same size, scaling it at this stage is better than scaling it using the gl.Scale function so that we don't have to worry about the object normals being scaled.

Scaling is a simple task, which just requires the x, y, and z values for each vertex to be multiplied by the provided scale factors. Just as with gl.Scale, a scale factor of 1 will leave the size unchanged; 2 will double it; 0.5 will halve it, and so on. The ScaleObject code is shown in Listing 13–8.

Listing 13–8. The ScaleObject Function

```
/// <summary>
/// Scale the object by the specified amounts
/// </summary>
/// <param name="scalex">The amount by which to scale on the x axis</param>
/// <param name="scaley">The amount by which to scale on the y axis</param>
/// <param name="scalez">The amount by which to scale on the z axis</param>
public void ScaleObject(float scalex, float scaley, float scalez)
{
    // Loop through the vertices...
    for (int i = 0; i < _vertices.Length; i += 3)
    {
        // Scale each vertex
        _vertices[i] *= scalex;
        _vertices[i + 1] *= scaley;
        _vertices[i + 2] *= scalez;
    }
}
```

CenterObject and ScaleObject both manipulate the values within the _vertices array, so these must be called before the vertex array is retrieved from the object.

Reading Geometry Data from .obj Files

With the base class ready, we can now derive a class from it so that .obj files can be read. The class that is created for this is called CGeomLoaderObj.

We won't go into too much detail about how this works, as it is essentially just a series of string-manipulation and array-handling functions. The class overrides the LoadFromString function and loops through each line of text contained in the provided content string. The text before the first space on each line is identified, and for v, vt, and vn lines, the following values are added to private List objects named _objDefinedVertices, _objDefinedTexCoords, and _objDefinedNormals.

When the loop finds an f line, it uses the indices provided to look inside these three lists, reading out the vertex locations, texture coordinates, and normals that have been added to them. These are then used to construct the final lists of values that will be put into the arrays when the loading is finished. The values are accumulated in the private _outputVertices, _outputTexCoords, and _outputNormals variables.

Once the entire file is processed, the output lists are copied into the float arrays ready to be retrieved by the calling procedure.

All of the code required to read .obj files can be found within the game engine project included with this chapter's download.

Using the Geometry Loader Class

With our .obj loader class ready, retrieving the geometry for a 3D model is very easy. The constructor of the CHouseObj class in the ImportingGeometry project in the accompanying download contains all the code required to do this, as shown in Listing 13–9.

Listing 13–9. *Loading the House Model*

```
public CObjHouse(CGeometryGame gameEngine)
    : base(gameEngine)
{
    // Store a reference to the game engine as its derived type
    _myGameEngine = gameEngine;

    // Set the initial object state
    XAngle = 90;
    YAngle = 180;
    ZAngle = 0;

    // Load the object
    GameEngine.CGeomLoaderObj objLoader = new GameEngine.CGeomLoaderObj();
    Assembly asm = Assembly.GetExecutingAssembly();
    objLoader.LoadFromStream(asm.GetManifestResourceStream(
                                    "ImportingGeometry.Geometry.House.obj"));

    // Center the object
    objLoader.CenterObject();
    // Scale the object to 1.5% of its original size
    objLoader.ScaleObject(0.015f, 0.015f, 0.015f);

    // Read the object details
    _vertices = objLoader.Vertices;
    _texCoords = objLoader.TexCoords;
    _normals = objLoader.Normals;

    // Were normals provided by the object?
    if (_normals == null)
    {
        // No, so generate them ourselves
        _normals = GenerateTriangleNormals(_vertices);
    }

    // Have we loaded our house texture?
    if (!_myGameEngine.GameGraphics.ContainsKey("House"))
    {
        // No, so load it now
        Texture tex = Texture.LoadStream(asm.GetManifestResourceStream(
                                    "ImportingGeometry.Graphics.House.jpg"), false);
        _myGameEngine.GameGraphics.Add("House", tex);
    }
}
```

The class itself stores its vertices, texture coordinates and normals in class-level arrays. This allows these to be set just once when its object initializes without any need to repeat this work during each render.

To read the geometry, the code first instantiates a CGeomLoaderObj object and calls its LoadFromStream method, passing in the Stream for the House.obj embedded resource. This loads all of the data for the model into the geometry loader object.

As the house object is off-center and much too big for our rendering environment, the code next centers it and scales it down to 1.5 percent of its original size.

Next the object normals are checked. If none are available (which they won't be for `.obj` files created by the SketchUp plug-in), they are calculated automatically using the `GenerateTriangleNormals` function that we developed in the previous chapter.

Finally, the object checks to see whether the object texture has been loaded. If not, it too is loaded from the project's embedded resources.

Take a look at the example project to see this all in action. Of course, the object geometry that we have used is extremely simple, but there is nothing stopping you from creating any object that you like for your game using exactly the same code and techniques that we have used here.

Moving the Camera

As well as moving objects around a 3D scene, it can sometimes be useful to move the *camera* around the scene, changing the position from which the player looks into the 3D world. The camera is not actually an OpenGL concept as such but rather another transformation that can be applied before objects are rendered. In practical terms, however, we can treat it as if it were a physical part of the game world.

In some ways, having a camera may seem unnecessary. After all, there wouldn't seem to be any visual difference between moving the camera toward an object and moving the object toward the camera. As soon as we start to build up complex multiobject scenes with lights, however, it becomes much more convenient to be able to calculate the object and light positions without having to worry about moving them all to simulate camera movement.

Let's look at the way in which the position of the camera can be changed in OpenGL.

Positioning the Camera

To move the camera, we need to figure out exactly how to set the transformation matrix required for the required camera position. Fortunately, the `glu` library takes care of this for us and provides a very useful function, `glu.LookAt`. This sets the model view matrix such that the objects subsequently rendered will be positioned as if the camera had moved to the requested location.

The `glu.LookAt` function requires three pieces of information to be provided:

- The current location of the camera as a coordinate in the 3D world (the *eye position*)

- A coordinate at which the camera is looking (the *center position*)

- A vector that tells OpenGL which way is up (the *up vector*)

The first two of these are fairly easy to understand. The eye position is the location within the world where the camera will actually be located. The scene will be rendered looking from this location. The center position defines the direction in which the camera is facing. The specified position will appear directly in the center of the rendered scene.

The up vector requires a little more explanation. In simple terms, it tells OpenGL which way is up relative to the camera position. In most cases you can provide a vector that simply points along the positive y axis: (0, 1, 0). The up vector does not need to be perpendicular to the camera's direction of view.

There are two situations where a different value for the up vector may need to be used. The first is if we want to be able to *roll* the camera. Rolling the camera rotates it around its z axis so that its own view of which way is up deviates from the world's view of up (rolling the camera by 180 degrees would result in everything appearing upside down). Figure 13–4 shows two views of the house object we imported earlier. The first shows the camera with an up vector of (0, 1, 0), the second with a modified up vector of (0.5, 1, 0).

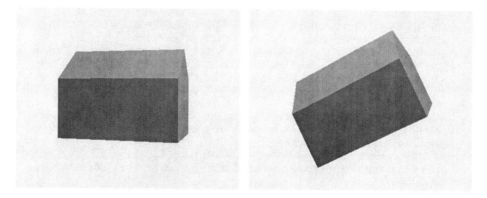

Figure 13–4. *Two views of a house, the first with an up vector pointing straight up and the second with an up vector of (0.5, 1, 0)*

Rolling the camera may not be useful in all games, but for some it is extremely handy. Any game that simulates the movement of an aircraft or spaceship, for example, will probably want to use it to allow the craft to bank to the sides as it flies.

The second situation where a different up vector is required is when the camera is looking directly along the y axis. If the camera were looking directly upward, we would be telling it that *forward* and *up* were both in exactly the same direction. This can't possibly be true, and so OpenGL's transformation matrix results in nothing displaying at all.

In all other cases, OpenGL is very tolerant of the values provided for the up vector and will cope fine with unnormalized vectors and vectors that are not perpendicular to the camera viewing angle.

Listing 13–10 shows a simple call to glu.LookAt that sets the camera so that it is located at position (0, 5, 5), is focused on position (0, 0, 0), and has an up vector of (0, 1, 0).

Listing 13–10. *Positioning the Camera*

```
glu.LookAt(0, 5, 5,     // eye position
           0, 0, 0,     // center position
           0, 1, 0);    // up vector
```

Adding Camera Objects to the Game Engine

When we decide to take control of the camera in one of our games, it is highly likely that we are going to want to move the camera. A moving camera will need to define all of the properties that we need to pass into the glu.LookAt function, be repositioned each time the game engine is updated, and be able to interpolate between positions so that it fits in with our timing model.

These features are all the standard features of our game objects, so it makes sense to allow the camera to be implemented as a game object too.

The camera is slightly special, however, as we must ensure that it is always processed before any objects are rendered. The camera is responsible for ensuring that various properties of the scene are initialized before any objects are rendered so that those scene properties apply to all objects that are rendered, rather than just those that are rendered after the light is processed. To ensure that this processing happens first, we add support for camera objects directly into the game engine.

First of all, we add a new base class called CGameObjectOpenGLCameraBase. This class derives from CGameObjectOpenGLBase, so it already has properties available for storing and updating its position. We can extend this class so that the same functionality is offered for the camera's center position (XCenter, YCenter, and ZCenter properties) and up vector (XUp, YUp, and ZUp properties). The UpdatePreviousPositions function is overridden to ensure that the previous values for each of these properties is updated, and functions for GetDisplayXCenter, GetDisplayXUp, and so forth are added so that the actual render values can be retrieved based on an interpolation factor.

All of this is exactly the same standard functionality that we have used for positions, angles, and scale factors already in our object base classes.

Now that the game engine is able to identify a camera object (an object derived from this camera base class) we can add a little extra code that ensures the camera is processed before any other objects. Inside the CGameEngineOpenGLBase class, the Advance function is modified so that it looks to see if a camera object is present. If the camera is not already the first object in the list, but a camera does exist in the list, the camera is moved so that it becomes the very first object. The code for the modified Advance function is shown in Listing 13–11.

Listing 13–11. The Advance Function with Camera Checking

```
/// <summary>
/// Advance the simulation by one frame
/// </summary>
public override void Advance()
{
    CGameObjectOpenGLCameraBase camera;

    // If the game form doesn't have focus, sleep for a moment and return without any
    // further processing
    if (!GameForm.Focused)
    {
        System.Threading.Thread.Sleep(100);
        return;
    }

    // Is the first object in the game objects list a camera?
    if (!(GameObjects[0] is CGameObjectOpenGLCameraBase))
    {
        // If we have a camera object, move it to the head of the object list.
        // This will ensure that the camera moves before any objects are rendered.
        camera = FindCameraObject();
        // Did we find a camera?
        if (camera != null)
        {
            // Remove the camera from the object list...
            GameObjects.Remove(camera);
            // ...and re-add it at the beginning of the list
            GameObjects.Insert(0, camera);
        }
    }

    // Call base.Advance. This will update all of the objects within our game.
    base.Advance();
```

```
        // Swap the buffers so that our updated frame is displayed
        egl.SwapBuffers(_eglDisplay, _eglSurface);
}
```

The FindCameraObject referred to in Advance is a simple loop that identifies the first GameObjects item that is derived from CGameObjectOpenGLCameraBase, and it can is shown in Listing 13–12.

Listing 13–12. Finding a Camera Object Within the GameObjects List

```
/// <summary>
/// Find a camera object (if there is one) within the GameObjects list.
/// </summary>
/// <returns>Returns the first camera object identified, or null if
/// no cameras are present within the list.</returns>
public CGameObjectOpenGLCameraBase FindCameraObject()
{
    foreach (CGameObjectBase obj in GameObjects)
    {
        if (obj is CGameObjectOpenGLCameraBase)
        {
            return (CGameObjectOpenGLCameraBase)obj;
        }
    }

    // No camera was found
    return null;
}
```

The final enhancement to the CGameEngineOpenGL class is the addition of a function called LoadCameraMatrix. This will be used in our derived object classes to reset their transformation matrix, in exactly the same way as they previously used gl.LoadIdentity. In fact, if no camera object is present, LoadCameraMatrix simply calls gl.LoadIdentity.

Assuming a camera object is found (once again using the FindCameraObject function), its display information is retrieved and passed into glu.LookAt to set the position of the camera. The LoadCameraMatrix code is shown in Listing 13–13.

Listing 13–13. Loading the Transformation Matrix for the Camera

```
/// Resets the projection matrix based upon the position of the
/// camera object within the object list. If no camera is present,
/// loads the identity matrix instead.
/// </summary>
/// <param name="interpFactor">The current render interpolation factor</param>
public void LoadCameraMatrix(float interpFactor)
{
    float eyex, eyey, eyez;
    float centerx, centery, centerz;
    float upx, upy, upz;
    CGameObjectOpenGLCameraBase camera;

    // Load the identity matrix.
    gl.LoadIdentity();
```

```
            // See if we have a camera object
            camera = FindCameraObject();
            if (camera != null)
            {
                // Get the camera's eye position
                eyex = camera.GetDisplayXPos(interpFactor);
                eyey = camera.GetDisplayYPos(interpFactor);
                eyez = camera.GetDisplayZPos(interpFactor);
                // Get the camera's center position
                centerx = camera.GetDisplayXCenter(interpFactor);
                centery = camera.GetDisplayYCenter(interpFactor);
                centerz = camera.GetDisplayZCenter(interpFactor);
                // Get the camera's up vector
                upx = camera.GetDisplayXUp(interpFactor);
                upy = camera.GetDisplayYUp(interpFactor);
                upz = camera.GetDisplayZUp(interpFactor);
                // Set the camera location
                glu.LookAt(eyex, eyey, eyez, centerx, centery, centerz, upx, upy, upz);
            }
        }
```

With all of these changes put into place within the game engine, we can now implement a camera in our game. To do so, we define a game object in exactly the same way as normal but derive it from the CGameObjectOpenGLCameraBase class. The complete implementation of a simple camera class is shown in Listing 13–14.

Listing 13–14. The Code for a Simple Camera Class

```
class CObjCamera : GameEngine.CGameObjectOpenGLCameraBase
{
    // Our reference to the game engine.
    private CCameraGame _myGameEngine;

    /// <summary>
    /// Constructor. Require an instance of our own game class as a parameter.
    /// </summary>
    public CObjCamera(CCameraGame gameEngine)
        : base(gameEngine)
    {
        // Store a reference to the game engine as its derived type
        _myGameEngine = gameEngine;

        // Set the initial camera position
        Update();
    }

    public override void Update()
    {
        base.Update();

        // Use the x and z angle to rotate around the y axis
        XAngle += 1.5f;
        ZAngle += 1.5f;
        XPos = (float)Math.Cos(XAngle / 360 * glu.PI * 2) * 5;
```

```
        ZPos = (float)Math.Sin(ZAngle / 360 * glu.PI * 2) * 5;
    }
}
```

This example camera class rotates its viewpoint around the y axis by using some simple trigonometry calculations to set the camera position. The center position remains unchanged at its default location of (0, 0, 0), and the up vector also remains at its default of (0, 1, 0).

One final modification is required for our camera to become effective. Each of the noncamera game objects needs to observe the camera position when it renders. So far, all of our objects have called gl.LoadIdentity prior to applying their transformations and rendering, but if we do that now, we will overwrite our camera transformation with the identity matrix, erasing its position.

In place of calling gl.LoadIdentity, each object's Render method should, therefore, call into the game engine function LoadCameraMatrix that we created back in Listing 13–13. This will perform the equivalent function to loading the identity matrix but ensure that the camera position is observed.

The modified Render function for an object is shown in Listing 13–15. The highlighted code shows the call to LoadCameraMatrix instead of loading the identity matrix.

Listing 13–15. Rendering an Object and Observing the Camera Position

```
/// <summary>
/// Render the object
/// </summary>
public override void Render(Graphics gfx, float interpFactor)
{
    base.Render(gfx, interpFactor);

    // Enable hidden surface removal
    gl.Enable(gl.GL_CULL_FACE);

    // Set the camera position
    _myGameEngine.LoadCameraMatrix(interpFactor);

    // Translate the object
    gl.Translatef(GetDisplayXPos(interpFactor),
                    GetDisplayYPos(interpFactor), GetDisplayZPos(interpFactor));

    // Rotate the object
    gl.Rotatef(GetDisplayXAngle(interpFactor), 1, 0, 0);
    gl.Rotatef(GetDisplayYAngle(interpFactor), 0, 1, 0);
    gl.Rotatef(GetDisplayZAngle(interpFactor), 0, 0, 1);

    // Render the object
    RenderTriangles(_vertices, null, _texCoords, _normals);
}
```

The camera can be seen in motion in the CameraControl example project in this chapter's accompanying download. The houses that are displayed within the animation are completely stationary, while the camera moves around them. Any transformations that are applied to the houses will be performed entirely independently of the camera; they continue to observe their own local coordinate system and are not affected by the camera position at all.

Lights, Camera, Action!

When we introduce moving cameras into a scene that also uses lighting, we encounter a problem: the lights move around the scene along with the camera. This is very unlikely to be the desired behavior. While it may be useful in some circumstances (for example, the light may represent a light source attached to the camera itself), the more likely requirement will be that the lights stay still while the camera moves independently.

The lights move because they have been set in the world space relative to the identity matrix. When the camera position is set into the transformation matrix, we are only simulating the movement of a camera and in actual fact are moving the objects within world space instead. Moving the camera forward by 10 units actually has the effect of transforming the objects towards the viewpoint by –10 units. As the lights are not being transformed as well, they remain stationary rather than being transformed alongside the objects that they are lighting.

Fortunately, this problem is easy to overcome. In fact, light positions are included as part of the transformation matrix. When we set the position of a light to be (0, 0, 2) in Listing 12-22 in the previous chapter, this was only set at this position in the world space because we had loaded the identity matrix prior to calling into the InitLight function.

The transformation matrix applies to lights as well as rendered objects, so we can get the lights to remain in position relative to the rest of the game objects by resetting their position each time the camera is moved. This results in the camera's transformation matrix affecting the position of the lights in exactly the same way as it affects the rendered objects. The effect of this is that the lights appear to be static within the game world, allowing the camera to move independently.

In the previous section, we modified the game engine so that camera objects are always processed before any other object in the GameObjects list. As a result, we can take advantage of its Render method (which is called before any other objects are rendered and currently does nothing at all) to update the positions of the lights, taking the camera position into account. Listing 13–16 shows the Render function in the CameraControl example project's CObjCamera class. The camera matrix is loaded just as it is when rendering objects (instead of loading the identity matrix), and the InitLight function is called to update the light positions.

Listing 13–16. Updating the Light Positions in the Camera Class's Render Function.

```
public override void Render(Graphics gfx, float interpFactor)
{
    base.Render(gfx, interpFactor);

    // Set the camera position
    _myGameEngine.LoadCameraMatrix(interpFactor);
    // Set the light positions
    _myGameEngine.InitLight(true);
}
```

InitLight itself has been slightly modified to reduce the amount of work required if we are just updating the light position. A Boolean parameter is passed in, indicating that the entire light configuration should be set (if the value false is passed) or that only the light positions should be updated (if true is passed). This prevents the function from repeatedly passing unchanged light and material data to OpenGL. The modified InitLight procedure is shown in Listing 13–17.

Listing 13–17. Initializing the Game Lights, Optionally Updating Just Their Position.

```
/// <summary>
/// Enable and configure the lighting to use within the OpenGL scene
/// </summary>
```

```
/// <param name="positionOnly">If true, only the light positions will be set</param>
internal void InitLight(bool positionOnly)
{
    if (positionOnly == false)
    {
        // Enable lighting
        gl.Enable(gl.GL_LIGHTING);

        // Set the ambient light color to dark gray
        SetAmbientLight(new float[] { 0.1f, 0.1f, 0.1f, 1 });

        // Set the material color
        SetMaterialParameter(gl.GL_FRONT_AND_BACK,gl.GL_AMBIENT,new float[] {1,1,1,1});
        SetMaterialParameter(gl.GL_FRONT_AND_BACK,gl.GL_DIFFUSE,new float[] {1,1,1,1});

        // Configure light 0.
        SetLightParameter(gl.GL_LIGHT0,gl.GL_DIFFUSE,new float[] {0.8f,0.8f,0.8f,1});
        gl.Enable(gl.GL_LIGHT0);
    }

    // Set the light positions
    SetLightParameter(gl.GL_LIGHT0, gl.GL_POSITION, new float[] { 2, 2, 2, 1 });
}
```

Try commenting out the rendering function in the example project's CObjCamera class and running the project. The house objects look as if they themselves are moving rather than the camera, as the way in which they reflect light changes as the camera moves around. Now, uncomment the code so that the light positions are updated once again. Observe that when the scene animates, the lighting on the houses is static, and the appearance is now one of camera movement rather than object movement.

Optimizing the Camera Calculation

The camera movement mechanism we have described so far requires each individual object to recalculate the camera position using the glu.LookAt function. As we are moving the camera just once per frame, this amounts to a potentially large number of repeated calculations. Once we have determined the camera transform for the first object, all the subsequent objects are performing identical repeat calculations over and over again.

We can eliminate this unnecessary processing by caching the camera transformation matrix after it has been calculated for the first time each frame. The transformation matrix is a 4 × 4–element array of float values, so we can read this each time a new camera position is calculated, store it in an array inside the camera, and restore it for all of the other calls to LoadCameraMatrix until the camera moves again.

The cache array is declared as a private 2D array inside CGameObjectOpenGLCameraBase with an accessor property with internal scope named CachedCameraMatrix. To ensure that this cache is cleared at the beginning of each frame, the class's Render method is overridden and used to set the cache array to null, as shown in Listing 13–18.

Listing 13–18. Clearing the Camera Matrix Cache At the Beginning of Each Frame

```
public override void Render(System.Drawing.Graphics gfx, float interpFactor)
{
    base.Render(gfx, interpFactor);
```

```
            // Clear the cached camera transformation matrix
            _cachedCameraMatrix = null;
    }
```

Next, the CGameEngineOpenGLBase.LoadCameraMatrix function is modified to support the use of this matrix cache. After determining that a camera is present, the code looks to see whether the cache array is available. If not (its value is null), the light position is calculated as before, and the camera transformation set using glu.LookAt. However, after setting the matrix, the code reads it back from OpenGL using a call to a new function named GetModelviewMatrix (which we'll add to the game engine class in a moment) and stores it into the camera object.

Alternatively, if the code finds that the cache array was available, it bypasses all of this code (skipping the near to perform both the camera interpolation calculations and the glu.LookAt calculations) and simply loads the cached matrix back into OpenGL using a call to another new function named SetModelviewMatrix (which we'll also add in a moment). The modified function code is shown in Listing 13–19.

Listing 13–19. Setting and Retrieving the Camera Transformation Matrix from the Cache

```
/// <summary>
/// Resets the projection matrix based upon the position of the
/// camera object within the object list. If no camera is present,
/// loads the identity matrix instead.
/// </summary>
/// <param name="interpFactor">The current render interpolation factor</param>
unsafe public void LoadCameraMatrix(float interpFactor)
{
    float eyex, eyey, eyez;
    float centerx, centery, centerz;
    float upx, upy, upz;
    CGameObjectOpenGLCameraBase camera;

    // Load the identity matrix.
    gl.LoadIdentity();

    // See if we have a camera object
    camera = FindCameraObject();
    if (camera != null)
    {
        // Do we already have a cached camera matrix?
        if (camera.CachedCameraMatrix == null)
        {
            // No, so calculate the camera position.
            // Get the camera's eye position
            eyex = camera.GetDisplayXPos(interpFactor);
            eyey = camera.GetDisplayYPos(interpFactor);
            eyez = camera.GetDisplayZPos(interpFactor);
            // Get the camera's center position
            centerx = camera.GetDisplayXCenter(interpFactor);
            centery = camera.GetDisplayYCenter(interpFactor);
            centerz = camera.GetDisplayZCenter(interpFactor);
            // Get the camera's up vector
            upx = camera.GetDisplayXUp(interpFactor);
            upy = camera.GetDisplayYUp(interpFactor);
```

```
            upz = camera.GetDisplayZUp(interpFactor);

            // Calculate the transformation matrix for the camera
            glu.LookAt(eyex, eyey, eyez, centerx, centery, centerz, upx, upy, upz);

            // Now we will store the calculated matrix into the camera object.
            camera.CachedCameraMatrix = GetModelviewMatrix();
        }
        else
        {
            // The camera has not moved since its matrix was last calculated
            // so we can simply restore the cached matrix.
            SetModelviewMatrix(camera.CachedCameraMatrix);
        }
    }
}
```

The current model-view matrix is retrieved from OpenGL into an array by calling the gl.Get function. It is set back into OpenGL using the gl.LoadMatrixf function. The GetModelviewMatrix and SetModelviewMatrix functions wrap around these to simplify their use, and are shown in Listing 13–20.

Listing 13–20. Getting and setting OpenGL's Model-View Matrix

```
/// <summary>
/// Retrieve the current modelview matrix as a 4x4 array of floats
/// </summary>
/// <returns></returns>
unsafe public float[,] GetModelviewMatrix()
{
    float[,] ret = new float[4, 4];

    // Fix a pointer to the array
    fixed (float* matrixPointer = &ret[0,0])
    {
        // Retrieve the model view matrix into the array
        gl.GetFloatv(gl.GL_MODELVIEW_MATRIX, matrixPointer);
    }

    return ret;
}

/// <summary>
/// Set the current modelview matrix from a 4x4 array of floats
/// </summary>
/// <param name="matrix"></param>
unsafe public void SetModelviewMatrix(float[,] matrix)
{
    // Fix a pointer to the array
    fixed (float* matrixPointer = &matrix[0, 0])
    {
        // Load the array data into OpenGL's modelview matrix
        gl.LoadMatrixf(matrixPointer);
    }
}
```

While this has no immediate visible effect on the simulation, the number of unnecessary repeat calculations is substantially reduced. The reduction becomes more significant as more game objects are added, which will lead to a small performance gain in complex scenes.

Cameras and the Projection Matrix

Keep in mind that, as we have already discussed, the model transformation matrix—not the projection matrix—is being updated when the camera moves around. There are two things to bear in mind as a result of this.

The first is that any transformations that are made to the projection matrix will still be effective when the camera moves and will always be relative to the camera position. For example, the code present in the `CGameEngineOpenGLBase.InitGLViewport` function transforms the projection matrix using a call to `gl.Translate` so that the objects move forward relative to the projection (which gives the appearance of having moved the camera backward). This transformation will still be present when the camera is moved and will apply relative to the generated camera position.

Second, don't forget the near and far clip planes that have been defined for the viewing frustum. If you move the camera far enough away from an object that it falls behind the far clip plane, it will disappear.

Rendering Fog

A useful facility provided by OpenGL is the ability to add fog to a rendered scene. This provides a simple simulation of real-world fog, making objects that are further away from the camera gradually fade away until they are no longer visible.

Figure 13–5 shows some examples of a scene rendered in OpenGL using fog. The image in the left has fog disabled, while the remaining two images show increasing levels of fog. The distant buildings in the image on the right have completely vanished into the background.

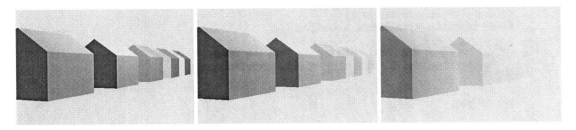

Figure 13–5. A scene rendered with increasing levels of fog

Fog can be useful for providing a sense of closeness and claustrophobia to a game, as it stops the player from being able to see into the distance. It is also useful as a way of masking objects that are being clipped by the far clipping plane. Instead of having a hard barrier beyond which objects become invisible, fog can be applied to the rear of the viewing frustum so that objects fade away smoothly instead.

OpenGL implements fog using a simple but effective trick. As it calculates the color for each vertex being rendered, it determines how far away the vertex is from the viewpoint. As the vertex becomes more distant and is therefore affected to a greater degree by the fog, OpenGL gradually fades the vertex color towards the defined fog color. If the object is sufficiently distant, its vertex colors will be fully set to the defined fog color causing the object to fade completely away into the background.

Adding Fog Support to the Game Engine

Fog is very easy to use, requiring just a small number of parameters to be set. Just as with lighting and materials however, one of the fog parameters (the fog color) requires an array to be passed and therefore relies on unsafe code.

To simplify passing the array and allow fog to be more easily used in VB.NET, we will once again wrap the fog parameter calls inside simple functions within CGameEngineOpenGLBase. The SetFogParameter function requires three versions, all of which accept the fog parameter name, followed by either an int, a float or a float array. The SetFogParameter functions are shown in Listing 13–21.

Listing 13–21. The Implementations of the SetForParameter Function

```
/// <summary>
/// Set a fog parameter to the provided value
/// </summary>
public void SetFogParameter(uint parameter, float value)
{
    gl.Fogf(parameter, value);
}

/// <summary>
/// Set a fog parameter to the provided value
/// </summary>
public void SetFogParameter(uint parameter, int value)
{
    gl.Fogx(parameter, value);
}

/// <summary>
/// Set a fog parameter to the provided value array
/// </summary>
unsafe public void SetFogParameter(uint parameter, float[] value)
{
    fixed (float* valuePointer = &value[0])
    {
        gl.Fogfv(parameter, valuePointer);
    }
}
```

Using Fog

Actually using the fog feature requires just a few lines of code. The first thing that we need to do is enable fog and tell OpenGL the fog's color, which is the color that OpenGL will fade the vertex colors toward as the objects get further from the camera. Generally, fog looks best when this color is set to be the same color as the environment's background color.

Next, we need to tell OpenGL which fog algorithm to use. Three algorithms are available: GL_EXP, GL_EXP2, and GL_LINEAR. The first two of these, the exponential fog algorithms, apply fog to all objects within the scene. The fog is given a density, which controls how quickly the fog takes effect as objects move into the distance. A density value of 0 disables fog completely, whereas higher values make the fog appear thicker and thicker. A density value of 5 produces fog that is virtually impenetrable. GL_EXP and GL_EXP2 are very similar in function, the difference being that GL_EXP2 causes the objects to fade away more rapidly as they move away from the viewpoint.

The remaining linear algorithm calculates fog slightly differently. Instead of a density, values are provided for the near and far elements of the fog distance calculation. Vertices that are closer to the viewpoint than the specified near value will be unaffected by fog; vertices that are further away from the viewpoint than the specified far value will be entirely obscured by fog. This allows for much finer control over the positioning of fog within the scene.

Exactly which of the algorithms is best will depend on how they appear within your rendered scene. Try each of them with various parameter values until you find a combination that works well.

The code required to implement exponential fog is shown in Listing 13–22.

Listing 13–22. Switching On and Configuring Exponential Fog

```
private void InitFog()
{
    // Enable fog
    gl.Enable(gl.GL_FOG);

    // Set the fog color. We'll set this to match our background color.
    SetFogParameter(gl.GL_FOG_COLOR, ColorToFloat4(BackgroundColor));

    // Use exponential fog
    SetFogParameter(gl.GL_FOG_MODE, gl.GL_EXP);
    SetFogParameter(gl.GL_FOG_DENSITY, 0.25f);
}
```

The code required for linear fog is shown in Listing 13–23.

Listing 13–23. Switching On and Configuring Linear Fog

```
private void InitFog()
{
    // Enable fog
    gl.Enable(gl.GL_FOG);

    // Set the fog color. We'll set this to match our background color.
    SetFogParameter(gl.GL_FOG_COLOR, ColorToFloat4(BackgroundColor));

    // Use linear fog
    SetFogParameter(gl.GL_FOG_MODE, gl.GL_LINEAR);
    SetFogParameter(gl.GL_FOG_START, 2.0f);
    SetFogParameter(gl.GL_FOG_END, 4.0f);
}
```

■ **CAUTION** The values for the GL_FOG_START, GL_FOG_END, and GL_FOG_DENSITY parameters must all be provided as float values. It is very easy to inadvertently pass int values instead, but these are not what OpenGL is expecting and will not produce the expected results.

An example of fog in action can be seen in the Fog example project. Try experimenting with different fog parameters in the CFogGame.InitFog function to see the effects that they have on the generated scene.

Working with Billboards

Billboards are simple quadrilaterals rendered in the game world such that they face directly toward the camera. They have a number of potential uses, including rendering lens flares around bright points of light, basic trees using a 2D image that always appears face-on to the camera, and particles systems (multiple small polygons that together make up a part of a scene, such as sparks from a fire or points of light from an exploding firework).

In this section, we will examine how billboards work and how they can be added to your games.

Rendering Billboards

All we need to do to render a simple billboard is rotate its quadrilateral so that it faces directly toward the camera. For many types of rendered object, this will give the appearance of depth even though the object is actually completely flat.

For example, imagine that you wish to render an untextured and unlit spherical object in your game. Such a sphere looks exactly the same from all angles, so if we can simply render a flat drawing of a sphere and keep it angled directly toward the camera, it will be indistinguishable from an actual sphere.

Billboard quadrilaterals are very useful for particle systems. If we wish to render fireworks, we need to ensure that all of the points of light that are rendered are actually visible. If we do not use billboarding, the quadrilaterals that make up the firework could be drawn edge-on to the camera, causing them to become virtually invisible.

Quadrilaterals rendered as billboards are still placed within the 3D scene, however. They will still retain their position within the game world, observe the perspective transformation, and be affected by the z buffer just as any normal quadrilateral would.

Figure 13–6 demonstrates the way in which quadrilaterals are oriented in order for them to appear as billboards. The arrows show the direction in which they are facing. You will notice that all of the arrows are aligned directly along the camera's z axis. As the camera moves, the quadrilaterals rotate so that they are always facing it.

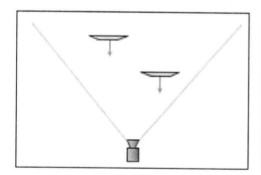
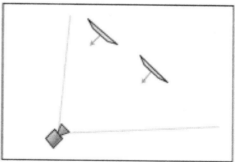

Figure 13–6. A scene viewed from above with billboard quadrilaterals rotated toward two different camera locations

Getting quadrilaterals to rotate in this way is actually fairly straightforward, but it requires us to do something that we have not done before—manually manipulate the transformation matrix.

Every time we perform a transformation on the object's position—be it a translation, rotation, or scaling operation—OpenGL fulfils the request by manipulating the model-view matrix. This is a 4×4 array of values. We have already interacted directly with this matrix back in the camera movement section, where we retrieved the matrix from OpenGL and set the matrix back to restore the camera position. An example matrix is shown in Figure 13–7.

$$
\begin{bmatrix}
0,0 & 1,0 & 2,0 & 3,0 \\
0,1 & 1,1 & 2,1 & 3,1 \\
0,2 & 1,2 & 2,2 & 3,2 \\
0,3 & 1,3 & 2,3 & 3,3
\end{bmatrix}
$$

Figure 13–7. The 4×4 array of values that form the transformation matrix

The transformation matrix actually stores the object's position in cells (3, 0) through (3, 2), shown in dark grey in Figure 13–7. The rotation and scaling of the object are stored in the grid of cells between (0, 0) and (2, 2), shown in light grey in Figure 13–7. If we can modify the matrix so that the values in the rotation and scaling part are reset to the identity matrix, the quadrilateral will realign itself to the camera's z axis.

Figure 13–8 shows a matrix that has been modified in this way. The rotation and scaling cells have been set to the identity matrix (all 0 except for the diagonal which is set to 1), while the rest of the matrix is left alone.

$$
\begin{bmatrix}
1 & 0 & 0 & x \\
0 & 1 & 0 & y \\
0 & 0 & 1 & z \\
a & b & c & d
\end{bmatrix}
$$

Figure 13–8. The modified transformation matrix with the rotation and scaling elements set to the identity

matrix

If we load this modified matrix back into OpenGL's transformation matrix, the quadrilaterals will be aligned in the way that we want.

There is one other consideration that we might want to take into account with our billboards. While aligning the quadrilateral toward the camera works well for some types of billboard, it doesn't work quite so well for others, for example, with trees.

Trees are complicated to render using 3D geometry, and in many cases, it is more efficient to simply render a 2D image of a tree displayed on a billboard. The problem with the billboard mechanism that we have described is that it rotates the object toward the camera on all of its axes. This means that if the camera moves into the air, the tree will appear to lean backward. If the camera moves lower toward the ground, the tree will appear to lean forward.

Figure 13–9 shows two side-on views of a scene with tree billboards behaving in this way. As the camera moves up and down, the tree rotates to keep facing it. This is not something that trees normally do!

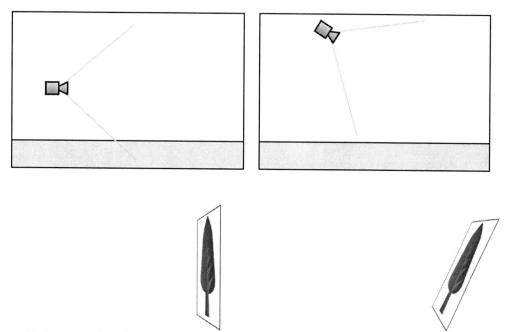

Figure 13–9. *Tree billboards rotating incorrectly to stay facing the camera.*

We can stop the billboard from doing this by leaving part of the matrix unchanged. The first three values in the second column, cells (1, 0) through to (1, 2) in Figure 13–7, control the quadrilateral's up vector. By leaving these alone, we can continue to ensure that the shape rotates toward the camera's x and z positions, but ignores its y position. Trees will then remain upright regardless of the height of the camera.

■ **NOTE** This simple implementation of trees will begin to fail if the camera reaches a height whereby it can look down on the trees from above. If a camera looks directly down at such a tree, it will see it as just a line, as that is all that the tree really is. The closer the camera gets to looking vertically, the more distorted the tree will become. As long as the camera remains at a reasonable height relative to the tree, however, the illusion should be sustained.

Adding Billboard Support to the Game Engine

Very little code is required to implement billboarding into the game engine. We already have the GetModelviewMatrix and SetModelviewMatrix functions that we created for camera movement, so these can retrieve the matrix for us to modify and pass it back to OpenGL once the modification is complete.

To simplify the manipulation of the matrix, we add a new function called RotateMatrixToCamera into CGameEngineOpenGLBase. Two overloads of this are provided: the first takes no parameters and rotates the matrix on all of its axes, while the second takes a bool parameter named keepUpVector, which will leave the matrix up vector intact for scenarios such as rendering trees.

The two overloads of RotateMatrixToCamera are shown in Listing 13–24.

Listing 13–24. The RotateMatrixToCamera Function

```
/// <summary>
/// Rotate the current modelview matrix so that it is facing towards
/// the camera.
/// </summary>
public void RotateMatrixToCamera()
{
    RotateMatrixToCamera(false);
}
/// <summary>
/// Rotate the current modelview matrix so that it is facing towards
/// the camera.
/// </summary>
/// <param name="keepUpVector">If true, the object's Up vector will be left
/// unchanged</param>
public void RotateMatrixToCamera(bool keepUpVector)
{
    // Retrieve the current modelview matrix
    float[,] matrix = GetModelviewMatrix();

    // Reset the first 3x3 elements to the identity matrix
    for (int i = 0; i < 3; i++)
    {
        for (int j = 0; j < 3; j++)
        {
            // Are we skipping the up vector (the values where i == 1)
            if (keepUpVector == false || i != 1)
            {
                // Set the element to 0 or 1 as required
                if (i == j)
                {
                    matrix[i, j] = 1;
                }
                else
                {
                    matrix[i, j] = 0;
                }
            }
        }
    }

    // Set the updated modelview matrix
    SetModelviewMatrix(matrix);
}
```

A demonstration of this in action can be seen in the Fireworks example project, a screenshot from which is shown in Figure 13–10. The trees on the ground and all of the firework elements are rotated toward the camera, which itself moves around the edge of the scene. All that is required to perform this alignment is to make a call to the _myGameEngine.RotateMatrixToCamera function from within each object's Render code. Remember to call this after any translations have taken place but before any rotation or scaling operations, as these will be erased by the billboard function.

Figure 13–10. Billboards used for trees and fireworks in the Fireworks example project

Learning More about OpenGL ES

Over the last few chapters, you have learned a lot about how to work with OpenGL ES and have advanced from simple 2D projects up to complex 3D scenes. While the power available to current Windows Mobile devices is fairly limited, especially when compared with the immense power available in desktop PC graphics cards, Windows Mobile is, nevertheless, still a flexible graphics environment with a huge amount of potential for mobile games. As new hardware is released, the processing capabilities available to OpenGL ES applications should continue to spiral upward at a rapid pace.

While we've covered a lot of OpenGL ES functionality, it is a very rich and flexible environment and there's a great deal more that you can learn about it if you wish to extend your knowledge further.

For many years, http://nehe.gamedev.net has provided one of the Internet's best sources for readable and accessible OpenGL tutorials. These are all aimed at OpenGL rather than OpenGL ES but still make for an interesting and useful read. The QOpenCD web site contains a page within which the majority of these tutorials can be found converted for OpenGL ES; point your web browser to http://embedded.org.ua/opengles/lessons.html to find these. The tutorials are all written for C/C++, but the techniques along with NeHe's tutorial descriptions should make for easy translation into .NET CF.

Visit http://www.khronos.org/opengles/sdk/1.1/docs/man/ to find the full OpenGL ES documentation. It includes detailed information about all of the available OpenGL ES commands and their expected parameters.

Also, many online discussion boards cover OpenGL and OpenGL ES.
`http://www.gamedev.net/community/forums/forum.asp?forum_id=25` is an example of an active community discussion group on this subject. Such discussion boards are useful both for browsing existing content and for posting questions of your own if you need any help or assistance.

I wish you many days of happy coding using OpenGL ES!

■ ■ ■

CHAPTER 14

Distributing Your Game

Over the course of this book, we have now covered a wide range of different game programming techniques and technologies, from coping with device diversity through to 3D graphics to using sound and input and lots more. I hope you are now ready and eager to start writing your own games using everything that you have learned.

But there is one further important aspect of creating a game—getting it on to other people's devices to that they can play it.

In this chapter, we will cover some of the problems and challenges that you will face in distributing your game and explore everything that you will need to create packages to distribute, sell, and market the games that you have created.

Preparing a Game for Distribution

Before you begin creating installation packages for your game, some background requirements need to be met first. While these have no direct impact on the way your game executes, they are all still important to ensure that your game installs properly and can be managed as later versions of the game are released.

Let's look at what we need to do to prepare for distributing a game.

Settings the Assembly Properties

The first place to start when preparing your game for release is the Assembly Information window. This allows information about the game's title, author, company, version number, and more to be provided. All of this information is built into the executable file that is created by Visual Studio.

The Assembly Information window is accessed by opening your game's Properties window and clicking the Assembly Information button within the Application tab, as shown in Figure 14–1.

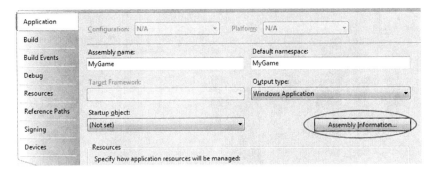

Figure 14-1. Opening the Assembly Information window

The Assembly Information window itself is shown in Figure 14-2.

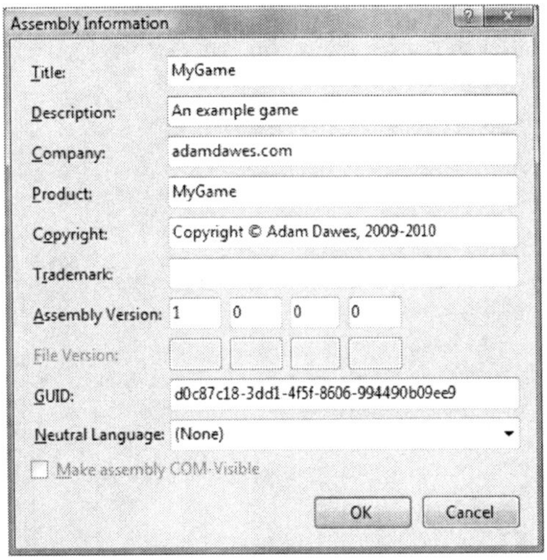

Figure 14-2. The Assembly Information window

The fields available within this form are as follows:

- *Title* allows the assembly title to be specified. Generally, this will be the same as the assembly name.

- *Description* allows a longer description of the assembly to be provided.

- *Company* details the name of the company that produced the assembly.

- *Product* identifies the overall product to which the assembly belongs. For example, if your game Invaders From Mars contains several separate assemblies, all of them can specify Invaders From Mars as their project.

- *Copyright* allows a copyright message to be entered. This normally takes the form `Copyright © name, year`.

- *Trademark* allows any relevant trademark to be specified.

- *Assembly Version* contains information about the version number of the assembly. We will discuss version numbers in more detail in a moment.

- *GUID* contains a unique identification number for the assembly. Visual Studio will automatically provide a value for this, and it will not normally need to be modified.

- *Neutral Language* specifies which culture the assembly supports. This can be left at its default value, None.

With the exception of the Assembly Version, GUID, and Neutral Language, all of these values are optional and can be left blank if you wish.

Alternatively, you may edit this data directly within the normal source editor window by editing the AssemblyInfo.cs file (AssemblyInfo.vb for VB.NET projects). This can be found inside Solution Explorer's Properties node for C# projects or inside the My Project node in VB.NET (though you will need to switch on the Show All Files option in Solution Explorer before the My Project node can be expanded). Attribute settings within this source file exist for each of the fields in the Assembly Information window.

Project Versioning

An important aspect of managing your games is keeping track of each assembly's version number. This is also accessed via the Assembly Information window or the AssemblyInfo file, as detailed in the previous section. Having distinct version numbers for each release of your game executables and DLLs will make it much easier for you to determine exactly what code is running and for users of your software to report problems that they experience in a way that you can diagnose.

Version numbers are formed by four numeric values separated by periods. For example, 1.0.0.0 might be the first version of a released executable. The four parts of the version number, from left to right, are:

- Major version

- Minor version

- Build number

- Revision

Each of these can contain a value in the range of 0 to 65535. Exactly how you use these is really up to you, but here is a suggested strategy:

- The major version is incremented each time a whole new version of a product is released (for example, the game has been rewritten or is substantially different from a previous version). Setting the major version to zero means that the product is still in a test state and has not yet been released as a finished product.

- The minor version is incremented each time a new version of an application is released, and the application is still the same basic product as the previous release. For example, this number would be incremented when new features have been added to a product, but the product has not been rewritten or substantially modified such that the major version would be increased. The minor version would be reset to zero if the major version number increases.

- The build number indicates revisions within the current minor version. If trivial enhancements or bug fixes are released that don't have any significant impact on the product, the build number can be incremented and the minor version left alone. The build number would be reset to zero if the major or minor version number increases.

- The revision is simply incremented by one for each new version of a product released. This will essentially form a release count and will not be reset even if the other version number elements are changed.

■ **NOTE** It is important to remember that the periods in version numbers are just field separators and not decimal separators. Incrementing the revision of a version string set to 1.0.0.9 results in a version string of 1.0.0.10, not 1.0.1.0.

By default, Visual Studio will create projects with a version string of either 1.0.0.0 or 1.0.*. The 1.0.* syntax tells Visual Studio to automatically provide values for the build number and revision each time it builds. While this syntax provides a simple way of obtaining a new version number, it also results in unpredictable values in this field and is better avoided. A preferable approach is to simply increment the version number manually each time you are ready to compile an assembly ready for release.

■ **CAUTION** When Visual Studio is deploying your application to a device for debugging, it will not replace existing DLLs or executables on the device if they have a higher version number than the version being deployed. No explanation will be given for this; the file simply won't deploy. If you ever need to lower the version number of an assembly (which will be the case if the version is changed from 1.0.* to 1.0.0.0), manually delete the existing files from the device to ensure that Visual Studio continues to deploy your modified assembly as expected.

If you recall the About box component that we created back in Chapter 9, you may remember that it has support built in for displaying the running assembly's version number. Passing {VersionNumber} anywhere within one of the strings added to the About box will cause the current version number to be displayed in its place. This is a simple and useful mechanism for displaying your game's current version to the player.

Creating an Icon

When your game is installed on a device, the end user will almost certainly access it through the Start menu or via the Programs application. Both of these display icons for installed applications. So that your game stands out and grabs the user's attention, it needs an attractive and appropriate icon.

Icons are created as .ico files, just as they are for desktop applications. These .ico files actually contain more than just a simple image. They are able to contain multiple images at different sizes and using different numbers of colors, and they also are able to store alpha transparency information.

Creating attractive icons with full alpha channels can be an intricate task and will definitely require some level of graphical ability, but simple icons can be created if needed that will still provide a useful representation for your game when it is shown on screen.

Icon images can be created within the .ico file at the sizes described in Table 14–1.

Table 14–1. Icon Image Sizes

Size in Pixels	Used For
16 16	Small icons on low-resolution screens
21×21	Small icons on square low-resolution screens
22×22	Small icons on smart phone screens
32×32	Large icons on low-resolution screens and small icons on high-resolution screens
43×43	Large icons on square high-resolution screens
44×44	Large icons on smart phone screens
45×45	Small icons in Windows Mobile 6.5
60×60	Large icons on square screens in Windows Mobile 6.5
64×64	Large icons on high-resolution screens
90×90	Large icons in Windows Mobile 6.5

Not all of these sizes need necessarily be included, because Windows Mobile will scale one of the existing images up or down in size to match whatever it needs. This scaling will not always produce attractive results however, so providing specific icons for each size will ensure that you have control over exactly what is displayed.

Most icon applications will allow you to create an icon at one size and use that image as the basis for the other icon sizes that are subsequently added. To use this feature, create an icon at the largest size you want to include, and then create smaller icons based on the large icon. When you add lots of different sizes, ensure that you base them all on the largest icon rather then any other smaller icons that you have previously created.

Many applications are available for creating and editing .ico files, and Visual Studio has a simple icon editor built in. Third-party applications are available that are much more sophisticated than this however. One such program that is very flexible and also free is IcoFX; visit http://icofx.ro to download the latest version. It has full support for setting an icon's alpha channel, using multiple image sizes within a single .ico file, and creating new icons sizes from existing images within the icon. Figure 14–3 shows IcoFX in operation.

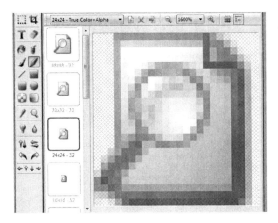

Figure 14–3. IcoFX being used to edit an icon file containing multiple images

Once you have created your icon, save it as an .ico file into your project's directory, alongside the main .csproj or .vbproj file. The icon can then be added to your executable project.

You can add the icon in C# projects by opening the project properties window and clicking the browse button (marked with the ellipses) to the right of the Icon field in the Resources panel. Browse to and select your .ico file and its name will be selected in the Icon field. This will also add the icon to the project so that it appears in Solution Explorer. A configured icon in a C# project is shown in Figure 14–4.

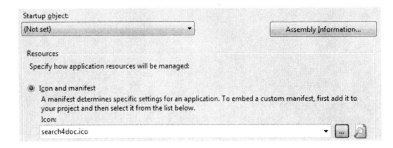

Figure 14–4. A C# project configured with an icon

Setting the icon for projects created in VB.NET is slightly different, as shown in Figure 14–5. The icon is still set in the project properties window but is selected by dropping open the Icon drop-down list and selecting the Browse item within. The icon can be selected in the resulting dialog and will be displayed in the Icon field and added to the project just as in C#.

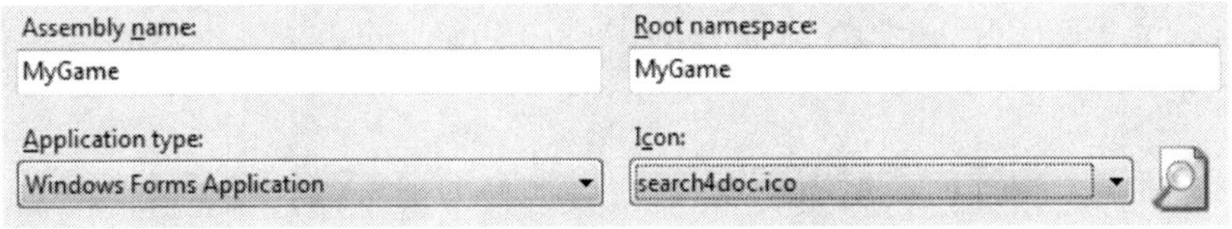

Figure 14–5. A VB.NET project configured with an icon

With the project configured in this way, the icon will be built into the resulting executable on all subsequent compilations.

Building Distribution Packages

With the steps from the previous sections complete, the project is now ready to be packaged for distribution.

Historically, there have been two different systems for packaging up applications for distribution: as CAB installers or as executable installers.

CAB files ("CAB" is short for "cabinet") are a compressed file archive, just like a ZIP file—in fact, many ZIP file applications (WinZip, 7-Zip, and WinRAR to name but three) are capable of interacting with these files. When CAB files are used to install Windows Mobile applications, they are set up with a particular structure that Windows Mobile natively recognizes. Attempting to execute a CAB file in a Windows Mobile device will initiate installation of the application.

When an executable is used for installation, the executable actually needs to run on a desktop PC rather than on the device itself. The device must be connected to the PC at the time the executable is launched. This gives a more standard feel to installing Windows Mobile applications, as the user is likely to be familiar with installing applications in this way on their computer.

The big advantage that CAB files have over executables is that they can be installed directly on the device. If the user is away from a PC (which for a mobile device is a fairly common scenario) or does not have a Windows PC at all, CAB files are still easy to download and install.

For this reason, CAB files have now become the standard method for distributing mobile applications. They are used for Microsoft's own Windows Marketplace for Mobile, as well as by other alternative marketplaces applications such as the community-developed OpnMarket that can be downloaded from the http://www.freewarepocketpc.com web site.

Visual Studio offers support for building CAB files within its IDE, so we will use this feature to create the installer for us. The following sections show how to create and configure a setup project ready for use by your game.

Switching into Release Mode

Before we start to create our setup project, we will first set Visual Studio to build in Release mode rather than in Debug mode. When compiling in Debug mode, the Visual Studio compiler adds extra data into the output DLLs and executables that allow the interactive debugger to work. When we release a finished application, we don't want to include this, as it is of no use on an end user's device. It also increases the sizes of the executables and has an impact on performance.

When we switch Visual Studio into Release mode, this debugging data is removed from the output binaries. We can switch Visual Studio between Debug and Release builds by selecting the appropriate option from the Solution Configurations box in the standard Visual Studio toolbar. Figure 14–6 shows this setting being changed to the Release configuration.

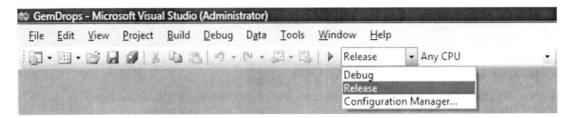

Figure 14–6. Selecting the Release configuration

Note that this setting affects the whole Visual Studio environment, not just the selected project.

Once you have changed to Release mode, ensure that your solution still compiles. You may need to make some configuration changes (for example, resetting the "Allow unsafe code" option within the Assembly Properties window), as many of the project properties are specific to the configuration in which they are set. You may also need to fix the references to external DLLs. Make sure that all of your code builds without any errors before continuing.

Creating the Setup Project

We are now ready to add a setup project to the solution. This project builds CAB files for use on mobile devices. Although it is added to your solution just like a normal project, it doesn't have a programming languages associated with it and is, therefore, identical for both C# and VB.NET projects.

With your game solution already open in Visual Studio, add a setup project by choosing the File ➤ Add ➤ New Project item from Visual Studio's main menu. When the Add New Project window shown in Figure 14–7 opens, select the Other Project Types / Setup and Deployment item in the Project types tree on the left and a Smart Device CAB Project in the Templates selection on the right. Give your setup project a name and location, and click OK to create and add the project.

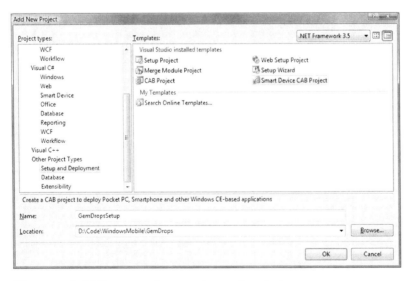

Figure 14–7. Adding a new Setup project to the solution.

The setup project will be added to your solution. The project has just a main window that appears in the IDE, which allows you to control which files to deploy to the device when the CAB is installed and where to place those files. The window is split vertically, with a folder tree shown in the left panel and the files within the selected folder shown on the right. The default content of this window for a new setup project is shown in Figure 14–8.

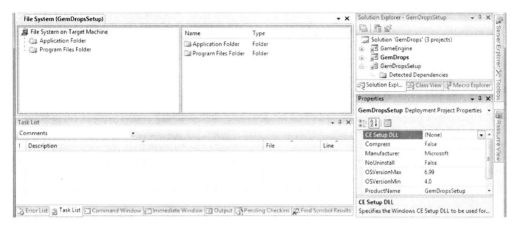

Figure 14–8. An empty setup project window

■ **NOTE** If you close the setup project window and need to reopen it, right-click the setup project's main node in Solution Explorer and choose View ➤ File System from the menu.

When the setup project node is selected in Solution Explorer, a number of properties will become available in the Properties window. Set the Manufacturer property to your name (or your company's name) and the ProductName property to the name of your game. It is important to set these appropriately, as the ProductName defines the name of the folder that will be created inside the device's \Program Files folder when the game is installed. Both of these values will also appear in the Remove Programs list if a user selects to uninstall applications from a device.

The remaining setup project properties can be left with their default values.

Adding the Setup Project's Files

Now, we are ready to begin adding some content to the CAB file. The first thing we add is our game itself. Add it by right-clicking the setup project node in Solution Explorer and selecting Add ➤ Project Output from the menu, as shown in Figure 14–9.

Figure 14–9. Selecting to add files to the setup project

This displays the Add Project Output Group window, shown in Figure 14–10. In this window, select the project for your game. Ensure that Primary Output is selected below this, and click the OK button. Visual Studio will add the project and all of its dependent files to the setup project contained within the Application Folder branch of the install tree. The output for the GemDrops example is shown in Figure 14–11.

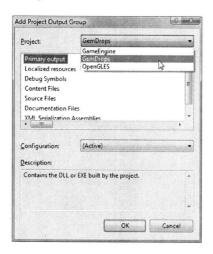

Figure 14–10. Selecting the main project to add to the setup project

Figure 14–11. The files added to the setup project by the Add Project Output Group window

This is Visual Studio's best guess at the files that we want to appear inside the application's install folder (the directory that will be created inside the device's \Program Files folder). In this example, Visual Studio has understood some of our requirements but is not entirely correct.

First of all, we need to add bass.dll to the project. Because bass.dll is an unmanaged DLL file, Visual Studio was unable to detect it and did not include it as part of the installation. To manually add a file, right-click the Application Folder item in the panel on the left, and select Add ➤ File from the menu. Browse to the file to be included, and it will appear in the file list.

The second thing we need to change is the presence of OpenGLES.dll. This file is used by GameEngine.dll to support OpenGL ES games, but GemDrops is a GDI game, so this is not required. We can remove the file by finding its entry in Solution Explorer. It will appear inside the setup project, under the Detected Dependencies node. Right-click OpenGLES.dll, and select Exclude from the menu, as shown in Figure 14–12. The selected file will disappear from the file list in the main window.

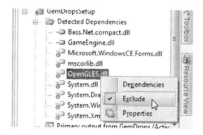

Figure 14–12. *Excluding a dependent file from the setup project*

Files need to be excluded in this way only if they are automatically added to the project by Visual Studio as a dependency of your main project. Files that have been manually added to the setup, such as bass.dll in this example, can simply be deleted from the file list panel.

■ **NOTE** It is also possible to configure registry keys as part of your setup project. Should you wish to do this, right-click the setup project in Solution Explorer and select View ➤ Registry from the menu. Registry keys may then be added to the project as required.

Creating a Programs Menu Shortcut

The setup project now contains everything it needs to install your game to a target device. The current project configuration does not add a shortcut icon to the Programs menu however, so the user will be unable to find the game on a device.

Adding a shortcut icon is achieved by right-clicking the File System on Target Machine node in the left panel of the setup project and selecting Add Special Folder ➤ Programs Folder from the menu, as shown in Figure 14–13. A new empty folder named Programs will be added to the left panel alongside the existing folders.

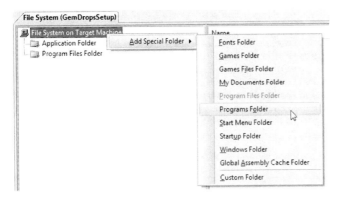

Figure 14–13. Adding the Programs folder to the setup project

If we want, we can add our shortcut directly to this `Programs` folder. This will cause it to appear in the top level of the Programs menu. It is common for games to be placed in a Programs menu subdirectory named Games, however, and we will follow this standard for our project. Right-click the `Programs` folder item, and select Add Folder from the menu. Set the folder's name to `Games`.

Select the new `Games` folder, and right-click the empty file list panel to the right. Select the Create New Shortcut item from the menu. This will open a file selection window showing all of the content that has been created within your setup project. Browse into the Application Folder directory, and select the Primary output item from the list, as shown in Figure 14–14. After clicking OK, a new shortcut will be added to the `Programs/Games` folder. Rename the shortcut to whatever you want to appear in the Programs menu (`GemDrops`, in this case).

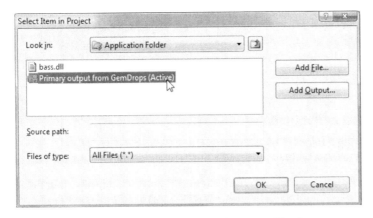

Figure 14–14. Selecting the file that our shortcut will reference.

The icon that will actually be displayed in the menu will be taken from the selected application. As we added an icon for our game back in the "Creating an Icon" section, this icon will be used for the shortcut.

Building the CAB File

The setup project is now fully configured and ready to build our CAB file. To perform the build, right-click the setup project in Solution Explorer, and select Build from the menu. Visual Studio will recompile all of the projects in your solution, ending with the setup project itself.

Once this build is complete, take a look in the setup project's folder on disk. You will see that it contains a sub-directory called Release, inside which is your CAB file.

The CAB file's name will initially be set to match that of your setup project (GemDropsSetup.CAB in this example). It is a good idea to rename this to include your game's major and minor version numbers—for example, GemDrops_1_0.CAB—prior to distribution. If you release multiple versions of your game, this approach will make it much easier to determine exactly which version of the game each CAB file will install.

It is strongly advisable to spend some time testing the CAB file before you think about distributing it publicly. The first places to test it are on the emulators and your own devices. Ensure that any existing game files are deleted from wherever you are performing the test, install the CAB, and start the game from the Programs menu. Ensure that the Programs menu icon and description appear correctly, everything starts as expected, and no errors occur. Also, use File Explorer to view the files that have been added for your game to the \Program Files directory and ensure that everything is how you would expect with no additional files or unexpected file names. If there are any problems, uninstall from the device, update your setup project as needed to ensure that everything gets installed to the correct locations, and then build and test your CAB file again.

When you are satisfied with testing on your own device, it can be useful to get friends or colleagues to test installation on their devices too. The larger range of devices you can test on the better. If you are unable to do this, the emulators and your own device should be sufficient to provide a solid test environment.

Your game is now ready to be released to the world!

Selling Games

Sometimes, game authors decide to release games as *freeware*, allowing others to download and distribute them free of charge. You may instead decide to try to sell your game, selling it using a commercial or *shareware* model. In this section, we'll look at some ways of achieving this.

Creating Evaluation Applications

Persuading a potential customer to actually purchase your game can be a difficult task. A huge variety of competing titles are available for Windows Mobile devices, and to make a sale, you will need to first enable your customers to realize that your game exists. Then, you must persuade them to try it out and, finally, convince them to actually pay for it.

Once someone finds out about your game (and we'll look at how you can help them to do so in the in the :Promoting Your Game: section later on), you ideally need to give them the opportunity to evaluate your game. Most people will be reluctant to hand over any money unless they know exactly what they are going to receive. There is enough low-quality software around that consumers quickly learn to be cautious in their purchases.

The easiest way to convince someone to buy your game is to provide an evaluation copy. The main ways to approach this follow:

- *Offer a limited version of the game.* Perhaps only allow the first level to be played, or make just the most basic game mode available. This scaled-down version will give the player a chance to decide whether the quality of the game is acceptable and whether they actually like the game. A player who has positive feelings in these two areas will be much more likely to purchase.

- *Offer a time-limited version of the game.* The game itself is unrestricted in terms of functionality, but it stores the date of first launch in an encrypted file on the system (possibly in the registry). Once a certain period of time has elapsed, the game stops working and requires the user to register. This option is more difficult to achieve, because you need to stop the user from just reinstalling the game in order to reset their evaluation time.

The first approach is by far the simpler to implement and will usually be quite sufficient to give players an idea of exactly what they are buying. Providing an evaluation version of your game is a very important thing to consider: you should not allow yourself to lose sales just because your target audience is unaware of what your game is and does.

Upgrading to Full Versions

Once you have sold a copy of your game, you need to deliver a copy of the full, unlocked game to their device. The two main methods of achieving this follow:

- Provide the user with a separate download that contains the full version of the game.

- Provide a registration code that *unlocks* the existing installed application to provide access to the restricted functionality.

The first of these options is easier to achieve but is less convenient for the players, because they have to install an entirely new application before they can continue playing the game. The simplicity of this approach may outweigh its disadvantages however.

The second option is nicer for the player but a lot more work to implement. Generally speaking, this kind of algorithm will generate a code based on the user's name and will use this code as the registration code. When the user's name and registration code are entered into the system, the two will be compared to test whether they match. If so, the game unlocks; if not, the user is informed that the code is invalid. The user is discouraged from giving the code to other people by the fact that it is associated with his or her name.

The CodeGenerator example project provides a simple implementation of a code generation and verification algorithm. It has a simple user interface that allows a code to be generated for a name in the top half of the form, and a name and code to be verified in the bottom half.

Codes are generated for names by following a number of steps. First of all, the name is encrypted using the TEA algorithm that you first saw in the high score table code back in Chapter 9. This results in the name being converted to an unreadable series of characters.

These characters are then placed into a 6-byte array. The first six characters are written directly into the six-array element, and the remaining characters are combined with those existing values using an *exclusive or* operator. The encrypted characters continue to be combined, looping through the 6-byte array as many times as is necessary for all of the characters to be processed.

Finally the 6-byte array is converted into a string of hexadecimal numbers, using two hexadecimal digits (with values 00 to ff) to represent each of the bytes. This code is presented to the user as the activation code. It is important to ensure that codes are readable and not too long: 12 alphanumeric characters is fine in this respect.

The example project performs all of this encoding in a function called GenerateCode and is shown in Listing 14–1.

Listing 14–1. Creating Activation Codes from a User-Entered Name

```
/// <summary>
/// Create an activation code from the supplied name.
/// </summary>
/// <param name="Name"></param>
/// <returns></returns>
private string GenerateCode(string Name)
{
    string encrypted;
    byte[] encryptedBytes;
    byte encryptedByte;
    int encryptedBytesIndex = 0;
    string result = "";

    // Make sure the name is at least 4 characters
    if (Name == null || Name.Length < 4)
    {
        throw new Exception("Name must be at least 4 characters long.");
    }

    // First encrypt the name
    encrypted = CEncryption.Encrypt(Name, "CodeGenerator");

    // Copy the encrypted string into a byte array.
    // After each 6 bytes, loop back to the start of the array and combine
    // the new bytes with those already present using an XOR operation.
    encryptedBytes = new byte[6];
    for (int i = 0; i < encrypted.Length; i++)
    {
        // Convert the character into a byte
        encryptedByte = (byte)encrypted[i];
        // Xor the byte with the existing array content
        encryptedBytes[encryptedBytesIndex] ^= encryptedByte;
        // Move to the next array index
        encryptedBytesIndex += 1;
        // If we reach the end of the array, loop back to the start
        if (encryptedBytesIndex == encryptedBytes.Length) encryptedBytesIndex = 0;
    }

    // Now we have a byte array, convert that to a string of hex digits
    foreach (byte b in encryptedBytes)
    {
        result += b.ToString("x2");
    }

    // Return the finished string
    return result;
}
```

Because of the way the data has been encoded, it is impossible to convert the generated code back into the original name, even if you know the algorithm used to generate the code. So how can we verify that a name and code that the user may enter actually match?

We check this simply be reencoding the supplied name. If the generated code matches the one that the user has entered, we accept the name and code combination as valid and allow access to the full game. If the generated code does not match the user-entered code, we reject it and continue to restrict the available functions.

Some very important considerations must be borne in mind if you decide to use this approach:

- It is absolutely essential that you *obfuscate* the project that contains the code-generation function. We will look at obfuscation in the "Implementing Reverse Engineering" section later in this chapter. Without obfuscation, it will be a simple matter for even an inexperienced hacker to not only retrieve the coding algorithm from your project to bypass the security check but also to generate codes themselves—the coding algorithm is, after all, present within your game.

- Do not expose access to this function via a public API. While it is perfectly possible for .NET applications to query and call private functions in an assembly, keeping its score set to `internal` or `private` makes it much more difficult to locate. If this were added as a public function to a DLL, everyone could reference your DLL and use it for their own code-generation purposes.

- Do not use the example presented here unmodified. At the very least, you should change the encryption key specified in the call to `CEncryption.Encrypt`, but it would be much better to use this just as inspiration for your own algorithm that can be developed from scratch.

- When the user enters an incorrect validation code, pause for a couple of seconds before stating that it is invalid. After a set number of incorrect attempts, close the application. These changes will make it harder for someone to automate a brute-force attack on your game's activation function.

- Also, be aware of case sensitivity. It may be sensible to convert the supplied name to lowercase before encrypting so that legitimately entered codes don't fail simply because the capitalization was not as expected.

No matter how hard you try to protect the algorithm in your project, it is always possible that more experienced hackers could reverse engineer it and be able to create their own activation code generators. All you can really do is put up sufficient barriers so that the average user is unable to pass them dishonestly. We will talk about this subject a little more in the "Minimizing Piracy" section shortly.

Using Windows Marketplace for Mobile

One of the more recent developments in the Windows Mobile world is the arrival of Microsoft's Windows Marketplace for Mobile. This is a centralized catalog of applications, available to browse both online and via a Marketplace program on the device itself. The Marketplace application is installed by default on all Windows Mobile 6.5 devices and can be installed manually on Windows Mobile 6.0 and 6.1 devices.

You can browse the available applications by visiting `http://marketplace.windowsphone.com` in your web browser. Applications are divided into categories (one of which is for games) and can also be displayed based on how recently they were added to the marketplace and how popular they are.

Getting an application listed in Marketplace is something that you should seriously consider if you plan to sell your game. Before you can get an application listed, you must first join the Microsoft Developer Program. This costs (at the time of this writing) $99 per year. In addition to your membership, you are also given five *submission credits* along with your membership. These can be used to submit applications into the marketplace. Each application submitted will use one of the credits. Further credits cost $99 each.

Applications submitted to the marketplace do not appear automatically, but are instead first submitted to a series of tests by Microsoft. These cover all sorts of areas of functionality, from checking that the program is stable and does not crash or leak memory, to ensuring that programs do not alter system settings without the user's permission, through to checking that there is no malicious software contained within the application.

You can visit http://developer.windowsphone.com/ to find out all the information you need about the Developer Program, submission guidelines, and testing. Included on the site are tutorials, video walkthroughs, and many other useful resources.

One of the things that will be tested during submission is how the game behaves when run alongside a Microsoft stress-testing application called Hopper. Hopper continuously sends random keystrokes and screen taps to the device in an attempt to force unexpected crashes or other undesirable behavior. Hopper will be left running against submitted applications for two hours and must not cause any problems at all. It can be downloaded from Microsoft (details are in the Application Submission Requirements document) so that you can use it yourself prior to submission. It is well worth ensuring that this can run against your games for extended periods of time without causing problems—leaving it running overnight is a useful way to test this.

If your application fails Microsoft's testing, its entry into the Marketplace will be refused. Unfortunately, the submission credit that was used to submit the failed application is not refunded. It is, therefore, essential that you thoroughly test your application and review the Submission Requirements prior to sending your game to Microsoft for testing. Silly mistakes can otherwise end up costing you money.

The Marketplace operates across a number of different *markets*, one per country. There are over 30 different markets supported within the marketplace at the moment, many of which use different currencies to allow users to purchase applications. When an application is submitted, a *primary market* is identified into which the application will be added. Microsoft used to charge an additional $10 fee to add the application to further markets, but this fee has now been dropped, and the application can be added to as many markets as needed without incurring any additional charges.

If you need assistance with Marketplace submissions or have any questions about how it works, the Marketplace forum at http://social.msdn.microsoft.com/Forums/en-US/mktplace/ is very active and is an ideal place to ask for help.

The installation of applications from Marketplace is handled entirely within the Marketplace software itself. Security mechanisms are built in to this to prevent purchased games from being executed on other devices without authorization. This provides a reasonable degree of security for your applications.

Marketplace applications do not get to include a demonstration or evaluation version as part of their submission. If you want to include a free evaluation version of your game, this will require a further submission credit. This does leave users in the unfortunate position of being unable to properly evaluate an application before buying it, which could present a barrier to sales. Providing an evaluation version is well worth considering so that you can build the trust of your audience.

In the absence of this, Microsoft will permit refunds on applications if the buyer decides that the product is not suitable. Refunds are only available for 24 hours after installation however and are limited to one refund per calendar month, so this is far from an ideal "try before you buy" strategy.

While the Windows Marketplace for Mobile has not seen the huge volumes of applications that the equivalent application stores have seen in some other mobile platforms, it is still well worth considering as a sales channel for your games.

Minimizing Piracy

Software piracy has always been a problem for software developers, and unfortunately this is also the case for Windows Mobile software. It is inevitable that there will be a degree of piracy on any popular commercial application.

Exactly how you plan to respond to this is, of course, entirely up to you, but do bear in mind that putting users through too much pain to validate and verify their legitimate software can be self-defeating. If users get so frustrated with your anti-piracy measures, they may be put off using your software or could even decide that the pirated version is actually better than the genuine version.

The middle ground here would seem to be to put sufficient measures in place to reduce or eliminate *casual* piracy (for example, simply copying executables between devices) but not to spend time attempting to defeat determined or professional software hackers. It costs money to develop antipiracy measures, and these expenses will eat into your revenue. If these measures are ultimately circumvented anyway, that money is wasted.

Accepting piracy as an inevitability may seen counterproductive, but in many cases, it actually allows you to focus your efforts into being creative rather than engaging in potentially futile intellectual battles.

Implementing Reverse Engineering

Even if you are giving your game away (and especially if you are asking people to pay for it), you should be aware of how easy it is to *reverse engineer* .NET CF applications. Powerful free tools such as the free and exceptionally easy to use Reflector.NET (http://reflector.red-gate.com) allow compiled .NET and .NET CF applications to be converted from executables and DLLs back into source code. The resulting source code is not identical the original code but is usually quite clear enough to read. If you have any sensitive code included within your game (such as activation code generation algorithms), it is essential to consider how you can stop others from decompiling your game.

Figure 14–15 shows Reflector.NET running with the compiled CodeGenerator.exe that was built from the example project we looked at earlier. You can see that the code is clearly visible, even down to the variable names, and it was compiled in Release mode too.

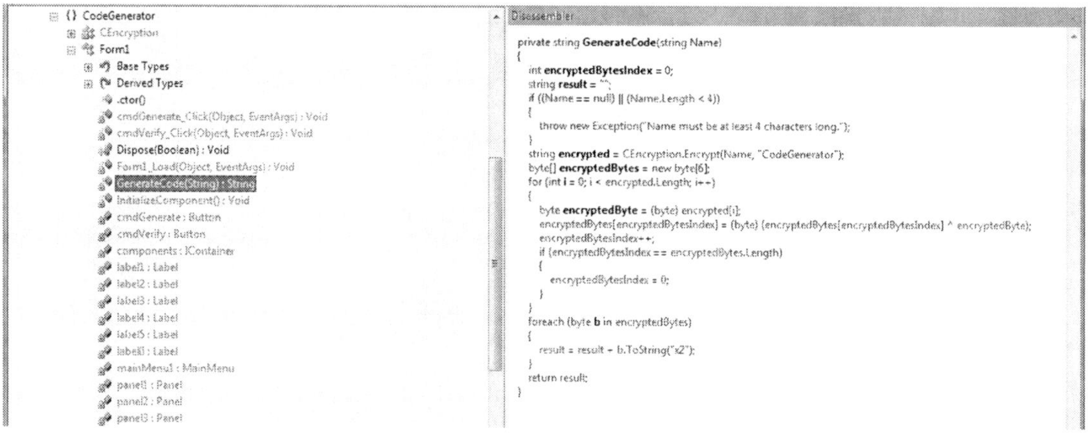

Figure 14–15. An example disassembly using Reflector.NET

Reflector.NET is not some kind of hacking tool but is simply using .NET's built-in Reflection functionality to examine the compiled executable. As well as decompiling code, it is able to provide information about all of the classes within the project and the fields, properties, and methods contained inside each. Clearly, if we want to protect our source code, we need to do something to hide our code from prying eyes.

The strategy that we can employ to achieve this is to use obfuscation. If we obfuscate our executables and DLLs, we obscure their inner workings, making it harder for them to be reverse engineered.

Microsoft provides a copy of PreEmptive Solutions's Dotfuscator Community Edition free with Visual Studio. Let's take a look at how this can be used to apply some protection to our games.

Obfuscating with Dotfuscator Community Edition

When Visual Studio is installed, it offers the option of including Dotfuscator Community Edition (hereafter simply referred to as Dotfuscator) as part of the installed environment. Dotfuscator is started externally to Visual Studio and appears with its own icon on the Start menu. If you can't find it, check and update your Visual Studio installation to ensure that it is actually installed.

Before you start Dotfuscator, you must first launch Visual Studio. Dotfuscator interacts with Visual Studio in the background and needs it to be running to facilitate this interaction.

When Dotfuscator launches, it will prompt you to either create a new project or open an existing project. A Dotfuscator project contains information about which assemblies are to be obfuscated and the type of obfuscation to apply to them. As we do not yet have a project, select to create a new one.

Dotfuscator initially displays its Input tab, showing the assemblies that are to be obfuscated. Click the leftmost toolbar button within the tab (that is, "Browse and add assembly to list") and locate the assembly that you wish to obfuscate (this should be a release build as discussed earlier in this chapter). The assembly will appear within the assembly list as shown in Figure 14–16.

Figure 14–16. Dotfuscator's Input tab with an assembly added

You can if you wish add multiple assemblies to the project at this stage in order to obfuscate them all at once.

When all the requested assemblies have been added, select File / Build from the main application menu. After prompting you to save the Dotfuscator project file, the obfuscation process will begin. This will take a few seconds, after which an obfuscation status window will appear as shown in Figure 14–17. This indicates that the obfuscation is finished: the obfuscated output file can be found in a subdirectory called Dotfuscated located wherever your Dotfuscator project file was saved.

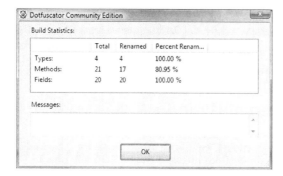

Figure 14–17. Dotfuscator's obfuscation completion status window.

If we now open the Dotfuscated executable in Reflector, we can see what it has done. All of the classes, fields, properties, and functions have been renamed. Our application's form is no longer called Form1, but now is simply called d. The GenerateCode procedure has been renamed as b. Immediately, this increases the amount of effort required to understand what the project is trying to do.

Similarly, the decompiled code is much harder to read. Variable names have changed; for example, the string named encrypted is now called str, and the byte array named encryptedBytes is now called buffer. These names are much less meaningful and again make ascertaining what the code is trying to do more difficult. The obfuscated executable open in Reflector is shown in Figure 14–18.

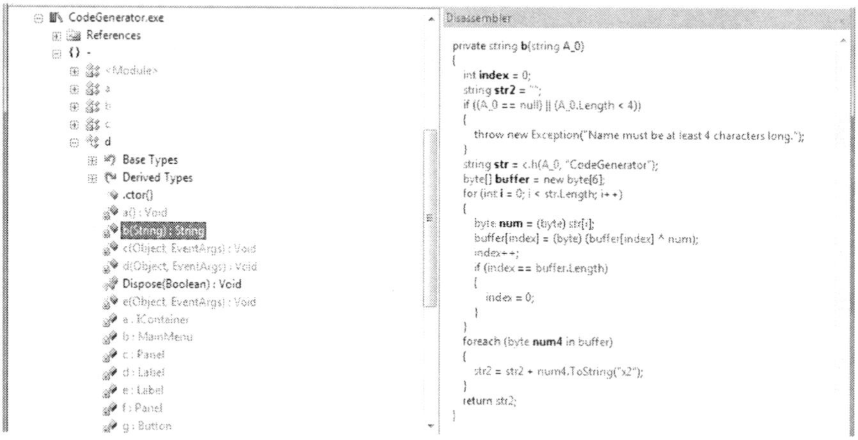

Figure 14–18. The Dotfuscated executable disassembled in Reflector.NET.

You may have noticed a potential issue with this however: if we rename all of the classes and methods, no external assemblies will be able to call into the code any more. If, for example, we obfuscate GameEngine.dll, all of the classes and methods that our games would expect to find would be renamed and would, therefore, result in errors when the game tries to call them.

We can work around this by putting Dotfuscator into *library mode*. When this mode is active, all public classes, fields, properties, and methods and all virtual functions will have their names left unchanged. Only private and internal elements of the assembly will be renamed. This provides as much renaming as possible without breaking any code that needs to use the library. You will need to use this for all DLLs that you obfuscate, but you do not need to use it for executables (unless they are themselves referenced from other assemblies).

Library mode is activated by clicking the corresponding toolbar button within Dotfuscator's Input tab, as shown in Figure 14–19. The Library check box for all of your assemblies will be toggled on or off each time this is clicked. The Community Edition of Dotfuscator allows this mode to be set only at project level rather then for individual assemblies, so if you wish to obfuscate some assemblies with library mode on and others with it off, you will need to create two separate projects.

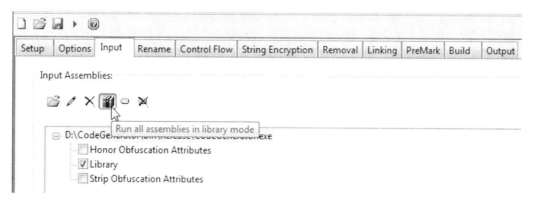

Figure 14–19. *Selecting to obfuscate in library mode.*

After applying obfuscation to your executable and DLL files, it is, of course, essential to make sure that they still work. Don't allow all your careful testing to be let down by accidentally obfuscating your DLLs so that they can no longer be called by your application!

You will also need to exercise caution if you use reflection to interrogate the classes and class members inside your project. Because these items would all have different names after obfuscation, your reflection will probably fail to find whatever it is looking for. If this is the case in your project, you can use Dotfuscator's Rename tab to exclude specific classes and class members from the renaming scheme.

Using Advanced Obfuscation

The previous section covers the full extent of the capabilities offered by Dotfuscator Community Edition. Other third-party obfuscators are able to perform more advanced obfuscation than this, however. If you decide that you need more powerful obfuscation, you will need to identify a suitable application to use; Google will provide lots of shareware and commercial options to explore.

Visiting http://en.wikipedia.org/wiki/Comparison_of_.NET_obfuscators will reveal a large list and comparison table of .NET obfuscators, though others not shown in this table are available too. Don't forget to ensure that any obfuscator you choose does support .NET CF assemblies. Most will, but some applications include this feature only in more expensive versions.

Some of the features that you can expect to find in more powerful obfuscators are shown in the following sections. None of these techniques will make it completely impossible to reconstruct your source code, but as more of these are used, doing so will become less and less practical and cost-effective.

Control Flow Obfuscation

One of the most useful types of obfuscation that can be applied is *control flow* obfuscation. This makes small changes in the instructions that form your code so that decompilers such as Reflector are no longer able to disassemble the program code at all.

This type of obfuscation works by inserting additional instructions into your assembly. Most .NET instructions are formed from multiple bytes of data within the compiled assembly. Control flow obfuscation will introduce a *jump* instruction so that the program flow moves to an instruction later within the procedure and will then insert a partial instruction (missing some of its bytes) into the area that has been jumped over. The .NET runtime will never attempt to execute this partial instruction, because it was told to jump past it, but the disassembler doesn't follow the jump and instead attempts to disassemble the partial instruction. This results in it getting out of step with the actual instructions, so part of the code disappears or, in most cases, the disassembly fails altogether.

This provides a significant improvement in the quality of protection added to your code. While the renaming scheme makes it more difficult to understand your code, the code itself is still visible. Control flow obfuscation will in most cases completely hide the code from prying eyes.

String Encryption

Figure 14–18 shows that the exception message "Name must be at least 4 characters long" is still clearly visible within the code disassembly, so it gives a vital clue to the purpose of the function.

Obfuscators that offer support for string encryption will remove all such readable strings from the compiled assembly and replace each with a function call that passes a random-looking number as a parameter. The function that is called will use that number to retrieve the string in an encrypted form, decrypt it, and return it back to the calling procedure.

These steps could be followed to determine what the message actually was, but this adds a significant amount of effort to the task of understanding each and every string that is contained within the compiled assembly, dramatically increasing the amount of time required to understand the purpose of the code.

Symbol Renaming Schemes

Dotfuscator Community Edition provided a simple symbol-renaming scheme, whereby each class and class member was renamed to a letter of the alphabet. Other obfuscators offer enhanced versions of this that are much more impenetrable than that offered by Dotfuscator CE.

Typical schemes will use unprintable characters for element names so that they do not display at all in Reflector and will identify multiple functions that have different parameters and rename them to all have the same name. .NET is still perfectly happy with these changes (it doesn't care about unreadable names at all and can work out which of the same-named functions to call by seeing the types of parameter they expect), but a human being will find this naming scheme to be extremely difficult to follow.

Reflector.NET Protection

Some obfuscators have code that specifically targets Reflector.NET to prevent it from interacting with the compiled assembly at all. They can manipulate the data contained within an assembly so that Reflector encounters an error simply opening the obfuscated assembly. This, used in combination with the other obfuscation options, can provide another level of protection to keep others out of your private code.

Resource Protection

Your code is not the only thing of value contained within your compiled assemblies: your game graphics, sound effects, and music are all present too.

While implementing your own encryption schemes for embedded resources is certainly possible, allowing an obfuscator to take care of this for you is much more convenient. Access to the resources will be unchanged as far as your code is concerned, but attempts to access them outside of your assembly will result in files that cannot be accessed. You may also find features, such as compression of embedded resources, reducing the overall file size of your compiled assemblies.

Adding Obfuscated Files to CAB Setup Projects

Some obfuscators are able to integrate themselves into the build process, meaning that each time Visual Studio compiles an executable or DLL, it will be automatically obfuscated. When an obfuscator works in this way, no additional steps are required to put the obfuscated file into the setup CAB, as the setup project will already be accessing the obfuscated files when the CAB is constructed.

Other obfuscators, including Dotfuscator Community Edition, cannot be integrated into the build process in this way and, therefore, present a slight project in terms of getting the obfuscated assemblies into your CAB file.

The resolution to this is simple, though slightly awkward. When building your CAB file setup project, instead of using the Add ➤ Project Output menu item, you must instead add individual files using the Add ➤ File option. After selecting this, browse to the obfuscated file on disk to add it to the CAB.

The two main implications of this approach follow:

- Visual Studio will not automatically detect the dependencies of the selected assembly. You will need to ensure that any required dependencies are manually added to the setup project using the same Add ➤ File option.

- As the file you are adding is the obfuscated file and not the output file compiled by Visual Studio, you will need to remember to reobfuscate your selected assemblies prior to each build of the setup project. Otherwise, the CAB file will be built using obfuscated assemblies that are out of date.

Releasing New Versions of Your Game

The release of a game to the public is rarely the end of that game's development. You may wish to release new versions of your game containing new game features, enhancements, or bug fixes. Once you have an established user base running your game, simplifying the process of informing users about the update and getting it on to their devices will encourage update of the your new game revisions.

If you release your game through Windows Marketplace for Mobile, the Marketplace application will automatically tell users that have your game installed about any new version that is released into the Marketplace. If you are not using Marketplace, you can simplify the update notification process by adding a *version check* feature to your game.

The check is very simple. It downloads an XML file from the Internet that you would host on your own web site and that contains a number indicating the assembly revision of the latest released version of the game. Once this revision number is retrieved, the code compares it to its own assembly revision number. If the retrieved value is greater, the user is informed that a new version of the application is available. If users want to know more, they can then be taken to your web site to explain what is new in the updated software version and can download the new version to install on their device.

An example of how to achieve this can be found in the UpdateCheck example project. The code of interest is contained within the CheckForUpdate function. The very first thing it does it confirm that the user is willing to connect to the Internet to retrieve this information. You should always obtain such confirmation before connecting to the Internet to avoid the user being unexpectedly charged for data access, which can be particularly expensive if users are roaming outside of their home areas or countries.

Once permission has been granted by the user, the code retrieves the XML file from the Internet. The example uses the URL http://www.adamdawes.com/windowsmobile/LatestVersion.xml to look for this update information. A version information file is available at this URL and contains the content shown in Listing 14–2.

Listing 14–2. The LatestVersion.xml File Content

```
<LatestVersion>
 <Revision>5</Revision>
</LatestVersion>
```

The retrieved revision (5 in this case) is compared against the assembly's own revision (which is set to 2 in the example). If the retrieved revision is greater, users are told about the availability of a new version. They may then choose to see more information, which launches the web browser to an appropriate page for such information to be seen.

The code for the CheckForUpdate function is in Listing 14–3. The highlighted code lines will, of course, need to change to refer to the appropriate locations on your own web site.

Listing 14–3. Checking for Updated Versions of the Application

```
/// <summary>
/// Check to see if a newer version of this game is available online.
/// </summary>
private void CheckForUpdate()
{
    XmlDocument xmlDoc = new XmlDocument();
    int latestRevision;

    // Make sure the user is OK with this
    if (MessageBox.Show("This will check for updates by connecting to the internet. "
        + "You may incur charges from your data provider as a result of this. "
        + "Are you sure you wish to continue?", "Update Check",
        MessageBoxButtons.YesNo, MessageBoxIcon.Asterisk,
        MessageBoxDefaultButton.Button1) == DialogResult.No)
    {
        // Abort
        return;
    }

    try
    {
        // Display the wait cursor while we check for an update
        Cursor.Current = Cursors.WaitCursor;

        // Try to open the xml file at the specified URL
        xmlDoc.Load("http://www.adamdawes.com/windowsmobile/LatestVersion.xml");

        // Remove the wait cursor
        Cursor.Current = Cursors.Default;
```

```
        // Read the revision from the retrieved document
        latestRevision = int.Parse(
                xmlDoc.SelectSingleNode("/LatestVersion/Revision").InnerText);

        // Is the retrieved version later than this assembly version?
        if (latestRevision > Assembly.GetExecutingAssembly().GetName().Version.Revision)
        {
            // Yes, notify the user and allow them to visit a web page with more info
            if (MessageBox.Show("A new version of this application is available. "
                + "Would you like to see more information?", "New Version",
                MessageBoxButtons.YesNo, MessageBoxIcon.Asterisk,
                MessageBoxDefaultButton.Button1) == DialogResult.Yes)
            {
                // Open the information page
                Process.Start("http://www.adamdawes.com", "");
            }
        }
        else
        {
            // No newer version is available
            MessageBox.Show("You are already running the latest version.");
        }
    }
    catch
    {
        // Something went wrong, tell the user to try again
        Cursor.Current = Cursors.Default;
        MessageBox.Show("Unable to retrieve update information at the moment. "
            + "Please check your internet connection or try again later.");
    }
}
```

Promoting Your Game

Your game may be brilliant, but if no one knows about it, no one will play or buy it. There are plenty of opportunities to raise awareness of your game; here are some suggestions:

- Create a web site, and use it to advertize your game. Make sure your site looks attractive, and be sure to include information about what the game is about and how to play it. Also add screenshots, purchase or download information, and anything else you think your audience may find useful or interesting.

- If you release a game as freeware, many popular sites will provide information and download links for you. Because these sites get large numbers of users each day, they can be a great way to build awareness of your game. Popular freeware sites include http://www.freewarepocketpc.net/ (which also hosts the very handy OpnMarket application for browsing and installing software directly on the device) and http://freewareppc.com/. Getting free software out into the world raises awareness and trust of you and your web site. Be aware that these sites will generally not include games that feature advertising or cut-down versions of paid applications.

- List your game in online catalogs. Getting your game included in Windows Marketplace for Mobile or other online stores such as http://www.pocketgear.com/ can raise awareness of your project and offer potential sales channels. However, make sure you aware of how much commission each site will keep on sales that you make through its store.

- Get your game reviewed. A number of sites will review your software, including http://www.bestwindowsmobileapps.com/. Be prepared for an honest review however. Make sure that everything is polished and working before review submission so that you maximize your chances of positive results.

- Inform Windows Mobile news sites about your new game. Not all sites will be interested in this kind of news item, but it doesn't hurt to ask. One site that you might wish to approach is http://wmpoweruser.com/; it has a user-submitted Page 2 section into which you can submit a news story yourself. You may also want to check out http://www.wmexperts.com/.

Go Create!

The only thing you need to add to your tool set now is your imagination. There are huge opportunities for gaming on Windows Mobile, so let your creativity run free. I wish you many happy days of writing games for Windows Mobile devices.

Please let me know about the games that you create. I'd also love to hear any feedback that you have about this book. You can contact me by sending e-mail to adam@adamdawes.com.

Index

B

Breinigsville, PA USA
13 April 2010
236091BV00003B/2/P